Year 5C

A Guide to Teaching for Mastery

Series Editor: Tony Staneff

Contents

Introduction

Foreword by the series editor and author, Tony Staneff

For far too long in the UK, maths has been feared by learners – and by many teachers, too. As a result, most learners consistently underachieve. More crucially, negative beliefs about ability, aptitude and the nature of maths are entrenched in children's thinking from an early age.

Yet, as someone who has loved maths all my life, I've always believed that every child has the capacity to succeed in maths. I've also had the great pleasure of leading teams and departments who share that belief and passion. Teaching for mastery, as practised in China and other South-East Asian jurisdictions since the 1980s, has confirmed my conviction that maths really is for everyone and not just those who have a special talent. In recent years, my team and I at Trinity Academy, Halifax, have had the privilege of researching with and working alongside some of the finest mastery practitioners from the UK and beyond, whose impact on learners' confidence, achievement and attitude is an inspiration.

The mastery approach recognises the value of developing the power to think rather than just do. It also recognises the value of making a coherent journey in which whole-class groups tackle concepts in very small steps, one by one. You cannot build securely on loose foundations – and it is just the same with maths: by creating a solid foundation of deep understanding, our children's skills and confidence will be strong and secure. What's more, the mindset of learner and teacher alike is fundamental: everyone can do maths … EVERYONE CAN!

I am proud to have been part of the extensive team responsible for turning the best of the world's practice, research, insights, and shared experiences into *Power Maths*, a unique teaching and learning resource developed especially for UK classrooms. *Power Maths* embodies our vision to help and support primary maths teachers to transform every child's mathematical and personal development. 'Everyone can!' has become our mantra and our passion, and we hope it will be yours, too.

Now, explore and enjoy all the resources you need to teach for mastery, and please get back to us with your *Power Maths* experiences and stories!

What is *Power Maths*?

Created especially for UK primary schools, and aligned with the new National Curriculum, *Power Maths* is a whole-class, textbook-based mastery resource that empowers every child to understand and succeed. *Power Maths* rejects the notion that some people simply 'can't do' maths. Instead, it develops growth mindsets and encourages hard work, practice and a willingness to see mistakes as learning tools.

Best practice consistently shows that mastery of small, cumulative steps builds a solid foundation of deep mathematical understanding. *Power Maths* combines interactive teaching tools, high-quality textbooks and continuing professional development (CPD) to help you equip children with a deep and long lasting understanding. Based on extensive evidence, and developed in partnership with practising teachers, *Power Maths* ensures that it meets the needs of children in the UK.

Power Maths and Mastery

Power Maths makes mastery practical and achievable by providing the structures, pathways, content, tools and support you need to make it happen in your classroom.

To develop mastery in maths children need to be enabled to acquire a deep understanding of maths concepts, structures and procedures, step by step. Complex mathematical concepts are built on simpler conceptual components and when children understand every step in the learning sequence, maths becomes transparent and makes logical sense. Interactive lessons establish deep understanding in small steps, as well as effortless fluency in key facts such as tables and number bonds. The whole class works on the same content and no child is left behind.

Power Maths

- Builds every concept in small, progressive steps.
- Is built with interactive, whole-class teaching in mind.
- Provides the tools you need to develop growth mindsets.
- Helps you check understanding and ensure that every child is keeping up.
- Establishes core elements such as intelligent practice and reflection.

The *Power Maths* approach

Child-centred learning

Children master concepts one step at a time in lessons that embrace a Concrete-Pictorial-Abstract (C-P-A) approach, avoid overload, build on prior learning and help them see patterns and connections. Same-day intervention ensures sustained progress.

Everyone can!

Founded on the conviction that every child can achieve, *Power Maths* enables children to build number fluency, confidence and understanding, step by step.

Continuing professional development

Embedded teacher support and development offer every teacher the opportunity to continually improve their subject knowledge and manage whole-class teaching for mastery.

Whole-class teaching

An interactive, whole-class teaching model encourages thinking and precise mathematical language and allows children to deepen their understanding as far as they can.

Introduction to the author team

Power Maths arises from the work of maths mastery experts who are committed to proving that, given the right mastery mindset and approach, **everyone can do maths**. Based on robust research and best practice from around the world, *Power Maths* was developed in partnership with a group of UK teachers to make sure that it not only meets our children's wide-ranging needs but also aligns with the National Curriculum in England.

Tony Staneff, Series Editor and author

Vice Principal at Trinity Academy, Halifax, Tony also leads a team of mastery experts who help schools across the UK to develop teaching for mastery via nationally recognised CPD courses, problem-solving and reasoning resources, schemes of work, assessment materials and other tools.

A team of experienced authors, including:

- **Josh Lury** – a specialist maths teacher, author and maths consultant with a passion for innovative and effective maths education

- **Trinity Academy, Halifax** (Michael Gosling CEO, Tony Staneff, Emily Fox, Kate Henshall, Rebecca Holland, Stephanie Kirk, Stephen Monaghan, Beth Smith and Rachel Webster)

- **David Board, Belle Cottingham, Jonathan East, Tim Handley, Derek Huby, Neil Jarrett, Timothy Weal, Paul Wrangles** – skilled maths teachers and mastery experts

- **Cherri Moseley** – a maths author, former teacher and professional development provider

Professors Liu Jian and Zhang Dan, Series Consultants and authors, and their team of mastery expert authors:

- **Wei Huinv, Huang Lihua, Zhu Dejiang, Zhu Yuhong, Hou Huiying, Yin Lili, Zhang Jing, Zhou Da and Liu Qimeng**

Used by over 20 million children, Professor Liu Jian's textbook programme is one of the most popular in China. He and his author team are highly experienced in intelligent practice and in embedding key maths concepts using a C-P-A approach.

A group of 15 teachers and maths co-ordinators

We have consulted our teacher group throughout the development of *Power Maths* to ensure we are meeting their real needs in the classroom.

Your *Power Maths* resources

To help you teach for mastery, *Power Maths* comprises a variety of high-quality resources.

Pupil Textbooks

Discover, Share, and Think together sections promote discussion and introduce mathematical ideas logically, so that children understand more easily.

Using a Concrete-Pictorial-Abstract approach, clear mathematical models help children to make connections and grasp concepts.

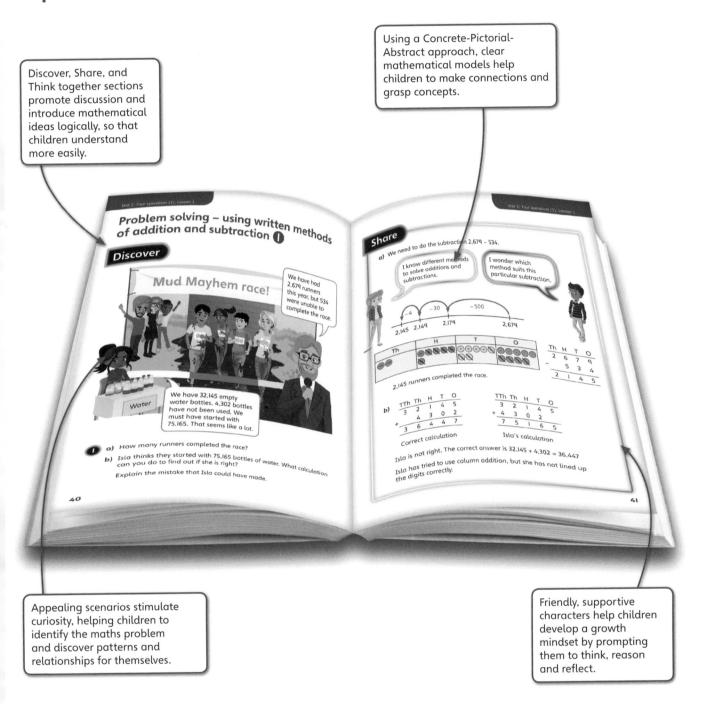

Appealing scenarios stimulate curiosity, helping children to identify the maths problem and discover patterns and relationships for themselves.

Friendly, supportive characters help children develop a growth mindset by prompting them to think, reason and reflect.

The coherent *Power Maths* lesson structure carries through into the vibrant, high-quality textbooks. Setting out the core learning objectives for each class, the lesson structure follows a carefully mapped journey through the curriculum and supports children on their journey to deeper understanding.

Pupil Practice Books

The Practice Books offer just the right amount of intelligent practice for children to complete independently in the final section of each lesson.

The practice questions are for everyone – each question varies one small element to move children on in their thinking. Look at the different parts in question **1**!

Calculations are connected so that children think about the underlying concept. In question **3**, children have to write out the calculation to find the answer. Concepts are presented differently again in question **4** to challenge children.

Practice questions are finely tuned to move children forward in their thinking and to reveal misconceptions.

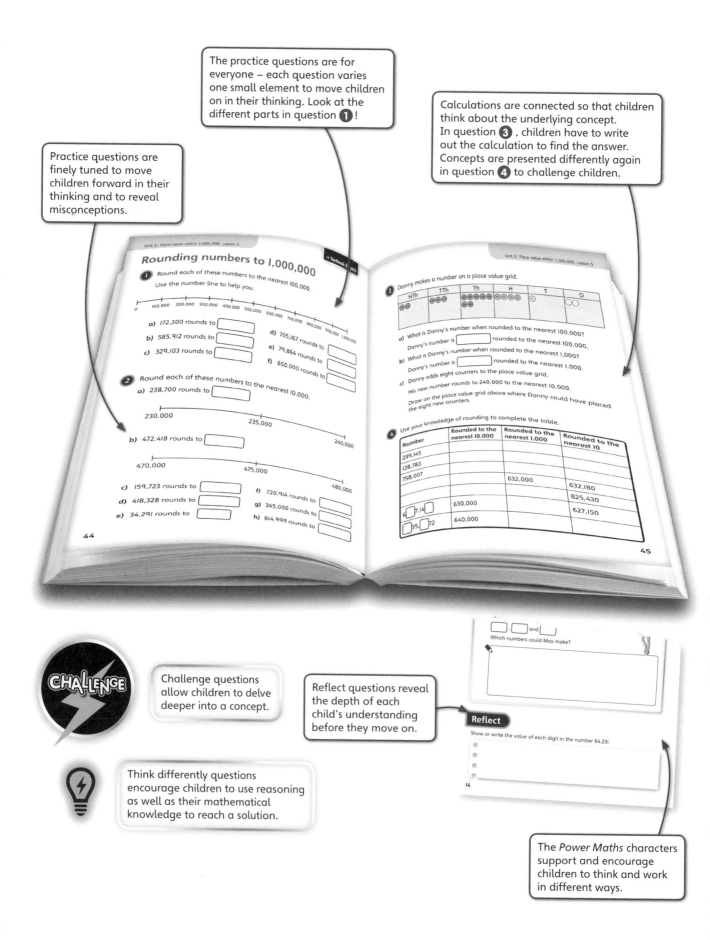

Challenge questions allow children to delve deeper into a concept.

Reflect questions reveal the depth of each child's understanding before they move on.

Think differently questions encourage children to use reasoning as well as their mathematical knowledge to reach a solution.

The *Power Maths* characters support and encourage children to think and work in different ways.

Online subscriptions

The online subscription will give you access to additional resources.

eTextbooks

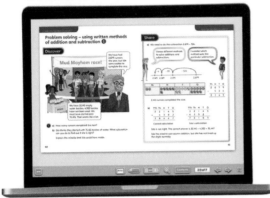

Digital versions of *Power Maths* Textbooks allow class groups to share and discuss questions, solutions and strategies. They allow you to project key structures and representations at the front of the class, to ensure all children are focusing on the same concept.

Teaching tools

Here you will find interactive versions of key *Power Maths* structures and representations.

Power Ups

Use this series of daily activities to promote and check number fluency.

Online versions of Teacher Guide pages

PDF pages give support at both unit and lesson levels. You will also find help with key strategies and templates for tracking progress.

Unit videos

Watch the professional development videos at the start of each unit to help you teach with confidence. The videos explore common misconceptions in the unit, and include intervention suggestions as well as suggestions on what to look out for when assessing mastery in your children.

End of unit Strengthen and Deepen materials

Each Strengthen activity at the end of every unit addresses a key misconception and can be used to support children who need it. The Deepen activities are designed to be 'Low Threshold High Ceiling' and will challenge those children who can understand more deeply. These resources will help you ensure that every child understands and will help you keep the class moving forward together. These printable activities provide an optional resource bank for use after the assessment stage.

Underpinning all of these resources, *Power Maths* is infused throughout with continual professional development, supporting you at every step.

The *Power Maths* teaching model

At the heart of *Power Maths* is a clearly structured teaching and learning process that helps you make certain that every child masters each maths concept securely and deeply. For each year group, the curriculum is broken down into core concepts, taught in units. A unit divides into smaller learning steps – lessons. Step by step, strong foundations of cumulative knowledge and understanding are built.

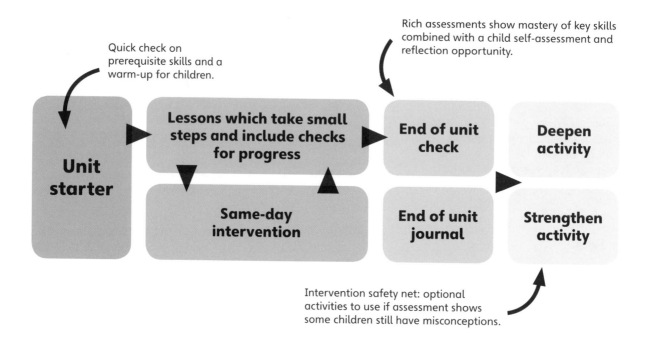

Quick check on prerequisite skills and a warm-up for children.

Rich assessments show mastery of key skills combined with a child self-assessment and reflection opportunity.

Intervention safety net: optional activities to use if assessment shows some children still have misconceptions.

Unit starter

Each unit begins with a unit starter, which introduces the learning context along with key mathematical vocabulary, structures and representations.

- The Textbooks include a check on readiness and a warm-up task for children to complete.

- Your Teacher Guide gives support right from the start on important structures and representations, mathematical language, common misconceptions and intervention strategies.

- Unit-specific videos develop your subject knowledge and insights so you feel confident and fully equipped to teach each new unit. These are available via the online subscription.

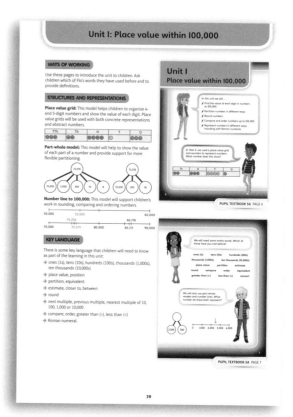

Lesson

Once a unit has been introduced, it is time to start teaching the series of lessons.

- Each lesson is scaffolded with Textbook and Practice Book activities and always begins with a Power Up activity (available via online subscription).
- *Power Maths* identifies lesson by lesson what concepts are to be taught.
- Your Teacher Guide offers lots of support for you to get the most from every child in every lesson. As well as highlighting key points, tricky areas and how to handle them, you will also find question prompts to check on understanding and clarification on why particular activities and questions are used.

Same-day intervention

Same-day interventions are vital in order to keep the class progressing together. Therefore, *Power Maths* provides plenty of support throughout the journey.

- Intervention is focused on keeping up now, not catching up later, so interventions should happen as soon as they are needed.
- Practice questions are designed to bring misconceptions to the surface, allowing you to identify these easily as you circulate during independent practice time.
- Child-friendly assessment questions in the Teacher Guide help you identify easily which children need to strengthen their understanding.

End of unit check and journal

The End of unit check presents six to nine multiple-choice questions. These questions are designed to reveal misconceptions and help you target areas that need strengthening.

At the end of a unit, summative assessment tasks reveal essential information on each child's understanding. An End of unit check in the Pupil Textbook lets you see which children have mastered the key concepts, which children have not and where their misconceptions lie. The Practice Book includes an End of unit journal in which children can reflect on what they have learnt.
Each unit also offers Strengthen and Deepen activities, available via the online subscription.

The Teacher Guide offers support with handling misconceptions.

The End of unit journal is an opportunity for children to test out their learning and reflect on how they feel about it. Tackling the 'journal' problem reveals whether a child understands the concept deeply enough to move on to the next unit.

In KS2, the End of unit assessment will also include at least one SATs-style question.

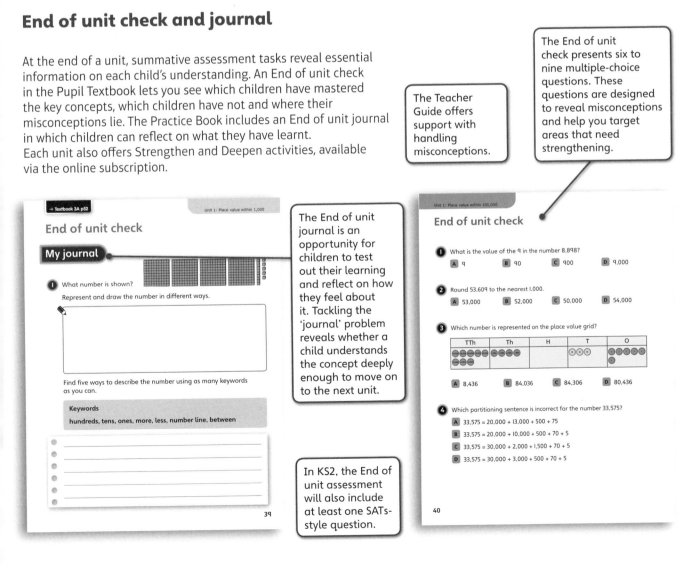

The *Power Maths* lesson sequence

At the heart of *Power Maths* is a unique lesson sequence designed to empower children to understand core concepts and grow in confidence. Embracing the National Centre for Excellence in the Teaching of Mathematics' (NCETM's) definition of mastery, the sequence guides and shapes every *Power Maths* lesson you teach.

Flexibility is built into the *Power Maths* programme so there is no one-to-one mapping of lessons and concepts meaning you can pace your teaching according to your class. While some children will need to spend longer on a particular concept (through interventions or additional lessons), others will reach deeper levels of understanding. However, it is important that the class moves forward together through the termly schedules.

Power Up ⏱ 5 minutes

Each lesson begins with a Power Up activity (available via the online subscription) which supports fluency in key number facts.

The whole-class approach depends on fluency, so the Power Up is a powerful and essential activity.

TOP TIP
If the class is struggling with the task, revisit it later and check understanding.

Power Ups reinforce key skills such as times-tables, number bonds and working with place value.

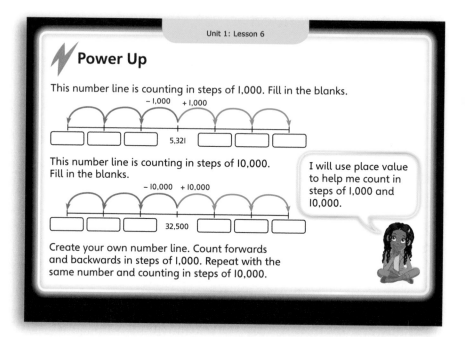

Discover ⏱ 10 minutes

A practical, real-life problem arouses curiosity. Children find the maths through story-telling.

A real-life scenario is provided for the Discover section but feel free to build upon these with your own examples that are more relevant to your class.

TOP TIP
Discover works best when run at tables, in pairs with concrete objects.

Question ❶ a) tackles the key concept and question ❶ b) digs a little deeper. Children have time to explore, play and discuss possible strategies.

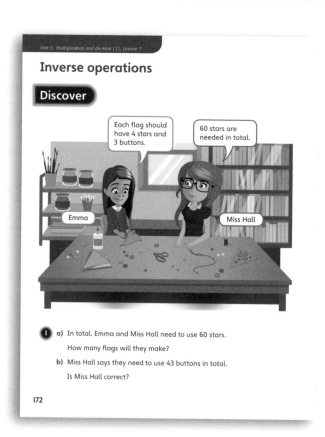

Share ⏱ 10 minutes

Teacher-led, this interactive section follows the Discover activity and highlights the variety of methods that can be used to solve a single problem.

TOP TIP
Ask children to discuss their methods. Pairs sharing a textbook is a great format for this!

Your Teacher Guide gives target questions for children. The online toolkit provides interactive structures and representations to link concrete and pictorial to abstract concepts.

TOP TIP
Bring children to the front to share and celebrate their solutions and strategies.

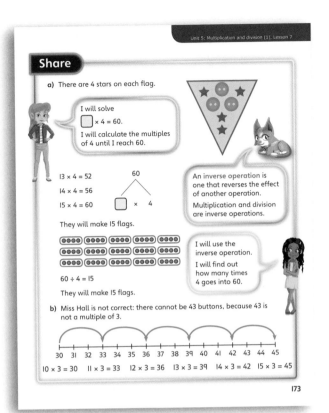

Think together

⏱ 10 minutes

Children work in groups on the carpet or at tables, using their textbooks or eBooks.

TOP TIP
Make sure children have mini whiteboards or pads to write on if they are not at their tables.

Unit 5: Multiplication and division (1), Lesson 7

Think together

1. Write multiplication and division facts related to the squares and circles on these flags.

a) Squares
☐ × ☐ = ☐
☐ ÷ ☐ = ☐
☐ ÷ ☐ = ☐

b) Circles
☐ × ☐ = ☐
☐ ÷ ☐ = ☐
☐ ÷ ☐ = ☐

2. Amelia is sewing more bunting. Each flag has 2 stars and some buttons.

a) So far she has used 36 stars.
How many flags has she made?
She has made ☐ flags.

b) She shares her buttons equally, and there are 6 for each flag.
How many buttons did she have?
She had ☐ buttons.

174

Using the Teacher Guide, model question ① for your class.

Question ② is less structured. Children will need to think together in their groups, then discuss their methods and solutions as a class.

In questions ③ and ④ children try working out the answer independently. The openness of the challenge question helps to check depth of understanding.

Practice ⏱ 15 minutes

Unit 5: Multiplication and division (1), Lesson 7

→ Textbook 5A p172

Using their Practice Books, children work independently while you circulate and check on progress.

Questions follow small steps of progression to deepen learning.

TOP TIP
Some children could work separately with a teacher or assistant.

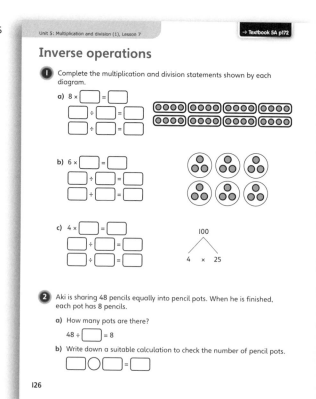

Inverse operations

1 Complete the multiplication and division statements shown by each diagram.

a) 8 × ☐ = ☐
☐ ÷ ☐ = ☐
☐ ÷ ☐ = ☐

b) 6 × ☐ = ☐
☐ ÷ ☐ = ☐
☐ ÷ ☐ = ☐

c) 4 × ☐ = ☐
☐ ÷ ☐ = ☐
☐ ÷ ☐ = ☐

100
4 × 25

2 Aki is sharing 48 pencils equally into pencil pots. When he is finished, each pot has 8 pencils.

a) How many pots are there?
48 ÷ ☐ = 8

b) Write down a suitable calculation to check the number of pencil pots.
☐ ◯ ☐ = ☐

126

Are some children struggling? If so, work with them as a group, using mathematical structures and representations to support understanding as necessary.

There are no set routines: for real understanding, children need to think about the problem in different ways.

Reflect ⏱ 5 minutes

Unit 5: Multiplication and division (1), Lesson 7

'Spot the mistake' questions are great for checking misconceptions.

The Reflect section is your opportunity to check how deeply children understand the target concept.

6 a) What number did Reena start with?

Reena **CHALLENGE**

Reena started with ☐.

I divide my number by 8 and get the answer 2 remainder 7.

b) What number did Andy divide by?

Andy

Andy divided by ☐.

I start with 69. I divide by a number and get the answer 9 remainder 6.

c) What numbers could Jamie have started with?

Jamie

Jamie could have started with ☐ or ☐.

I am thinking of a prime number between 50 and 100. I divide by 6 and get a remainder of 1.

Reflect

Show the different strategies required to find the missing values of the following calculations.

18 ÷ ☐ = 3   ☐ ÷ 3 = 18

128

The Practice Books use various approaches to check that children have fully understood each concept.

Looking like they understand is not enough! It is essential that children can show they have grasped the concept.

Using the *Power Maths* Teacher Guide

Think of your Teacher Guides as *Power Maths* handbooks that will guide, support and inspire your day-to-day teaching. Clear and concise, and illustrated with helpful examples, your Teacher Guides will help you make the best possible use of every individual lesson. They also provide wrap-around professional development, enhancing your own subject knowledge and helping you to grow in confidence about moving your children forward together.

There is a Teacher Guide per year group for every term with unit and lesson level guidance and support.

Tips and advice on key elements such as C-P-A approaches, misconceptions, language, modelling growth mindsets and same-day intervention.

Annotations for every Pupil Textbook and Practice Book page, providing prompts for key questions to ask to expose understanding and explanations as to why key questions have been chosen.

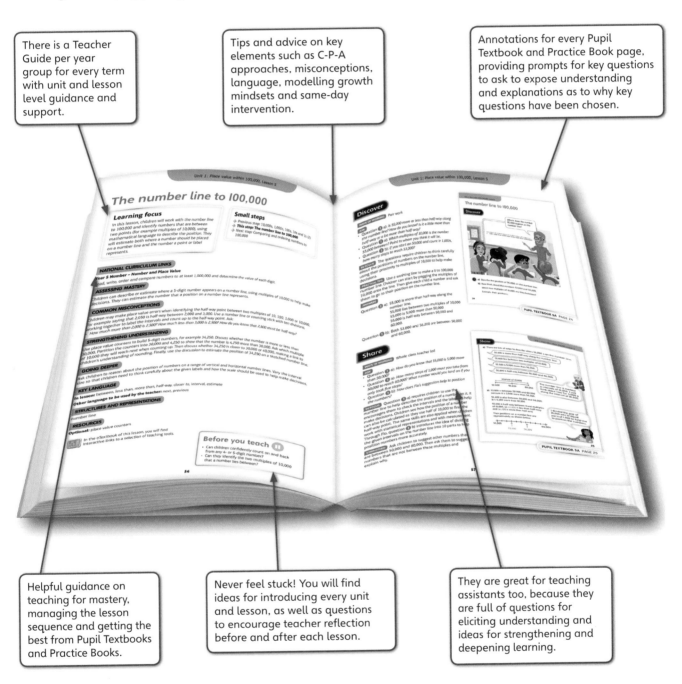

Helpful guidance on teaching for mastery, managing the lesson sequence and getting the best from Pupil Textbooks and Practice Books.

Never feel stuck! You will find ideas for introducing every unit and lesson, as well as questions to encourage teacher reflection before and after each lesson.

They are great for teaching assistants too, because they are full of questions for eliciting understanding and ideas for strengthening and deepening learning.

At the end of each unit, your Teacher Guide helps you identify who has fully grasped the concept, who has not and how to move every child forward. This is covered later in the Assessment strategies section.

Power Maths Year 5, yearly overview

Textbook	Strand	Unit		Number of Lessons
Textbook A / Practice Book A (Term 1)	Number – number and place value	1	Place value within 100,000	8
	Number – number and place value	2	Place value within 1,000,000	8
	Number – addition and subtraction	3	Addition and subtraction	10
	Statistics	4	Graphs and tables	5
	Number – multiplication and division	5	Multiplication and division (1)	10
	Measurement	6	Measure – area and perimeter	7
Textbook B / Practice Book B (Term 2)	Number – multiplication and division	7	Multiplication and division (2)	11
	Number – fractions (including decimals and percentages)	8	Fractions (1)	8
	Number – fractions (including decimals and percentages)	9	Fractions (2)	12
	Number – fractions (including decimals and percentages)	10	Fractions (3)	7
	Number – fractions (including decimals and percentages)	11	Decimals and percentages	12
Textbook C / Practice Book C (Term 3)	Number – fractions (including decimals and percentages)	12	Decimals	15
	Geometry – properties of shapes	13	Geometry – properties of shapes (1)	7
	Geometry – properties of shapes	14	Geometry – properties of shapes (2)	5
	Geometry – position and direction	15	Geometry – position and direction	4
	Measurement	16	Measure – converting units	10
	Measurement	17	Measure – volume and capacity	4

Power Maths Year 5, Textbook 5C (Term 3) Overview

Strand 1	Strand 2	Unit	Lesson number	Lesson title	NC Objective 1	NC Objective 2	NC Objective 3	NC Objective 3
Number – fractions (including decimals and percentages)		Unit 12	Decimals	1	Adding and subtracting decimals (1)	Solve problems involving number up to three decimal places		
Number – fractions (including decimals and percentages)		Unit 12	Decimals	2	Adding and subtracting decimals (2)	Solve problems involving number up to three decimal places		
Number – fractions (including decimals and percentages)		Unit 12	Decimals	3	Adding and subtracting decimals (3)	Solve problems involving number up to three decimal places		
Number – fractions (including decimals and percentages)		Unit 12	Decimals	4	Adding and subtracting decimals (4)	Solve problems involving number up to three decimal places		
Number – fractions (including decimals and percentages)		Unit 12	Decimals	5	Adding and subtracting decimals (5)	Solve problems involving number up to three decimal places		
Number – fractions (including decimals and percentages)		Unit 12	Decimals	6	Adding and subtracting decimals (6)	Solve problems involving number up to three decimal places		

Strand 1	Strand 2	Unit	Lesson number	Lesson title	NC Objective 1	NC Objective 2	NC Objective 3	NC Objective 3
Number – fractions (including decimals and percentages)		Unit 12	Decimals	7	Adding and subtracting decimals (7)	Solve problems involving number up to three decimal places		
Number – fractions (including decimals and percentages)		Unit 12	Decimals	8	Adding and subtracting decimals (8)	Solve problems involving number up to three decimal places		
Number – fractions (including decimals and percentages)		Unit 12	Decimals	9	Decimal sequences	Read, write, order and compare numbers with up to three decimal places		
Number – fractions (including decimals and percentages)		Unit 12	Decimals	10	Problem solving – decimals (1)	Solve problems involving number up to three decimal places		
Number – fractions (including decimals and percentages)		Unit 12	Decimals	11	Problem solving – decimals (2)	Solve problems involving number up to three decimal places		
Number – fractions (including decimals and percentages)		Unit 12	Decimals	12	Multiplying decimals by 10	Recognise and use thousandths and relate them to tenths, hundredths and decimal equivalents	Solve problems involving number up to three decimal places	
Number – fractions (including decimals and percentages)		Unit 12	Decimals	13	Multiplying decimals by 10, 100 and 1,000	Recognise and use thousandths and relate them to tenths, hundredths and decimal equivalents	Solve problems involving number up to three decimal places	
Number – fractions (including decimals and percentages)		Unit 12	Decimals	14	Dividing decimals by 10	Recognise and use thousandths and relate them to tenths, hundredths and decimal equivalents	Solve problems involving number up to three decimal places	
Number – fractions (including decimals and percentages)		Unit 12	Decimals	15	Dividing decimals by 10, 100 and 1,000	Recognise and use thousandths and relate them to tenths, hundredths and decimal equivalents	Solve problems involving number up to three decimal places	
Geometry – properties of shapes		Unit 13	Geometry – properties of shapes (1)	1	Measuring angles in degrees	Identify: –angles at a point and one whole turn (total 360°) –angles at a point on a straight line and $\frac{1}{2}$ a turn (total 180°) –other multiples of 90°	Know angles are measured in degrees: estimate and compare acute, obtuse and reflex angles	
Geometry – properties of shapes		Unit 13	Geometry – properties of shapes (1)	2	Measuring with a protractor (1)	Know angles are measured in degrees: estimate and compare acute, obtuse and reflex angles	Draw given angles, and measure them in degrees (°)	
Geometry – properties of shapes		Unit 13	Geometry – properties of shapes (1)	3	Measuring with a protractor (2)	Identify: –angles at a point and one whole turn (total 360°) –angles at a point on a straight line and $\frac{1}{2}$ a turn (total 180°) –other multiples of 90°	Know angles are measured in degrees: estimate and compare acute, obtuse and reflex angles	Draw given angles, and measure them in degrees (°)
Geometry – properties of shapes		Unit 13	Geometry – properties of shapes (1)	4	Drawing lines and angles accurately	Draw given angles, and measure them in degrees (°)		
Geometry – properties of shapes		Unit 13	Geometry – properties of shapes (1)	5	Calculating angles on a straight line	Identify: –angles at a point and one whole turn (total 360°) –angles at a point on a straight line and $\frac{1}{2}$ a turn (total 180°) –other multiples of 90°		
Geometry – properties of shapes		Unit 13	Geometry – properties of shapes (1)	6	Calculating angles around a point	Identify: –angles at a point and one whole turn (total 360°) –angles at a point on a straight line and $\frac{1}{2}$ a turn (total 180°) –other multiples of 90°		

Strand 1	Strand 2	Unit	Lesson number	Lesson title	NC Objective 1	NC Objective 2	NC Objective 3	NC Objective 3
Geometry – properties of shapes		Unit 13	Geometry – properties of shapes (1)	7	Calculating lengths and angles in shapes	Use the properties of rectangles to deduce related facts and find missing lengths and angles		
Geometry – properties of shapes		Unit 14	Geometry – properties of shapes (2)	1	Recognising and drawing parallel lines	Use the properties of rectangles to deduce related facts and find missing lengths and angles	Identify: –angles at a point and one whole turn (total 360°) –angles at a point on a straight line and <stacked fraction> $\frac{1}{2}$ a turn (total 180°) –other multiples of 90°	
Geometry – properties of shapes		Unit 14	Geometry – properties of shapes (2)	2	Recognising and drawing perpendicular lines	Use the properties of rectangles to deduce related facts and find missing lengths and angles	Identify: –angles at a point and one whole turn (total 360°) –angles at a point on a straight line and <stacked fraction> $\frac{1}{2}$ a turn (total 180°) –other multiples of 90°	
Geometry – properties of shapes		Unit 14	Geometry – properties of shapes (2)	3	Reasoning about parallel and perpendicular lines	Draw given angles, and measure them in degrees (o)	Identify: –angles at a point and one whole turn (total 360°) –angles at a point on a straight line and <stacked fraction> $\frac{1}{2}$ a turn (total 180°) –other multiples of 90°	
Geometry – properties of shapes		Unit 14	Geometry – properties of shapes (2)	4	Regular and irregular polygons	Distinguish between regular and irregular polygons based on reasoning about equal sides and angles		
Geometry – properties of shapes		Unit 14	Geometry – properties of shapes (2)	5	Reasoning about 3D shapes	Identify 3D shapes, including cubes and other cuboids, from 2D representations		
Geometry – position and direction		Unit 15	Geometry – position and direction	1	Reflection	Identify, describe and represent the position of a shape following a reflection or translation, using the appropriate language, and know that the shape has not changed		
Geometry – position and direction		Unit 15	Geometry – position and direction	2	Reflection with coordinates	Identify, describe and represent the position of a shape following a reflection or translation, using the appropriate language, and know that the shape has not changed		
Geometry – position and direction		Unit 15	Geometry – position and direction	3	Translation	Identify, describe and represent the position of a shape following a reflection or translation, using the appropriate language, and know that the shape has not changed		
Geometry – position and direction		Unit 15	Geometry – position and direction	4	Translation with coordinates	Identify, describe and represent the position of a shape following a reflection or translation, using the appropriate language, and know that the shape has not changed		
Measurement		Unit 16	Measure – converting units	1	Metric units (1)	Convert between different units of metric measure (for example, kilometre and metre; centimetre and metre; centimetre and millimetre; gram and kilogram; litre and millilitre)		
Measurement		Unit 16	Measure – converting units	2	Metric units (2)	Convert between different units of metric measure (for example, kilometre and metre; centimetre and metre; centimetre and millimetre; gram and kilogram; litre and millilitre)		
Measurement		Unit 16	Measure – converting units	3	Metric units (3)	Use all four operations to solve problems involving measure [for example, length, mass, volume, money] using decimal notation, including scaling	Convert between different units of metric measure (for example, kilometre and metre; centimetre and metre; centimetre and millimetre; gram and kilogram; litre and millilitre)	

Strand 1	Strand 2	Unit	Lesson number	Lesson title	NC Objective 1	NC Objective 2	NC Objective 3	NC Objective 3
Measurement		Unit 16	Measure – converting units	4	Metric units (4)	Use all four operations to solve problems involving measure [for example, length, mass, volume, money] using decimal notation, including scaling	Convert between different units of metric measure (for example, kilometre and metre; centimetre and metre; centimetre and millimetre; gram and kilogram; litre and millilitre)	
Measurement		Unit 16	Measure – converting units	5	Imperial units of length	Understand and use approximate equivalences between metric units and common imperial units such as inches, pounds and pints		
Measurement		Unit 16	Measure – converting units	6	Imperial units of mass	Understand and use approximate equivalences between metric units and common imperial units such as inches, pounds and pints		
Measurement		Unit 16	Measure – converting units	7	Imperial units of capacity	Understand and use approximate equivalences between metric units and common imperial units such as inches, pounds and pints		
Measurement		Unit 16	Measure – converting units	8	Converting units of time	Solve problems involving converting between units of time		
Measurement		Unit 16	Measure – converting units	9	Timetables	Solve problems involving converting between units of time		
Measurement		Unit 16	Measure – converting units	10	Problem solving – measure	Use all four operations to solve problems involving measure [for example, length, mass, volume, money] using decimal notation, including scaling		
Measurement		Unit 17	Measure – volume and capacity	1	What is volume?	Estimate volume [for example, using 1 cm³ blocks to build cuboids (including cubes)] and capacity [for example, using water]		
Measurement		Unit 17	Measure – volume and capacity	2	Comparing volumes	Estimate volume [for example, using 1 cm³ blocks to build cuboids (including cubes)] and capacity [for example, using water]		
Measurement		Unit 17	Measure – volume and capacity	3	Estimating volume	Estimate volume [for example, using 1 cm³ blocks to build cuboids (including cubes)] and capacity [for example, using water]		
Measurement		Unit 17	Measure – volume and capacity	4	Estimating capacity	Estimate volume [for example, using 1 cm³ blocks to build cuboids (including cubes)] and capacity [for example, using water]		

Mindset: an introduction

Global research and best practice deliver the same message: learning is greatly affected by what learners perceive they can or cannot do. What is more, it is also shaped by what their parents, carers and teachers perceive they can do. Mindset – the thinking that determines our beliefs and behaviours – therefore has a fundamental impact on teaching and learning.

Everyone can!

Power Maths and mastery methods focus on the distinction between 'fixed' and 'growth' mindsets (Dweck, 2007).[1] Those with a fixed mindset believe that their basic qualities (for example, intelligence, talent and ability to learn) are pre-wired or fixed: 'If you have a talent for maths, you will succeed at it. If not, too bad!' By contrast, those with a growth mindset believe that hard work, effort and commitment drive success and that 'smart' is not something you are or are not, but something you become. In short, everyone can do maths!

Key mindset strategies

A growth mindset needs to be actively nurtured and developed. *Power Maths* offers some key strategies for fostering healthy growth mindsets in your classroom.

It is okay to get it wrong

Mistakes are valuable opportunities to re-think and understand more deeply. Learning is richer when children and teachers alike focus on spotting and sharing mistakes as well as solutions.

Praise hard work

Praise is a great motivator, and by focusing on praising effort and learning rather than success, children will be more willing to try harder, take risks and persist for longer.

Mind your language!

The language we use around learners has a profound effect on their mindsets. Make a habit of using growth phrases, such as, 'Everyone can!', 'Mistakes can help you learn' and 'Just try for a little longer'. The king of them all is one little word, 'yet …
I cannot solve this … yet!'
Encourage parents and carers to use the right language too.

Build in opportunities for success

The step-by-small-step approach enables children to enjoy the experience of success. In addition, avoid ability grouping and encourage every child to answer questions and explain or demonstrate their methods to others.

[1]Dweck, C (2007) *The New Psychology of Success*, Ballantine Books: New York

The *Power Maths* characters

The *Power Maths* characters model the traits of growth mindset learners and encourage resilience by prompting and questioning children as they work. Appearing frequently in the Textbooks and Practice Books, they are your allies in teaching and discussion, helping to model methods, alternatives and misconceptions, and to pose questions. They encourage and support your children, too: they are all hardworking, enthusiastic and unafraid of making and talking about mistakes.

Meet the team!

Flexible Flo is open-minded and sometimes indecisive. She likes to think differently and come up with a variety of methods or ideas.

Determined Dexter is resolute, resilient and systematic. He concentrates hard, always tries his best and he'll never give up – even though he doesn't always choose the most efficient methods!

'Let's try again.'

'Mistakes are cool!'

'Have I found all of the solutions?'

'Let's try it this way …'

'Can we do it differently?'

'I've got another way of doing this!'

'I'm going to try this!'

'I know how to do that!'

'Want to share my ideas?'

Curious Ash is eager, interested and inquisitive, and he loves solving puzzles and problems. Ash asks lots of questions but sometimes gets distracted.

'What if we tried this …?'

'I wonder …'

'Is there a pattern here?'

Miaow!

Sparks the Cat

Brave Astrid is confident, willing to take risks and unafraid of failure. She is never scared to jump straight into a problem or question, and although she often makes simple mistakes she is happy to talk them through with others.

Mathematical language

Traditionally, we in the UK have tended to try simplifying mathematical language to make it easier for young children to understand. By contrast, evidence and experience show that by diluting the correct language, we actually mask concepts and meanings for children. We then wonder why they are confused by new and different terminology later down the line! *Power Maths* is not afraid of 'hard' words and avoids placing any barriers between children and their understanding of mathematical concepts. As a result, we need to be planned, precise and thorough in building every child's understanding of the language of maths. Throughout the Teacher Guides you will find support and guidance on how to deliver this, as well as individual explanations throughout the Pupil Textbooks.

Use the following key strategies to build children's mathematical vocabulary, understanding and confidence.

Precise and consistent

Everyone in the classroom should use the correct mathematical terms in full, every time. For example, refer to 'equal parts', not 'parts'. Used consistently, precise maths language will be a familiar and non-threatening part of children's everyday experience.

Full sentences

Teachers and children alike need to use full sentences to explain or respond. When children use complete sentences, it both reveals their understanding and embeds their knowledge.

Stem sentences

These important sentences help children express mathematical concepts accurately, and are used throughout the *Power Maths* books. Encourage children to repeat them frequently, whether working independently or with others. Examples of stem sentences are:

'4 is a part, 5 is a part, 9 is the whole.'

'There are … groups. There are … in each group.'

Key vocabulary

The unit starters highlight essential vocabulary for every lesson. In the Pupil Textbooks, characters flag new terminology and the Teacher Guide lists important mathematical language for every unit and lesson. New terms are never introduced without a clear explanation.

Mathematical signs

Mathematical signs are used early on so that children quickly become familiar with them and their meaning. Often, the *Power Maths* characters will highlight the connection between language and particular signs.

The role of talk and discussion

When children learn to talk purposefully together about maths, barriers of fear and anxiety are broken down and they grow in confidence, skills and understanding. Building a healthy culture of 'maths talk' empowers their learning from day one.

Explanation and discussion are integral to the *Power Maths* structure, so by simply following the books your lessons will stimulate structured talk. The following key 'maths talk' strategies will help you strengthen that culture and ensure that every child is included.

Sentences, not words

Encourage children to use full sentences when reasoning, explaining or discussing maths. This helps both speaker and listeners to clarify their own understanding. It also reveals whether or not the speaker truly understands, enabling you to address misconceptions as they arise.

Working together

Working with others in pairs, groups or as a whole class is a great way to support maths talk and discussion. Use different group structures to add variety and challenge. For example, children could take timed turns for talking, work independently alongside a 'discussion buddy', or perhaps play different *Power Maths* character roles within their group.

Think first – then talk

Provide clear opportunities within each lesson for children to think and reflect, so that their talk is purposeful, relevant and focused.

Give every child a voice

Where the 'hands up' model allows only the more confident child to shine, *Power Maths* involves everyone. Make sure that no child dominates and that even the shyest child is encouraged to contribute – and is praised when they do.

Assessment strategies

Teaching for mastery demands that you are confident about what each child knows and where their misconceptions lie: therefore, practical and effective assessment is vitally important.

Formative assessment within lessons

The Think together section will often reveal any confusions or insecurities: try ironing these out by doing the first Think together question as a class. For children who continue to struggle, you or your teaching assistant should provide support and enable them to move on.

Performance in Practice can be very revealing: check Practice Books and listen out both during and after practice to identify misconceptions.

The Reflect section is designed to check on the all-important depth of understanding. Be sure to review how children performed in this final stage before you teach the next lesson.

End of unit check – Textbook

Each unit concludes with a summative check to help you assess quickly and clearly each child's understanding, fluency, reasoning and problem-solving skills. In KS2 this check also contains a SATs-style question to help children become familiar with answering this type of question.

In KS2 we would suggest the End of unit check is completed independently in children's exercise books, but you can adapt this to suit the needs of your class.

End of unit check – Practice Book

The Practice Book contains further opportunities for assessment, and can be completed by children independently whilst you are carrying out diagnostic assessment with small groups. Your Teacher Guide will advise you on what to do if children struggle to articulate an explanation – or perhaps encourage you to write down something they have explained well. It will also offer insights into children's answers and their implications for the next learning steps. It is split into three main sections, outlined below.

My journal

My journal is designed to allow children to show their depth of understanding of the unit. It can also serve as a way of checking that children have grasped key mathematical vocabulary. Children should have some time to think about how they want to answer the question, and you could ask them to talk to a partner about their ideas. Then children should write their answer in their Practice Book.

Power check

The Power check allows children to self-assess their level of confidence on the topic by colouring in different smiley faces. You may want to introduce the faces as follows:

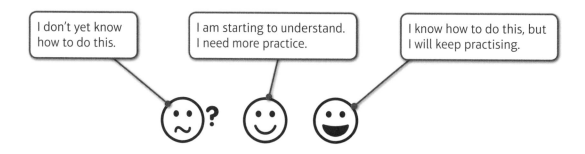

I don't yet know how to do this.

I am starting to understand. I need more practice.

I know how to do this, but I will keep practising.

Power play or Power puzzle

Each unit ends with either a Power play or a Power puzzle. This is an activity, puzzle or game that allows children to use their new knowledge in a fun, informal way. In Key Stage 2 we have also included a deeper level to each game to help challenge those children who have grasped a concept quickly.

How to use diagnostic questions

The diagnostic questions provided in *Power Maths* Textbooks are carefully structured to identify both understanding and misconceptions (if children answer in a particular way, you will know why). The simple procedure below may be helpful:

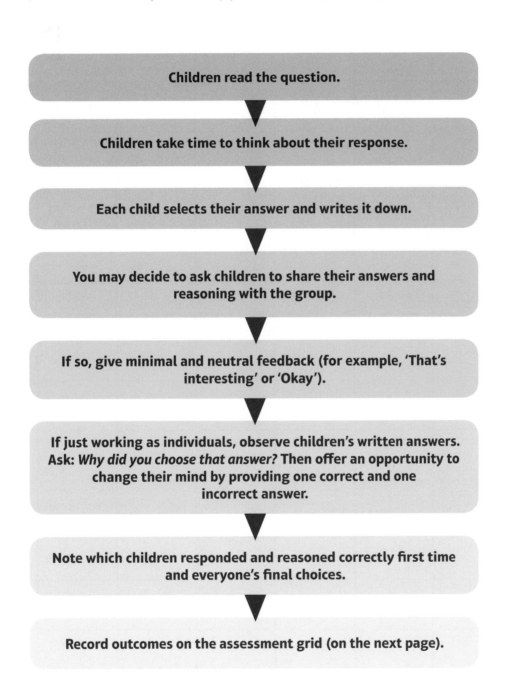

Children read the question.

Children take time to think about their response.

Each child selects their answer and writes it down.

You may decide to ask children to share their answers and reasoning with the group.

If so, give minimal and neutral feedback (for example, 'That's interesting' or 'Okay').

If just working as individuals, observe children's written answers. Ask: *Why did you choose that answer?* Then offer an opportunity to change their mind by providing one correct and one incorrect answer.

Note which children responded and reasoned correctly first time and everyone's final choices.

Record outcomes on the assessment grid (on the next page).

Power Maths unit assessment grid

Year ___   **Unit** ___ _____

Record only as much information as you judge appropriate for your assessment of each child's mastery of the unit and any steps needed for intervention.

Name	Diagnostic questions	SATs-style question	My journal	Power check	Power play/puzzle	Mastery	Intervention/ Strengthen

Keeping the class together

Traditionally, children who learn quickly have been accelerated through the curriculum. As a consequence, their learning may be superficial and will lack the many benefits of enabling children to learn with and from each other.

By contrast, *Power Maths'* mastery approach values real understanding and richer, deeper learning above speed. It sees all children learning the same concept in small, cumulative steps, each finding and mastering challenge at their own level. Remember that when you teach for mastery, EVERYONE can do maths! Those who grasp a concept easily have time to explore and understand that concept at a deeper level. The whole class therefore moves through the curriculum at broadly the same pace via individual learning journeys.

For some teachers, the idea that a whole class can move forward together is revolutionary and challenging. However, the evidence of global good practice clearly shows that this approach drives engagement, confidence, motivation and success for all learners, and not just the high flyers. The strategies below will help you keep your class together on their maths journey.

Mix it up

Do not stick to set groups at each table. Every child should be working on the same concept, and mixing up the groupings widens children's opportunities for exploring, discussing and sharing their understanding with others.

Recycling questions

Reuse the Pupil Textbook and Practice Book questions with concrete materials to allow children to explore concepts and relationships and deepen their understanding. This strategy is especially useful for reinforcing learning in same-day interventions.

Strengthen at every opportunity

The next lesson in a *Power Maths* sequence always revises and builds on the previous step to help embed learning. These activities provide golden opportunities for individual children to strengthen their learning with the support of teaching assistants.

Prepare to be surprised!

Children may grasp a concept quickly or more slowly. The 'fast graspers' won't always be the same individuals, nor does the speed at which a child understands a concept predict their success in maths. Are they struggling or just working more slowly?

Depth and breadth

Just as prescribed in the National Curriculum, the goal of *Power Maths* is never to accelerate through a topic but rather to gain a clear, deep and broad understanding.

"Pupils who grasp concepts rapidly should be challenged through being offered rich and sophisticated problems before any acceleration through new content. Those who are not sufficiently fluent with earlier material should consolidate their understanding, including through additional practice, before moving on."

National Curriculum: Mathematics programmes of study: KS1 & 2, 2013

The lesson sequence offers many opportunities for you to deepen and broaden children's learning, some of which are suggested below.

Discover

As well as using the questions in the Teacher Guide, check that children are really delving into why something is true. It is not enough to simply recite facts, such as '6 + 3 = 9'. They need to be able to see why, explain it, and to demonstrate the solution in several ways.

Share

Make sure that every child is given chances to offer answers and expand their knowledge and not just those with the greatest confidence.

Think together

Encourage children to think about how they found the solution and explain it to their partner. Be sure to make concrete materials available on group tables throughout the lesson to support and reinforce learning.

Practice

Avoid any temptation to select questions according to your assessment of ability: practice questions are presented in a logical sequence and it is important that each child works through every question.

Reflect

Open-ended questions allow children to deepen their understanding as far as they can by discovering new ways of finding answers. For example, *Give me another way of working out how high the wall is … And another way?*

My friends and I often ask questions that make children think more deeply!

Have I found all of the solutions?

Is that always true?

Online materials

For each unit you will find additional strengthening activities to support those children who need it and to deepen the understanding of those who need the additional challenge.

Same-day intervention

Since maths competence depends on mastering concepts one-by-one in a logical progression, it is important that no gaps in understanding are ever left unfilled. Same-day interventions – either within or after a lesson – are a crucial safety net for any child who has not fully made the small step covered that day. In other words, intervention is always about keeping up, not catching up, so that every child has the skills and understanding they need to tackle the next lesson. That means presenting the same problems used in the lesson, with a variety of concrete materials to help children model their solutions.

We offer two intervention strategies below, but you should feel free to choose others if they work better for your class.

Within-lesson intervention

The Think together activity will reveal those who are struggling, so when it is time for Practice, bring these children together to work with you on the first Practice questions. Observe these children carefully, ask questions, encourage them to use concrete models and check that they reach and can demonstrate their understanding.

After-lesson intervention

You might like to use Think together before an assembly, giving you or teaching assistants time to recap and expand with slow graspers during assembly time. Teaching assistants could also work with strugglers at other convenient points in the school day.

The role of practice

Practice plays a pivotal role in the *Power Maths* approach. It takes place in class groups, smaller groups, pairs and independently, so that children always have the opportunities for thinking as well as the models and support they need to practise meaningfully and with understanding.

Intelligent practice

In *Power Maths*, practice never equates to the simple repetition of a process. Instead we embrace the concept of intelligent practice, in which all children become fluent in maths through varied, frequent and thoughtful practice that deepens and embeds conceptual understanding in a logical, planned sequence. To see the difference, take a look at the following examples.

Traditional practice

- Repetition can be rote – no need for a child to think hard about what they are doing.

- Praise may be misplaced.

- Does this prove understanding?

Intelligent practice

- Varied methods – concrete, pictorial and abstract.

- Calculations expressed in different ways, requiring thought and understanding.

- Constructive feedback.

All practice questions are designed to move children on and reveal misconceptions.

Simple, logical steps build onto earlier learning.

C-P-A runs throughout – different ways of modelling and understanding the same concept.

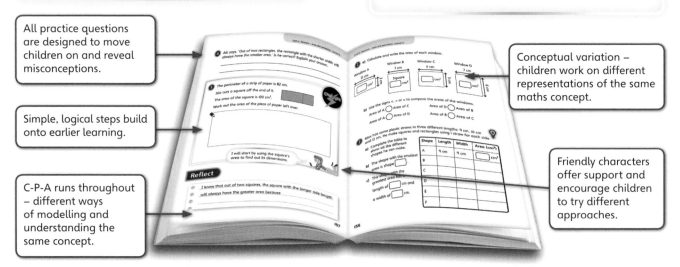

Conceptual variation – children work on different representations of the same maths concept.

Friendly characters offer support and encourage children to try different approaches.

A carefully designed progression

The Practice Books provide just the right amount of intelligent practice for children to complete independently in the final sections of each lesson. It is really important that all children are exposed to the Practice questions, and that children are not directed to complete different sections. That is because each question is different and has been designed to challenge children to think about the maths they are doing. The questions become more challenging so children grasping concepts more quickly will start to slow down as they progress. Meanwhile, you have the chance to circulate and spot any misconceptions before they become barriers to further learning.

Homework and the role of carers

While *Power Maths* does not prescribe any particular homework structure, we acknowledge the potential value of practice at home. For example, practising fluency in key facts, such as number bonds and times-tables, is an ideal homework task, and carers could work through uncompleted Practice Book questions with children at either primary stage.

However, it is important to recognise that many parents and carers may themselves lack confidence in maths, and few, if any, will be familiar with mastery methods. A Parents' and Carers' Evening that helps them understand the basics of mindsets, mastery and mathematical language is a great way to ensure that children benefit from their homework. It could be a fun opportunity for children to teach their families that everyone can do maths!

Structures and representations

Unlike most other subjects, maths comprises a wide array of abstract concepts – and that is why children and adults so often find it difficult. By taking a Concrete-Pictorial-Abstract (C-P-A) approach, *Power Maths* allows children to tackle concepts in a tangible and more comfortable way.

Non-linear stages

Concrete

Replacing the traditional approach of a teacher working through a problem in front of the class, the concrete stage introduces real objects that children can use to 'do' the maths – any familiar object that a child can manipulate and move to help bring the maths to life. It is important to appreciate, however, that children must always understand the link between models and the objects they represent. For example, children need to first understand that three cakes could be represented by three pretend cakes, and then by three counters or bricks. Frequent practice helps consolidate this essential insight. Although they can be used at any time, good concrete models are an essential first step in understanding.

Pictorial

This stage uses pictorial representations of objects to let children 'see' what particular maths problems look like. It helps them make connections between the concrete and pictorial representations and the abstract maths concept. Children can also create or view a pictorial representation together, enabling discussion and comparisons. The *Power Maths* teaching tools are fantastic for this learning stage, and bar modelling is invaluable for problem solving throughout the primary curriculum.

Abstract

Our ultimate goal is for children to understand abstract mathematical concepts, signs and notation and, of course, some children will reach this stage far more quickly than others. To work with abstract concepts, a child needs to be comfortable with the meaning of, and relationships between, concrete, pictorial and abstract models and representations. The C-P-A approach is not linear, and children may need different types of models at different times. However, when a child demonstrates with concrete models and pictorial representations that they have grasped a concept, we can be confident that they are ready to explore or model it with abstract signs such as numbers and notation.

Use at any time and with any age to support understanding.

Practical aspects of *Power Maths*

One of the key underlying elements of *Power Maths* is its practical approach, allowing you to make maths real and relevant to your children, no matter their age.

Manipulatives are essential resources for both key stages and *Power Maths* encourages teachers to use these at every opportunity, and to continue the Concrete-Pictorial-Abstract approach right through to Year 6.

The Textbooks and Teacher Guides include lots of opportunities for teaching in a practical way to show children what maths means in real life.

Discover and Share

The Discover and Share sections of the Textbook give you scope to turn a real-life scenario into a practical and hands-on section of the lesson. Use these sections as inspiration to get active in the classroom. Where appropriate, use the Discover contexts as a springboard for your own examples that have particular resonance for your children – and allow them to get their hands dirty trying out the mathematics for themselves.

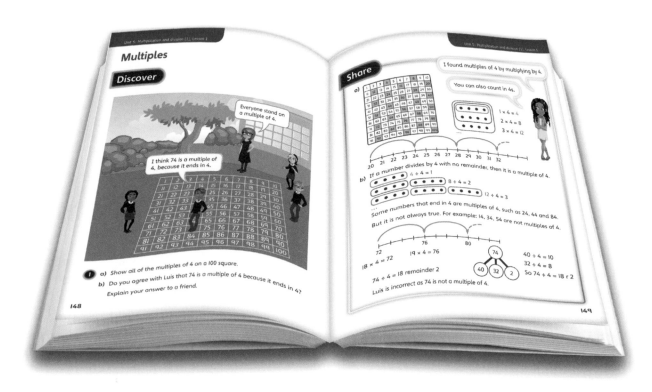

Unit videos

Every unit has a video which incorporates real-life classroom sequences.

These videos show you how the reasoning behind mathematics can be carried out in a practical manner by showing real children using various concrete and pictorial methods to come to the solution. You can see how using these practical models, such as part-whole and bar models, helps them to find and articulate their answer.

Mastery tips

Mastery Experts give anecdotal advice on where they have used hands-on and real-life elements to inspire their children.

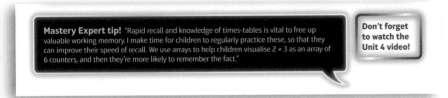

Mastery Expert tip! "Rapid recall and knowledge of times-tables is vital to free up valuable working memory. I make time for children to regularly practice these, so that they can improve their speed of recall. We use arrays to help children visualise 2 × 3 as an array of 6 counters, and then they're more likely to remember the fact."

Don't forget to watch the Unit 4 video!

Concrete-Pictorial-Abstract (C-P-A) approach

Each Share section uses various methods to explain an answer, helping children to access abstract concepts by using concrete tools, such as counters. Remember this isn't a linear process, so even children who appear confident using the more abstract method can deepen their knowledge by exploring the concrete representations. Encourage children to use all three methods to really solidify their understanding of a concept.

Pictorial representation – drawing the problem in a logical way that helps children visualise the maths.

Concrete representation – using manipulatives to represent the problem. Encourage children to physically use resources to explore the maths.

Abstract representation – using words and calculations to represent the problem.

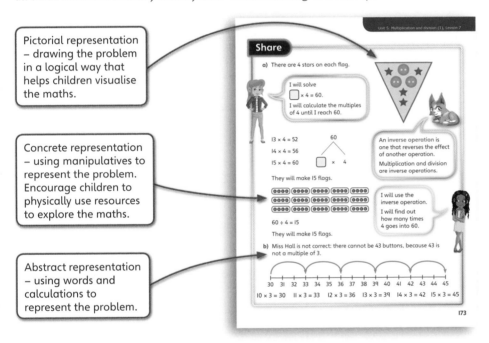

Practical tips

Every lesson suggests how to draw out the practical side of the Discover context.

You'll find these in the Discover section of the Teacher Guide for each lesson.

PRACTICAL TIPS You could use balls, counters or cubes under plastic cups to re-enact the artwork and help children get a feel for this activity.

Resources

Every lesson lists the practical resources you will need or might want to use. There is also a summary of all of the resources used throughout the term on page 34 to help you be prepared.

RESOURCES

Mandatory: cubes, counters, number lines

Optional: balls, plastic cups

List of practical resources

Year 5C Mandatory resources

Resource	Lesson
Base 10 equipment	**Unit 12** lessons 12, 13
Blank comparison bar models	**Unit 12** lesson 11
Containers of different sizes	**Unit 17** lesson 4
Cubes	**Unit 17** lessons 1, 2, 3, 4
Geoboards	**Unit 14** lesson 2
Isometric paper	**Unit 15** lesson 1 **Unit 17** lesson 1
Measuring jug (metric)	**Unit 12** lesson 8
Mirrors	**Unit 15** lessons 1, 2
Paper or card circles	**Unit 13** lesson 6
Paper strips	**Unit 14** lesson 3
Pictures of different jugs	**Unit 17** lesson 4
Place value counters	**Unit 12** lessons 1, 2, 3, 5, 6, 8, 12, 13, 14, 15
Protractor	**Unit 13** lessons 2, 3, 4, 5 **Unit 14** lessons 3, 4
Ruler	**Unit 13** lessons 2, 4, 7 **Unit 14** lessons 1, 3, 4 **Unit 15** lesson 1
Square dotted paper	**Unit 15** lessons 1, 3
Squared paper	**Unit 15** lessons 1, 2, 3, 4
Weighing scales (metric)	**Unit 12** lessons 8, 11

Year 5C Optional resources

Resource	Lesson
0–9 number cards	**Unit 12** lesson 7
2D shapes cut from squared paper	**Unit 15** lesson 3
Two different coloured dice	**Unit 15** lesson 4
3D shapes	**Unit 14** lesson 5
Analogue and digital clocks	**Unit 16** lesson 8
Analogue clock with moveable hands	**Unit 16** lessons 9, 10
Arrow spinner	**Unit 13** lesson 1
Blank bar models	**Unit 12** lesson 11 **Unit 16** lesson 3
Blank place value grid	**Unit 12** lessons 12, 13, 14, 15 **Unit 16** lessons 3, 4
Bottles with different capacities in ml	**Unit 16** lessons 2, 7 **Unit 17** lessons 1, 4
Building blocks	**Unit 12** lesson 13
Calendars	**Unit 16** lesson 8
Card strips	**Unit 14** lessons 3, 4
Chalk	**Unit 15** lesson 3
Cubes	**Unit 12** lesson 13 **Unit 16** lesson 8
Cylinders	**Unit 17** lesson 4
Decimal number cards	**Unit 12** lesson 9
Digit cards	**Unit 16** lessons 3, 4
Dried rice and pasta	**Unit 16** lesson 10 **Unit 17** lesson 4

Resource	Lesson
Flashcards	**Unit 16** lessons 3, 6, 10
Geoboards	**Unit 14** lessons 3, 4
Geostrips	**Unit 14** lessons 2, 4
Glue	**Unit 12** lesson 1
Images of reflections	**Unit 15** lesson 1
Imperial weights	**Unit 16** lesson 6
Isometric paper	**Unit 17** lesson 2
Large and small boxes	**Unit 12** lesson 15
Large sheets of paper	**Unit 16** lesson 2
Measuring jug (metric)	**Unit 16** lesson 2, 7
Measuring jug (imperial)	**Unit 16** lesson 7
Measuring tape (cm)	**Unit 16** lessons 5, 10
Measuring wheel	**Unit 16** lesson 1
Metre stick	**Unit 12** lessons 4, 7 **Unit 16** lesson 2
Mini whiteboards	**Unit 16** lesson 9
Modelling clay	**Unit 17** lesson 3
Number line	**Unit 12** lesson 9 **Unit 16** lesson 3
Paper	**Unit 12** lessons 1, 14 **Unit 16** lessons 9, 10
Paper angle measurer	**Unit 13** lesson 2
Paper semicircles	**Unit 13** lesson 5
Paper squares and rectangles	**Unit 13** lesson 7 **Unit 16** lesson 7
Place value counters	**Unit 12** lessons 7, 9
Plant growth chart	**Unit 12** lesson 9
Plastic or paper money	**Unit 12** lessons 5, 6
Pictures of items for sale in the shop	**Unit 12** lesson 5
Protractor	**Unit 13** lesson 6 **Unit 14** lesson 2
Ramp	**Unit 13** lesson 2
Ruler	**Unit 13** lesson 6 **Unit 16** lessons 2, 4, 10 **Unit 17** lesson 2
Ruler showing imperial units	**Unit 16** lesson 5
Sand	**Unit 17** lesson 4
Scissors	**Unit 12** lesson 14 **Unit 13** lesson 5
Split pins	**Unit 14** lessons 3, 4
Sticks	**Unit 14** lesson 1
Sticky labels	**Unit 16** lessons 5, 6
String	**Unit 16** lesson 10
Square dotted paper	**Unit 14** lesson 3 **Unit 17** lessons 2, 3
Squared paper	**Unit 14** lesson 4
Timetables	**Unit 16** lesson 9
Torch	**Unit 14** lesson 5
Toy items (fruit)	**Unit 12** lesson 6
Toy train tracks	**Unit 12** lesson 1
Variety of measuring items	**Unit 17** lesson 1
Weighing scales (metric)	**Unit 12** lessons 4, 10 **Unit 16** lessons 1, 6, 10
Weighing scales (imperial)	**Unit 16** lesson 6
Year planner	**Unit 16** lesson 8

Variation helps visualisation

Children find it much easier to visualise and grasp concepts if they see them presented in a number of ways, so be prepared to offer and encourage many different representations.

For example, the number six could be represented in various ways:

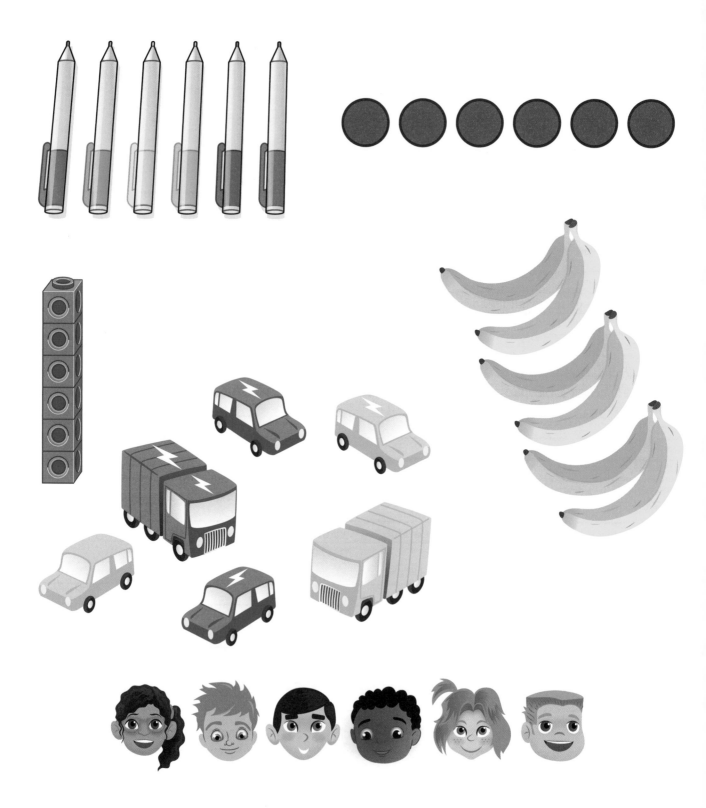

Getting started with *Power Maths*

As you prepare to put *Power Maths* into action, you might find the tips and advice below helpful.

STEP 1: Train up!

A practical, up-front, full-day professional development course will give you and your team a brilliant head-start as you begin your *Power Maths* journey. You will learn more about the ethos, how it works and why.

STEP 2: Check out the progression

Take a look at the yearly and termly overviews. Next take a look at the unit overview for the unit you are about to teach in your Teacher Guide, remembering that you can match your lessons and pacing to your class.

STEP 3: Explore the context

Take a little time to look at the context for this unit: what are the implications for the unit ahead? (Think about key language, common misunderstandings and intervention strategies, for example.) If you have the online subscription, don't forget to watch the corresponding unit video.

STEP 4: Prepare for your first lesson

Familiarise yourself with the objectives, essential questions to ask and the resources you will need. The Teacher Guide offers tips, ideas and guidance on individual lessons to help you anticipate children's misconceptions and challenge those who are ready to think more deeply.

STEP 5: Teach and reflect

Deliver your lesson – and enjoy!

Afterwards, reflect on how it went … Did you cover all five stages? Does the lesson need more time? How could you improve it? What percentage of your class do you think mastered the concept? How can you help those that didn't?

Unit 12
Decimals

Don't forget to watch the Unit 12 video!

Mastery Expert tip! "To build confidence with decimals, we invented a board game called 93. There were 93 children in Year 5. They each created one question where the answer was a decimal number. Children applied their learning from this unit to the game. We challenged children to add, subtract, multiply, divide and problem-solve with decimals to win points. They tried to make as many points as possible before reaching 'Finish'. The game really engaged children and was a great way to build confidence and fluency in working with decimals."

WHY THIS UNIT IS IMPORTANT

This unit is important because it applies the formal methods of addition and subtraction to numbers with up to three decimal places. It also teaches children to multiply and divide decimal numbers by 10, 100 and 1,000. The range of problem-solving questions in this unit will develop confidence and flexibility when exploring the most efficient ways to work with decimal numbers.

WHERE THIS UNIT FITS

→ Unit 11: Decimals and percentages

→ **Unit 12: Decimals**

→ Unit 13: Geometry – properties of shapes (1)

This unit builds on children's work in Years 4 and 5 of adding and subtracting whole numbers, and multiplying and dividing whole numbers by 10, 100 and 1,000. It also extends on children's work with number patterns. By considering the place value of each digit, children will broaden their understanding of adding and subtracting using formal written methods and of multiplying and dividing decimal numbers.

Before they start this unit, it is expected that children:

• can add and subtract numbers with up to 4 digits
• are able to solve addition and subtraction word problems
• can multiply and divide whole numbers by 10, 100 and 1,000
• understand what place value means and can use a place value grid to partition a decimal number.

ASSESSING MASTERY

Children who have mastered this unit children can add and subtract numbers with up to three decimal places using a variety of methods, including formal written methods. They can multiply and divide decimal numbers by 10, 100 and 1,000. They can confidently apply their knowledge of decimal numbers to solve word problems.

COMMON MISCONCEPTIONS	STRENGTHENING UNDERSTANDING	GOING DEEPER
When using column addition or subtraction, children may line the numbers up from right to the left rather than according to their place value.	Use a place value grid alongside the column addition or subtraction so that children can link the concrete and abstract representations.	Compare calculations laid out correctly and incorrectly. What is the difference between the correct and incorrect answer? Why?
Children may add the digits when adding decimals that make one, for example, 0·3 + 0·7, children 3 and 7 and give the answer 0·10.	Use a bar model or number line to help children understand whether the answer is 1 or not. Discuss that 0·3 means 3 tenths, and 0·7 means 7 tenths.	Ask increasingly difficult missing number questions. Give children a total and ask them to find the different ways they can make the total.

WAYS OF WORKING

As a whole class, discuss the unit starter pages. Talk through the key learning points and vocabulary mentioned by the characters. Use Ash's comment to remind children of the column method, noting the importance of setting out column addition neatly.

STRUCTURES AND REPRESENTATIONS

Place value grid: This model uses counters to show the value of each column. It supports the column method layout.

O	•	Tth	Hth	Thth
① ①	•	$\frac{1}{10}$ $\frac{1}{10}$ $\frac{1}{10}$ $\frac{1}{10}$	$\frac{1}{100}$ $\frac{1}{100}$	$\frac{1}{1,000}$

Column addition and subtraction: This model demonstrates the place value of each digit in addition and subtraction calculations and shows exchanges between columns.

$$
\begin{array}{r}
\text{O} \cdot \text{Tth} \ \text{Hth} \ \text{Thth} \\
2 \cdot 4 \quad 3 \quad 1 \\
+ \ 0 \cdot 0 \quad 8 \quad 0 \\
\hline
2 \cdot 5 \quad 1 \quad 1 \\
\end{array}
$$

$$
\begin{array}{r}
\text{O} \cdot \text{Tth} \ \text{Hth} \ \text{Thth} \\
{}^{7}\cancel{8} \cdot {}^{1}2 \ {}^{6}\cancel{7} \ {}^{1}0 \\
- \ 6 \cdot 6 \quad 5 \quad 3 \\
\hline
1 \cdot 6 \quad 1 \quad 7 \\
\end{array}
$$

Bar model: This model can be used to compare numbers and identify missing information. It can be used to represent the information in some addition and subtraction word problems.

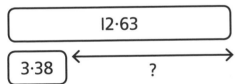

KEY LANGUAGE

There is some key language that children will need to know as part of the learning in this unit.

→ add, subtract, multiply, divide
→ ones, tenths, hundredths, thousandths
→ difference, group, share, compare, represent
→ decimal, decimal point, decimal place, digit
→ column, place value, exchange
→ mass, weight, length, width, cost, height

Adding and subtracting decimals

Learning focus

In this lesson, children will learn to add decimals, recognising the importance of place value.

Small steps

→ Previous step: Equivalent fractions, decimals and percentages
→ **This step: Adding and subtracting decimals (1)**
→ Next step: Adding and subtracting decimals (2)

NATIONAL CURRICULUM LINKS

Year 5 Number – Fractions (Including Decimals and Percentages)

Solve problems involving number up to three decimal places.

ASSESSING MASTERY

Children can add and subtract decimals where the answer is less than one. Children can answer abstract questions or those presented in a context and draw diagrams to express their thinking.

COMMON MISCONCEPTIONS

Children may not understand the importance of place value or what each digit represents. When adding decimals that total one, such as 0·3 + 0·7, children often add the digits 3 and 7 and give the answer as 0·10. Ask:
• *What does the 3 represent? Can you represent each number with place value counters?*
• *Can you simplify 0·10? Can you show the number on a number line? Can you show the sum on a number line?*

STRENGTHENING UNDERSTANDING

Children should practise adding 2 or 3 whole numbers before moving on to decimals. They may use a number line to visualise the calculation better. Discuss that 0·3 means 3 tenths, and 0·7 means 7 tenths. Ask: *What is the total of 3 tenths and 7 tenths?* If children say 10 tenths, revisit the concept of fractions. Encourage them to clearly describe the place value of each column and ensure they understand the importance of the decimal point, particularly in an exchange.

GOING DEEPER

Give children a total and ask how many different ways they can make the total, for example _ + _ = 0·9. This could also be represented on a part-whole model to help children to see the link between adding and subtracting. Change each decimal to a fraction and link both concepts together. Children know that $\frac{3}{10} + \frac{7}{10} = 1$. What other decimals and fractions can they find with a total of 1?

KEY LANGUAGE

In lesson: add, subtract, difference, total, tenths, part-whole, metres (m)

Other language to be used by the teacher: ones, hundredths, digit, column, place value, decimal point

STRUCTURES AND REPRESENTATIONS

bar model, number line, part-whole model

RESOURCES

Mandatory: place value counters

Optional: toy train tracks, paper, glue

In the eTextbook of this lesson, you will find interactive links to a selection of teaching tools.

Before you teach

• Do children know how to add and subtract 1- and 2-digit numbers?
• Do children understand what a decimal is?

Discover

Adding and subtracting decimals ❶

Discover

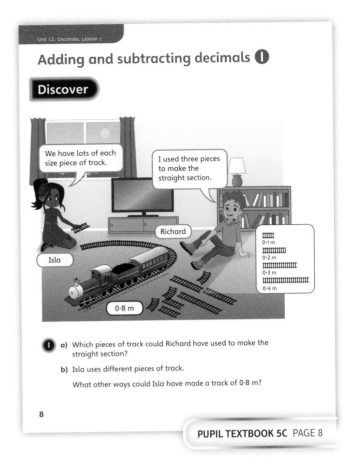

WAYS OF WORKING Pair work

ASK

• Question ❶ a): *What lengths are the different track pieces? What does 0·8 m show?*
• Question ❶ b): *How many track pieces can be used to make a track of 0·8 m? What does this depend on?*

IN FOCUS Question ❶ a) is important as it requires children to consider and identify three decimal numbers that have a total of 0·8. Question ❶ b) requires children to explore alternative ways that 0·8 can be made.

PRACTICAL TIPS Consider allowing children to assemble their own train tracks so that they feel fully involved in the context of the lesson. Bring in different length train tracks or make paper tracks. Children could link or glue the tracks together. This is a good opportunity to discuss the vocabulary needed for this lesson, such as: total, longer, shorter, difference and sum.

ANSWERS

Question ❶ a): Richard could have used 0·4 m, 0·3 m and 0·1 m track pieces to make the straight section [other possible answers can be accepted].

Question ❶ b): Isla could have used one 0·4 m and two 0·2 m pieces. Or she could have used two 0·3 m and one 0·2 m pieces to make a track of 0·8 m [other possible answers can be accepted – must be different to answer to a)].

❶ a) Which pieces of track could Richard have used to make the straight section?

b) Isla uses different pieces of track.

What other ways could Isla have made a track of 0·8 m?

8

Share

WAYS OF WORKING Whole class teacher led

ASK

• Question ❶ a): *How many decimal numbers do you need? What should they add up to (sum to)? What method could you use to add the two numbers together?*
• Question ❶ a): *Does it matter which number you start with?*
• Question ❶ b): *How many decimal numbers are you looking for? What method could you use to work out which numbers make the total? Is there a quicker way?*

IN FOCUS For question ❶ a), take the opportunity to discuss the use of the bar model above the number line. Demonstrate how a bar model helped Dexter work out the possible answers. Place value grids can also be used to reinforce the place value of each digit, for example ask: *What is 3 tenths add 4 tenths add 1 tenth?*

For question ❶ b), discuss the use of adding whole, numbers that make 8, emphasising the need to not miss any calculations. Discuss Flo's comment. To extend, children can investigate what their strategy would be if the total was 0·9 m or 1·0 m.

Share

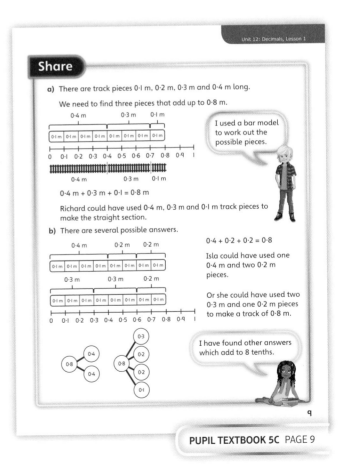

a) There are track pieces 0·1 m, 0·2 m, 0·3 m and 0·4 m long.

We need to find three pieces that add up to 0·8 m.

0·4 m + 0·3 m + 0·1 = 0·8 m

Richard could have used 0·4 m, 0·3 m and 0·1 m track pieces to make the straight section.

b) There are several possible answers.

0·4 + 0·2 + 0·2 = 0·8

Isla could have used one 0·4 m and two 0·2 m pieces.

Or she could have used two 0·3 m and one 0·2 m pieces to make a track of 0·8 m.

9

Think together

Whole class teacher led (I do, We do, You do)

ASK

- Question **1** a) and b): *What is the same and what is different about this question and the question in Discover?*
- Question **2** b): *Does the question only have one answer or is there more than one possible answer?*
- Question **3** b): *What strategy will you use? Can you use a number line to show the calculation?*

IN FOCUS Question **3** highlights the most common misconception in this lesson. Give children the opportunity to discuss what mistake Isla has made. Encourage them to use a bar model with a number line to support their answer. Discuss the methods Astrid and Flo used to find the difference between the decimal numbers in question **3** b). Decimals are numbers so children should realise that all the strategies used to add and subtract numbers can be applied to decimals.

STRENGTHEN Support understanding by representing calculations using counters on a place value grid. Revisit the vocabulary that children have already encountered when adding and subtracting numbers. Ask children to explain what each word means, for example: difference, total, more, less, sum.

DEEPEN Explore all the possible ways of making each of the numbers given in question **2**. Do children work systematically to find all the possible combinations? Children could explore more open-ended questions, for example, find five decimals with a sum of 1.

ASSESSMENT CHECKPOINT Can children explain how to add two or more decimals with a total less than or equal to 1? Can children find the difference between two decimal numbers? Can they draw a diagram to support their calculation?

ANSWERS

Question **1** a): 0·6 m + 0·2 m = 0·8 m.
The track is 0·8 m in total.

Question **1** b): 0·7 m − 0·1 m = 0·6 m.
Piece A is 0·6 m longer than piece B.

Question **2** a): 0·4 + 0·5 = 0·9

Question **2** b): Possible answers 0·3 − 0·2 = 0·1,
0·2 − 0·1 = 0·1, 0·4 − 0·3 = 0·1, 0·5 − 0·4 = 0·1

Question **2** c): 0·4 + 0·2 = 0·6

Question **3** a): 0·1 + 0·2 + 0·7 = 1 not 0·10

Question **3** b): 1 − 0·7 = 0·3 m

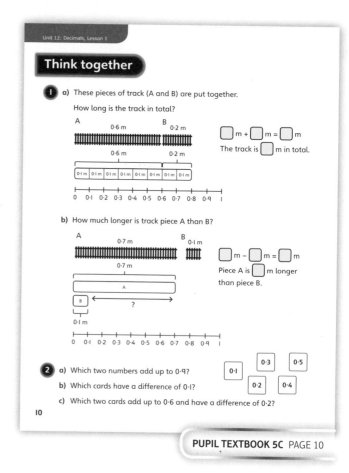

PUPIL TEXTBOOK 5C PAGE 10

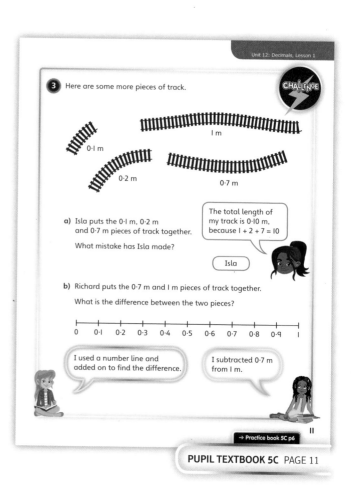

PUPIL TEXTBOOK 5C PAGE 11

Practice

WAYS OF WORKING Independent thinking

IN FOCUS Question ❶ consolidates understanding of adding two or more decimal numbers.

Question ❷ consolidates children's understanding of subtracting decimals and revisits the vocabulary that children have used previously to compare numbers.

For question ❻, children need to identify whether to add or subtract to find the missing numbers. To solve these questions, children need to understand that addition and subtraction are inverse operations. Ask children to write the number sentence they used to find each missing number.

STRENGTHEN Encourage children to use counters on a place value grid to support understanding and use the bar model to check their answers are correct. Ask: *Are number bonds important when adding decimals? Why?*

DEEPEN If children are comfortable solving question ❽, then ask them to solve the question in a different way. Ask: *What is your strategy? Do you start by finding the numbers in each vertex or do you complete one side at a time? What addition and subtraction statements can you write?*

THINK DIFFERENTLY Question ❼ will require children to think differently and work backwards from the answer to determine what the possible question might be. Discuss whether there might be more than one answer and then challenge children to find all the possible answers.

ASSESSMENT CHECKPOINT Children are confident adding and subtracting decimal numbers less than 1.

ANSWERS Answers for the **Practice** part of the lesson appear in the separate **Practice and Reflect answer guide**.

Reflect

WAYS OF WORKING Independent thinking

IN FOCUS This **Reflect** activity checks that children are recognising and adding decimals correctly. Encourage them to explain (without doing any calculations) why Emma is wrong. Children should recognise that Emma has added 0·1 to 0·4 rather than 1 and 0·4. Look for children who are able to spot the mistake without any prompting.

ASSESSMENT CHECKPOINT Assess if children can correctly explain how to find two decimal numbers that have a total of less than 1, emphasising the importance of place value and what each digit represents.

ANSWERS Answers for the **Reflect** part of the lesson appear in the separate **Practice and Reflect answer guide**.

After the lesson ⏸

- Can children add and subtract decimals less than 1?
- Can children find two or more decimals that equal a given total?
- Which children needed to use counters on a place value grid for support?
- Can children accurately draw or use a bar model to support their answers?

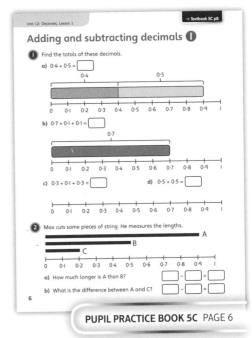

PUPIL PRACTICE BOOK 5C PAGE 6

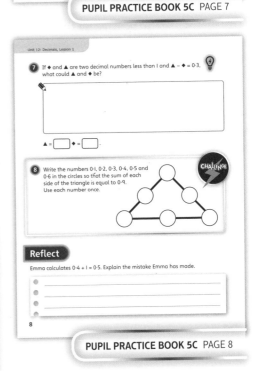

PUPIL PRACTICE BOOK 5C PAGE 7

PUPIL PRACTICE BOOK 5C PAGE 8

Adding and subtracting decimals ❷

Learning focus

In this lesson, children will add and subtract decimals less than one. They will use the written column method to add or subtract decimals.

Small steps

→ Previous step: Adding and subtracting decimals (1)
→ **This step: Adding and subtracting decimals (2)**
→ Next step: Adding and subtracting decimals (3)

NATIONAL CURRICULUM LINKS

Year 5 Number – Fractions (Including Decimals and Percentages)

Solve problems involving number up to three decimal places.

ASSESSING MASTERY

Children can add or subtract decimals less than one using the written column method.

COMMON MISCONCEPTIONS

Children may not set the column method out correctly when adding decimals with a zero as one of the digits. They ignore the zero and add the wrong number. For example, instead of adding 0·03 to a number they add 0·3. Ask:
• *What does each digit represent? What is the value of each digit? Do digits in the same column have the same value?*

STRENGTHENING UNDERSTANDING

Encourage children to use counters on a place value grid. This can be done alongside the column addition or subtraction so that children can see how the concrete and abstract methods link together. Ask children to estimate the answer, for example: *How different is the exact answer from your estimated one?*

GOING DEEPER

Ask children to create their own questions. They could find two numbers where their sum or difference is given, for instance: *Find two numbers that total 0·87 or find two numbers where one is 0·12 more than the other.* Encourage children to make the link between addition and subtraction when solving these kinds of calculations.

KEY LANGUAGE

In lesson: add, subtract, total, altogether, difference, sum, exchange, decimal, column, how much more, less than, tenths, hundredths, litres (l)

Other language to be used by the teacher: place value, ones

STRUCTURES AND REPRESENTATIONS

column addition and subtraction, place value grid, bar model, number line, part-whole model

RESOURCES

Mandatory: place value counters

 In the eTextbook of this lesson, you will find interactive links to a selection of teaching tools.

Before you teach

• Are children confident making an exchange when using the column addition method?
• Can children set out a column addition when one of the numbers is zero?

Discover

WAYS OF WORKING Pair work

ASK

- Question ❶ a): *Do you think this question is about addition or subtraction? Can you answer this question without doing a calculation? How do you know you are correct?*
- Question ❶ b): *What strategy could you use to find the answer?*

IN FOCUS Discuss with children the language used in **Discover** section. Usually, children link the words 'how much' and 'more' with addition, however in question ❶ b) they need to subtract. If children are unsure how to proceed, give real-life examples and use smaller numbers.

PRACTICAL TIPS Consider linking **Discover** to an art class. Discuss with children why it is important to know the measurements of red and yellow paint when mixing them. Children need to think about the container that they will use to store the paint and how much paint they may use. Use words like 'total', 'more' or 'less' when discussing the amount of paint that they will mix.

ANSWERS

Question ❶ a): Olivia and Luis can make 0·68 l of orange paint.

Question ❶ b): Olivia and Luis need 0·07 l more orange paint.

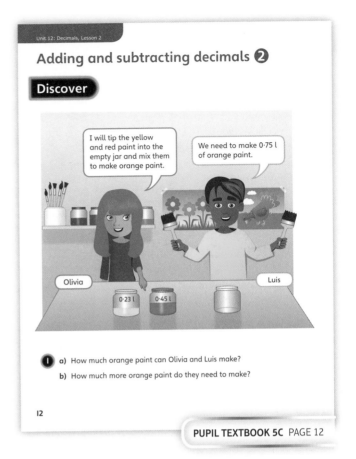

Share

WAYS OF WORKING Whole class teacher led

ASK

- Question ❶ a): *Look at the columns in the place value grid. What does each column represent? How can you use column addition of whole numbers to add decimal numbers?*
- Question ❶ a): *Why do we need to be careful how we write the numbers so that they are lined up?*
- Question ❶ b): *To answer this question, should you add or subtract? How do you know? What part of the question tells you this? What calculation could you do to prove your answer is correct?*

IN FOCUS In question ❶ b), children should be able to articulate why they have performed a subtraction and not an addition. Children can use bar models and number lines to prove their answers are correct. Show children the column method of addition and subtraction of decimal numbers. Use this question to reinforce the place value of each digit when carrying out the calculation and discuss the exchange that needs to take place of 1 tenth for 10 hundredths.

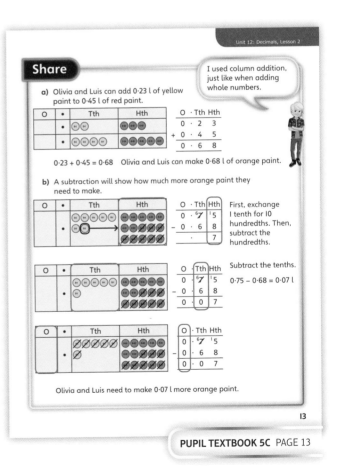

Think together

WAYS OF WORKING Whole class teacher led (I do, We do, You do)

ASK

- Question **1** a): *What is the same and different about this question and the one in* **Discover**?
- Question **1** b): *What is the question asking? What is the unit of measurement?*
- Question **3** a): *What do you need to know to find the amount of slime altogether? Do you know how much slime each child has? Can you work it out?*

IN FOCUS Questions **1** a) and b) apply learning from **Discover**. Use question **1** b) to reinforce the place value of each digit when adding the numbers together. Discuss the exchange of 10 hundredths for 1 tenth. Emphasise the use of the correct units of measurement. Question **3** introduces a two-step question. Children need to find how much slime Kate has before adding the amounts together to find the total. Some children may just add the two numbers given without fully reading the question. Encourage them to describe the question before finding a solution.

STRENGTHEN To support understanding, represent each calculation using counters on a place value grid and display these alongside the abstract calculations. For question **3**, ask children to use bar model to find the answer.

DEEPEN Challenge children to create their own addition and subtraction problems using the words 'more than', 'less than' and 'how much more?'. What language will they use to indicate a subtraction? Can they use a variety of different words? If children need support, provide them with an addition and subtraction example.

ASSESSMENT CHECKPOINT Can children use a bar model and a number line to explain their answers? Can children explore the best method to use to add or subtract two decimal numbers? If so, can they describe their strategy?

ANSWERS

Question **1** a): 0·41 l + 0·42 l = 0·83 l
 0·83 litres of orange paint can be made.

Question **1** b): 0·29 l + 0·22 l = 0·51 l
 0·51 litres of squash can be made.

Question **2** a): Jamilla has 0·91 l of soup in total.

Question **2** b): Jamilla needs 0·09 l more soup.

Question **3** a): 0·27 l + 0·22 l = 0·49 l.
 Kate has 0·49 l of slime.
 0·27 l + 0·49 l = 0·76 l.
 Ebo and Kate have 0·76 l of slime altogether.

Question **3** b): 1·00 l − 0·76 l = 0·24 l.
 They need another 0·24 l of slime.

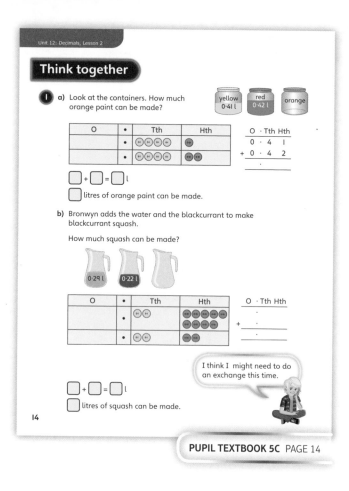

PUPIL TEXTBOOK 5C PAGE 14

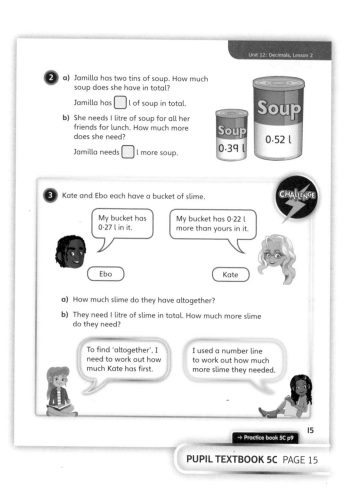

PUPIL TEXTBOOK 5C PAGE 15

Practice

WAYS OF WORKING Independent thinking

IN FOCUS Questions ❶ and ❸ aim to consolidate children's understanding of adding or subtracting two decimal numbers using the column method. The information is represented with counters on a place value grid, in a column and abstractly.

Questions ❺ and ❻ use different models to ensure a variety of representations and to demonstrate how the bar model and number line can both be used when adding or subtracting decimal numbers.

STRENGTHEN Ensure children have access to concrete materials and number lines throughout the exercise. Encourage all children to continuously explain their thought processes. Question ❷ provides a good opportunity to discuss a common misconception when adding decimals with 0 as one of the digits. Urge children to use counters on a place value grid to support their understanding.

DEEPEN Ask children to discuss how they tackled the challenge question. Is there only one way to approach it? Did they start with the hundredth or the tenth column? Why?

THINK DIFFERENTLY Question ❻ encourages children to link the visual representation and abstract calculation. Some children may add all the numbers at once; others may write two addition statements. To extend, ask children to write two word problems based on the number line. Ask: *Can this be a subtraction calculation? What words can you use to show that?*

ASSESSMENT CHECKPOINT Are children confident in using the addition and subtraction column methods to add or subtract decimals? Do they understand how they can use the link between addition and subtraction to find missing numbers?

ANSWERS Answers for the **Practice** part of the lesson appear in the separate **Practice and Reflect answer guide**.

Reflect

WAYS OF WORKING Independent thinking

IN FOCUS This **Reflect** activity checks that children can use the addition of two whole numbers to calculate the addition of two decimal numbers. Identify children who can use the link between the additions and are able to add decimal numbers mentally. Identify those who need further support in understanding the link between the additions, then explain the links by using concrete resources.

ASSESSMENT CHECKPOINT Check that children are able to explain the similarities between adding decimal numbers and whole numbers. Do children recognise that the methods of adding and subtracting of whole numbers can be adapted and used when working with decimal numbers?

ANSWERS Answers for the **Reflect** part of the lesson appear in the separate **Practice and Reflect answer guide**.

After the lesson

- Can children confidently use the column addition or subtraction to add two decimal numbers?
- Can children identify calculations that require exchanges and correctly solve them?
- Do children understand the importance of place value when adding decimal numbers?

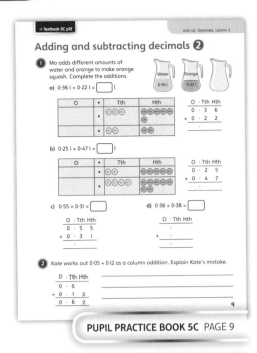

PUPIL PRACTICE BOOK 5C PAGE 9

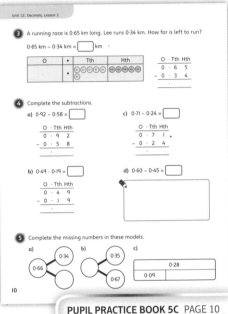

PUPIL PRACTICE BOOK 5C PAGE 10

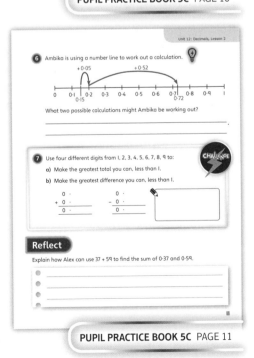

PUPIL PRACTICE BOOK 5C PAGE 11

Adding and subtracting decimals ❸

Learning focus

In this lesson, children will work out how much needs to be added to another decimal to make the whole: to find the complement to 1.

Small steps

→ Previous step: Adding and subtracting decimals (2)
→ **This step: Adding and subtracting decimals (3)**
→ Next step: Adding and subtracting decimals (4)

NATIONAL CURRICULUM LINKS

Year 5 Number – Fractions (Including Decimals and Percentages)

Solve problems involving number up to three decimal places.

ASSESSING MASTERY

Children can use number bonds to 10 and 100 and column addition and subtraction to find decimal numbers that add to make 1. Children can answer abstract questions or those presented in a context and draw diagrams to represent their thinking.

COMMON MISCONCEPTIONS

Children may not set the column method out correctly when subtracting decimals from 1. For example, they may think of 1 as 0·1 and subtract the smaller digit from the bigger digit, so when calculating 1 – 0·23 they may actually calculate 0·23 – 0·1. Ask:

• *What digit do you need to subtract? How many tenths are there in 1? How many hundredths are there in one tenth?*

STRENGTHENING UNDERSTANDING

Children should first practise subtracting whole numbers from 100 or 1,000 before progressing to subtracting decimals with two and three decimal places from 1. Children should be given the opportunity to use a hundredths grid (or a similar resource) to visually link what happens when different parts of the whole (that complement to make 1) are added together. To embed this process, move parts away from the whole to see where the two complementary parts come from.

GOING DEEPER

Challenge children to find three or four decimal numbers that add to make 1. They should write these as addition equations and derive the subtraction equations from them.

KEY LANGUAGE

In lesson: whole, place value, ones, tenths, hundredths, exchange, number bonds, column, add, subtract

Other language to be used by the teacher: parts, split, partitioned, thousandth, decimal point, 2 decimal places, 3 decimal places

STRUCTURES AND REPRESENTATIONS

bar model, part-whole model, hundredths grid, number line, column addition, column subtraction, place value grid

RESOURCES

Mandatory: place value counters

 In the eTextbook of this lesson, you will find interactive links to a selection of teaching tools.

Before you teach

• Do children know how to make an exchange when subtracting?
• Can children confidently add two or more whole numbers with two or more decimal places?

Discover

WAYS OF WORKING Pair work

ASK

- Question ❶ a): *How long are the two lengths of mirror Aki needs to decorate? What lengths of paper does he have?*
- Question ❶ b): *Will you add or subtract to find the answer?*

IN FOCUS Question ❶ a) asks children to find the pairs of numbers that have a total of 1. Ensure that children understand what the question requires. Question ❶ b) requires children to calculate how much ribbon is left from 1 m, so they will need to subtract a number with three decimal places from 1.

PRACTICAL TIPS Consider providing children with three different lengths of paper or ribbon, where two pieces add up to 1 m. Give them a 1 m stick. Ask them to measure each piece, write the measurements and put together the pieces that make 1 m. Provide children with a hundredths grid and discuss how it can be used.

ANSWERS

Question ❶ a): Aki can use the 0·7 m and 0·3 m pieces to decorate one side of the mirror and 0·57 m and 0·43 m to decorate the other side.

Question ❶ b): Aki has 0·765 m of ribbon left.

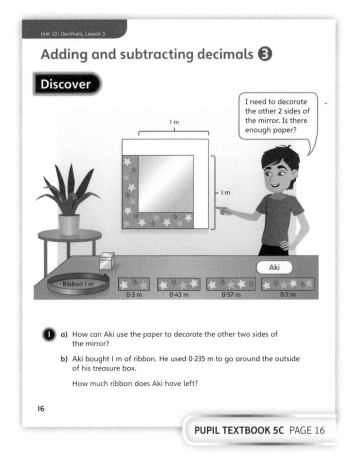

PUPIL TEXTBOOK 5C PAGE 16

Share

WAYS OF WORKING Whole class teacher led

ASK

- Question ❶ a): *How can you use number bonds to help? How did Astrid use the hundredths grid to help her?*
- Question ❶ b): *Why is it helpful to write 1 as 1·000 here? What exchanges do you need to make to find the difference?*

IN FOCUS In this section, children are shown how to find decimal numbers that have a total of 1. They are also introduced to subtracting a decimal number from 1. Show children the column method of subtraction. They should be able to explain which place value column they need to start with and how to exchange when subtracting a 3-digit number from 100. Draw similarities between subtracting 2- and 3-digit numbers from 100 and 1,000 and subtracting decimal numbers from 1.

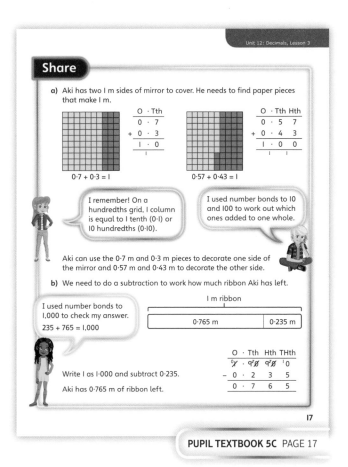

PUPIL TEXTBOOK 5C PAGE 17

Think together

ASK

- Question ❶: *How can you find the missing parts? What do you notice about the number pairs that add up to 1?*
- Question ❷: *What do the part-whole models and bar model show? What is the same about them? How do they differ?*

IN FOCUS In questions ❶ and ❷, children are exposed to a variety of different representations for adding decimals to make 1. Encourage children to try different methods, ensuring they use place value counters next to the diagrams. Discuss their preferred methods and clarify any questions or misconceptions. Question ❸ links the use of concrete resources to the abstract written calculation. Astrid and Ash present the most likely misconception children will encounter. Placing counters in each column will help children visualise the column addition better and understand the value of each digit in the calculation.

STRENGTHEN To support understanding, encourage children to find the answer using more than one method. Children could use the part-whole model or the bar model to find the answer.

DEEPEN After question ❸ b), children could produce their own calculations where two or more decimals are added together to make a whole. They could extend it even further by including both addition and subtraction in each calculation, for example, _ – _ + _ = 1.

ASSESSMENT CHECKPOINT Children should be able to verbalise how they know that their calculations are correct. Children should also be able to explain when and how they can do an exchange when adding decimal numbers that total 1.

ANSWERS

Question ❶ a): 1 m – 0·4 m = 0·6 m

Question ❶ b): 1 m – 0·49 m = 0·51 m

Question ❶ c): 1 m – 0·68 m = 0·32 m

Question ❷ a): 0·8

Question ❷ b): 0·29

Question ❷ c): 0·868

Question ❷ d): 0·479

Question ❸ a): 0·29 + 0·71 = 1

Question ❸ b): 0·724 + 0·276 = 1

Question ❸ c): 0·34 + 0·45 + 0·21 = 1
0·34 – 0·21 + 0·87 = 1
Possible answer: 0·234 + 0·123 + 0·643 = 1

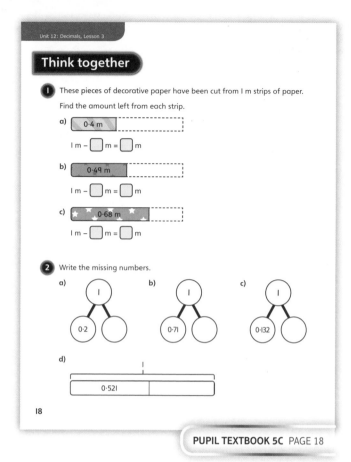

PUPIL TEXTBOOK 5C PAGE 18

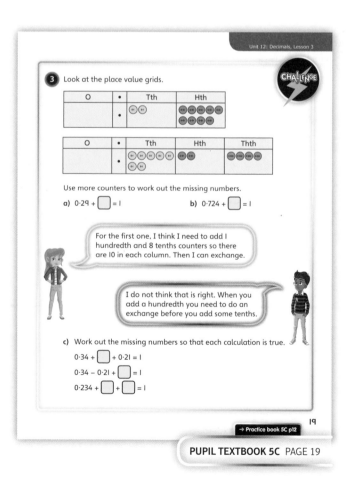

PUPIL TEXTBOOK 5C PAGE 19

Practice

WAYS OF WORKING Independent thinking

IN FOCUS Questions ① and ② aim to consolidate children's understanding of adding decimals that make 1.

In question ③, children need to explain Lexi's mistake. This will demonstrate their understanding of how to correctly display the calculation using a place value grid.

Question ④ links addition and subtraction. Children should be able to change an addition calculation to a subtraction and vice versa.

STRENGTHEN Strengthen understanding by using concrete manipulatives. Use counters, bar models, number lines or place value grids to help reinforce the concept in a more visual and relatable way.

DEEPEN The challenge question provides an opportunity for children to provide multiple solutions to the same question. To extend this, children can be presented with similar questions, varying the number of parts in the whole as relevant. Encourage them to find all of the different ways the calculation can be completed.

ASSESSMENT CHECKPOINT Children should be able to use resources to explain the calculations they have completed. Furthermore, they should also be able to draw different representations to show the solutions to the problems.

ANSWERS Answers for the **Practice** part of the lesson appear in the separate **Practice and Reflect answer guide**.

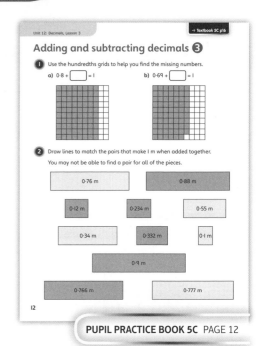

PUPIL PRACTICE BOOK 5C PAGE 12

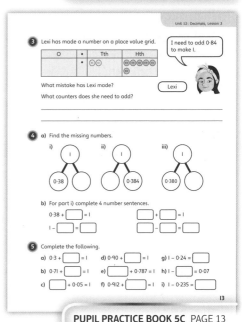

PUPIL PRACTICE BOOK 5C PAGE 13

Reflect

WAYS OF WORKING Independent thinking

IN FOCUS In this section of the lesson, children are required to reason whether Andy's calculation is correct or incorrect through the use of accurate vocabulary. They could also use diagrams or column addition to support their reasoning.

ASSESSMENT CHECKPOINT The strength of children's written response should allow assessments to be made about whether they have a secure understanding of the concept of adding decimals, including the addition of decimals that require one or more exchange.

ANSWERS Answers for the **Reflect** part of the lesson appear in the separate **Practice and Reflect answer guide**.

After the lesson

- What percentage of children mastered the lesson?
- Were children able to use a variety of different representations to show their solutions?
- Can children identify calculations that need exchange and correctly complete these calculations?

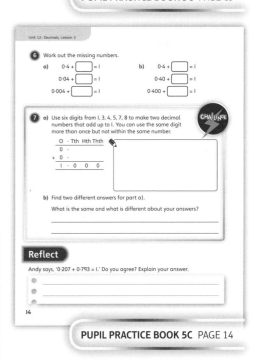

PUPIL PRACTICE BOOK 5C PAGE 14

Adding and subtracting decimals

Learning focus

In this lesson, children will add numbers less than 1 where the total is greater than 1.

Small steps

→ Previous step: Adding and subtracting decimals (3)
→ **This step: Adding and subtracting decimals (4)**
→ Next step: Adding and subtracting decimals (5)

NATIONAL CURRICULUM LINKS

Year 5 Number – Fractions (Including Decimals and Percentages)

Solve problems involving number up to three decimal places.

ASSESSING MASTERY

Children can add decimals less than 1 where the total is greater than 1. For example, when adding 0·5 + 0·7 they are able to explain why the answer is 1·2 and not 0·12. Children can answer abstract questions or those presented in a context and draw diagrams to explain their thinking.

COMMON MISCONCEPTIONS

Children may not exchange correctly when the sum of the decimals is greater than 1. For example, when adding 0·7 + 0·6, they think that the answer is 0·13 rather than 1·3. Ask:

• *How many tenths are there in 0·7? How many tenths are there in 0·6? How many tenths are there in total? How many tenths are there in one whole? How many tenths are left over?*

STRENGTHENING UNDERSTANDING

Encourage children to clearly describe the place value of each digit and ensure they understand the importance of it, in particular when making an exchange. Some children will benefit from using place value counters. Other children may find it useful to link decimals with fractions out of 10 and use concrete representations such as a metre stick or scale that is split into tenths. Seeing what happens when two decimals add to make a number greater than 1 will deepen children's understanding.

GOING DEEPER

Ask children to explore and explain different methods. Encourage children to decide which method is more efficient depending on the context. Children may represent their addition in more than one way, for example with bar models, number lines and place value counters.

KEY LANGUAGE

In lesson: add, total, column, decimal, whole, tenths, less than (<), greater than (>), equals (=), metres (m), kilograms (kg)

Other language to be used by the teacher: increased by, digit, exchange, ones, hundredths, place value

STRUCTURES AND REPRESENTATIONS

place value grid, column addition, number line, bar model

RESOURCES

Optional: metre stick, weighing scales

 In the eTextbook of this lesson, you will find interactive links to a selection of teaching tools.

Before you teach

• Can children add fractions with a sum greater than 1 and denominator of 10?
• Can children make an exchange when using the column addition method?

Discover

ASK

- Question **1** a): *What information does the table show?*
- Question **1** a): *Do all plants grow in the same away? What does 'grown by' mean?*
- Question **1** b): *What do the measurements on the stick go up by?*

IN FOCUS Question **1** a) helps to ensure that children can use a table to derive the relevant information and then interpret how to use it. Question **1** b) requires children to calculate how much taller the cactus is than the bamboo tree. Children build on prior learning of finding solutions to 'how much more' questions. Discuss possible methods of addition and subtraction that can be used to find solutions.

PRACTICAL TIPS Show children pictures of fast-growing and slow-growing plants. Investigate and discuss their growth rates and the maximum height they can grow to. Discuss the height that a bamboo can be each year and compare that to the height of a cactus or another slow-growing plant. The more curious children become, the more invested they will be in the task ahead.

ANSWERS

Question **1** a): At the end of the month the height of the bamboo tree is 1·6 m. At the end of the month the height of the cactus is 1·25 m.

Question **1** b): The bamboo tree is 0·35 m taller than the cactus.

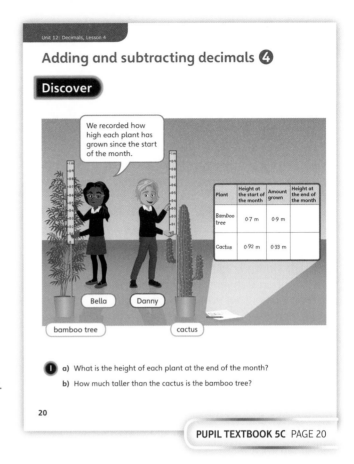

Share

ASK

- Question **1** a): *How much has the bamboo tree grown by? And the cactus? What calculation do you have to do to find the height of both plants at the end of the month?*
- Question **1** b): *How tall is the bamboo tree? What is the number line showing? How can you check your calculation is correct?*

IN FOCUS Question **1** a) requires children to add two decimal numbers where the total is greater than 1. These calculations necessitate one exchange when using the column addition method. Explore the different models and methods that can be used to find the total. Use the number line to further develop understanding of each step. Discuss the number of tenths of each number and the number of tenths that make 1 whole.

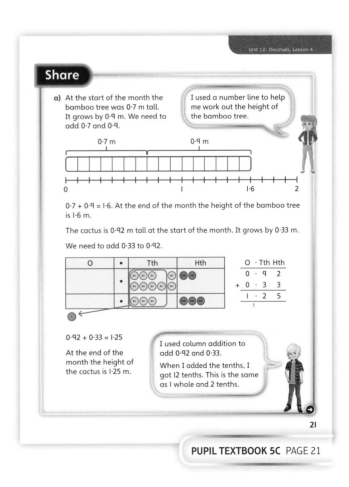

Think together

Whole class teacher led (I do, We do, You do)

ASK

- Question **1**: *What information do you need to find the height of the sunflower at the end of the month?*
- Question **2** a): *How many tenths are there in 0·5? And in 0·7? How many tenths altogether? How many tenths make one whole?*
- Question **2** b): *How many tenths are there in 0·48? And in 0·71? How many tenths make one whole?*
- Question **3** a): *How could Ash check his answer?*

IN FOCUS Question **2** focuses on a common misconception. If children use the column method, make sure that they lay out the columns correctly. Children should be able to explain which place value column they start with when adding numbers together and why. Use this question to reinforce the place value of each digit and discuss the exchange of 10 tenths for 1 one that takes place.

STRENGTHEN To support understanding in question **2** a), show children a weighing scale or a picture of scales showing 0·5 kg. Show children what happens when 0·7 kg is added. A number line can be used alongside the abstract calculation in order to link the concrete, pictorial and abstract representations together.

DEEPEN Take children further in question **3**. Ask them to write number stories or provide a context for each of the calculations. Children can share their stories and discuss how they can be solved. Encourage them to use diagrams in their explanation and answer any questions their peers may have. As an extension, children could create their own missing number question in the same style as those given.

ASSESSMENT CHECKPOINT Can children add numbers less than 1 with a sum greater than 1? In question **2** a) can children explain why 0·5 + 0·7 is not 0·12? Can children explain how they have found missing numbers to their partner?

ANSWERS

Question **1**: 0·67 + 0·75 = 1·42
At the end of the month the height of the sunflower is 1·42 m.

Question **2** a): 0·5 kg + 0·7 kg = 1·2 kg, not 0·12 kg.
Emma has made a mistake because she has neglected to exchange 10 tenths for 1 one.

Question **2** b): 0·48 + 0·71 = 1·19, not 0·119.
Max has also forgotten to exchange 10 tenths for 1 one.

Question **3** a): 0·8 + 0·5 = 1·3

Question **3** b): 0·92 + 0·35 = 1·27

Question **3** c): 0·454 + 0·685 = 1·139

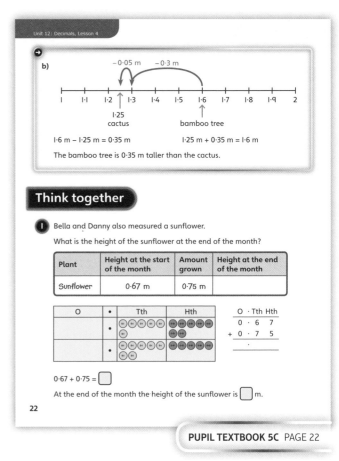

PUPIL TEXTBOOK 5C PAGE 22

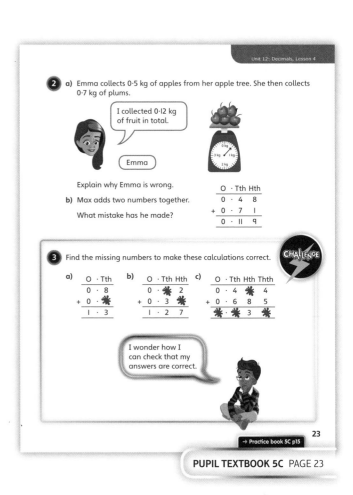

PUPIL TEXTBOOK 5C PAGE 23

Practice

WAYS OF WORKING Independent thinking

IN FOCUS Questions ❶ and ❷ aims to consolidate children's understanding of how to find the total of two decimal numbers where the answer exceeds 1.

Questions ❻ encourages children to compare two calculations. Ask children to pay attention to the hundredths and tenths digit on either side of the sign, rather than use the written method. To extend further, children should be encouraged to use their knowledge of number bonds to calculate or estimate the answer.

STRENGTHEN Encourage children to use counters on a place value grid to support their understanding and to make it clearer when to exchange 10 tenths for 1 one. Children can draw their own diagrams to check their answer is correct.

DEEPEN Question ❺ encourages children to problem solve and work out missing digits in addition calculations. This can be explored further by giving children more complex missing number problems. For example, children could find the calculation for two decimal numbers with a total of 1·23. Ask children to find more than one solution.

ASSESSMENT CHECKPOINT Children are confident in adding two numbers less than 1 with a total that is greater than 1. Pay attention to children's working out in question ❷ to assess whether they are confident adding two decimals and look for any misconceptions surrounding place value.

ANSWERS Answers for the **Practice** part of the lesson appear in the separate **Practice and Reflect answer guide**.

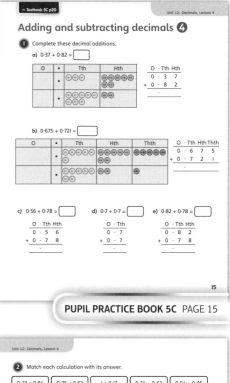

PUPIL PRACTICE BOOK 5C PAGE 15

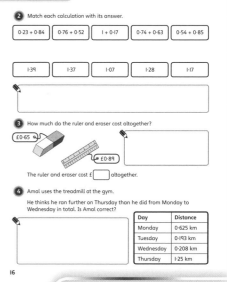

PUPIL PRACTICE BOOK 5C PAGE 16

Reflect

WAYS OF WORKING Independent thinking

IN FOCUS This question checks children's understanding of what they have learnt in the lesson and in particular of the misconception discussed in the lesson. Encourage children to explain their reasoning as well as calculate the answer.

ASSESSMENT CHECKPOINT This reflection will assess children's ability to add two decimals where the answer exceeds 1. Look for children who can clearly explain the exchange that takes place and the reason for it. Identify children who still need support to do this.

ANSWERS Answers for the **Reflect** part of the lesson appear in the separate **Practice and Reflect answer guide**.

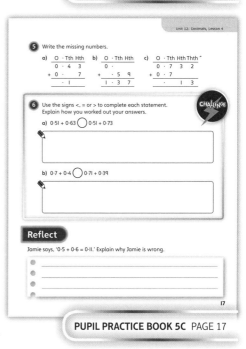

PUPIL PRACTICE BOOK 5C PAGE 17

After the lesson ⏸

- Can children explain how to add decimal numbers that exceed 1?
- Can children identify and solve calculations that require exchanges?
- Can children explain the importance of place value when adding? Are they aware of common mistakes they should attempt to avoid?

Adding and subtracting decimals ⑤

Learning focus

In this lesson, children will add two numbers that have the same number of decimal places, such as 2·56 + 7·75.

Small steps

- Previous step: Adding and subtracting decimals (4)
- **This step: Adding and subtracting decimals (5)**
- Next step: Adding and subtracting decimals (6)

NATIONAL CURRICULUM LINKS

Year 5 Number – Fractions (Including Decimals and Percentages)

Solve problems involving number up to three decimal places.

ASSESSING MASTERY

Children can use and explain different methods of adding two decimal numbers that have the same number of decimal places. Within a context, they can decide which method is the most efficient.

COMMON MISCONCEPTIONS

Children may not realise that zero is important as a place holder. For instance, when adding 8·02 and 5·01, they may write 8·02 as 8·2 and 5·01 as 5·1 and calculate 8·02 + 5·01 = 13·3. Ask:
- *Are 8·2 and 8·02 the same value? What does the '2' in the number represent? Are £8·20 and £8·02 the same amount?*

STRENGTHENING UNDERSTANDING

To strengthen learning in this lesson, ask children to place decimal numbers in a place value grid. When they have done this successfully, ask them what the value of each digit is. Use the context of money to explain the differences between £8 and 20p and £8 and 2p.

GOING DEEPER

Deepen learning in this lesson by counting backwards and forward in tenths and hundredths. Can children cross whole number boundaries such as 8·99, 9, 9·01?

KEY LANGUAGE

In lesson: add, total, digit, column, whole, part, place value, ones, tenths, hundredths, less than (<), greater than (>), equals (=), pounds (£)

Other language to be used by the teacher: decimal, decimal places, exchange, pence (p)

STRUCTURES AND REPRESENTATIONS

number line, place value grid, column addition, part-whole model, bar model

RESOURCES

Mandatory: place value counters

Optional: plastic or paper money, picture of items for sale in the shop

 In the eTextbook of this lesson, you will find interactive links to a selection of teaching tools.

Before you teach

- Children focused on decimal numbers less than 1 in the previous lesson. Do you need to revisit decimals greater than 1 prior to this lesson?
- Do children use efficient methods to add decimals?

Discover

ASK

- Question **1** a): *What is Max buying? How much money does he have? What do you need to know to calculate whether he has enough money to buy the items he wants?*
- Question **1** b): *Is Jamie paying more or less than Max? How do you know? What method can you use to find out how much Jamie's meal costs?*

IN FOCUS Question **1** a) is important because children have to work with decimal numbers above 1. This calculation requires children to make two exchanges when using the column addition method. Question **1** b) requires children to find the sum of two totals.

PRACTICAL TIPS Give children an opportunity to visualise the problem by using concrete representations. Each table could have its own shop or canteen to represent how children can come across this problem in their everyday lives. The items in the shop are labelled. Give children a certain amount to spend, for instance £4, and ask them to list the items that they can buy and the ones they cannot. Ask: *How much do these items cost? How much more money do you need to buy this item?*

ANSWERS

Question **1** a): Max's meal costs £4 in total, so he has enough money.

Question **1** b): The total cost of Jamie's meal is £5·35.

PUPIL TEXTBOOK 5C PAGE 24

Share

ASK

- Question **1** a): *What method can you use to add the two numbers together? Will the answer be different if you chose a different method?*
- Question **1** a): *Which place value column do you need to start with? Will you need to make an exchange?*
- Question **1** b): *Do you need to know the cost of each item Jamie buys? What is the key word in the question that can help you decide how to calculate the total?*

IN FOCUS Question **1** a) is important because children must represent the decimal numbers on a place value grid using place value counters. The use of place value grids in question **1** a) reinforces the place value of each digit in the calculation. Demonstrate why this is important when children are required to carry out the exchange of 10 hundredths for 1 tenth and 10 tenths for 1 one. Question **1** b) is important because children must represent the addition of a whole number and a decimal number with 2 decimal places on a number line. Doing this makes the learning both visual and practical.

Discuss the use of mental addition. Ask: *What would you do if you were in the canteen? How would you calculate the total cost to work out if you had enough money?*

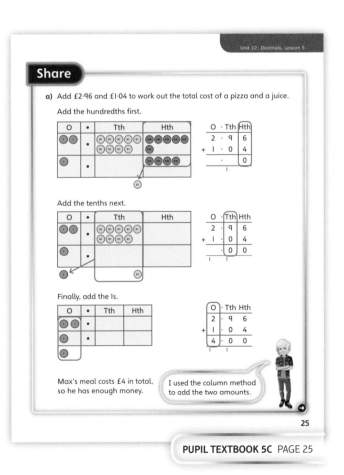

PUPIL TEXTBOOK 5C PAGE 25

Think together

WAYS OF WORKING **WAYS OF WORKING** Whole class teacher led (I do, We do, You do)

ASK

• Question **3** a): *How can the last digits help you determine whether you are correct?*
• Question **3** b): *What method can you use to check the answers?*

IN FOCUS Question **2** is important because children have an opportunity to use a part-whole model, a bar model and an abstract calculation to add decimal numbers. This will require a good understanding of what tenths and hundredths mean and how each of the models can be used to find the missing numbers. When working out which two numbers make a given total in question **2** a), encourage children to look at the last digit in each number instead of carrying out the full calculation.

STRENGTHEN For questions **2** a) and b), provide children with place value counters and a place value grid to use alongside the part-whole model and the bar model. This will help them to find the whole more readily. The place value grid and counters are particularly useful for question **2** c), allowing them to visualise each decimal number.

DEEPEN For question **3**, ask children to work out the total for other combinations of numbers or to imagine they bought four items instead of three items. Ask them to make their own questions based on the picture. What key words do they use?

ASSESSMENT CHECKPOINT Can children add decimal numbers with the same number of decimal places? Are children able to use the part-whole model and the bar model to find solutions?

ANSWERS

Question **1** a): The total cost is £4·49

Question **1** b): The total cost is £5·27

Question **2** a): 2·9 + 3·7 = 6·6

Question **2** b): 2·453 + 5·232 = 7·685

Question **2** c): 6 ones, 3 tenths and 4 hundredths plus 7 ones, 2 tenths and 9 hundredths is equal to 1 tens, 3 ones, 6 tenths and 3 hundredths. (6·34 + 7·29 = 13·63)

Question **3** a): £6·47 + £3·15 + £2·38 = £12·00. Jamilla chose colour pencils, marbles and a ruler.

Question **3** b): £3·15 + £4·26 = £0·94 + £6·47

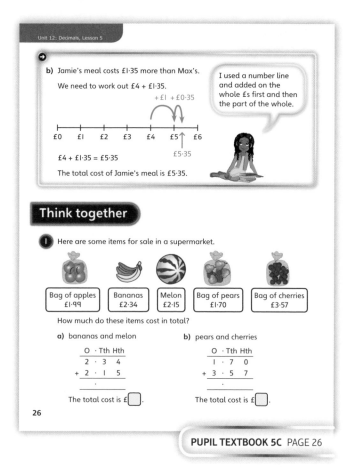

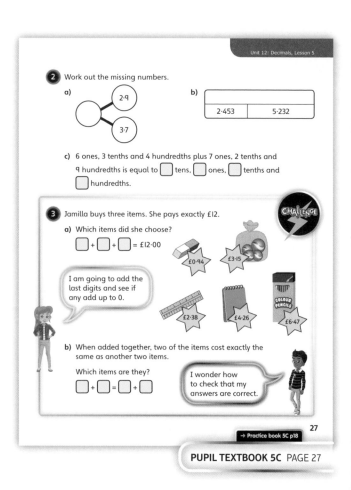

PUPIL TEXTBOOK 5C PAGE 26

PUPIL TEXTBOOK 5C PAGE 27

Practice

WAYS OF WORKING Independent thinking

IN FOCUS Questions ❶ and ❷ aims to consolidate children's understanding of adding two decimal numbers through the use of the column method and using counters on a place value grid.

In question ❸, children will need to use their preferred method to add numbers with two or three decimal places and then use appropriate signs to compare the amounts.

STRENGTHEN Question ❺ provides a good opportunity for children to locate decimal numbers on a number line and compare decimal numbers with each other. The number line will aid their visualisation of which numbers are smaller or larger. Can children accurately position a decimal number on the number line? For example, in finding 7·32, do they locate it just after the 7·3 mark? Children may need the support of number lines with greater detail.

DEEPEN The challenge question provides an opportunity for children to provide multiple solutions to the same question. Children need to read and understand the table of prices to solve this question. Explore this further by asking children to round the numbers to the nearest whole number before adding them mentally. Ask children to make their own table of prices and ask their partner to choose two or three activities that they want to complete.

THINK DIFFERENTLY Question ❺ will help children develop their confidence with ordering decimal numbers as well as understanding the place value of numbers with up to three decimal places as they estimate their position on the number line.

ASSESSMENT CHECKPOINT Children are confident in adding two decimal numbers which have the same number of decimal places.

ANSWERS Answers for the **Practice** part of the lesson appear in the separate **Practice and Reflect answer guide**.

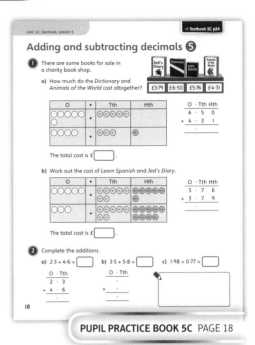

PUPIL PRACTICE BOOK 5C PAGE 18

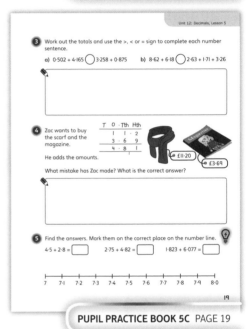

PUPIL PRACTICE BOOK 5C PAGE 19

Reflect

WAYS OF WORKING Independent thinking

IN FOCUS This activity is a great way for children to reflect on the learning of this lesson. Encourage children to explain how they would carry out the calculation as well as actually answering it. Look for children who are able to add the numbers without support and offer support or concrete apparatus to children that lack confidence when adding the numbers.

ASSESSMENT CHECKPOINT Assess if children can correctly explain how to find the total of two decimal numbers, emphasising the importance of the place value of each column and identifying the exchanges they need to make.

ANSWERS Answers for the **Reflect** part of the lesson appear in the separate **Practice and Reflect answer guide**.

After the lesson ⏸

- Can all children add decimals with two decimal places?
- Can they represent decimal numbers on a place value grid and a number line?
- Are children confident with the key vocabulary of the lesson?

PUPIL PRACTICE BOOK 5C PAGE 20

Adding and subtracting decimals 6

Learning focus

In this lesson, children will use the column method to subtract decimals in the context of taking away or finding the difference. This will include examples where an exchange is required.

Small steps

→ Previous step: Adding and subtracting decimals (5)
→ **This step: Adding and subtracting decimals (6)**
→ Next step: Adding and subtracting decimals (7)

NATIONAL CURRICULUM LINKS

Year 5 Number – Fractions (Including Decimals and Percentages)

Solve problems involving number up to three decimal places.

ASSESSING MASTERY

Children can subtract any two numbers that have the same number of decimal places, such as 12·56 – 7·75. They recognise why exchanges are needed when subtracting decimal numbers.

COMMON MISCONCEPTIONS

Children may, when subtracting two decimal numbers, subtract the smaller digit from the larger digit. For example, when working out 3·82 – 1·25 = 2·63, they may write 3 in the hundredth column as they have worked out 5 – 2 and not made the exchange. Ask:

• *Which digit do you need to subtract? What will you do if the digit you are subtracting is bigger than the digit you are subtracting from? How do you set out the column method when subtracting numbers?*

STRENGTHENING UNDERSTANDING

Children should first spend time practising subtracting whole numbers with 2 or 3 digits before moving on to subtracting decimals.

GOING DEEPER

Give children missing number problems such as _ – 0·78 = 1·65 or ask them to complete _ – _ = 2·34 in as many different ways as possible.

KEY LANGUAGE

In lesson: subtract, difference, efficient, exchange, greater, change, cheaper, ones, tenths, hundredths, column, inverse, predict, pounds (£), pence (p), kilometres (km)

Other language to be used by the teacher: place value, fewer, more, less

STRUCTURES AND REPRESENTATIONS

place value grid, column method subtraction, bar model, number line

RESOURCES

Mandatory: place value counters

Optional: paper money, toy items (fruit) to buy

 In the eTextbook of this lesson, you will find interactive links to a selection of teaching tools.

Before you teach

• Can children subtract 2- and 3-digit numbers?
• Do children understand key vocabulary such as 'greater', 'inverse', 'cost' and 'change'?

Discover

WAYS OF WORKING Pair work

ASK

- Question **1** a): *How much does a pineapple and a watermelon cost altogether? How much does the pineapple cost? How could you work out how much the watermelon costs?*
- Question **1** b): *When does the shopkeeper give you change? What information do you need to know to calculate the change Amelia will get?*

IN FOCUS Question **1** a) requires children to calculate one part when the other part and the whole is given. It requires children to subtract with two exchanges. Question **1** b) introduces another subtraction. If calculated as a column subtraction, this also requires two exchanges where two of the digits are 0.

PRACTICAL TIPS To assist children in visualising the scenario and in determining what calculations are required, give them paper money and ask them to role play. Ask how much change they would receive if they bought different items.

ANSWERS

Question **1** a): The watermelon costs £3·49.

Question **1** b): Amelia gets 26p change.

Share

WAYS OF WORKING Whole class teacher led

ASK

- Question **1** a): *In which column(s) do we need to make an exchange? How do you know?*
- Question **1** b): *Could you use either an addition or a subtraction on this number line and find the same answer? What would be a different method of presenting this information?*

IN FOCUS Question **1** a): Discuss the column subtraction and ensure children are confident in using this layout when subtracting. Check that children can explain how we know that we need to make an exchange. Use the column method to reinforce the place value of each digit when carrying out the calculation and explain the exchanges that take place. For question **1** b), show children the number line and ask: *Why might Flo have counted on to find the difference? How can this be presented as a subtraction?* Encourage children to try to show this as a column subtraction. Reinforce the exchange that happens when the hundredth and tenths digits are 0.

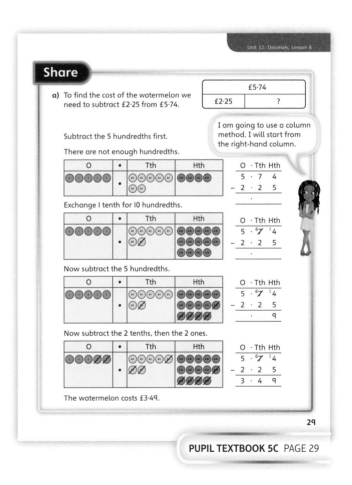

61

Think together

WAYS OF WORKING Whole class teacher led (I do, We do, You do)

ASK

- Question **1**: *What calculation do we need to do to calculate 'how much cheaper'? Which place value column should we start with? What exchange do we need to make?*
- Question **2** a): *What information do we need to find to predict the number of exchanges? Which digits should we look at first?*
- Question **3** a): *When do you have to exchange to complete the subtraction?*
- Question **3** b): *Can you find Reena's number in two different ways?*

IN FOCUS Question **1** requires children to subtract two decimal numbers. The use of place value counters and column method supports the calculation. Question **2** encourages children to look at the digits within each number and compare them. Children need to have a clear understanding of when an exchange happens to answer this question. Invite children to share their views. Write their answers on the board, including any mistakes, and use this opportunity to clarify any misconceptions children may still have. Question **3** encourages children to analyse the methods used and reason as to why Ebo is not correct. Encourage children to draw their own diagrams to visualise the question better and identify the subtractions they need to complete.

STRENGTHEN To help children visualise the calculations Reena must make, give children a similar version of the question using whole numbers. For instance: *I am thinking of a number. I add 1, then add 2. My answer is 7. What number was I thinking of?* Once children are clear on their strategy, they can apply this to find Reena's number.

DEEPEN Further develop understanding by presenting children with questions similar to question **2**, where they have to predict the number of exchanges. Extend this further by asking children to write their own 'predict' questions and ask them to think of how they can make them easier or harder.

ASSESSMENT CHECKPOINT Can children compare different methods to carry out a subtraction calculation? Are they able to explain their steps and the reasoning they used to find their answers?

ANSWERS

Question **1**: 5·15 − 3·52 = 1·63
The hat is £1·63 cheaper than the socks.

Question **2** a): 37·5 − 13·9 = 23·6

Question **2** b): 2·654 − 1·375 = 1·279

Question **3** a): Ebo is subtracting the smaller number from the bigger number (the 3 from the 7 instead of the 7 from the 3).
7·3 − 2·7 = 4·6. Lexi's number is 4·6.

Question **3** b): 12·65 − 3·92 = 8·73. Ebo's number is 8·73.
12·04 − 3·57 − 1·23 = 7·24. Reena's number is 7·24

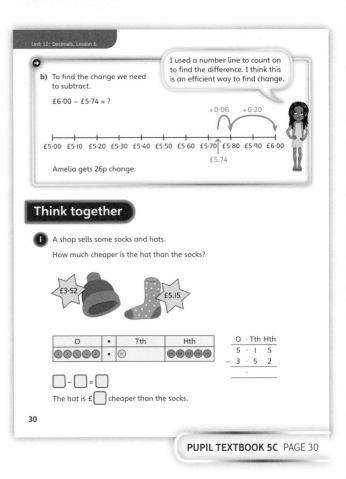

PUPIL TEXTBOOK 5C PAGE 30

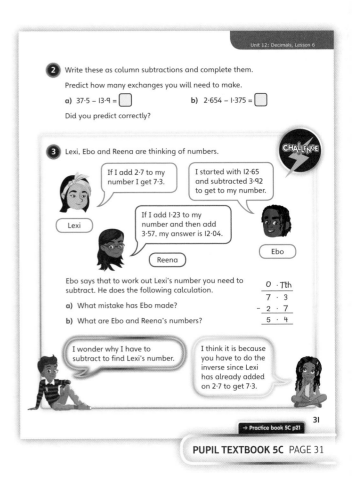

PUPIL TEXTBOOK 5C PAGE 31

Practice

WAYS OF WORKING Independent thinking

IN FOCUS Questions **1**, **2** and **3** aims to consolidate children's understanding of subtracting decimal numbers. Provide time for discussion of the different methods children used to find their answers.

Question **4** presents another misconception that occurs when subtracting from a number that has 0 as a hundredths digit. Use this opportunity to clarify the exchange of 1 tenth for 10 hundredths to make this calculation work.

Question **5** develops children's understanding of decimals as part of a whole in a problem-solving context. Encourage children to use a bar model to explain their answers and use the correct mathematical vocabulary when explaining their reasoning.

STRENGTHEN Ask children to think of the possible mistakes that could happen when subtracting decimals. Write their ideas on the board. Invite them to think of ways and strategies to avoid these mistakes. Write their suggestions on the board next to the mistakes with a different coloured pen. Children may find it easier to visualise question **4** if presented in a real-life scenario. Ask: *You have £6·20, you spent 59p. How much money do you have left?*

DEEPEN Provide children with missing number questions, similar in format to question **6**. These types of questions involve a problem-solving element and allow children to explore different paths to achieve the answer. Allow them to work through and discuss the additional problems and then pose questions of their own for a partner to answer.

THINK DIFFERENTLY Although the question text refers to additions, question **6** requires children to use the inverse operation in order to find the missing numbers. Look for children setting out the calculation correctly, and encourage them to use place value counters if they require extra support.

ASSESSMENT CHECKPOINT Can children subtract decimals? Are children's diagrams accurate and their written process fluent? Can they provide solutions by subtracting decimals?

ANSWERS Answers for the **Practice** part of the lesson appear in the separate **Practice and Reflect answer guide**.

Reflect

WAYS OF WORKING Independent thinking

IN FOCUS This highlights children's understanding of differentiating between subtractions that involve exchange and those that do not. Children need to look at the calculations and notice how the digits in each of the numbers differ. Encourage children to use key vocabulary and the correct place value terms when explaining their reasoning.

ASSESSMENT CHECKPOINT Can children explain how to subtract one decimal number from the another? Can children explain how they know that the subtraction calculation will necessitate an exchange?

ANSWERS Answers for the **Reflect** part of the lesson appear in the separate **Practice and Reflect answer guide**.

After the lesson

- Can children use the column method to subtract two decimal numbers?
- Can children identify where exchanges will occur in subtractions?
- Can children predict what the last digit of the answer will be when subtracting one decimal number from another?

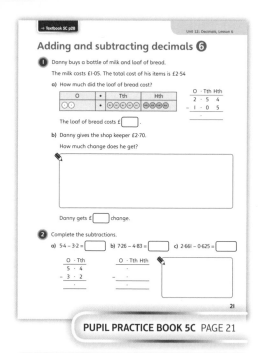

PUPIL PRACTICE BOOK 5C PAGE 21

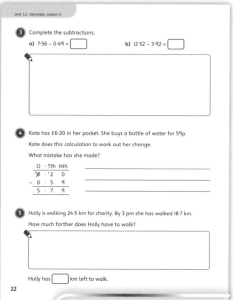

PUPIL PRACTICE BOOK 5C PAGE 22

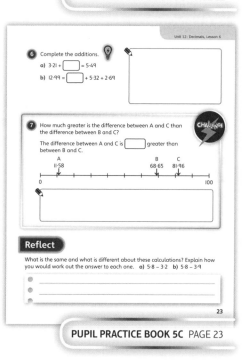

PUPIL PRACTICE BOOK 5C PAGE 23

Adding and subtracting decimals ⑦

Learning focus

In this lesson, children will add and subtract decimals with a different number of decimal places. This includes examples where an exchange is required or children must identify the mistake in a calculation.

Small steps

→ Previous step: Adding and subtracting decimals (6)
→ **This step: Adding and subtracting decimals (7)**
→ Next step: Adding and subtracting decimals (8)

NATIONAL CURRICULUM LINKS

Year 5 Number – Fractions (Including Decimals and Percentages)

Solve problems involving number up to three decimal places.

ASSESSING MASTERY

Children can add and subtract decimals that have a different number of decimal places. They can use addition and subtraction to check the answers to their calculations.

COMMON MISCONCEPTIONS

Children may make mistakes when using column addition or subtraction. They align the numbers from right to the left rather than according their place value, for example

$$\begin{array}{r} 2{\cdot}3 \\ +\ 4{\cdot}61 \\ \hline 4{\cdot}84 \\ \hline \end{array}$$

Ask:
• *Does the answer make sense? Can 2·3 and 4·61 added together to make 4·84? Which digits represent the ones, the tenths, the hundredths? Can 2 ones + 4 ones = 4 ones?*

STRENGTHENING UNDERSTANDING

Encourage children to use a place value grid to help them identify the calculations more readily. Do this alongside the column addition or subtraction so that children can see how the concrete and abstract representations link together.

GOING DEEPER

Give children six number cards, such as 0, 1, 2, 3, 4, 5. Ask them to use each digit only once to make two decimal numbers. Ask children to add the numbers. How many different answers can they find in 1 minute?

KEY LANGUAGE

In lesson: add, subtract, check, digit, decimal point, hundredths, column, difference, sum, shortest, less, further, addition pyramid

Other language to be used by the teacher: inverse, operation, ones, tenths, equal, exchange, place value, greatest

STRUCTURES AND REPRESENTATIONS

column addition, column subtraction, addition pyramid, place value grid, number line

RESOURCES

Optional: place value counters, 0–9 number cards, metre stick

 In the eTextbook of this lesson, you will find interactive links to a selection of teaching tools.

Before you teach

• Do children know how to accurately lay out a column addition and subtraction?
• Do children know how to exchange when adding and subtracting using the column method?

Discover

ASK

- Question **1** a): *What calculation do you need to do to calculate how far Ambika's paper plane flew? What operation will you use? What method will you use to complete the addition?*
- Question **1** b): *What calculation do you need to do to calculate the distance Lee's paper plane flew? What is the key word in the question? Will you add or subtract? Why?*

IN FOCUS Question **1** a) is used to find the sum of two decimals with a different number of decimal places. Question **1** b) is used to find the difference between two decimals with the same number of decimal places.

PRACTICAL TIPS Ask children to make paper aeroplanes. Invite three children to throw their paper planes and ask children to use a metre ruler to measure how far each plane flew. Write the three numbers on the board. Ask children to think of questions that you could ask them to solve using these numbers.

ANSWERS

Question **1** a): Ambika's paper plane flew 5·83 m.

Question **1** b): Lee's paper plane flies 3·81 m.

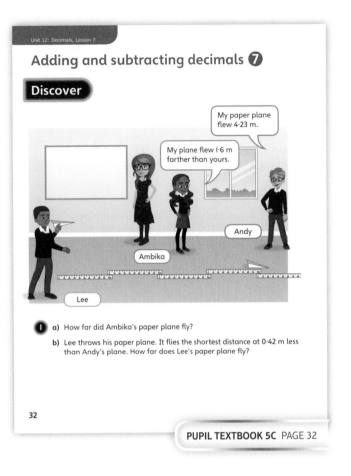

PUPIL TEXTBOOK 5C PAGE 32

Share

ASK

- Question **1** a): *Why do we need to add? What numbers should we add together?*
- Question **1** a): *Why it is important to line the numbers up at the decimal point?*
- Question **1** a): *Why has Dexter added a 0 in the hundredths column? Will this change the answer? Are 1·6 and 1·60 different? Why do we use 1·60?*
- Question **1** b): *Look at the methods used. How many cm are there in 1 m?*

IN FOCUS For question **1** a), it is vital that children fully understand that 1·6 and 1·60 are equal. Invite one child to use a metre ruler and measure 1·6 m from a fixed point, such as the door. Ask the child to stand at that point. Ask a second child to measure 160 cm or 1·60 m using a metre ruler, from the same starting point. Both children will be standing at the same point. This should enable them to recognise for themselves that 1·6 m and 1·60 m are the same distance. Now ask each child to walk 42 cm back towards the starting point. Again, both children should notice that they have reached at the same point. Ask children to calculate how far from the door they are. Write 1·6 − 0·42 = 1·18 m and 1·60 − 0·42 = 1·18 m. Ensure children understand why both calculations have the same answer.

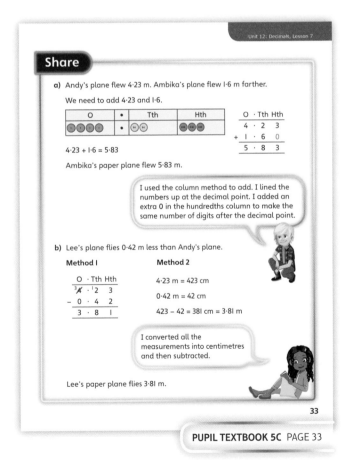

PUPIL TEXTBOOK 5C PAGE 33

Think together

Whole class teacher led (I do, We do, You do)

ASK

- Question **1**: *What is the same between this and the Discover question? What is different?*
- Question **2**: *How does an addition pyramid work? What do you have to do to calculate each missing step? Should you add or subtract?*
- Question **3** a): *Can you spot the mistakes? How do you know if an answer is wrong? Is each answer too big or too small?*

IN FOCUS Question **3** looks at different mistakes that children may make. Discuss whether 5·92 is a sensible answer to 4·74 + 11·8 and link this to the lesson about using rounding to check answers.

STRENGTHEN Encourage children to show their workings clearly for question **3**. If children are using the column method they need to ensure the digits are being lined up at the decimal point and that they add an extra 0 in the hundredth column so that there are the same number of digits after the decimal point.

DEEPEN Ask children to add the numbers in question **3** mentally. What method did they use? Did they round the numbers up or down? Discuss the methods with the whole class and encourage children to use estimating to check their answers.

ASSESSMENT CHECKPOINT Are children confident with laying the column method out neatly and accurately? Are they confident in using a variety of strategies when adding, subtracting or identifying mistakes that may happen?

ANSWERS

Question **1** a): 3·4 + 0·65 = 4·05 m.
Mo's second throw flew 4·05 m.

Question **1** b): 3·921 − 3·75 = 0·171 m.
Louis's plane flew 0·171 m further than Kate's plane.

Question **2** a): A = 0·78 (1·48 − 0·7 = 0·78)

Question **2** b): B = 0·54 (0·7 − 0·16 = 0·54)

Question **2** c): C = 2·432 (1·732 + 0·7 = 2·432)

Question **2** d): D = 3·912 (2·432 + 1·48 = 3·912)

Question **3** a): See correct workings below. Errors include not aligning the place value columns properly, not adding a placeholder zero, not aligning the decimal point in the correct place and not completing the exchange correctly (forgetting to remove a one and a tenth after they had already been exchanged).

Question **3** b):

```
  4 · 5 0        8 · 2 0
+ 1 · 3 4      − 1 · 8 6
  5 · 8 4        6 · 3 4
```

```
  8 2 · 4 3
−     1 · 8 9
  8 0 · 5 4
```

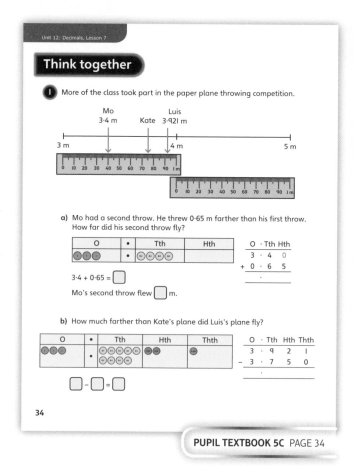

PUPIL TEXTBOOK 5C PAGE 34

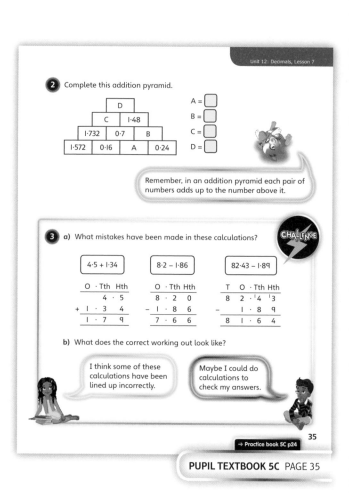

PUPIL TEXTBOOK 5C PAGE 35

Practice

→ Textbook 5C p32

WAYS OF WORKING Independent thinking

IN FOCUS Questions ❶, ❷ and ❸ provide practice in adding and subtracting decimals with a different number of decimal places.

Encourage children to use their preferred method in questions ❸ and ❹ to add and subtract the decimals.

In question ❺, focus the learning around identifying Zac's mistake rather than simply subtracting the numbers.

Question ❼ asks children to find the difference between A and B. Ask: *What is halfway between 4·1 and 4·2? Is point A closer to 4·1 or 4·2? What number is point B close to?*

STRENGTHEN Support children in question ❽ by giving them a number line with number 19·7 on it. Children could find the points that are 1·55 to the left and right of 19·7. It may help to break this down into steps, such as starting with 19·7, adding 1 whole and then adding a further 0·55. Ask: *Do you add or subtract? Why?*

DEEPEN Question ❻ can be explored further by asking children to make their own 'always, sometimes, never' questions based on what they have learnt so far in the lesson. Encourage children to support their answers with examples and/or diagrams.

THINK DIFFERENTLY Encourage children to explain what information is given in question ❼ and what they need to find. Ask: *Look at this question. What is different about this question compared to other ones you have solved so far? What does each point represent? What do you need to do to calculate the difference between the two numbers?*

ASSESSMENT CHECKPOINT Children are confident in using the column layout to add and subtract decimals with a different number of decimal places.

ANSWERS Answers for the **Practice** part of the lesson appear in the separate **Practice and Reflect answer guide**.

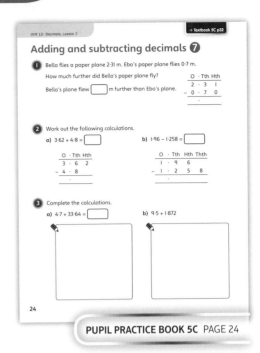

PUPIL PRACTICE BOOK 5C PAGE 24

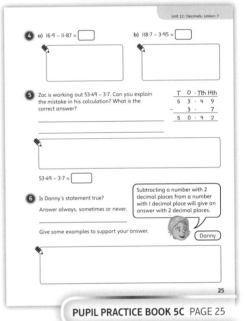

PUPIL PRACTICE BOOK 5C PAGE 25

Reflect

WAYS OF WORKING Independent thinking

IN FOCUS This **Reflect** activity checks children's understanding of how to add or subtract decimals with a different number of decimal places. Encourage children to explain their ideas clearly, paying attention to mistakes that might happen and the misconception discussed in the lesson.

ASSESSMENT CHECKPOINT Children should be able to articulate the methods they use to add or subtract decimals with a different number of decimal points. They are able to explain their reasoning.

ANSWERS Answers for the **Reflect** part of the lesson appear in the separate **Practice and Reflect answer guide**.

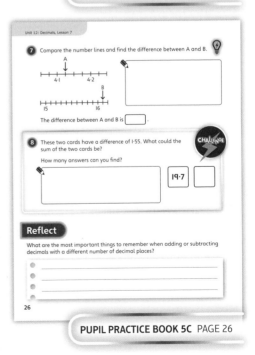

PUPIL PRACTICE BOOK 5C PAGE 26

After the lesson

- Do children understand the importance of setting up the column method correctly?
- Can children employ a variety of strategies to solve problems?
- Can children describe the mistakes that may happen when adding or subtracting decimals?

Adding and subtracting decimals 8

Learning focus

In this lesson, children will add and subtract decimal numbers with up to 4 digits from whole numbers. They will perform exchanges when there are zeros in the columns.

Small steps

→ Previous step: Adding and subtracting decimals (7)
→ **This step: Adding and subtracting decimals (8)**
→ Next step: Decimal sequences

NATIONAL CURRICULUM LINKS

Year 5 Number – Fractions (Including Decimals and Percentages)

Solve problems involving number up to three decimal places.

ASSESSING MASTERY

Children can add or subtract a whole number and a decimal. They can talk through their methods, demonstrating a clear understanding of place value when zero is in the column in which an exchange is required. Finally, children can show their addition or subtraction using place value counters and column method addition or subtraction.

COMMON MISCONCEPTIONS

Children may try to make an exchange but see that there is a 0 in the next column. They may exchange the hundredths but not change the tenths or ones. Ask:

• *What should we do if there is a 0 in a column we need for an exchange?*

Children may also think that when you subtract from 0 the answer is 0 or the number itself, for instance *0 – 2 = 2*. Ask:

• *Can you show me 0 – 2? Can the answer be 2? Can you buy a notebook for £2 if you have no money?*

STRENGTHENING UNDERSTANDING

Children should gain confidence by subtracting whole numbers with 1, 2 or 3 digits from multiples of 100 and 1,000 before moving on to subtracting decimals from whole numbers. Children should be able to work methodically and solve questions such as 100 – 235, 1,000 – 342. Revisit subtraction of decimals from 1. Ask: *What is 1 – 0·2? 1 – 0·23? 1 – 0·456?*

GOING DEEPER

Deepen learning in this lesson by providing children with subtractions that have exchange mistakes in them. Can they spot the mistakes and reason why the mistakes may have been made?

KEY LANGUAGE

In lesson: place value, digits, mass, decimal, take away, minus, add, subtract, column addition, column subtraction, whole, part

Other language to be used by the teacher: difference, fewer, exchange, less than, greater than, thousandths, hundredths, tenths, ones

STRUCTURES AND REPRESENTATIONS

place value grid, column addition, column subtraction, number line

RESOURCES

Mandatory: place value counters, weighing scales, measuring jug

 In the eTextbook of this lesson, you will find interactive links to a selection of teaching tools.

Before you teach

• How will you explain what to do if there is a 0 in a column required for an exchange?
• Do children know how to accurately lay out a column subtraction?

Discover

WAYS OF WORKING Pair work

ASK

- Question **1** a): *How much juice is in each bottle? Why would you need to know the total amount? What calculation do you need to do?*
- Question **1** b): *How much flour was there in the bag to start with? How much flour is on the scales?*

IN FOCUS Question **1** a) requires children to add a whole number and a decimal. Question **1** b) introduces the subtraction of a decimal from a whole number. Children are focusing on exploring what happens when an exchange is needed but there is a 0 in the column they need to exchange from.

PRACTICAL TIPS You may want to use digital weighing scales and/or a 2 or 3 litre measuring jug. Ask children to first measure 2 litres of water or weigh 2 kg. Allow children to be curious and explore what happens when the weight or the capacity change. Write the number statements on the board and discuss what happens in each instance. Are the numbers getting bigger or smaller?

ANSWERS

Question **1** a): There is 6·25 l of juice in the two bottles in total.

Question **1** b): There is 1·704 kg of flour left in the bag.

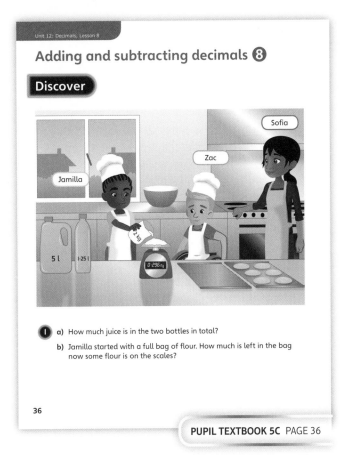

Adding and subtracting decimals **8**

Discover

1 a) How much juice is in the two bottles in total?

b) Jamilla started with a full bag of flour. How much is left in the bag now some flour is on the scales?

36

PUPIL TEXTBOOK 5C PAGE 36

Share

WAYS OF WORKING Whole class teacher led

ASK

- Question **1** a): *Why are there red zeros after the 5 in 5·00 + 1·25? What is their purpose?*
- Question **1** b): *Where do you start the column subtraction?*
- Question **1** b): *What steps do you need to go through when there is a 0 in the column you need to use for an exchange? How many exchanges do we have to do? What does the small '1' mean? Where does the '9' come from?*

IN FOCUS For question **1** b), model the subtraction in the column method format. Show children the importance of the layout, how to strike through the numbers being exchanged, and how to put the small 1 for the exchanged number. Ensure that children understand every step of the calculation and reinforce the place value of each digit. Use place value counters to reinforce that 1 = 10 tenths, 1 tenth = 10 hundredths and 1 hundredth = 10 thousandths.

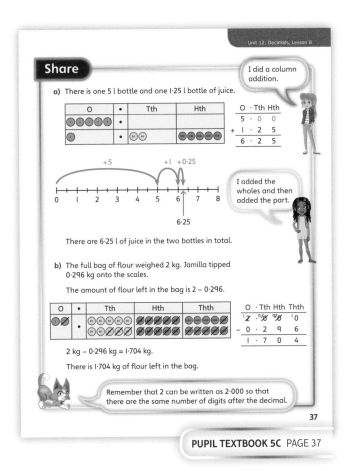

Share

a) There is one 5 l bottle and one 1·25 l bottle of juice.

There are 6·25 l of juice in the two bottles in total.

b) The full bag of flour weighed 2 kg. Jamilla tipped 0·296 kg onto the scales.

The amount of flour left in the bag is 2 − 0·296.

2 kg − 0·296 kg = 1·704 kg.

There is 1·704 kg of flour left in the bag.

I did a column addition.

I added the wholes and then added the part.

Remember that 2 can be written as 2·000 so that there are the same number of digits after the decimal.

37

PUPIL TEXTBOOK 5C PAGE 37

Think together

WAYS OF WORKING Whole class teacher led (I do, We do, You do)

ASK

- Question **1** a): *Can you write 5 so that 5 and 2·8 have the same number of digits after the decimal point?*
- Question **2**: *How many tenths and hundredths does each weight have? How many in each answer?*
- Question **3**: *What do both methods have in common? How do you decide what you should change each number to? Which method will you use?*

IN FOCUS Question **1** offers an opportunity to link subtraction and addition. Challenge children to tell you the associated addition or subtraction in each instance. Question **2** introduces problem solving to find the missing weights. Ask children to write down the number sentences for each calculation. To extend further, ask children to think of other ways that each amount can be made by using as many weights as needed.

STRENGTHEN Provide children with place value counters in question **3** and ask them to set out each of Jamilla's calculations. Ask them to first set out 2 − 0·296, then demonstrate what they need to do to change to 1·999 − 0·2995. If necessary, simplify to whole numbers such as 20 − 3 and ask them to think why that is the same as 19 − 2 or 19 − 3 + 1. Allow time for children to explore these methods before progressing to question **3** b).

DEEPEN Question **3** offers a great opportunity to link back to previous work on adding and subtracting whole numbers using knowledge of place value. Children should be able to spot the links between all the calculations. Challenge them to think of other ways that they can use to complete each calculation. Ask: *What method would you use if you subtracted 296 from 2,000? Can you use the same method to work out 2 − 0·296?*

ASSESSMENT CHECKPOINT Can children accurately add whole numbers and decimals? Can they subtract when there are zeroes in columns that require exchange?

ANSWERS

Question **1** a): 5 + 2·8 = 7·8 kg
There is 7·8 kg of pasta in total.

Question **1** b): 2 + 2 + 2 + 0·65 = 6·65 kg
There is 6·65 kg of porridge in total.

Question **1** c): 3·00 − 0·35 = 2·65 l
2·65 l are left in the bottle.

Question **2**: 4 kg + 0·75 kg = 4·75 kg;
1 kg + 0·05 kg = 1·05 kg;
15 kg + 0·5 kg + 0·05 kg = 15·55 kg;
5 kg + 4 kg + 0·5 kg + 0·425 kg = 9·925 kg

Question **3** a): Method 1: Jamilla reduces 2 by 0·001 and then adjusts the answer by adding 0·001 back.
Method 2: Jamilla reduces both numbers by 0·001, so the difference is the same but the numbers are easier.

Question **3** b): 5·99 − 3·45 = 2·54, 2·54 + 0·01 = 2·55
2·999 − 0·914 = 2·085, 2·085 + 0·001 = 2·086
25·9 − 2·8 = 23·1, 23·1 + 0·1 = 23·2

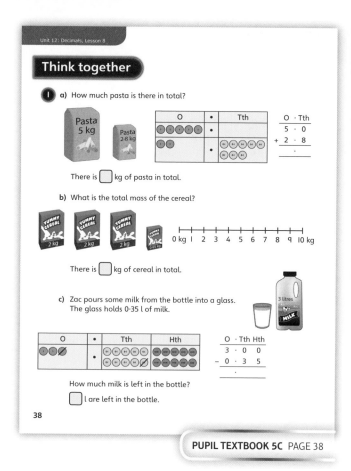

PUPIL TEXTBOOK 5C PAGE 38

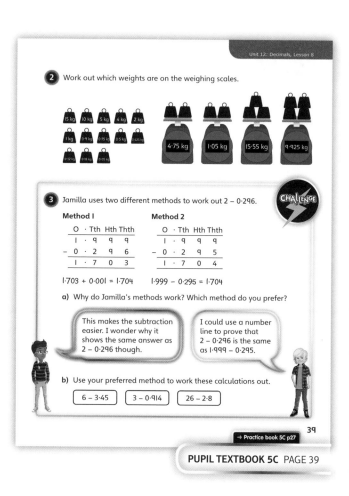

PUPIL TEXTBOOK 5C PAGE 39

Practice

→ Textbook 5C p36

WAYS OF WORKING Independent thinking

IN FOCUS Question **2** asks children to find solutions and work out the missing numbers whilst linking addition and subtraction. This will focus children's thinking and push them to work backwards. Support them by asking them to talk you through where they should start and how they can check that their answer is correct.

Question **4** offers another opportunity to subtract a decimal from a whole number by manipulating the numbers to simplify the calculation.

Questions **5** and **7** introduce a context for adding or subtracting a whole number with a decimal. Ask children to write the appropriate units of measurement with their answer.

STRENGTHEN Encourage children to use counters on a place value grid and number lines to support their learning. When the calculation in not given in a column layout, encourage them to write it in columns and offer support and feedback on their efforts.

DEEPEN Explore the Challenge question in more depth by providing similar missing number problems. To extend their learning, ask children to calculate mentally rather than with a written method.

ASSESSMENT CHECKPOINT Children are confident in adding or subtracting whole numbers and decimals. They can use different ways to find solutions to missing number problems and are able to explain the calculations they have completed.

ANSWERS Answers for the **Practice** part of the lesson appear in the separate **Practice and Reflect answer guide**.

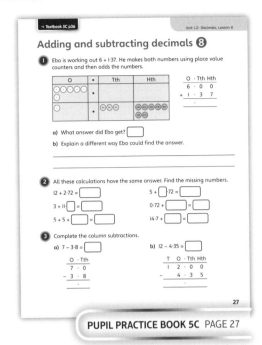

PUPIL PRACTICE BOOK 5C PAGE 27

Reflect

WAYS OF WORKING Independent thinking

IN FOCUS This **Reflect** activity checks children's understanding of applying the method where they manipulate the numbers to calculate the difference. Encourage children to explain by demonstrating the calculation on the number line. Focus their attention not only in the answer but on noticing what is the same and what is different between the calculations. Children should explain that both numbers (6·9 and 2·3) are 0·1 less than the original numbers, hence the difference between the numbers will be the same.

ASSESSMENT CHECKPOINT Can children explain how a subtraction between a whole number and a decimal can be manipulated in order to make it easier to solve? Can children use a number line to support their answer?

ANSWERS Answers for the **Reflect** part of the lesson appear in the separate **Practice and Reflect answer guide**.

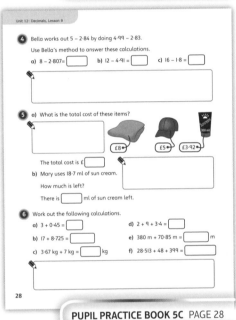

PUPIL PRACTICE BOOK 5C PAGE 28

After the lesson ⏸

- Can children explain how to exchange when there is a 0 in a column required for the exchange?
- Do children employ a variety of strategies to complete the calculations?
- Are children able to use a variety of different representations to show their solutions?
- Can they accurately manipulate numbers in order to make a calculation more efficient to solve?

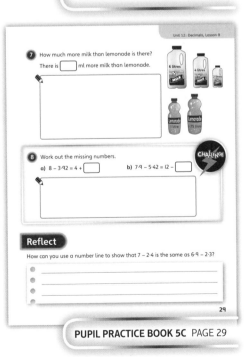

PUPIL PRACTICE BOOK 5C PAGE 29

Decimal sequences

Learning focus

In this lesson, children will use their understanding of decimal numbers to count and complete decimal sequences. They will describe the rule that the sequence follows and use it to calculate missing terms.

Small steps

→ Previous step: Adding and subtracting decimals (8)
→ **This step: Decimal sequences**
→ Next step: Problem solving – decimals (1)

NATIONAL CURRICULUM LINKS

Year 5 Number – Fractions (Including Decimals and Percentages)

Read, write, order and compare numbers with up to three decimal places.

ASSESSING MASTERY

Children can reliably count in decimals and continue the count accurately. They can order and complete number sequences and write down the rule that the decimal sequence follows.

COMMON MISCONCEPTIONS

Children may make mistakes when ordering the numbers in a sequence if they neglect to consider the place value of each digit. For example, they may say that the next number in the sequence 0, 0·4, 0·8 is 0·12 rather than 1·2. Ask:
• *What is the rule that the sequence follows? How many tenths do you have? How many tenths are you adding? What happens if you add another 4 tenths?*

STRENGTHENING UNDERSTANDING

To support children as they complete the number sequences in this lesson, it may help to revisit what they have learnt so far about the addition and subtraction of decimals. Show children a concrete representation of the number sequence using place value counters. Ask: *What do you notice about how the number of counters change?* Randomly hide one of the numbers and its concrete representation and ask: *Which number have I hidden? How do you know?*

GOING DEEPER

Give children two decimal numbers and ask them to create number sequences that include the two numbers without them being next to each other in the sequence. Children can challenge a partner to complete their number sequence. Ask: *Can you write your sequence so that the numbers increase? How would the sequence change if the numbers decreased instead?*

KEY LANGUAGE

In lesson: decimal, add, subtract, sequence, order, rule, amount, count up, pattern

Other language to be used by the teacher: count backwards, count forward, count back, steps of

STRUCTURES AND REPRESENTATIONS

number line, tables

RESOURCES

Optional: place value counters, plant growth chart, number lines, decimal number cards

 In the eTextbook of this lesson, you will find interactive links to a selection of teaching tools.

Before you teach

• How can you link sequences to children's real-life experiences or other areas of the curriculum?
• What concrete resources could you use to demonstrate the order of the numbers children will be studying?

Discover

WAYS OF WORKING Pair work

ASK

- Question ❶ a): *How tall is the rose bush to start with? How can you find how tall the rose bush will be next month?*
- Question ❶ a): *What pattern or rule do the numbers follow?*
- Question ❶ b): *What is the height of the rose bush? What operation do you need to do to find its height last month?*
- Question ❶ b): *How could you predict the number of months it took to grow from 60 cm to 87·2 cm?*

IN FOCUS Question ❶ a) invites children to write down a sequence of decimal numbers when the rule is given, without specifically mentioning the word 'sequence'. Children have written sequences of numbers before so they should notice that the numbers follow a rule. Discuss the meaning of 'sequence' and ensure they all recognise and understand how a sequence can be represented. Questions ❶ a) and b) link to previous learning. Children should be able to use their understanding of adding and subtracting decimals to work out the heights of the plants over the next few months or previous months.

PRACTICAL TIPS Give children a growth chart of different plants showing how much each plant grows every month or year. Ask them to investigate what will happen to the height of each plant. They could draw a plant for each month and label each picture with its increasing height month-on-month. Discuss which plants grow faster or slower.

ANSWERS

Question ❶ a):

Month	April	May	June	July	Aug	Sept	Oct
Height	15·4	17·9	20·4	22·9	25·4	27·9	30·4

Question ❶ b): The rose bush has been over 60 cm tall for the last 10 months.

Share

WAYS OF WORKING Whole class teacher led

ASK

- Question ❶ a): *What do the jumps show? How are the number line, table and **Discover** picture linked?*
- Question ❶ a): *What other sequences have you encountered?*
- Question ❶ b): *Which way do you count on the number line?*
- Question ❶ b): *Does the size of the jumps change when you count backwards?*

IN FOCUS Through questions ❶ a) and b) it will be important for children to recognise how adding and subtracting decimals is essential for completing the number sequences. The importance of using a number line and being systematic by organising the data in a table is made explicit through these diagrams and examples. The use of jumps forwards and backwards highlights the fact that the inverse of addition is subtraction and vice versa.

Decimal sequences

Discover

These rose bushes grow 2·5 cm every month.

Mo   Olivia

❶ a) The rose bush Mo and Olivia are planting is 15·4 cm tall in April. How tall will it be each coming month for the next 6 months?

b) The other rose bush is 87·2 cm. For how many months has the rose bush been over 60 cm tall?

40

PUPIL TEXTBOOK 5C PAGE 40

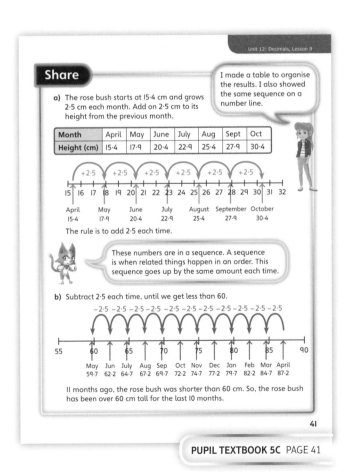

Share

I made a table to organise the results. I also showed the same sequence on a number line.

a) The rose bush starts at 15·4 cm and grows 2·5 cm each month. Add on 2·5 cm to its height from the previous month.

Month	April	May	June	July	Aug	Sept	Oct
Height (cm)	15·4	17·9	20·4	22·9	25·4	27·9	30·4

The rule is to add 2·5 each time.

These numbers are in a sequence. A sequence is when related things happen in an order. This sequence goes up by the same amount each time.

b) Subtract 2·5 each time, until we get less than 60.

11 months ago, the rose bush was shorter than 60 cm. So, the rose bush has been over 60 cm tall for the last 10 months.

41

PUPIL TEXTBOOK 5C PAGE 41

Think together

Whole class teacher led (I do, We do, You do)

ASK

- Question ❶: *How does the table help show the sequence clearly?*
- Question ❶: *What do you need to know to find the missing values for each sequence?*
- Question ❷: *How will you know what number the sequences count in?*
- Question ❷: *Will you add or subtract to find the missing number?*
- Question ❸: *Why do you need to put the decimal cards in order?*

IN FOCUS Question ❶ requires children to extract the necessary information from the table to find the next term. Children need to use the clues given in the partially completed sequences to find the rules. Discuss with children how to go about finding the rule first, using the correct language such as 'the tenths increase by' to describe it.

STRENGTHEN To help children to complete the sequence in question ❷, ask: *How many equal intervals are there between one number and the next? If there are five equal intervals, what decimal would each interval represent?*

DEEPEN Question ❷ c) deepens children's fluency in recognising sequences of decimals on a number line. To extend further, ask children to reverse the numbers, so the first number in the sequence is 8 and the last is 7. Ask: *Will the rule change now? Will the size of the jump be different?*

ASSESSMENT CHECKPOINT Children are able to use tables and number lines to represent a number sequence. They can describe the rule that decimals follow, predict the next term and complete the missing terms in a given sequence.

ANSWERS

Question ❶:

	April	May	June	July	Aug	Sept	Oct
White rose	15·1	15·2	15·3	15·4	15·5	15·6	15·7
Climbing rose	10·0	12·6	15·2	17·8	20·4	23·0	25·6
Wild rose	12·429	12·43	12·431	12·432	12·433	12·434	12·435

Question ❷ a): 20·5, 20·75, 21, 21·25, 21·5, 21·75, 22

Question ❷ b): 0·65, 0·68, 0·71, 0·74, 0·77, 0·8, 0·83, 0·86

Question ❷ c): 7·0, 7·2, 7·4, 7·6, 7·8, 8

Question ❸ a): 3·5, 3·6, 3·7, 3·8, 3·9, 4·0
(Goes up by 1 tenth each time)

Question ❸ b): 29·4, 32·5, 35·6, 38·7, 41·8, 44·9, 48
(Goes up by 3·1 each time)

Question ❸ c): 51·1

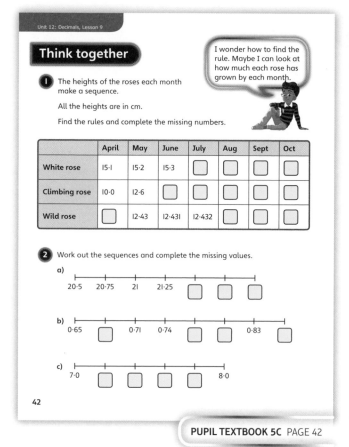

PUPIL TEXTBOOK 5C PAGE 42

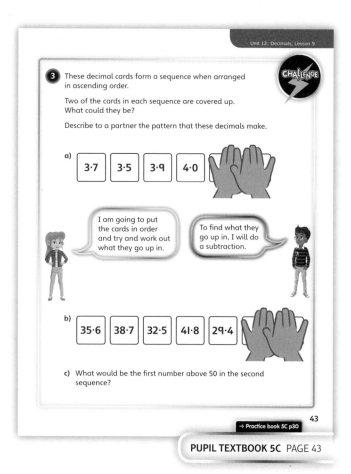

PUPIL TEXTBOOK 5C PAGE 43

Practice

WAYS OF WORKING Independent thinking

IN FOCUS Questions ❶ and ❷ present number sequences with missing numbers in different positions. This is important as it not only develops children's fluency in calculating the term-to-term rule and finding the next or previous term, but also makes them consider which operation they need to use. Children should be able to decide whether they add or subtract in each instance.

STRENGTHEN For question ❺, children may find it difficult to add multiples of 0·2, particularly when crossing 0, for example 12·85 + 0·2. Ensure that children have access to number lines and place value counters. Look for children who say 12·87 and ask them to use a concrete resource to model the sequence. By this point, children should be able to independently choose a number line to demonstrate the sequence. Write examples of mistakes on the white board and invite the class to discuss the calculations and correct the mistakes.

DEEPEN Extend the context of question ❼ by asking children to explore how many rounds it would take Toshi to run a total of 30 m. Alternatively, change the distance of 0·4 m to 0·48 m and ask children to describe how the total distance travelled changes from one round to the next.

ASSESSMENT CHECKPOINT Are children confident in recognising and understanding how a number sequence can be represented? Are children able to complete the missing numbers in the sequences? Can they recognise the rule a number sequence is following?

ANSWERS Answers for the **Practice** part of the lesson appear in the separate **Practice and Reflect answer guide**.

Reflect

WAYS OF WORKING Pair work

IN FOCUS This question offers a good opportunity to assess children's fluency with the concepts covered in both this and previous lessons. Encourage children to consider using multiple ways of representing the number sequence that they have made, including a number line and a table. Ask children to use the correct mathematical vocabulary when describing the rule their sequence follows.

ASSESSMENT CHECKPOINT Are there children who use mixed whole and decimal numbers, numbers with more than one decimal place or pictures to represent their number sequence? Do they simplify the decimal numbers in their sequences, for instance 0·6, 0·8, 1, 1·2? Children should begin to recognise that there is a limitless amount of possible ways to represent their number sequence.

ANSWERS Answers for the **Reflect** part of the lesson appear in the separate **Practice and Reflect answer guide**.

After the lesson

- Do children understand what a decimal sequence is?
- What concrete resources would have supported the learning in this lesson?

→ Textbook 5C p40

Unit 12: Decimals, Lesson 9

Decimal sequences

❶ Work out the missing numbers in each sequence.

a) 4·6, 4·7, 4·8, ☐ . ☐ . ☐ . ☐

b) 11·5, 11·9, ☐ , 12·7, ☐ , 13·5, ☐ . ☐

c) ☐ . ☐ , 15·65, 15·6, 15·55, ☐ . ☐

❷ Complete the numbers on the number line.

a) 0·76 0·77 ☐☐☐☐☐

b) 5·615 5·620 ☐ 5·630 ☐☐ 5·645 ☐

❸ Kate is counting up by the same amount each time.

> 0, 0·3, 0·6, 0·9, 0·12, 0·15

Kate

What mistake has Kate made?

_____

30

PUPIL PRACTICE BOOK 5C PAGE 30

Unit 12: Decimals, Lesson 9

❹ Complete the sequence and write whether each rule is true or false.

a) 10·1, 10·3, 10·5, 10·7, ☐

The rule is 'add 0·2'.

c) 3·0, 2·25, 1·5, 0·75, ☐

The rule is 'subtract 0·25'.

b) 39·57, 39·60, 39·63, 39·66, ☐

The rule is 'add 0·3'.

d) 0·4, 0·52, 0·64, 0·76, ☐

The rule is 'add 0·12'.

❺ Max is counting up by 0·02 each time. He starts at 12·45.

a) What are the next three numbers Max will say?

> 12·45, 12·47 …

Max

The next three numbers Max will say are ☐ . ☐ . ☐ .

b) Max stopped when he reached the first number above 18.

What number did Max stop on? ☐

❻ Complete the sequences. Write the rule for each sequence.

a) 0·21, 0·42, 0·63, ☐ , 1·05, 1·26,

b) 11·3, ☐ , 12·1, ☐ . ☐ , 13·3, 13·7

c) 7·68, 7·61, 7·54, 7·47, ☐ . ☐ , 7·26

Rules:
a)
b)
c)

31

PUPIL PRACTICE BOOK 5C PAGE 31

Unit 12: Decimals, Lesson 9

❼ Seven cones are spaced equally apart for a running race.

CHALLENGE

A   B   C   D   E   F   G
0·4 km 0·4 km 0·4 km 0·4 km 0·4 km 0·4 km

In round 1, Toshi starts at A, runs to B and then back to A.

In round 2, he then runs from A to C and back to A.

He continues in the same pattern until round 6, when he runs A to G and back to A.

Complete the table to show how far Toshi runs each round and in total.

Round	1	2	3	4	5	6
Distance travelled in round (km)						
Total distance travelled so far (km)						

Reflect

Make a sequence using decimal numbers. Ask a partner to continue the sequence. What rule did you use?

- _____
- _____
- _____
- _____

32

PUPIL PRACTICE BOOK 5C PAGE 32

Problem solving – decimals ①

Learning focus

In this lesson, children will learn strategies for solving problems involving adding and subtracting numbers with up to three decimal places.

Small steps

→ Previous step: Decimal sequences
→ **This step: Problem solving – decimals (1)**
→ Next step: Problem solving – decimals (2)

NATIONAL CURRICULUM LINKS

Year 5 Number – Fractions (Including Decimals and Percentages)

Solve problems involving number up to three decimal places.

ASSESSING MASTERY

Children can solve problems that involve a combination of adding and subtracting numbers with up to three decimal places and making multiple exchanges.

COMMON MISCONCEPTIONS

Sometimes, children assume that certain words always indicate a particular calculation without considering the context. For example, they may think that 'more' always means adding and 'less' always mean subtracting. Ask:

• *What are you trying to find out? What kind of answer are you expecting to get? Have you used all the information from the question? How can you check your answer is correct? If you substitute the answer back into the question, does it make sense?*

STRENGTHENING UNDERSTANDING

Children should focus on finding solutions to problems with either addition or subtraction first, before combining them. Encourage children to use a bar model or number line to aid their understanding or to check their answer. Use different contexts with smaller numbers. Ask: *What operation should you use?*

GOING DEEPER

Give children multi-step problems that can be solved in two or more different ways. Ask them to draw diagrams and bar models and generalise where possible. Challenge them to find all of the different ways of finding solutions to problems.

KEY LANGUAGE

In lesson: more than, difference, total, method, efficient, mass, weigh, heavier, kilogram (kg)

Other language to be used by the teacher: altogether, addition, subtraction, combine, compare

STRUCTURES AND REPRESENTATIONS

bar model, column addition, column subtraction

RESOURCES

Optional: weighing scales

 In the eTextbook of this lesson, you will find interactive links to a selection of teaching tools.

Before you teach

• Do children know how to lay out column additions and subtractions and make multiple exchanges?
• Do children understand key vocabulary such as 'more than' and 'less than'?
• Do they consider the context in which the vocabulary has been used?

Discover

Unit 12: Decimals, Lesson 10

WAYS OF WORKING Pair work

ASK

- Question **1** a): *How much does the astronaut weigh on Earth? And on the moon? What does 'how much more' mean?*
- Question **1** b): *What do you need to know to find the mass of the life support? What do you know about the mass of the life support?*

IN FOCUS Question **1** a) requires children to subtract to calculate the difference between the mass of the astronaut on Earth and on the moon. Question **1** b) is a two-step addition problem that involves working out the mass of the life support and then the total combined mass of the spacesuit and life support.

PRACTICAL TIPS Discuss the changes in the astronaut's mass on Earth and on the moon. Show examples of a variety of objects and their mass on Earth, for example a car, TV and a melon. Ask children to predict what their mass might be on the moon. Will it be more or less? Why is it important for the astronauts to know what the mass of different objects will be? Pay attention to vocabulary used, such as 'more than', 'less than', 'difference', 'how much more?', 'how much less?'. Discuss the calculations that children need to do in each instance.

ANSWERS

Question **1** a): The weight of the astronaut on Earth is 64·05 kg more than on the moon.

Question **1** b): The total mass of the spacesuit and the life support is 189·98 kg.

Share

WAYS OF WORKING Whole class teacher led

ASK

- Question **1** a): *What calculation do you need to do if you are finding 'how much more'? Are you adding or subtracting?*
- Question **1** b): *If the mass of life support is 90·2 kg heavier than the spacesuit, how could you work out its mass? What is the mass of the spacesuit? How can you work out the total mass?*

IN FOCUS For question **1** a), show children the bar model and ask how they know that finding the difference leads us to performing a subtraction. Ensure children are confident of the correct column layout for a decimal subtraction. For question **1** b), look for children who just add the numbers together, instead of finding the mass of the life support first. Highlighting the bar model should help children realise why this will not work. Discuss the key words in the question and how they could work out the mass of the life support. Emphasise the importance of reading the question carefully. Reinforce the place value of each digit when carrying out the calculations and address the need for an exchange.

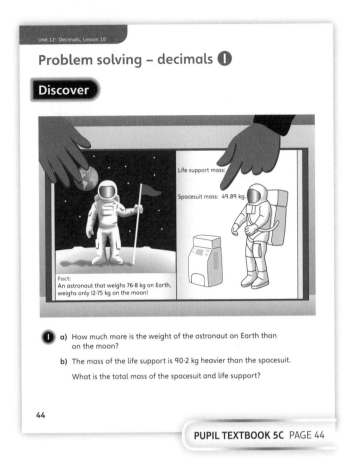

PUPIL TEXTBOOK 5C PAGE 44

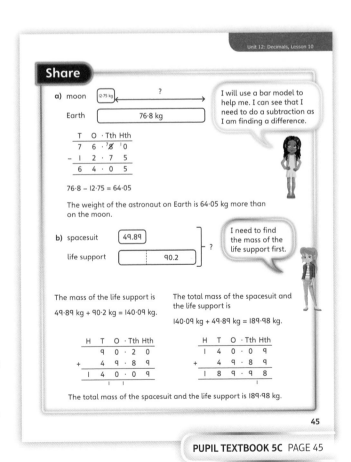

PUPIL TEXTBOOK 5C PAGE 45

Think together

Think together

WAYS OF WORKING Whole class teacher led (I do, We do, You do)

ASK

- Question **1**: *What calculation do you need to do? What word(s) tell you this?*
- Question **2**: *How much does each magazine cost? Look at the bar model. What do you need to do to find the total?*
- Question **3**: *What do you need to do? What is the mass of rock B?*

IN FOCUS In question **1**, children may not understand why 'how much farther' is being associated with a subtraction. Use the bar model to show why they need to subtract. Encourage children to use the column subtraction method. Question **2** requires children to find solutions with more than two decimal numbers. Show the bar model and discuss how they need to carry out an addition calculation. Discuss the different methods that could be used; adding all three numbers at once in a column addition, or adding two numbers in a column addition then adding the other number to this answer, or carrying out the addition calculations mentally. Could they manipulate any of the numbers to make the calculation simpler?

STRENGTHEN To support understanding, children should be able to describe a question and represent it using a bar model or diagram. They should write the information they know on the bar diagram and use a question mark to show what they are trying to find out.

DEEPEN Question **3** can be explored further by changing the mass of rock B and asking children to find the new mass of rocks A and C. Alternatively, give a mass difference between two of the three rocks and see if children can identify what the mass of each rock could be.

ASSESSMENT CHECKPOINT Can children solve problems that involve addition, subtraction and a combination of the two, with decimal numbers? Confident answers to question **3** will indicate that children have a firm grasp of the learning in this section.

ANSWERS

Question **1**: Lexi could jump 7·644 m farther on the moon.

Question **2**: £4·99 + £2·99 + £5·88 = £13·86

Question **3** a): The total mass of the three rocks is 37·15 kg.

Question **3** b): Rock C weighs 8·35 kg more than rock A.

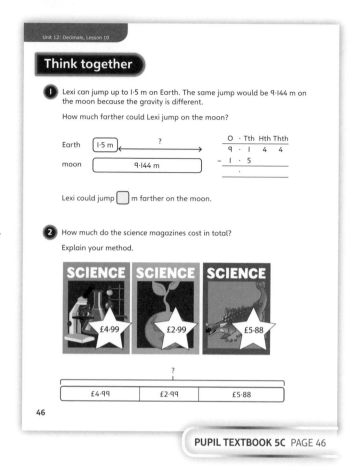

Think together

1 Lexi can jump up to 1·5 m on Earth. The same jump would be 9·144 m on the moon because the gravity is different.

How much farther could Lexi jump on the moon?

Lexi could jump ☐ m farther on the moon.

2 How much do the science magazines cost in total?

Explain your method.

46

PUPIL TEXTBOOK 5C PAGE 46

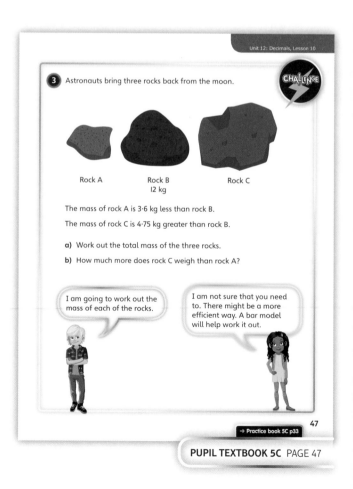

PUPIL TEXTBOOK 5C PAGE 47

Practice

WAYS OF WORKING Independent thinking

IN FOCUS For question ❶, ask children to focus on the calculations that arise from each bar model and to show their method for solving them. Encourage children to discuss the different ways they could find a solution to question ❶ c). Questions ❷ and ❸ aims to consolidate children's understanding of problem solving within a context. Urge children to draw a bar model and to add in any information as they complete the calculation.

STRENGTHEN Use the same context as question ❹ but substitute the decimals for whole numbers. For example, find two numbers that add up to 5 but have a difference of 1. Ask children to use a bar model. From this, lead on to identifying what children need to do to answer the actual question.

DEEPEN Question ❷ can be explored in greater depth by asking children to create their own word problem based on the numbers used in question ❷. For instance, Bella throws a javelin 26·3 m. Her second throw travels a further 6·85 m. How far did Bella throw the second javelin? Ask: *What will the key words in your word problem be? Can you put the key words into a context? Are you going to create an addition or subtraction problem?*

THINK DIFFERENTLY In question ❺, children are asked to subtract four numbers with varying decimal places. Support children by asking them to pay attention to the place value of each digit in the calculation. Encourage children to use counters on a place value grid to support their understanding. Challenge children to work out the calculation mentally and share their strategy with the whole class.

ASSESSMENT CHECKPOINT Can children confidently add and subtract decimals and solve problems that involve combinations of these calculations?

ANSWERS Answers for the **Practice** part of the lesson appear in the separate **Practice and Reflect answer guide**.

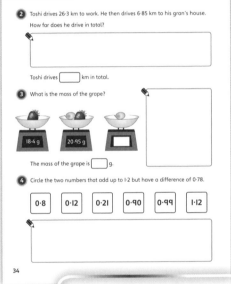

PUPIL PRACTICE BOOK 5C PAGE 33

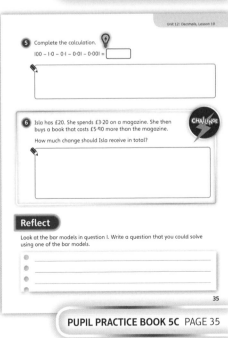

PUPIL PRACTICE BOOK 5C PAGE 34

Reflect

WAYS OF WORKING Independent thinking

IN FOCUS This **Reflect** activity checks children's understanding of using bar models to solve addition and subtraction problems. Encourage children to write a two-step problem. Pay close attention to the vocabulary they use. Ask children to also find solutions once they have written it. As an extension, are they able to find solutions to problem in a different way?

ASSESSMENT CHECKPOINT Can children use the appropriate vocabulary to write a two-step problem that requires the use of both addition and subtraction to solve it?

ANSWERS Answers for the **Reflect** part of the lesson appear in the separate **Practice and Reflect answer guide**.

After the lesson ⏸

- Can children apply what they know about addition and subtraction of decimal numbers in problem solving contexts?
- Are children confident identifying each step that is required to solve a two-step problem?

PUPIL PRACTICE BOOK 5C PAGE 35

Problem solving – decimals ②

Learning focus

In this lesson, children will learn how to solve more complex addition and subtraction multi-step problems. They will interpret and identify the information necessary to solve the problem.

Small steps

→ Previous step: Problem solving – decimals (1)
→ **This step: Problem solving – decimals (2)**
→ Next step: Multiplying decimals by 10

NATIONAL CURRICULUM LINKS

Year 5 Number – Fractions (Including Decimals and Percentages)

Solve problems involving number up to three decimal places.

ASSESSING MASTERY

Children can solve more complex multi-step problems that involve adding and subtracting decimals where the information is represented in tables or needs to be extracted from sentences.

COMMON MISCONCEPTIONS

Children may not understand what calculation a problem requires them to undertake and so will just guess whether to add or subtract. This is particularly the case where the question is long. Ask:

• *What is the question about? Can you describe it? Why do you think this information is provided? What can you find from it? What model could you draw to help you?*

STRENGTHENING UNDERSTANDING

Encourage children to sketch, act-out situations or use concrete materials; whatever helps solidify the concept for them. Remind them to read the problem carefully a number of times until they fully understand what is needed. Encourage them to discuss the problem with their partner or rewrite the question in their own words.

GOING DEEPER

Ask children to consider solving the problem in a different way. Can they simplify it at all? Encourage them to think 'what if?' and see if they can draw on the strategies used to find the solution to a problem to help them with another. Encourage the use of their logical thought processes and generalisation where possible.

KEY LANGUAGE

In lesson: how much, balance, distance, decimal, multiply, more than (>), less than (<), total, mass, weight, add, remove, reduce, difference, kilogram (kg)

Other language to be used by the teacher: greatest, fewer, compare, increase, identical

STRUCTURES AND REPRESENTATIONS

bar model, number line, column subtraction

RESOURCES

Mandatory: weighing scales, blank comparison bar models

 In the eTextbook of this lesson, you will find interactive links to a selection of teaching tools.

Before you teach

• Are children confident with breaking a problem into smaller parts?
• Can children select the information they know and decide what is unknown or needs to be discovered?

Discover

WAYS OF WORKING Pair work

ASK

- Question ① a): *What can you see in the picture? What do all the scales have in common? How do they differ? Which one is the balance scale?*
- Question ① a) *What is the mass of the oats? What is the mass of the pears? What is their combined mass?*
- Question ① b): *When does a scale balance? What happens if the left-hand side is heavier than the right-hand side? What do Emma and Ebo need to do to get the scales to balance?*

IN FOCUS Question ① a) requires children to identify what will happen to the scale when the mass at either side changes. In question ① b), children can use two different methods to balance the scales. They could either increase the mass of sugar (on one side of the balance) or reduce the mass of oats (on the other side of the balance).

PRACTICAL TIPS Use a scale to reinforce the concept of mass measured in kilograms. Gradually change the mass of one of the items you are weighing and note what happens to the scales when you do so. Allow children to explore what would happen if they increase both sides by the same amount, or reduce both sides by different amounts.

ANSWERS

Question ① a): 3·49 kg > 3 kg, so the scales will not move. The sugar bag is not heavy enough to tip the balance.

Question ① b): 3·49 − 3 = 0·49. Emma and Ebo can add 0·49 kg of sugar to the bag or they can remove 0·49 kg of oats to balance the scales.

Share

WAYS OF WORKING Whole class teacher led

ASK

- Question ① a): *What increments does the scale go up in? What number is half-way between 2·4 kg and 2·8 kg?*
- Question ① b): *How could you balance the scales? What calculation do you need to do to so that both sides have an equal mass?*

IN FOCUS For question ① a) show all the scales. Discuss how they know the arrow is pointing to 2·6 kg on the analogue scales. Discuss with children the methods that can be used to find the combined mass of 2·6 + 0·89 (the oats plus the pears). Children could count on from 2·6 or use column addition. The sugar weighs 3 kg. Discuss whether the combined oats and pears weigh more than 3 kg. Ask: *Which side of the scales will be heavier?* Question ① b) could be further demonstrated using a comparison bar model. Ask children what calculation they need to do so that the bars are of equal length. The use of the bar model will help children visualise why they need to either add 0·49 kg of sugar or subtract 0·49 kg of oats to balance the scales or do the calculation.

Unit 12: Decimals, Lesson 11

Problem solving – decimals ❷

Discover

① a) What will happen to the balance scale when Ebo puts the bag of sugar in the empty balance pan?

b) By adding or removing some sugar or oats to or from the bags, how can Emma and Ebo get the scales to balance?

48

PUPIL TEXTBOOK 5C PAGE 48

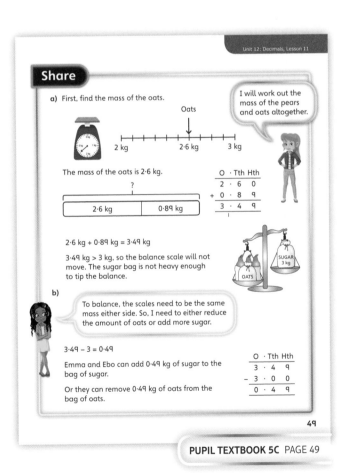

Unit 12: Decimals, Lesson 11

Share

a) First, find the mass of the oats.

I will work out the mass of the pears and oats altogether.

Oats

2 kg   2·6 kg   3 kg

The mass of the oats is 2·6 kg.

2·6 kg	0·89 kg

?

O	·	Tth	Hth
2	·	6	0
+ 0	·	8	9
3	·	4	9

2·6 kg + 0·89 kg = 3·49 kg

3·49 kg > 3 kg, so the balance scale will not move. The sugar bag is not heavy enough to tip the balance.

b)

To balance, the scales need to be the same mass either side. So, I need to either reduce the amount of oats or add more sugar.

3·49 − 3 = 0·49

Emma and Ebo can add 0·49 kg of sugar to the bag of sugar.

Or they can remove 0·49 kg of oats from the bag of oats.

O	·	Tth	Hth
3	·	4	9
− 3	·	0	0
0	·	4	9

49

PUPIL TEXTBOOK 5C PAGE 49

Think together

WAYS OF WORKING Whole class teacher led (I do, We do, You do)

ASK

- Question **1**: *How much sugar was in the bag to start with? How much sugar has been used?*
- Question **2**: *What do you need to know to find the total mass? What calculation could you do to work out the mass of the flour on each spoon?*
- Question **3**: *What is the distance between the 1st and 2nd lamp post? How can you use this information?*

IN FOCUS Question **1** requires children to find the solution involving addition and comparison. Ask them to find a different way to find the solution and share their ideas with the class. To find the solution to question **2**, children will need to both add and subtract decimals. Discuss what 'less' means and encourage children to draw a comparison bar model (like the example) to identify what calculations are needed. They can use the column method for their calculations. For question **3**, children may find it useful to draw a line and mark each of the lamp posts on the line and label the distances between them. They should use a bar model and write the numbers on each of the bars. Discuss the need to add 5·85 m three times and the different strategies that children may use.

STRENGTHEN Provide a blank comparison bar model in question **2** and ask children to fill in the information they know. Reinforce the link between the information in the word problem and how it can be represented on a model. Look for children that add or subtract the numbers in the question but are unsure of why they need to do so. Break the question into smaller parts. Ask: *What does that mean? What can you find from this information?*

DEEPEN Question **3** can be explored further by asking children to find the total distance between all the posts or compare the distance between each pair of lamp posts. Take the opportunity to challenge children to practise all the different strategies they have learned so far to add and subtract decimals.

ASSESSMENT CHECKPOINT Can children recognise mathematical language within problems? Can they correctly identify which operation needs to be used? Are children able to use addition and subtraction of decimals to find the solutions to multi-step problems or do they need further practice?

ANSWERS

Question **1**: There is 1·61 kg of sugar left in the bag.

Question **2**: The total mass of the flour on the two spoons is 21·3 g.

Question **3**: The distance between the 3rd and 4th lamp posts is 5·511 m.

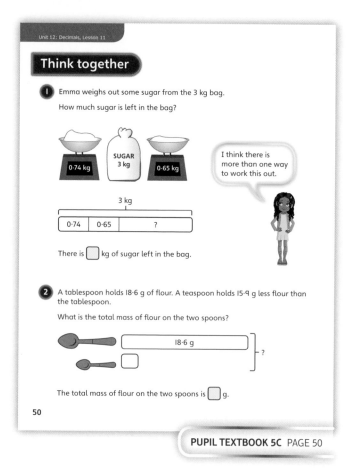

PUPIL TEXTBOOK 5C PAGE 50

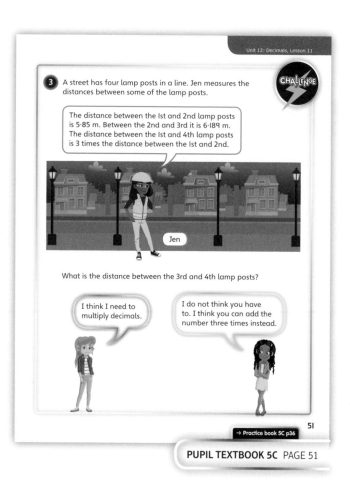

PUPIL TEXTBOOK 5C PAGE 51

Practice

WAYS OF WORKING Independent thinking

IN FOCUS Questions **2** and **3** consolidate children's understanding of problem solving within a context. Encourage children to use a comparison bar model, asking questions to help them do this correctly. Ask: *Which bar will be longest? How do you know? Which bar will be shortest?* Ensure children are sure which operation is required and that they do not just add or subtract the numbers given in the question.

STRENGTHEN Suggest children draw a bar model to help them grasp which calculations are needed in question **6**. Alternatively, provide blank bar models so they can fill the numbers in themselves.

DEEPEN Ask children to find the solution to question **7** using number lines and a bar model to support their answer. Ask children to compare both models and strategies and discuss which other types of question both models could be used for.

THINK DIFFERENTLY Children have come across questions similar to question **5** when calculating the perimeter of shapes. Some children may find it challenging to link the shapes and decimals together. Ask children to consider what they would do if they were working with whole numbers instead of the decimals. For example, what if the length of the rectangle was 10 cm and the width was 4 cm?

ASSESSMENT CHECKPOINT Look at children's responses and working out for question **3**. Can children identify the relevant information needed to confidently solve a multi-step problem involving addition and subtraction of decimals? Do children follow a logical and systematic approach to their problem solving?

ANSWERS Answers for the **Practice** part of the lesson appear in the separate **Practice and Reflect answer guide**.

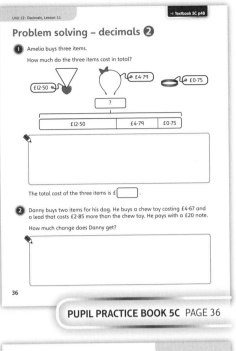

PUPIL PRACTICE BOOK 5C PAGE 36

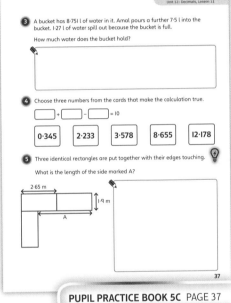

PUPIL PRACTICE BOOK 5C PAGE 37

Reflect

WAYS OF WORKING Pair work

IN FOCUS This question allows children to self-assess their learning. Children need to note the language and numbers used in the question. They need to think of the operations and strategy they will use to reach the solution 3·21 kg. This is a good opportunity to identify children that need extra support and clarify any misconceptions that they may have.

ASSESSMENT CHECKPOINT Can children create their own addition and subtraction problem-solving questions? What calculations will they provide that will solve their question?

ANSWERS Answers for the **Reflect** part of the lesson appear in the separate **Practice and Reflect answer guide**.

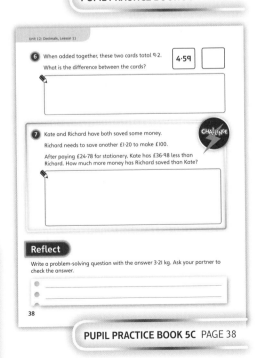

PUPIL PRACTICE BOOK 5C PAGE 38

After the lesson

- Can children identify the important mathematical language within a problem?
- Can children identify the correct operation and employ a suitable, efficient method?

Multiplying decimals by 10

Learning focus

In this lesson, children will use their understanding of place value to develop fluency in multiplying decimals by 10.

Small steps

→ Previous step: Problem solving decimals (2)
→ **This step: Multiplying decimals by 10**
→ Next step: Multiplying decimals by 10, 100 and 1,000

NATIONAL CURRICULUM LINKS

Year 5 Number – Fractions (Including Decimals and Percentages)
• Recognise and use thousandths and relate them to tenths, hundredths and decimal equivalents.
• Solve problems involving number up to three decimal places.

ASSESSING MASTERY

Children can reliably and fluently multiply decimals by 10. They can link their understanding of place value to their calculations and can confidently represent their thinking using concrete, pictorial and abstract representations.

COMMON MISCONCEPTIONS

A common misconception when multiplying decimals by 10 is that children assume they should just 'add a zero' onto the end of whatever number they start with. For example, they write the answer to 4·5 × 10 as 4·50. Ask:
• *Can you show me what you mean by 'add a zero'? What does 'add zero' actually mean? What is the same between 4·5 and 4·50? Can you show me both numbers using place value counters?*

STRENGTHENING UNDERSTANDING

Provide children with different items, each with a price, for instance a notebook for £2·50, a pen for £1·20. Ask children to calculate the price of 10 notebooks or 10 pens. Children can change the price from pounds to pence before completing their calculations. Write all the number sentences on the board. £2·50 × 10 = £25, £1·20 × 10 = £12. Use a place value grid next to each calculation. Ask: *What happens to each digit when multiplying by 10? Five tenths are the same as how many hundredths?*

GOING DEEPER

Get children to work out the price for 1 item when presented with the price for 10 items. For instance, 10 × ? = £63·50 or ? × 10 = 26·90. Challenge them to create contextual word problems for each calculation.

KEY LANGUAGE

In lesson: multiply, multiplication, column, exchange, place value, digit, double

Other language to be used by the teacher: ones, tens, hundreds, thousands, tens of thousands, tenth, hundredth, thousandth

STRUCTURES AND REPRESENTATIONS

place value grid, number lines

RESOURCES

Mandatory: base 10 equipment, place value counters

Optional: printed place value grids

 In the eTextbook of this lesson, you will find interactive links to a selection of teaching tools.

Before you teach

• How confident are children with place value and using base place value grids?
• How confident are children when multiplying whole numbers by 10, 100 and 1,000?

Discover

Pair work

ASK

- Question **1** a): *How can Kate and Richard show 0·1 in the place value grid? How many tenths are in 0·1?*
- Question **1** b): *How many tenths are there in 0·11? How many hundredths?*
- Question **1** a) and b): *What happens to a number when multiplied by 10?*

IN FOCUS Questions **1** a) and b) will give children their first experience of multiplying a decimal number by 10. This will offer a good opportunity to pre-assess children's confidence before starting the main part of the lesson.

PRACTICAL TIPS Write $0·1 = \frac{1}{10}$. Display a rectangle made of 10 squares. Ask children to colour one of the squares. Ask: *What fraction of the rectangle is 1 small square? How can you write this? Now shade 10 squares. How can you write this as a fraction? How can you write this as a decimal? What is 0·1 × 10?*

ANSWERS

Question **1** a): 0·1 × 10 = 1. The answer to Kate and Richard's multiplication is 1.

Question **1** b): The correct answer to Reena and Aki's multiplication is 1·1.

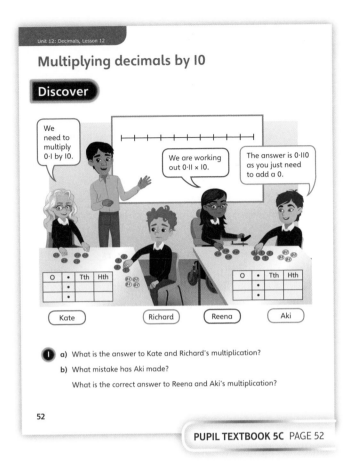

PUPIL TEXTBOOK 5C PAGE 52

Share

Whole class teacher led

ASK

- Question **1** a): *How does the place value grid and counters help clarify the multiplication?*
- Question **1** a): *What exchange do you need to make?*
- Question **1** b): *How do the numbers change when you multiply by 10?*
- Question **1** b): *Discuss Sparks's advice. Why don't you need to write 1·10? What can you simplify it to?*

IN FOCUS Give children place value grids and place value counters and ask them to make the numbers in the question. Ask children to multiply the number by 10. Ensure that children understand that now there will be 10 tenths (0·1) counters. Discuss the exchange of ten tenths for one. In question **1** b), discuss the misconception that you add a 0 to the end of a decimal. Ask children to show you 1·1 and 1·10 in a number line. Link decimals and fractions and ask children to compare 1 tenth and 10 hundredths. Provide more examples such as 1·8 × 10 = ?, 2·3 × 10 = ? and encourage generalisation.

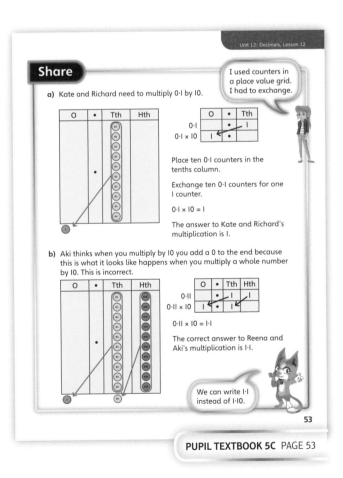

PUPIL TEXTBOOK 5C PAGE 53

Think together

Whole class teacher led (I do, We do, You do)

ASK

- Question ❶: *What is being shown by the counters in the place value grids? Have they already been multiplied by 10?*
- Question ❷: *What happens to each digit when multiplied by 10? Why does it move to the left on the grid?*
- Question ❸ b): *What do all the answers have in common? What happens when a decimal is multiplied by 10?*

IN FOCUS Question ❷ moves to a more abstract way of recording the multiplication with numbers instead of counters in a partially completed place value grid. It offers a good opportunity for children to recognise how a product is similar and different when numbers with the same number of digits after the decimal place are multiplied by 10. Questions ❸ and ❹ encourage children to generalise. They use the idea of exchange to develop the concept that when a number moves from the tenths column to the ones column or from the hundredths column to the tenths column (in the place value grid) it is being multiplied by 10, rather than 'just adding a zero'.

STRENGTHEN If children are finding it difficult to generalise in question ❸, it may help them to build the calculations using concrete resources.

DEEPEN Deepen children's fluency in multiplying decimals by 10 by asking them to make up word problems within the context of measures for a partner to solve. Ask: *What information is given? How can you answer this question?*

ASSESSMENT CHECKPOINT Are children able to multiply decimal numbers by 10? Can they use a place value grid to show their calculations? Look at children's responses to question ❷ to help you evaluate their understanding.

ANSWERS

Question ❶ a): $0.14 \times 10 = 1.4$

Question ❶ b): $2.3 \times 10 = 23$

Question ❷ a): $3.7 \times 10 = 37$

Question ❷ b): $4.5 \times 10 = 45$

Question ❷ c): $2.39 \times 10 = 23.9$

Question ❷ d): $0.196 \times 10 = 1.96$

Question ❸ a): 1; 12; 57; 191

Question ❸ b): 7.2; 12.5; 57.1; 191.6

Question ❸ c): 2.56; 12.56; 311.26

Question ❸ d): Answers will vary but may include:
The digits move 1 place to the left.
The digits are the same but the decimal place has moved; the 0 has disappeared.

Question ❹ a): $10 \times 3.9 = 39$

Question ❹ b): $10 \times 11.6 = 116$

Question ❹ c): $0.456 \times 10 = 4.56$

Question ❹ d): $1.262 \times 10 = 12.62$

Question ❹ e): $0.32 \times 10 = 3.2$

Question ❹ f): $1.586 \times 10 = 15.86$

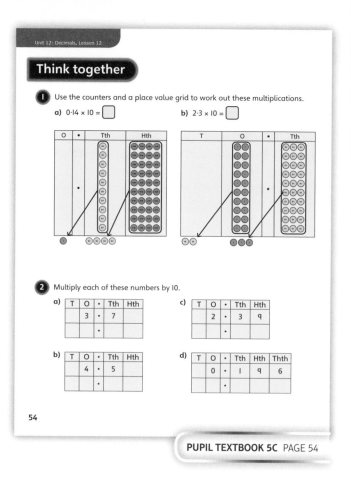

PUPIL TEXTBOOK 5C PAGE 54

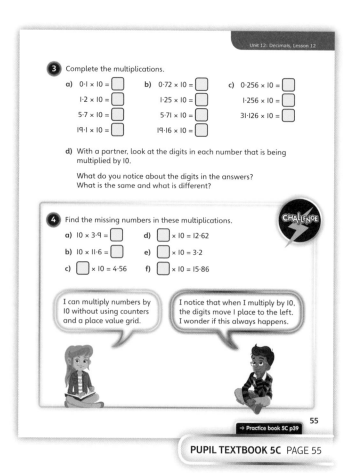

PUPIL TEXTBOOK 5C PAGE 55

Practice

WAYS OF WORKING Independent thinking

IN FOCUS Questions ❶ and ❷ develop children's ability to multiply by 10 while scaffolding their understanding with a place value grid. In order to develop their fluency, children need to recognise how multiplying by 10 can be represented. Question ❸ provides an opportunity to check for any misconceptions surrounding 'adding a zero' and place value in general. Question ❻ a) requires children to diagnose Luis's mistake. It is valuable to develop children's written reasoning. Ask them to identify and describe the mistake, then write their advice to Luis on how to avoid the mistake next time. Question ❼ is an excellent opportunity for children to develop their ability to reason and problem solve. Children can use the associative property of multiplying to double the numbers first, then multiply by 10. Other children may add two strides first, then multiply by 10, or multiply one stride by 10 and then double the answer.

STRENGTHEN Support children when completing the calculations in question ❻ b) by encouraging them to insert the answer in the question and check whether it is correct. Ask: *Can you spot any patterns in the numbers that will help you complete the next calculation?*

DEEPEN Deepen children's work on question ❼ by exploring the different ways the question can be answered. Write all the methods and answers on the board and encourage children to explain each other's answers. Ask: *What is this calculation finding? Where does this number come from?*

ASSESSMENT CHECKPOINT Children can multiply a decimal number by 10. They are able to use multiplication of decimals to reason and problem-solve.

ANSWERS Answers for the **Practice** part of the lesson appear in the separate **Practice and Reflect answer guide**.

Reflect

WAYS OF WORKING Independent thinking

IN FOCUS This question brings with it an opportunity for children to generalise based on what they have learned in this lesson. Encourage children to offer examples of numbers with one, two and three decimal places. If necessary, remind them of the misconception of 'just adding zero'. They should use their understanding of place value to support their answer.

ASSESSMENT CHECKPOINT Look for children fluently explaining what happens to the digits of a decimal number when it is multiplied by 10. Children can confidently use concrete representations and place value grids to support generalising and their reasoning.

ANSWERS Answers for the **Reflect** part of the lesson appear in the separate **Practice and Reflect answer guide**.

After the lesson ⏸

- Which concrete manipulatives were most effective in this lesson?
- Do children have a robust understanding of how to multiply by 10 before progressing to multiplying by 100 and 1,000?

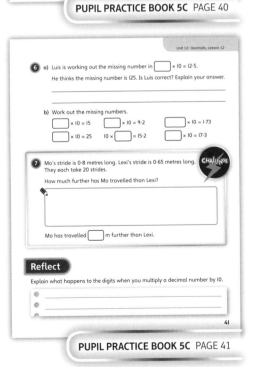

PUPIL PRACTICE BOOK 5C PAGE 39

PUPIL PRACTICE BOOK 5C PAGE 40

PUPIL PRACTICE BOOK 5C PAGE 41

Multiplying decimals by 10, 100 and 1,000

Learning focus

In this lesson, children will use their understanding of place value to develop fluency in multiplying decimals by 10, 100 and 1,000.

Small steps

→ Previous step: Multiplying decimals by 10
→ **This step: Multiplying decimals by 10, 100 and 1,000**
→ Next step: Dividing decimals by 10

NATIONAL CURRICULUM LINKS

Year 5 Number – Fractions (Including Decimals and Percentages)
• Recognise and use thousandths and relate them to tenths, hundredths and decimal equivalents.
• Solve problems involving number up to three decimal places.

ASSESSING MASTERY

Children can reliably and fluently multiply decimal numbers by 10, 100 and 1,000. They can link their understanding of place value to their calculations and confidently represent their thinking using concrete, pictorial and abstract representations.

COMMON MISCONCEPTIONS

Children may get confused about which way the digits 'move' when multiplying by 10, 100 and 1,000 and instead of multiplying by 10, 100 or 1,000, they actually divide by 10, 100 or 1,000. For example, $4·32 \times 100 = 0·0432$ rather than 432. Ask:
• *Can you show me what you mean by 'moving the digits'? Do numbers get bigger or smaller when multiplied by 100?*

STRENGTHENING UNDERSTANDING

Using a place value grid and place value counters will help children better visualise what happens when a decimal number is multiplied by 10, 100 or 1,000.

GOING DEEPER

Children could create contextual word problems that require someone to multiply by 10, 100 or 1,000. Using real-life situations will help children to better see what happens to each decimal when becoming 10, 100 or 1,000 times bigger.

KEY LANGUAGE

In lesson: multiply, place value, weight, digit, column, kilogram (kg), mass

Other language to be used by the teacher: tenth, hundredth, thousandth, ones, tens, hundreds, thousands, tens of thousands

STRUCTURES AND REPRESENTATIONS

place value grid

RESOURCES

Mandatory: base 10 equipment, place value counters

Optional: printed place value grids, building blocks, cubes

 In the eTextbook of this lesson, you will find interactive links to a selection of teaching tools.

Before you teach

• How confident are children at multiplying decimals by 10?

Discover

WAYS OF WORKING Pair work

ASK

- Question ❶ a): *How many kg of potatoes are there in a bag? How many bags are there in each sack?*
- Question ❶ a): *What is a pallet? How many sacks are on a pallet?*
- Question ❶ b): *How many pallets are on each lorry?*
- Question ❶ a) and b): *What patterns can you spot in the numbers?*

IN FOCUS Question ❶ a) and b) will give children their first opportunity to multiply decimals by 10, 100 and 1,000. Children will use a place value grid and the associative property of multiplication $100 = 10 \times 10$ and $1,000 = 10 \times 10 \times 10$ to work out each multiplication.

PRACTICAL TIPS Use place value counters, building blocks or cubes to act out the question. For example, to represent 2·5 kg you could make a tower with 2 yellow blocks to show the ones and 5 blue blocks to show the tenths. Put 10 of the towers into a box or bag. Show children 10 boxes or bags. By seeing 10 groups of 10 towers, children will visualise the question better and understand that multiplying by 100 is the same as multiplying by 10 and 10.

ANSWERS

Question ❶ a): The mass of 10 sacks or 100 bags on one pallet is 250 kg.

Question ❶ b): The mass of all the potatoes on the lorry is 2,500 kg.

Share

WAYS OF WORKING Whole class teacher led

ASK

- Question ❶ a): *What does the arrow show? How many bags are there in a sack?*
- Question ❶ a) and b): *How do the numbers change and stay the same as you multiply by 10 and 100?*
- Question ❶ b): *Why are there extra zeros in the calculations?*

IN FOCUS It will be important in questions ❶ a) and b) to ensure children recognise that when multiplying, each digit becomes 10, 100 or 1,000 times bigger. This should be supported with the use of concrete resources so children can manipulate and experience the difference between multiplying by 10 once, twice or three times.

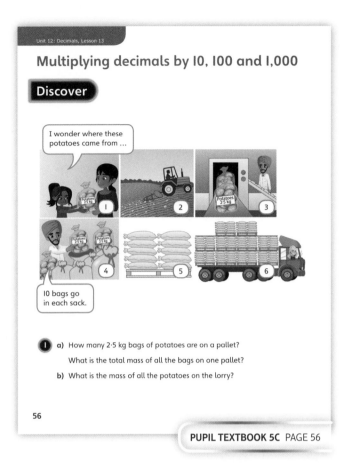

PUPIL TEXTBOOK 5C PAGE 56

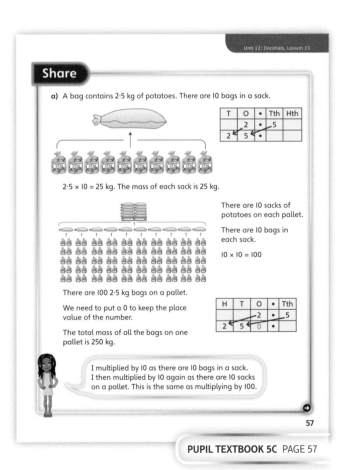

PUPIL TEXTBOOK 5C PAGE 57

Think together

Whole class teacher led (I do, We do, You do)

ASK

- Question **1**: *What do the arrows show?*
- Question **2**: *What happens when you repeatedly multiply by 10? How can you multiply by 100 and 1,000 without using the place value grid? Does it work for all decimal numbers?*
- Question **3**: *How does the place value grid show the multiplication clearly? Do you need to draw a place value grid for all parts of this question?*

IN FOCUS Question **1** moves to a more abstract way of recording the multiplication by showing it using a partially completed place value grid. Encourage children to recognise how a product is similar and different when the same number is multiplied by 10, 100 and 1,000. Question **2** encourages children to generalise. Children should notice the links between multiplying the same decimal number by 100 and 1,000. They also will notice what happens when numbers with one, two and three decimal places are multiplied by 100 and 1,000.

STRENGTHEN If children are finding it difficult to generalise in question **2**, it may help them to build the calculations using concrete representations. Draw a 3 × 2 grid on the board. Write some different lengths in metres, for example 0·12 m, 1·35 m, 0·45 m. Ask children to copy the grid but write each length in cm instead of m: 12 cm, 135 cm, 45 cm. Give them a metre ruler to check their answers.

DEEPEN Deepen children's fluency with multiplying by 10, 100 and 1,000 by asking them to make up problems with a measurement context for a partner to solve. Ask: *What information is given? How can you answer this question?*

ASSESSMENT CHECKPOINT Can children multiply decimal numbers by 10, 100 and 1,000? Can they use place value grids to show this? Evaluate children's answers to question **3** as an indication of their understanding.

ANSWERS

Question **1** a): 3·7 × 10 = 37; 3·7 × 100 = 370;
3·7 × 1,000 = 3,700

Question **2** a): 1·72 × 10 = 17·2; 1·72 × 100 = 172;
1·72 × 1,000 = 1,720

Question **2** b): 4·13 × 1,000 = 4,130; 0·413 × 1,000 = 413;
0·041 × 1,000 = 41

Question **2** c): 39·3 × 100 = 3,930; 3·93 × 100 = 393;
0·393 × 100 = 39·3

Question **3** a): 0·12 × 100 = 12; 0·12 × 1,000 = 120;
7·35 × 100 = 735; 7·35 × 1,000 = 7,350;
16·9 × 100 = 1,690; 16·9 × 1,000 = 16,900;
0·384 × 100 = 38·4; 0·384 × 1,000 = 384
When multiplying by 100, the digits move two places to the left. When multiplying by 1,000 the digits move three places to the left.

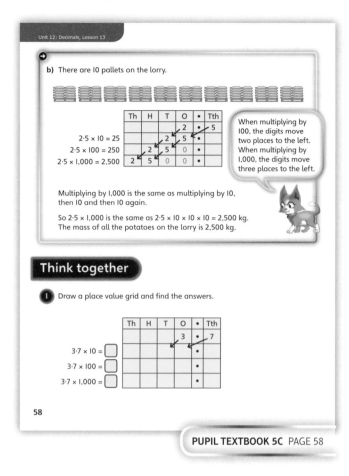

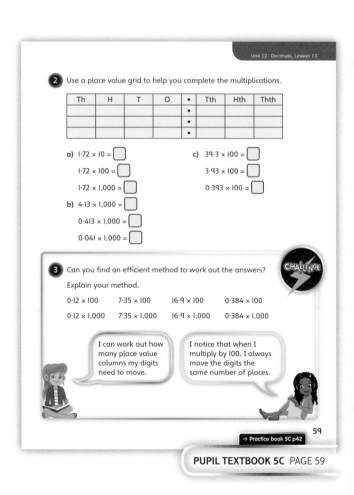

→ Practice book 5C p42

PUPIL TEXTBOOK 5C PAGE 58

PUPIL TEXTBOOK 5C PAGE 59

Practice

IN FOCUS Question ① develops children's ability to multiply by 10, 100 and 1,000 while scaffolding their learning with a place value grid. In question ② the scaffolding is removed and children are required to find the missing numbers when decimals are multiplied by 100 and 1,000. Question ③ develops children's fluency and reasoning, by presenting them with a real-life context.

STRENGTHEN For question ④ a), encourage children to build the calculations first with concrete materials, then look for patterns to help them complete the rest. Ask: *Can you complete the first calculation? How about the second? Can you spot any patterns in the numbers that will help you complete the next two calculations? How can you apply what you have noticed to the next column?*

DEEPEN Deepen the learning from question ⑤ by asking children to find three ways to complete ? × ? > ? × ?. Ask: *Can you convince your partner that you are correct? What resources can you use to support your answer?*

ASSESSMENT CHECKPOINT Children use their understanding of place value and the associative properties of multiplication to multiply decimal numbers by 10, 100 and 1,000. They understand that multiplying by 100 means they need to multiply by 10 and 10 again, whilst multiplying by 1,000 means that they need to multiply by 10, 10 and 10 again.

ANSWERS Answers for the **Practice** part of the lesson appear in the separate **Practice and Reflect answer guide**.

Reflect

IN FOCUS This question brings with it an opportunity for children to combine their learning from the previous lessons with their learning from this lesson. Children do not simply repeat rules and procedures but are able to use a place value grid to demonstrate what happens when a number is multiplied by 100 and 1,000. Children should confidently recognise the multiplication facts they have focussed on in this lesson and are able to use them to multiply by 10, 100 and 1,000. This also provides an opportunity for children to relate their understanding to a peer in their own words.

ASSESSMENT CHECKPOINT Look for fluency in children when recognising and interpreting the concrete representations of a number being multiplied by 10, 100 and 1,000. Children should be able to confidently link the representation to an appropriate calculation.

ANSWERS Answers for the **Reflect** part of the lesson appear in the separate **Practice and Reflect answer guide**.

After the lesson ⏸

- Did children recognise the usefulness of the properties of multiplication when multiplying by 10, 100 and 1,000?
- Have children mastered the concept of multiplying decimals by 10, 100 and 1,000? Are they able to multiply fluently?

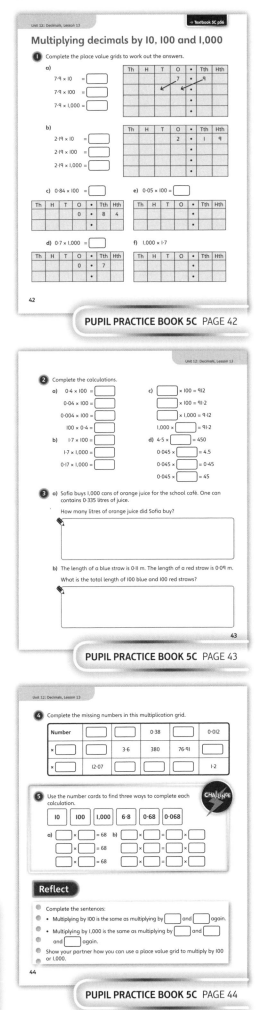

PUPIL PRACTICE BOOK 5C PAGE 42

PUPIL PRACTICE BOOK 5C PAGE 43

PUPIL PRACTICE BOOK 5C PAGE 44

Dividing decimals by 10

Learning focus

In this lesson, children will use their understanding of place value to develop fluency in dividing decimal numbers by 10.

Small steps

→ Previous step: Multiplying decimals by 10, 100 and 1,000
→ **This step: Dividing decimals by 10**
→ Next step: Dividing decimals by 10, 100 and 1,000

NATIONAL CURRICULUM LINKS

Year 5 Number – Fractions (Including Decimals and Percentages)
• Recognise and use thousandths and relate them to tenths, hundredths and decimal equivalents.
• Solve problems involving number up to three decimal places.

ASSESSING MASTERY

Children can reliably and fluently divide decimal numbers by 10. They can link their understanding of place value to their calculations and can confidently represent their thinking using concrete, pictorial and abstract representations.

COMMON MISCONCEPTIONS

Children may recognise dividing by 10, 100 and 1,000 as just 'taking away a zero' and as a consequence become confused when there aren't any zeros or they subtract the wrong zero. For instance, $0.3 \div 10 = 3$. Ask:
• *What does it mean to 'take away a zero'? What happens to a number when you divide it by 10? Does the number get bigger or smaller?*

STRENGTHENING UNDERSTANDING

It may be beneficial to recap division of whole numbers by 10 before this lesson. Give children different opportunities to experience this concept through sharing objects into groups of 10 and linking this action to the division calculation.

GOING DEEPER

Give children this statement to investigate: *Is it always, sometimes or never true that when you divide a decimal number by 10, the answer is a number less than 1?*

KEY LANGUAGE

In lesson: divide, digit, division, place value, mass, share, group, width, difference, column, metres (m), kilograms (kg), pounds (£), pence (p), litres (l)

Other language to be used by the teacher: ones, tenth, hundredth, thousandth

STRUCTURES AND REPRESENTATIONS

place value grid, bar model

RESOURCES

Mandatory: place value counters

Optional: printed place value grids, paper, scissors

 In the eTextbook of this lesson, you will find interactive links to a selection of teaching tools.

Before you teach

• How confident were children with multiplying decimals by 10? Are there any misconceptions that may slow progress in this lesson?
• How will you clarify the link between this lesson and the last to strengthen children's understanding of the inverse relationship between multiplication and division?

Discover

WAYS OF WORKING Pair work

ASK

- Question ❶ a): *How many handspans have Danny and Lexi each measured? What is the width of Danny's 10 handspans?*
- Question ❶ a): *How can you work out the width of one handspan if you know the width of 10?*
- Question ❶ b): *Do you think the width of Lexi's handspan is equal to the width of Danny's handspan? How do you know?*

IN FOCUS Questions ❶ a) and b) are important as they provide children with their first opportunity to understand the effect of dividing a decimal number by 10. Children find the difference between both results in question ❶ b).

PRACTICAL TIPS To help engage children in this area of learning, you could ask them to draw their handspan on a piece of paper. Make copies of it and use scissors to cut around each handspan. Choose two children, place their 10 handspans next to each other on the board for all to see. Compare the lengths of each line they make. Which one is wider or narrower? This activity will contextualise the main concept of the lesson. It may also give an opportunity to consider when division is used.

ANSWERS

Question ❶ a): The width of one of Danny's handspans is 0·15 m.

Question ❶ b): Lexi's handspan is 0·06 m narrower than Danny's.

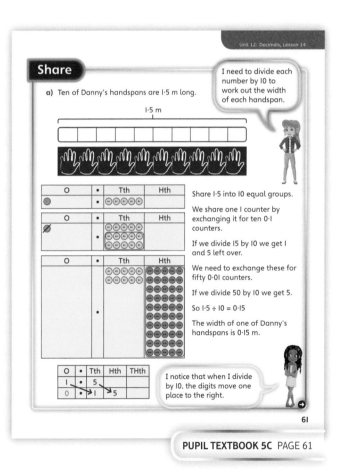

Dividing decimals by 10

Discover

> I wonder how wide just one of my handspans is?

Danny

1·5m

0·9m

Lexi

❶ a) What is the width of one of Danny's handspans in metres?

b) In metres, how much narrower is Lexi's handspan than Danny's?

60

PUPIL TEXTBOOK 5C PAGE 60

Share

WAYS OF WORKING Whole class teacher led

ASK

- Question ❶ a): *What calculation does the bar model show?*
- Question ❶ a): *What happens to the digits of a number when divided by 10?*
- Question ❶ a): *Do you agree with Flo? Why do you think the digits move to the right?*
- Question ❶ b): *Is Flo's method correct? Will you achieve the same answer?*
- Question ❶ b): *What do you need to pay attention to when subtracting the decimals? What is the red zero for?*

IN FOCUS It is important to focus on question ❶ b) as it offers two different potential ways of finding a solution. Making this clear will help children explore different approaches and develop their fluency when solving similar calculations.

Share

> I need to divide each number by 10 to work out the width of each handspan.

a) Ten of Danny's handspans are 1·5 m long.

1·5 m

Share 1·5 into 10 equal groups.

We share one 1 counter by exchanging it for ten 0·1 counters.

If we divide 15 by 10 we get 1 and 5 left over.

We need to exchange these for fifty 0·01 counters.

If we divide 50 by 10 we get 5.

So 1·5 ÷ 10 = 0·15

The width of one of Danny's handspans is 0·15 m.

> I notice that when I divide by 10, the digits move one place to the right.

61

PUPIL TEXTBOOK 5C PAGE 61

Think together

WAYS OF WORKING Whole class teacher led (I do, We do, You do)

ASK

- Question **1**: *How can the place value grid help you solve this?*
- Question **2**: *What patterns can you spot in these calculations? What can you say about what happens every time you divide by 10?*
- Question **3** a): *If Danny mixes the orange and the water, how much squash will he make?*
- Question **3** b): *How many ml are there in 1 l?*
- Question **3** c): *How many g are there in 1 kg?*

IN FOCUS Question **2** offers an excellent opportunity for children to start generalising about dividing by 10. It is important to discuss what they notice and link what they know of place value and dividing whole numbers to the division of decimals. In question **3** c), children can explore dividing by 2 and then by 10 or vice versa. It is important to discuss how dividing by 10 and then 2 is equivalent to dividing by 20, much like how multiplying by 10 and then 2 is the same as multiplying by 20.

STRENGTHEN In question **3**, it may be beneficial to encourage children to use a bar model and place value grid. The bar model should help them visualise the steps that they need to take and the information they need to identify in order to calculate the answer. The place value grid should help divide the decimal numbers.

DEEPEN When solving question **2**, deepen children's understanding by encouraging them to generalise. Ask: *What do you notice? What happens to the numbers when dividing by 10? How can this help you solve similar calculations more quickly in the future?*

ASSESSMENT CHECKPOINT Question **3** will provide good evidence of children's understanding of the concepts in this lesson and their ability to link them to prior learning on multiplying decimals and their learning about place value.

ANSWERS

Question **1**: $2 \cdot 6 \div 10 = 0 \cdot 26$ m.
Each of Toshi's footsteps is $0 \cdot 26$ m.

Question **2** a): $0 \cdot 92 \div 10 = 0 \cdot 092$

Question **2** b): $53 \cdot 6 \div 10 = 5 \cdot 36$

Question **2** c): $95 \div 10 = 9 \cdot 5$

Question **2** d): $58 \cdot 6 \div 10 = 5 \cdot 86$

Question **2** e): $89 \cdot 02 \div 10 = 8 \cdot 902$

Question **2** f): $10 \cdot 02 \div 10 = 1 \cdot 002$

Question **3** a): $2 \cdot 25 + 0 \cdot 7 = 2 \cdot 95$ l, $2 \cdot 95 \div 10 = 0 \cdot 295$ l
There is $0 \cdot 295$ l in each glass.

Question **3** b): £1·20 ÷ 10 = 12p. 100 ml of milk costs 12p; 12p × 2 = 24p. 200 ml of milk costs 24p.

Question **3** c): 16 kg ÷ 20 = 0·8 kg or half of 16 kg is 8 kg.
$8 \div 10 = 0 \cdot 8$ kg

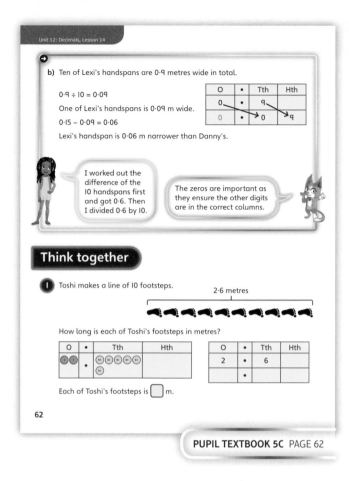

PUPIL TEXTBOOK 5C PAGE 62

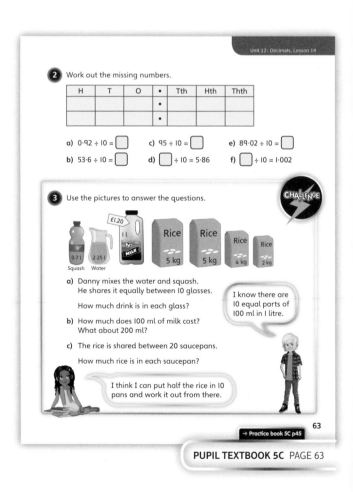

PUPIL TEXTBOOK 5C PAGE 63

Practice

WAYS OF WORKING Independent thinking

IN FOCUS Questions **4**, **6**, **7** and **8** show children how their learning can be used in real-life contexts, applying units of measurement to their current learning. Children need to pay attention not only to their calculations, but also the units of measurement used in each part of the question. When solving question **5**, it will be beneficial to remind children of the patterns and generalisations they noticed earlier in the lesson. This question encourages children to think algebraically, considering what they know about each side of the calculation and how they can use known information to find the unknown number.

STRENGTHEN To strengthen understanding when solving question **8**, ask children to draw a bar model. Ask: *What do you need to know to find the mass of hot chocolate in one cup? How can you use the bar model to find the number of cups Toshi makes from 2·5 kg of powder?*

DEEPEN Ask children to use division by 10 to calculate the price of 100 ml of juice if the price for a bottle of 500 ml is 76p. Then find the price of 100 g of sugar if the price of 2 kg of sugar is £1·48. Listen for the different strategies that children use and share and discuss the answers with the whole class.

THINK DIFFERENTLY Children need to use the information shown on the picture and their understanding of division by 10 to find the price of different measurements. In question **7** b), look for children who calculate the price of 2,000 g of cocoa first and then divide the answer by 10.

ASSESSMENT CHECKPOINT Using responses to questions **4** and **6**, evaluate whether children are able to divide decimal numbers by 10. Can they solve missing number questions and use the division of decimals to problem-solve and answer questions presented in different real-life contexts?

ANSWERS Answers for the **Practice** part of the lesson appear in the separate **Practice and Reflect answer guide**.

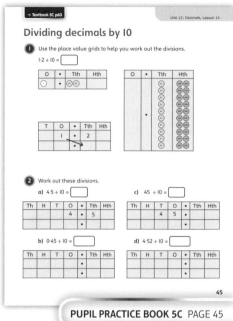

PUPIL PRACTICE BOOK 5C PAGE 45

PUPIL PRACTICE BOOK 5C PAGE 46

Reflect

WAYS OF WORKING Independent thinking

IN FOCUS This question will help assess whether children can explain how to divide decimal numbers by 10. Encourage children to use the accurate vocabulary they have been exposed to during the lesson. They can support their reasoning with the use of place value grids.

ASSESSMENT CHECKPOINT Look for children who can fluently and clearly explain how they can divide a number by 10. Do children understand of the concept or have they adopted a shortcut to find the answer?

ANSWERS Answers for the **Reflect** part of the lesson appear in the separate **Practice and Reflect answer guide**.

After the lesson

- Are children equally confident with dividing by 10 as they were with multiplying by 10?
- Are children confident in using the inverse relationship between multiplication and division to check their answers?

PUPIL PRACTICE BOOK 5C PAGE 47

Dividing decimals by 10, 100 and 1,000

Learning focus

In this lesson, children will use their understanding of place value and division of decimals by 10, to develop fluency in dividing decimal numbers by 10, 100 and 1,000.

Small steps

→ Previous step: Dividing decimals by 10
→ **This step: Dividing decimals by 10, 100 and 1,000**
→ Next step: Measuring angles in degrees

NATIONAL CURRICULUM LINKS

Year 5 Number – Fractions (Including Decimals and Percentages)
- Recognise and use thousandths and relate them to tenths, hundredths and decimal equivalents.
- Solve problems involving number up to three decimal places.

ASSESSING MASTERY

Children can reliably and fluently use their knowledge of division by 10 to divide decimal numbers by 100 and 1,000. They can confidently represent their thinking using concrete, pictorial and abstract representations.

COMMON MISCONCEPTIONS

Children may link dividing by 10, 100 or 1,000 as always having a set number of zeroes after the decimal point. For example, they know that 0·6 ÷ 10 = 0·06, and so assume that 1·6 ÷ 10 = 0·016. Ask:
- *Can you show me what dividing by 10 would look like in place value grid? Why is there a '0' in the answer of 0·6 ÷ 10 = 0·06?*

STRENGTHENING UNDERSTANDING

Give children a strip of paper 16 cm long. Say: *Let's check whether when 16 is divided by 10, the answer is 1·6, 0·16 cm or 0·016 cm.* Discuss where the number 0·016 could be. Children should establish that the lengths of 0·16 and 0·016 are too small to be a tenth of the length of the strip.

GOING DEEPER

Give children these statements to complete. 5 ÷ ? = 0·5 ÷ 10, 0·4 ÷ 100 = ? ÷ 1,000. Ask: *Is there only one answer?*

KEY LANGUAGE

In lesson: divide, place, share, mass, rule, equal, represent, kilograms (kg), litres (l), kilometres (km)

Other language to be used by the teacher: place value, ones, grouping, ten, tenth, hundredth, thousandth

STRUCTURES AND REPRESENTATIONS

place value grid, bar model

RESOURCES

Mandatory: place value counters

Optional: printed place value grids, 1 large and 10 small boxes

 In the eTextbook of this lesson, you will find interactive links to a selection of teaching tools.

Before you teach

- How confident were children with multiplying by 10, 100 and 1,000? Are there any misconceptions that need addressing first?
- How will you make clear the link between this lesson and the last?
- How can you strengthen children's understanding of the inverse relationship between multiplication and division?

Discover

WAYS OF WORKING Pair work

ASK

- Question **1** a): *What is a sachet? What is a carton? How many sachets are there in a carton?*
- Question **1** a): *How many cartons are there in a large box? What calculation do you need to do to work out how many sachets are in a large box?*
- Question **1** b): *How can you work out the mass of each sachet?*

IN FOCUS For question **1** a), discuss the sizes and names of the containers in the picture (namely 'sachet', 'carton' and 'large box') so that children are comfortable with what each container is, and what it is called. Some children may assume that the answer is 10 or are unsure what to do, as they simply look at the picture and not at the information it provides. Highlight the importance of looking carefully at the information and deciding how to use it. Question **1** b) gives children the first opportunity to understand the effect of dividing a decimal by 100 by dividing by 10 and 10 again.

PRACTICAL TIPS To help engage children, create a 'magic box'. Put 10 smaller boxes inside a large 'magic box'. Each of the smaller boxes holds 10 counters (or sweets). Ask: *If the magic box has a mass of 1·2 kg, what is the mass of each small box?* This activity will give children hands-on, contextualised experience to relate to the problem in the lesson and should help them to identify a strategy to find the solution.

ANSWERS

Question **1** a): There are 100 sachets of curry powder in the large box.

Question **1** b): There is 0·085 kg of curry powder in each sachet.

Share

WAYS OF WORKING Whole class teacher led

ASK

- Question **1** a): *What information do you need to know to find the number of sachets in the large box? What calculation do you need to do?*
- Question **1** b): *What calculation does the 1st bar model show? Explain how.*
- Question **1** b): *What calculation does the 2nd bar model show? What does the place value grid show?*
- Question **1** b): *How is Flo's method of dividing by 100 the same or different to Astrid's? Whose is more efficient?*

IN FOCUS Make sure children understand the place value grids in question **1** b) and that they are confident in how to use them. Draw children's attention to the calculation of dividing by 10, then dividing by 10 again and ask them to think of a single calculation that they may use instead. Show them Flo's method of dividing by 100. If children are unsure, provide examples with whole numbers, such as 700 ÷ 10 = 70, 70 ÷ 10 = 7. Ask: *What number can you divide 700 by that gives the answer 7?*

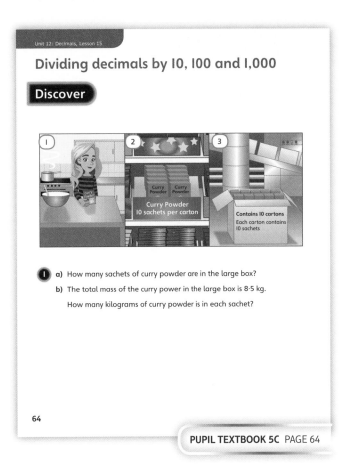

Dividing decimals by 10, 100 and 1,000

Discover

1 a) How many sachets of curry powder are in the large box?

b) The total mass of the curry power in the large box is 8·5 kg.

How many kilograms of curry powder is in each sachet?

64

PUPIL TEXTBOOK 5C PAGE 64

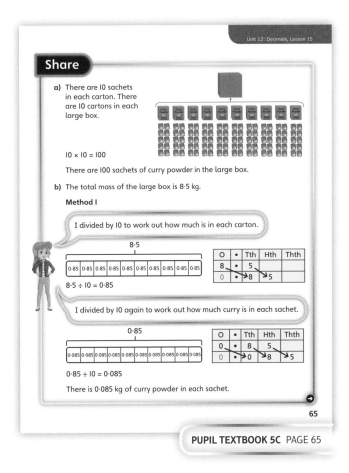

PUPIL TEXTBOOK 5C PAGE 65

Think together

WAYS OF WORKING Whole class teacher led (I do, We do, You do)

ASK

- Question **1**: *How can a place value grid help you find solutions to these calculations?*
- Question **2**: *What do you notice about what happens every time you divide by 100?*
- Question **3**: *How does your knowledge of dividing by 10 help you with this question?*

IN FOCUS Question **2** offers further opportunity for children to divide by 100. It is important to discuss the method that children may use and clarify any misconceptions. Question **3** requires children to use place value when dividing by 10, 100 and 1,000, to problem-solve. It will be important to discuss how (similar to multiplying by 10, 10 and 10 again) dividing by 10, 10 and then by 10 again is equivalent to dividing by 1,000.

STRENGTHEN To help children with question **3**, it may be useful for them to use place value counters and a place value grid. Emphasise that when dividing by 100 or 1,000, the numbers will become 100 or 1,000 times smaller.

DEEPEN Deepen children's understanding by asking them to create their own word problems based on the calculations in question **3**. Pay attention to the language they use. Ask: *Can you find the solutions in more than one way?*

ASSESSMENT CHECKPOINT Question **3** will provide solid evidence of children's understanding of the concepts in this lesson and their ability to link to prior learning from the previous lesson and their work on place value. Look for children's recognition that, for example, dividing by 10 and then by 10 and 10 again is equivalent to dividing by 1,000.

ANSWERS

Question **1**: 12·8 kg ÷ 100 = 0·128 kg; 128 ÷ 100 = 1·28; 2·52 m ÷ 100 = 0·0252 m; 0·9 ÷ 100 = 0·009

Question **2**: 4 ÷ 100 = 0·04 litres. There is 0·04 litres of milk in each scone.

Question **3** a): 12 ÷ 1,000 = 0·012

Question **3** b): 6·2 ÷ 1,000 = 0·0062

Question **3** c): 718 km ÷ 1,000 = 0·718 km (718 m)

Question **3** d): 0·7 ÷ 1,000 = 0·0007

Question **4** a): 46 kg ÷ 1,000 = 0·046 kg. A single slice of bread weighs 0·046 kg.

Question **4** b): Answers will vary but may include 'divide by 1,000' or 'divide by 10, then 10, then 10 again'.

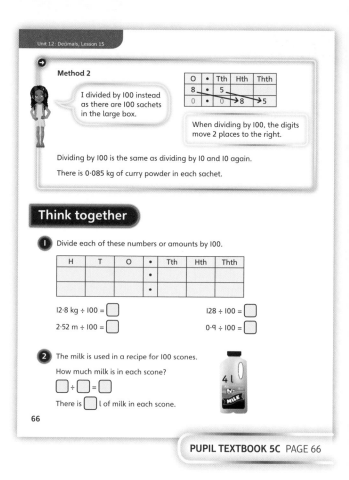

PUPIL TEXTBOOK 5C PAGE 66

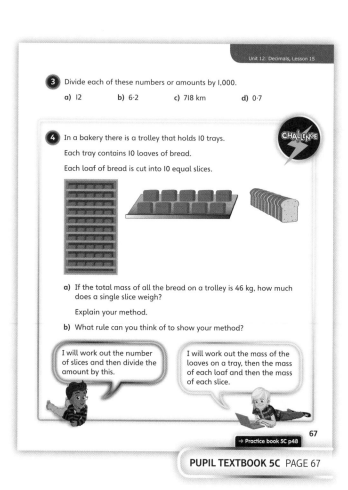

PUPIL TEXTBOOK 5C PAGE 67

Practice

WAYS OF WORKING Independent thinking

IN FOCUS Question **1** offers children a scaffolded activity where they can begin to independently use the place value grid to divide by 100 and 1,000. Question **2** offers another opportunity for children to generalise the rule that they can use on how to divide by 100. Discuss with children how they can use the square to prove Bella's theory. Question **7** is important as it encourages children to think algebraically, considering what they know about each side of the equation and working forwards and backwards to find the missing numbers, developing their fluency, reasoning and problem-solving skills.

STRENGTHEN To strengthen understanding when solving question **6**, ask children to use a bar model. Ask: *How can you use the bar model to find the amount of money they save each day? What calculations will you use? Can you find the solution to the question in two ways?*

DEEPEN Explore question **7** by giving other missing number problems, such as $3.56 \div ? = 0.0356 \times ? = 35.6$. Encourage children to explain their method clearly using the correct mathematical vocabulary.

ASSESSMENT CHECKPOINT Children are confident in dividing by 10, 100 and 1,000. They use their knowledge of multiplying and dividing decimals to find the missing numbers in problems.

ANSWERS Answers for the **Practice** part of the lesson appear in the separate **Practice and Reflect answer guide**.

Reflect

WAYS OF WORKING Independent thinking

IN FOCUS This question will help you assess whether children have fully understood the effect that dividing by 10, 100 and 1,000 has on the place value of digits in a number.

ASSESSMENT CHECKPOINT Look for children who use place value accurately and can fluently and clearly explain which calculation is correct and why. The question prompts children to check Reena's answer. Look for children using multiplication and division, and demonstrating their understanding of the inverse relationship between multiplication and division to check their calculations.

ANSWERS Answers for the **Reflect** part of the lesson appear in the separate **Practice and Reflect answer guide**.

After the lesson

- Are children equally confident with dividing by 10, 100 and 1,000 as they were when multiplying?
- Are children confident using the inverse relationship between multiplication and division?
- Can children confidently use place value grids and bar models to model their thinking?

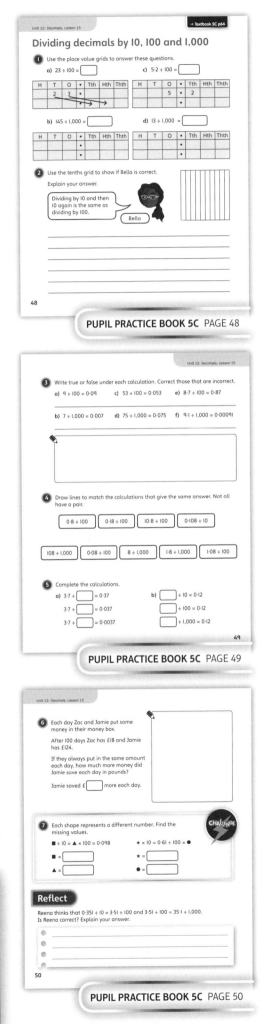

PUPIL PRACTICE BOOK 5C PAGE 48

PUPIL PRACTICE BOOK 5C PAGE 49

PUPIL PRACTICE BOOK 5C PAGE 50

End of unit check

Don't forget the *Power Maths* unit assessment grid on p26.

WAYS OF WORKING Group work adult led

IN FOCUS These questions cover the whole unit and are designed to draw out misconceptions and misunderstandings. Check that children can use the formal method for addition and subtraction and can correctly align the numbers. Children should realise that to find a missing number they will need to use an inverse operation. When children are solving word problems, including those with several steps, encourage them to represent each situation using a bar model to help them work out if they need to add or subtract, multiply or divide.

Children should use a place value grid to support their calculations.

ANSWERS AND COMMENTARY Children who have mastered this unit understand the place value of each digit in numbers with three decimal places. They can look for key language to see if they are requested to multiply or divide by 10, 100 or 1,000. They also will have confidence in selecting efficient methods to solve addition and subtraction problems with decimal numbers.

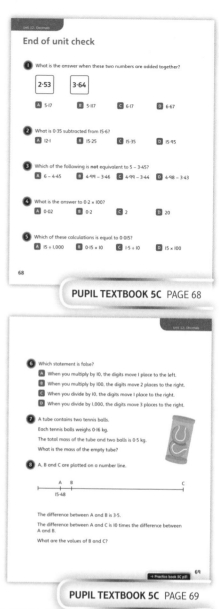

PUPIL TEXTBOOK 5C PAGE 68

PUPIL TEXTBOOK 5C PAGE 69

Q	A	WRONG ANSWERS AND MISCONCEPTIONS	STRENGTHENING UNDERSTANDING
1	C	A shows exchanging in the wrong direction, left to right. B suggests incorrectly lining up numbers and exchanging. D suggests an incorrect exchange.	Use place value grids and counters to support column methods of addition and subtraction. Work through step-by-step showing any counter exchanges and linking the place value grid to the column method.
2	B	A suggests they have lined the numbers up incorrectly.	
3	B	A, C, and D suggest the child has not realised that the difference between the numbers has not changed.	
4	D	A, B or C suggest the child has made a mistake with the place value of 0·2 or 100.	Use a bar model to represent each situation and help children decide if they need to add or subtract, multiply or divide.
5	A	B suggests the child has multiplied instead of dividing.	
6	B	A, C and D suggest insecure knowledge of multiplying and dividing by 10, 100 and 1,000.	
7	0·18kg	Some children will start with the mass of the tennis balls, some may find the mass of the two balls first.	
8	B is 18·98 C is 50·48	Look for children who are systematic in their approach and find the answer as they move along.	If children are unsure ask them to re-read the question.

My journal

WAYS OF WORKING Independent thinking

ANSWERS AND COMMENTARY

Question **1** a): Max could do this as a column subtraction (see example).

Or he could do 12 – 4·35 = 11·99 – 4·34 = 7·65.
• Encourage children to work out the missing number first using the methods they have encountered in this unit.

T	O	·	Tth	Hth
$^0\cancel{1}$	$\cancel{2}$	·	$^9\cancel{\cancel{0}}$	$^1 0$
–	4	·	3	5
	7	·	6	5

Question **1** b): Max should be careful to avoid mistakes when setting up the column method. He could also make mistakes when exchanging. Max may ignore the digit of '0' and not do any exchange at all or do the wrong exchange.

Question **2** a): All the sums are equal to 27·95.

Question **2** b): The first calculation shows the sum of a whole number and a decimal number. The second calculation is the sum of two decimal numbers with one exchange. The third calculation is that of two numbers with a different number of decimal places.

Power check

WAYS OF WORKING Independent thinking

ASK
• Are you confident in adding and subtracting using the column method?
• Are you confident in multiplying and dividing decimals by 10, 100 and 1,000?
• Can you solve word problems by working out what information you have and what you need to find?

Power play

WAYS OF WORKING Independent thinking

IN FOCUS Children are presented with a puzzle which requires them to complete a sequence of calculations that to leave them on their target number or 0·002 or 2. They can work independently or in pairs.

ANSWERS AND COMMENTARY Encourage children to double-check the calculations on every row and column and to write all the number sentences.

2	÷ 100	÷ 10	× 100	× 10	÷ 100
÷ 1,000	× 100	× 10	÷ 10	× 100	× 10
× 10	÷ 100	× 10	÷ 10	× 100	÷ 1,000
× 100	÷ 10	× 1,000	× 100	× 10	0·002

2	÷ 100	÷ 10	× 100	× 10	÷ 100
÷ 1,000	× 100	× 10	÷ 10	× 100	× 10
× 10	÷ 100	× 10	÷ 10	× 100	÷ 1,000
× 100	÷ 10	× 1,000	× 100	× 10	2

After the unit ⏸

• Can all children confidently add and subtract using formal column methods?
• Can they generalise their method of multiplying and dividing by 10, 100 and 1,000?

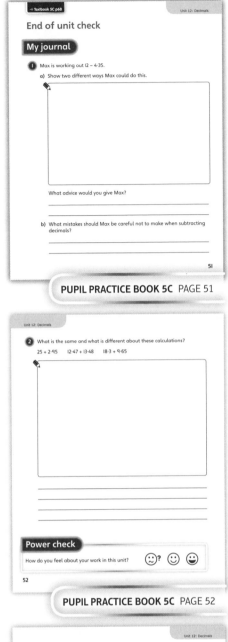

PUPIL PRACTICE BOOK 5C PAGE 51

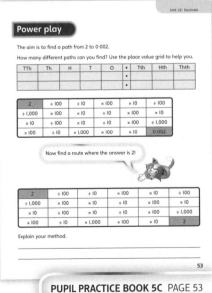

PUPIL PRACTICE BOOK 5C PAGE 52

PUPIL PRACTICE BOOK 5C PAGE 53

Strengthen and **Deepen** activities for this unit can be found in the *Power Maths* online subscription.

Unit 13
Geometry – properties of shapes ①

Mastery Expert tip! "When teaching this unit, I encourage children to explore the properties of angles physically and visually, by showing angles using their arms, or by drawing sketches of their ideas to justify their reasoning. It is important to give them opportunities to link their calculations and measurements to the meaning in physical terms."

Don't forget to watch the Unit 13 video!

WHY THIS UNIT IS IMPORTANT

This unit is important because it develops geometric reasoning alongside key measurement skills. Many children find the protractor a difficult tool to master, so it is important that they practice in a meaningful context. The skill of measurement is developed alongside reasoning and calculating to allow children to make predictions, to check their calculations and to discuss the properties of shapes and angles that they are to explore.

WHERE THIS UNIT FITS

→ Unit 12: Decimals

→ **Unit 13: Geometry – properties of shapes (1)**

→ Unit 14: Geometry – properties of shapes (2)

This unit builds on children's work from Year 4 where they identified properties of angles. They will also be given the grounding to work on the following unit where they will be asked to reason about the lengths and angles of quadrilaterals.

Before they start this unit, it is expected that children:

· know the difference between clockwise and anticlockwise turns
· understand the concept of an angle as a measure of turn
· can structure calculations with more than one step
· are familiar with right angles.

ASSESSING MASTERY

Children who have mastered this unit will be able to measure angles accurately in degrees, create given angles and calculate missing angles. They will also be able to justify logical reasoning about missing angles and lengths based on the properties of shapes and angles that they have learnt.

COMMON MISCONCEPTIONS	STRENGTHENING UNDERSTANDING	GOING DEEPER
Children may find the protractor difficult to use if the angle is not presented with a horizontal 'base'.	Encourage children to rotate the page to help them position the protractor. This encourages them to think of how to manipulate a problem in a way that supports understanding.	Explore the possibilities of drawing shapes and designs with greater accuracy, by using the protractor to measure to the nearest degree. Children may create their own designs.
Once children master the skill of measurement, they may revert to using that at times when it may be more efficient and accurate to calculate based on known properties.	Encourage children to look for what is known and what is unknown before deciding how best to tackle the problem.	Children can investigate general statements about the angles around a point and on a straight line.

WAYS OF WORKING

Use these pages to introduce the focus of the unit to children. You can use the characters to explore different ways of working too.

STRUCTURES AND REPRESENTATIONS

Angle diagrams: Use these to help children justify reasoning based on the fractions of a turn.

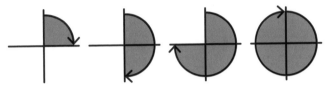

Right angles: The properties of right angles will recur and be important as the unit progresses.

Protractor: Children will spend much of the unit developing their understanding of angles through the use of a protractor to measure and draw acute and obtuse angles.

KEY LANGUAGE

There is some key language that children will need to know as part of the learning in this unit.

→ angle, turn
→ whole turn, half turn, quarter turn
→ acute angle, right angle, obtuse angle, reflex angle
→ degrees (°)
→ 90 degrees
→ 180 degrees, 360 degrees
→ interior angle
→ protractor

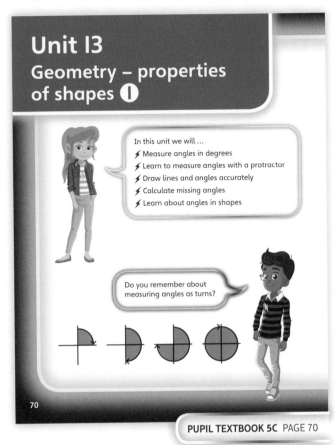

PUPIL TEXTBOOK 5C PAGE 70

PUPIL TEXTBOOK 5C PAGE 71

Measuring angles in degrees

Learning focus

In this lesson, children will learn to use degrees as a unit for measure of turn, focusing on common angles of 90, 180, 270 and 360° linking with their understanding of whole turns, half turns and quarter turns. They will also encounter turns in multiples of 45°.

Small steps

→ Previous step: Dividing decimals by 10, 100 and 1,000
→ **This step: Measuring angles in degrees**
→ Next step: Measuring with a protractor (1)

NATIONAL CURRICULUM LINKS

Year 5 Geometry – Properties of Shapes
- Identify:
  – angles at a point and one whole turn (total 360°)
  – angles at a point on a straight line and $\frac{1}{2}$ a turn (total 180°)
  – other multiples of 90°.
- Know angles are measured in degrees: estimate and compare acute, obtuse and reflex angles.

ASSESSING MASTERY

Children can describe and follow turns in multiples of 90°, and also in multiples of 45°. They can explain their reasoning based on fractions of a whole turn.

COMMON MISCONCEPTIONS

Children may be confused by the fact that degrees are also used as a unit of measure for temperature. Ask:
- *Have you heard 'degrees' used before?*

STRENGTHENING UNDERSTANDING

Ask children to act out the turns themselves, by standing on a point with an arm stretched out in front. They should then perform different turns by rotating on the spot, noticing the sweep of their arm as they rotate.

GOING DEEPER

The lesson challenges children to recognise and explore angles in an eight-point grid, which requires a deep understanding of angles with different start and end positions, and in different orientations. Children can extend this activity by adding new turns to the table or by making up their own similar problem for a partner to solve.

KEY LANGUAGE

In lesson: degrees (°), clockwise, anticlockwise, half turn, quarter turn, whole turn, right angle

STRUCTURES AND REPRESENTATIONS

angle diagrams

RESOURCES

Optional: arrow spinner, mini-figures

 In the eTextbook of this lesson, you will find interactive links to a selection of teaching tools.

Before you teach

- Can children define 90-degree angles from their work in Years 3 and 4?
- Are children confident in identifying angles?

Discover

WAYS OF WORKING Pair work

ASK

- Question ❶ a): *What is Lexi facing to begin with?*
- Question ❶ a): *Have you heard of a 180-degree turn before? What do you think 180° means? What about a 360-degree turn?*
- Question ❶ b): *What direction could Lexi turn?*

IN FOCUS Questions ❶ a) and b) are the first time that children encounter the word 'degrees' as a unit for the measure of turn. They may very well have heard phrases such as 'do a 180' or 'turn 360' or '90-degree angle' in other contexts such as sport, design and technology, gymnastics, skateboarding or video games. These questions cement this vocabulary within geometry.

PRACTICAL TIPS A practical version of this problem could very simply be acted out by children, perhaps in the school hall, on the playground or by cleared space in the classroom.

All children could practise turning by different fractions of a turn, especially to revise the difference between clockwise and anticlockwise turns.

Likewise, it may help to use a mini-figure to act out the turns, or to use an arrow spinner.

ANSWERS

Question ❶ a): After a 180-degree turn Lexi will be facing Lee.

Question ❶ b): Lexi could turn 90° clockwise or 90° anticlockwise. She could be facing the flowers or the bench now.

Share

WAYS OF WORKING Whole class teacher led

ASK

- Question ❶ a): *What do you notice about the numbers 180 and 360?*
- Question ❶ a): *Does it matter whether you turn 180° clockwise or anticlockwise? Why?*
- Question ❶ b): *What is another name for a 90-degree turn?*

IN FOCUS In this lesson, children are learning how to use degrees as an accurate measure of turn. In question ❶ a) the key angles 180° and 90° are described. The focus is on understanding the measure of degrees for common angles in terms of the fractions of a whole turn. Children may ask why 360° for a whole turn instead of perhaps 100 or 1? One reason is that 360 divides exactly into more fractions than 100. Some children might use division to explore this at a later stage.

Think together

Whole class teacher led (I do, We do, You do)

ASK

- Question ② : *What is the starting position? What is the turn? What is the end position?*
- Question ③ : *Show me a 90-degree turn. What is half of the 90-degree turn?*

IN FOCUS Question ③ introduces an eight-point grid, so that children explore the turns in different orientations, and also includes an understanding of turns that are 45° and 135°. This challenges them to solve problems where different pieces of information are missing, either start direction, turn in degrees, or end direction. This requires a deep understanding rather than simple procedural rote understanding.

STRENGTHEN Encourage children to use a pencil or a mini-figure, or an arrow to act out the turn on the page, as a way of being able to envisage the turn from the perspective of the problem.

DEEPEN Children could make up their own problems involving turns and then swap with a partner or share with the class.

ASSESSMENT CHECKPOINT Answers to question ③ will indicate whether or not children are using the terms clockwise and anticlockwise correctly.

ANSWERS

Question ① a): Lexi has turned 360°. She is now facing Lee.

Question ② : Amelia has turned 270°.

Question ③ a):

start	turn	finish
facing B	180°	facing F
facing A	90° anticlockwise	facing G
facing E	90° anticlockwise	facing C
facing G	90° clockwise	facing A
facing G	45° clockwise	facing H
facing A	45° clockwise	facing B

Question ③ b): Mo could turn 225° anticlockwise or 135° clockwise.

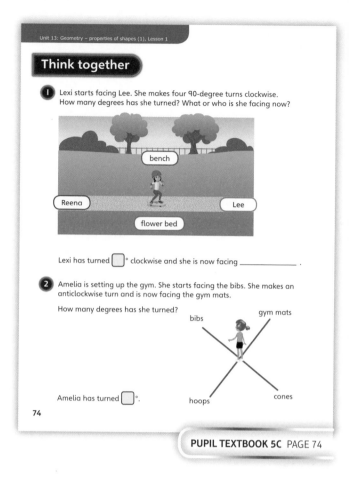

Think together

① Lexi starts facing Lee. She makes four 90-degree turns clockwise. How many degrees has she turned? What or who is she facing now?

Lexi has turned ☐° clockwise and she is now facing _____ .

② Amelia is setting up the gym. She starts facing the bibs. She makes an anticlockwise turn and is now facing the gym mats.

How many degrees has she turned?

Amelia has turned ☐°.

74

PUPIL TEXTBOOK 5C PAGE 74

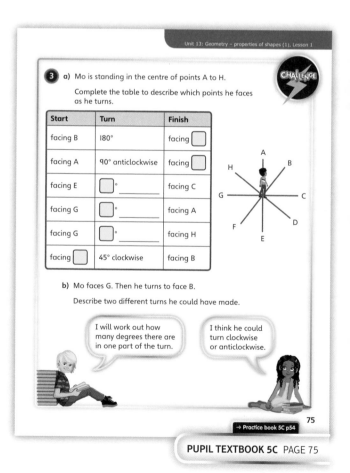

③ a) Mo is standing in the centre of points A to H.

Complete the table to describe which points he faces as he turns.

Start	Turn	Finish
facing B	180°	facing ☐
facing A	90° anticlockwise	facing ☐
facing E	☐° _____	facing C
facing G	☐° _____	facing A
facing G	☐° _____	facing H
facing ☐	45° clockwise	facing B

b) Mo faces G. Then he turns to face B.

Describe two different turns he could have made.

I will work out how many degrees there are in one part of the turn.

I think he could turn clockwise or anticlockwise.

75

→ Practice book 5C p54

PUPIL TEXTBOOK 5C PAGE 75

Practice

WAYS OF WORKING Independent thinking

IN FOCUS Question ❶ gives practice for recognition of common turns measured in degrees, and requires children to recognise the turns in different orientations.

Question ❷ deepens understanding by asking for different aspects of the information, including start position, turn, and end position.

Question ❸ looks at describing turns on an eight-point grid, including 45-degree turns or multiples of 45°.

STRENGTHEN Children could use mini-figures, or even act out the turns using role-play on the playground or in the school hall.

DEEPEN Extend question ❹ by asking children to find new combinations using the buttons if the robot move from two different points on the grid.

ASSESSMENT CHECKPOINT Accurate answers to questions ❷ and ❸ show good understanding of the key skills. Look at incorrect answers to check whether children have a secure knowledge of clockwise and anticlockwise. Question ❸ asks them to calculate turns from different starting positions – incorrect answers here might indicate that children have not fully grasped this visualisation.

ANSWERS Answers for the **Practice** part of the lesson appear in the separate **Practice and Reflect answer guide**.

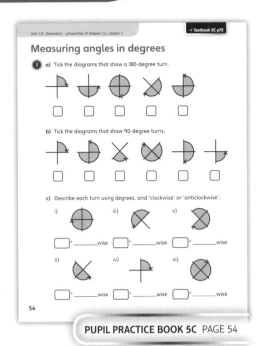

PUPIL PRACTICE BOOK 5C PAGE 54

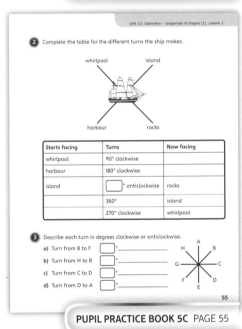

PUPIL PRACTICE BOOK 5C PAGE 55

Reflect

WAYS OF WORKING Independent thinking

IN FOCUS This **Reflect** question allows children to draw their own diagrams of the key angles covered in the lesson. This ensures they understand how each angle looks and how they correspond to each other in terms of size.

ASSESSMENT CHECKPOINT Children's diagrams should show understanding of the relationship between the different angles.

ANSWERS Answers for the **Reflect** part of the lesson appear in the separate **Practice and Reflect answer guide**.

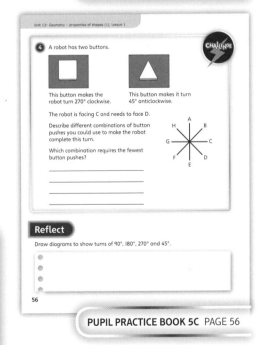

PUPIL PRACTICE BOOK 5C PAGE 56

After the lesson

- Could children follow turns from different starting positions, rather than always from a north position?
- Were children confident explaining how the fractions of a turn relate to 45-, 90- and 180-degree turns?

Measuring with a protractor ❶

Learning focus

In this lesson, children will be introduced to the protractor and how to use it to measure acute angles.

Small steps

→ Previous step: Measuring angles in degrees
→ **This step: Measuring with a protractor (1)**
→ Next step: Measuring with a protractor (2)

NATIONAL CURRICULUM LINKS

Year 5 Geometry – Properties of Shapes
- Know angles are measured in degrees: estimate and compare acute, obtuse and reflex angles.
- Draw given angles, and measure them in degrees (°).

ASSESSING MASTERY

Children can measure acute angles in different orientations and are able to explain which scale to use for a given angle.

COMMON MISCONCEPTIONS

Children may need support to measure angles where there is not a horizontal 'base' line to orient the protractor. Ask:
- *What would you do first to measure this angle?*

Children may find it difficult to know how to place the protractor accurately, with the cross-hairs precisely on the turn and the base lined up with one of the angles. Ask:
- *How would you place the protractor to measure this angle?*

STRENGTHENING UNDERSTANDING

Encourage children to decide whether an angle to be measured is acute or obtuse by making a visual judgement and then use this to support their choice of scale on the protractor.

GOING DEEPER

Challenge children to measure precisely and to explain their reasoning when selecting a measure between multiples of 10 on a protractor scale.

KEY LANGUAGE

In lesson: protractor, degrees (°), acute, angle, scale

Other language to be used by the teacher: obtuse

STRUCTURES AND REPRESENTATIONS

angle diagrams

RESOURCES

Mandatory: protractor, ruler

Optional: ramp, paper angle measurer

 In the eTextbook of this lesson, you will find interactive links to a selection of teaching tools.

Before you teach ❚❚

- Are children confident with the terminology of acute and obtuse angles?
- How confidently do children measure angles? Do they measure accurately?

Discover

Unit 13: Geometry – properties of shapes (1), Lesson 2

Measuring with a protractor ❶

Discover

Amal   Holly

❶ a) Amal and Holly are using a ramp to test the grip of some new trainers. What angle is the ramp at now?

b) Amal records the angle as 150°. Explain his mistake.

76

WAYS OF WORKING Pair work

ASK

- Question ❶ a): *Does the angle look greater than or less than 90°? What about 45°?*
- Question ❶ a): *Can you estimate the angle the ramp makes with the table?*
- Question ❶ a): *What tool could you use to measure the angle? Would a ruler help, or does it require a different tool?*

IN FOCUS Questions ❶ a) and b) are important as this is the first introduction to the protractor as a tool. Many children find it very challenging to use a protractor to measure angles accurately and so may need plenty of practice over the course of this lesson. Encourage them to make an estimate, based on their understanding of 90° and 45°.

PRACTICAL TIPS This is a version of a simple experiment that children can try in class. They could lift a ramp to a different angle, and then test at which point an object begins to slip. However, it is difficult to measure an angle exactly using a practical ramp. It may make sense to create an angle measure from a large sheet of paper, which can be held up against the ramp, rather than having to use a protractor on a practical experiment. The angle measurer could be marked in multiples of 10°, from 0° up to 90°.

Children could then be introduced to the protractor as a tool for measuring angles precisely on a drawing.

ANSWERS

Question ❶ a): The ramp is now at an angle of 30°.

Question ❶ b): Protractors often have two scales, so you can start measuring from the left or from the right. Amal's mistake is reading the wrong scale.

Share

WAYS OF WORKING Whole class teacher led

ASK

- Question ❶ a): *Where should you place the protractor?*
- Question ❶ a): *Where is the turning point of the angle?*
- Question ❶ b): *Which scale on the protractor is correct for this angle?*

IN FOCUS The key point of question ❶ a) is to learn the correct procedure for using the protractor accurately. Make sure that children know that they need to line up the base line with one of the lines of the angle, line up the cross-hair with the exact turning point of the angle and then read the correct scale on the protractor.

Unit 13: Geometry – properties of shapes (1), Lesson 2

Share

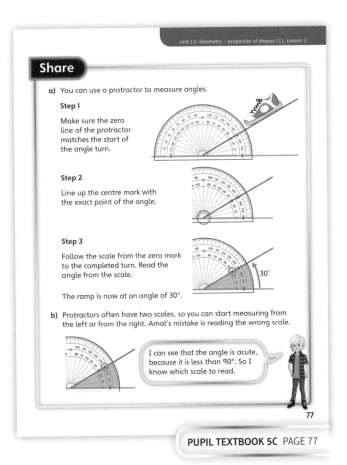

a) You can use a protractor to measure angles.

Step 1

Make sure the zero line of the protractor matches the start of the angle turn.

Step 2

Line up the centre mark with the exact point of the angle.

Step 3

Follow the scale from the zero mark to the completed turn. Read the angle from the scale.

30°

The ramp is now at an angle of 30°.

b) Protractors often have two scales, so you can start measuring from the left or from the right. Amal's mistake is reading the wrong scale.

I can see that the angle is acute, because it is less than 90°. So I know which scale to read.

77

Think together

Whole class teacher led (I do, We do, You do)

ASK

- Question **2**: *Show me how you would find the starting position for measuring this angle.*
- Question **2**: *How would you decide which scale to use to measure these angles?*

IN FOCUS Question **2** introduces angles in different orientations from a horizontal line and includes an angle that is not a multiple of 10°.

Question **3** includes angles in different orientations that are not multiples of 10 and are angles inside a shape. It also encourages children to question whether the orientation of an angle affects the size of the angle.

STRENGTHEN Encourage children to rotate the page when measuring angles in different orientations.

DEEPEN Ask children to measure to the nearest degree. This requires them to ensure that they are following the three steps for correct measuring to get a precise measurement.

ASSESSMENT CHECKPOINT If children are able to measure the angles in the triangles in question **3** accurately enough to discover that the triangles are similar, they have accurate measuring skills.

ANSWERS

Question **1**: The trainer could have slipped down the ramp between 51° and 70°.

Question **2**: a = 60°
b = 50°
c = 45°

Question **3**: 77°, 77° and 26°. There may be some error margin in these measurements (of 0–3°). Ash is correct, all the angles are acute as they are less than 90°.

Practice

→ Textbook 5C p76

WAYS OF WORKING Independent thinking

IN FOCUS Question ❶ practises the skill of measuring angles where there is a horizontal base, and the first two examples are multiples of 10°, and the protractor is already placed correctly. This pictorially reinforces how children should use a protractor before reaching question ❷ where they must use a protractor themselves.

STRENGTHEN For question ❺, suggest that children can extend one line by drawing with a pencil and ruler to allow them to measure more accurately.

DEEPEN Can children draw angles using a protractor, for a partner to accurately measure?

THINK DIFFERENTLY Question ❹ shows two common errors when placing the protractor for children to spot and explain. By explaining these misconceptions they will become more aware of avoiding this when doing the measuring themselves.

ASSESSMENT CHECKPOINT Questions ❷ and ❸ will show that children can confidently use a protractor themselves to measure angles accurately. Responses to question ❹ will reveal any potential misconceptions children have when using protractors.

ANSWERS Answers for the **Practice** part of the lesson appear in the separate **Practice and Reflect answer guide**.

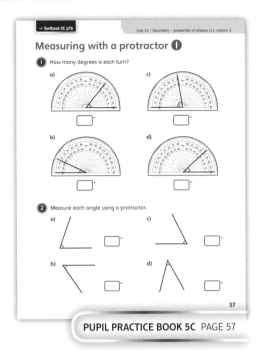

PUPIL PRACTICE BOOK 5C PAGE 57

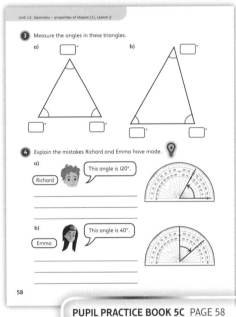

PUPIL PRACTICE BOOK 5C PAGE 58

Reflect

WAYS OF WORKING Independent thinking

IN FOCUS The practical skill of measuring is procedural in nature, and this challenges children to explain the process in their own words.

ASSESSMENT CHECKPOINT Can children explain how each step ensures that they measure accurately?

ANSWERS Answers for the **Reflect** part of the lesson appear in the separate **Practice and Reflect answer guide**.

After the lesson ⏸

- Were children able to place the protractor accurately when angles were presented in different orientations?
- Can children explain which scale to use on the protractor to measure accurately, by considering the zero line, and also in terms of acute and obtuse angles?

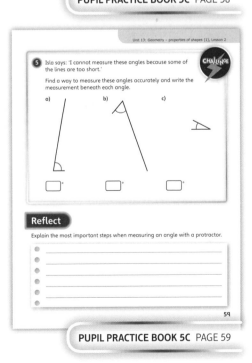

PUPIL PRACTICE BOOK 5C PAGE 59

Measuring with a protractor ②

Learning focus

In this lesson, children will continue to develop their protractor skills by measuring obtuse angles accurately.

Small steps

→ Previous step: Measuring with a protractor (1)
→ **This step: Measuring with a protractor (2)**
→ Next step: Drawing lines and angles accurately

NATIONAL CURRICULUM LINKS

Year 5 Geometry – Properties of Shapes
• Identify:
  – angles at a point and one whole turn (total 360°)
  – angles at a point on a straight line and $\frac{1}{2}$ a turn (total 180°)
  – other multiples of 90°.
• Know angles are measured in degrees: estimate and compare acute, obtuse and reflex angles.
• Draw given angles, and measure them in degrees (°).

ASSESSING MASTERY

Children can measure obtuse angles accurately, and can select the correct scale to use, by considering the size of the angle in relation to 90°.

COMMON MISCONCEPTIONS

Children may need support to see which scale to use when measuring a given angle. Ask:
• *Would you use the inside or the outside scale for this angle? How do you know?*

Children may need support to measure accurately when the angle is not a multiple of 10. Ask:
• *What is this angle to the nearest 10°?*

STRENGTHENING UNDERSTANDING

Encourage children to count from the zero mark on the protractor, and follow the scale in multiples of 10 until they reach the completed angle.

GOING DEEPER

Challenge children to use their knowledge of acute and obtuse angles to make predictions on the angle size then justify or check answers based on their reasoning.

KEY LANGUAGE

In lesson: obtuse, angle, protractor, greatest, smallest, hexagon, scale

Other language to be used by the teacher: acute, interior angle, right angle, degrees (°)

STRUCTURES AND REPRESENTATIONS

angle diagrams, 2D shapes

RESOURCES

Mandatory: protractors

 In the eTextbook of this lesson, you will find interactive links to a selection of teaching tools.

Before you teach

• Are children familiar with the difference between acute and obtuse angles?
• Can children confidently use a protractor?

Discover

Measuring with a protractor ❷

WAYS OF WORKING Pair work

ASK

- Question ❶ a): *Is the angle less than or greater than 90°?*
- Questions ❶ a) and b): *What are the main things to remember when measuring angles with a protractor?*
- Question ❶ b): *Can you make a reasoned estimate of that angle?*

IN FOCUS Questions ❶ a) and b) prompt children to think about measuring angles inside a shape (interior angles) and to notice that the angles are greater than 90°. Children should make estimates of the angles and consider different justifications for those estimates. Encourage children to discuss how this relates to their learning in the previous lesson, especially with reference to any difficulties they encountered, such as knowing which scale to use or placing a protractor accurately in order to measure the angle.

PRACTICAL TIPS The context in the **Discover** image can be recreated in the classroom and could be modelled as a game of pass the parcel or passing a ball around the group. Children should make exaggerated turn movements, like robots passing boxes with arms straightened out in front. The idea is to sense that the turn they are making is the angle to be measured and to feel that it is greater than 90°.

ANSWERS

Question ❶ a): Mo turns an angle of 120°.

Question ❶ b): Emma turns an angle of 120°.

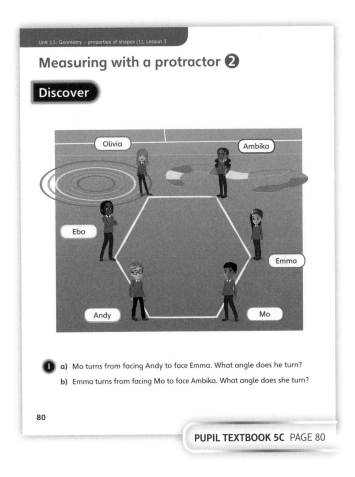

Discover

❶ a) Mo turns from facing Andy to face Emma. What angle does he turn?

b) Emma turns from facing Mo to face Ambika. What angle does she turn?

80

Share

WAYS OF WORKING Whole class teacher led

ASK

- Question ❶ a): *Where is the correct point to place the protractor?*
- Question ❶ a): *Which scale would you use to measure this angle?*

IN FOCUS The main focus is to recognise that the angle is obtuse and use this to support a judgement about which scale to use when measuring with the protractor.

Children may explore whether all angles are equal in this shape, and discuss whether this is true for all hexagons.

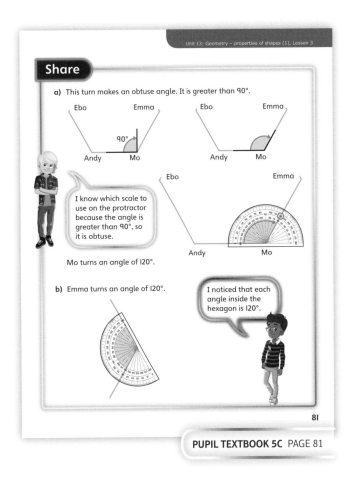

Share

a) This turn makes an obtuse angle. It is greater than 90°.

I know which scale to use on the protractor because the angle is greater than 90°, so it is obtuse.

Mo turns an angle of 120°.

b) Emma turns an angle of 120°.

I noticed that each angle inside the hexagon is 120°.

81

113

Think together

WAYS OF WORKING Whole class teacher led (I do, We do, You do)

ASK

- Question **①** : *Where would you place the protractor for this angle?*
- Question **②** : *Would it help to rotate the page?*
- Question **②** : *Can you make a reasoned estimate before measuring?*
- *How can you read the angle correctly if it is between two 10-degree marks?*

IN FOCUS Question **①** is important as it provides basic practice at reading angles in different orientations. It refreshes understanding of working with protractors from the last lesson.

Question **②** encourages children to estimate first. It can be partially solved by reasoning about the acute and right angles, then measuring to check the two obtuse angles.

Question **③** challenges children to consider angles that reverse a turn.

STRENGTHEN Encourage children to rotate the page when measuring angles in different orientations. Support children with placing the protractor by modelling how to find the 'baseline' first, then slide to line up the cross-hair.

DEEPEN With question **③** , challenge children to explain how the angle for a turn from A to C is the same as the turn from C to F, even though F is further away than A.

ASSESSMENT CHECKPOINT Question **②** will show whether children are confident measuring angles at different orientations as well as showing their reasoning skills when judging angle size.

ANSWERS

Question **①** : a is 120°; b is 170°

Question **②** : d, a, b, c

Question **③** a): Amelia turns 140° clockwise or 220° anticlockwise.

Question **③** b): Amelia turns 220° clockwise or 140° anticlockwise. The angles are the same as when she turned from point A. Although F is further away it is still the same angle.

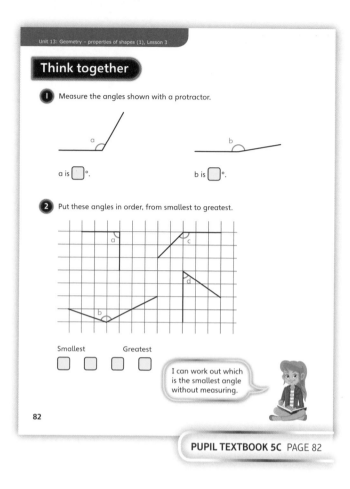

PUPIL TEXTBOOK 5C PAGE 82

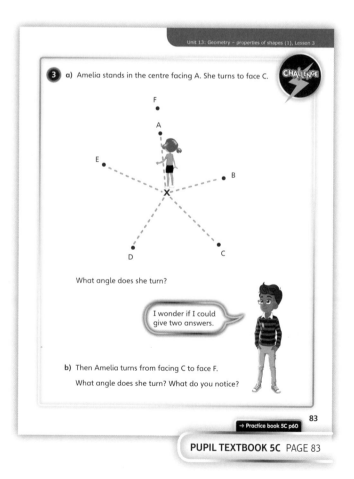

PUPIL TEXTBOOK 5C PAGE 83

Practice

WAYS OF WORKING Independent thinking

IN FOCUS Questions ❶ and ❷ focus on the correct placement of the protractor, especially when measuring in different orientations. This reinforces the learning from this and the previous lesson.

Question ❸ extends learning by introducing the concept of reasoning as well as measurement, though children may compare the two obtuse angles by measuring.

Question ❹ asks children to measure angles inside a polygon, ensuring that they understand the concept of interior angles and are able to measure angles in all orientations.

STRENGTHEN Ask children to talk through the different steps of using a protractor with their partner. Fully explaining each step will help cement the process.

DEEPEN Extend question ❺ by adding more turns to the table for children to measure and complete.

THINK DIFFERENTLY Children may spot that there are symmetries in the shapes in question ❹ which can reduce the amount of measurement they need to do.

ASSESSMENT CHECKPOINT Questions ❷ and ❹ test the core skill of measuring using a protractor. Incorrect answers here indicate that children's learning of the steps for accurate measurement is not secure and needs reinforcing.

ANSWERS Answers for the **Practice** part of the lesson appear in the separate **Practice and Reflect answer guide**.

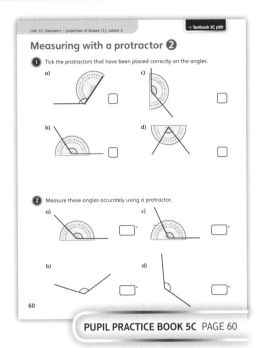

PUPIL PRACTICE BOOK 5C PAGE 60

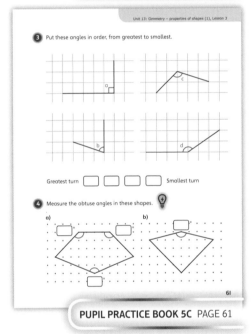

PUPIL PRACTICE BOOK 5C PAGE 61

Reflect

WAYS OF WORKING Independent thinking

IN FOCUS The **Reflect** question ensures children are confident with key terms such as 'obtuse angle' and relate this to their knowledge of how to accurately use a protractor.

ASSESSMENT CHECKPOINT Can children verbalise the link between obtuse and acute angles with the two scales on a protractor?

ANSWERS Answers for the **Reflect** part of the lesson appear in the separate **Practice and Reflect answer guide**.

After the lesson

- Could children recognise obtuse angles?
- Could children read angles that fall between multiples of 10°?
- How did children manipulate the page or the protractor when the angles were presented in different orientations?

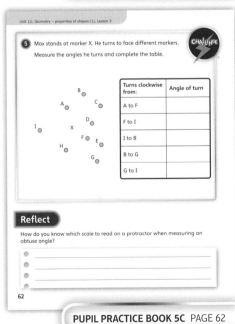

PUPIL PRACTICE BOOK 5C PAGE 62

Drawing lines and angles accurately

Learning focus

In this lesson, children will continue to use a protractor to draw angles accurately. They combine this with drawing lines accurately to the nearest millimetre.

Small steps

→ Previous step: Measuring with a protractor (2)
→ **This step: Drawing lines and angles accurately**
→ Next step: Calculating angles on a straight line

NATIONAL CURRICULUM LINKS

Year 5 Geometry – Properties of Shapes

Draw given angles, and measure them in degrees (°).

ASSESSING MASTERY

Children can draw angles accurately up to 180°. They can draw lines to the nearest millimetre, given measurements in units of cm and mm, and can follow instructions to create a design.

COMMON MISCONCEPTIONS

Children will need to have mastered protractor skills from the previous two lessons before tackling this. They might still need support with positioning the protractor accurately and choosing the appropriate scale to read. Ask:
• *Explain how to measure accurately using a protractor. What are the key points you need to think about?*

STRENGTHENING UNDERSTANDING

This lesson practises drawing angles in different orientations by following a design, in order to give some purpose to the activity. Some children may need to practise more basic angle drawing before tackling the independent work. Give children a range of challenges for drawing angles in different orientations before moving on.

GOING DEEPER

Challenge children to explain how small errors at the start of a design can cause quite large differences in the finished results.

KEY LANGUAGE

In lesson: angle, protractor, millimetre (mm), to scale, centimetre (cm)

Other language to be used by the teacher: acute angle, degrees (°)

STRUCTURES AND REPRESENTATIONS

angle diagrams

RESOURCES

Mandatory: protractor, ruler

 In the eTextbook of this lesson, you will find interactive links to a selection of teaching tools.

Before you teach

• How will you ensure that children are confident and accurate when using a protractor?
• How will you refer back to previous learning to explore with children what is the same and what is different about, for example, 55 mm and 5.5 cm?

Discover

ASK

- *What does 'Not to scale' mean on the diagram?*
- Question ❶ a): *What tools will you need?*
- Question ❶ a): *Which line would you draw first? Why?*
- Question ❶ b): *What mistakes might someone make when measuring this angle?*

IN FOCUS For questions ❶ a) and b) Children are building on the skills from the previous two lessons, and now add the skill of drawing a given angle. The difficulty level builds up over the course of the design, to allow children to build the skill set gradually.

PRACTICAL TIPS This lesson is built around one design, which requires a progression of practical skills in measuring and drawing angles in different orientations. It may help some children to work in pairs on a design, taking it in turns to place the protractor and agreeing the angle required before marking it.

ANSWERS

Diagrams match the design.

Share

ASK

- Question ❶ a): *How is this related to the measuring skills you learnt in the last two lessons?*
- Question ❶ a): *What extra skills do you need to finish this step?*
- Question ❶ a): *How can you draw the new line to the exact length required?*

IN FOCUS Questions ❶ a) and b) build on skills from the previous two lessons. The major new skill is marking the correct angle on the edge of the protractor, then using the ruler to join the point of the angle with the new mark and drawing a line of the exact length required. This is a difficult skill for children to master, so encourage them to have more than one go at it where necessary. Reassure them that it is a very tricky skill that takes a good deal of practice. Mistakes are good learning points here!

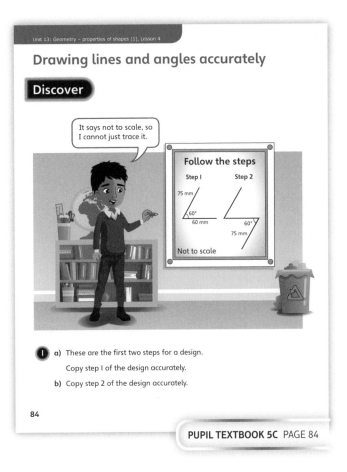

PUPIL TEXTBOOK 5C PAGE 84

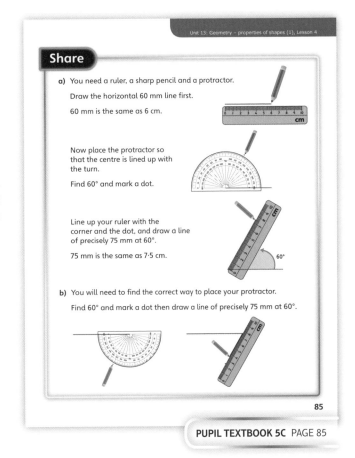

PUPIL TEXTBOOK 5C PAGE 85

Think together

WAYS OF WORKING Whole class teacher led (I do, We do, You do)

ASK

- Question **2**: *You need to draw an angle between two 10-degree marks. How should you use the protractor to do this?*
- Question **2**: *Would it be easier if you rotated the page?*

IN FOCUS Question **2** requires a different orientation so children will need to work out the correct placement of the protractor. It is also the first time that children are asked to draw an angle that is not a multiple of 10 and therefore not labelled on the protractor.

Question **3** progresses to include the drawing of an obtuse angle.

STRENGTHEN Encourage children to rotate the page, and to work in pairs to agree on the placement of the protractor before drawing. All children could work on scrap paper, as mistakes are very likely.

DEEPEN Once step 6 has been completed, ask children to label each angle as 'acute' or 'obtuse'.

ASSESSMENT CHECKPOINT If there are errors in children's designs, can they spot and explain the errors by measuring to check? Can children identify how and where errors may have occurred and suggest changes for their next try?

ANSWERS Questions **1**, **2** and **3**: designs should be close to the instructions given, though there will be variation due to small errors being compounded as the drawing continues.

Question **3** c): Upper angle 50°; lower angle 55°; line 60 mm.

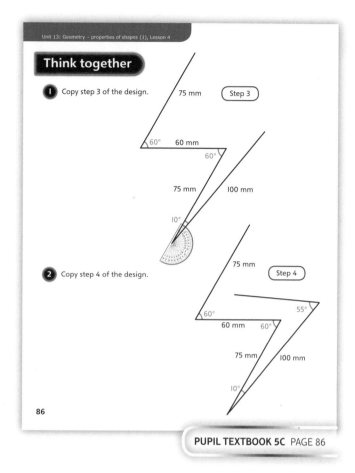

PUPIL TEXTBOOK 5C PAGE 86

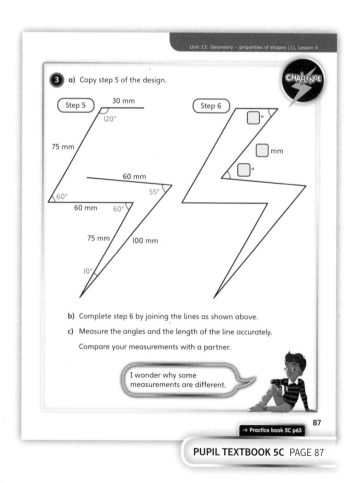

PUPIL TEXTBOOK 5C PAGE 87

Practice

WAYS OF WORKING Independent thinking

IN FOCUS Questions ❶ and ❷ reinforce the learning with protractors by asking children to complete the angles given in multiples of 10° from a given line and then drawing the same angle in different orientations.

Question ❸ challenges children to follow the steps of a design to ensure they accurately use a protractor and ruler together.

STRENGTHEN Encourage children to work on scrap paper to try out their designs, as they may need to redraft if errors creep in, which is a likely occurrence given the practical difficulty of this skill.

DEEPEN Children could experiment by changing the angle by a small amount and seeing what happens to the design. This would give additional practice in drawing accurately, and also underline the importance of accurate measurement.

THINK DIFFERENTLY Question ❹ asks children to consider whether the sides of a triangle can all be the same length if the angles are different. Encourage children to use trial and error to investigate the question.

ASSESSMENT CHECKPOINT Correctly following the steps of question ❸ requires very good protractor skills. Errors here could be caused by inaccurate measurements or by children not remembering that 'not to scale' means they can't find the missing angles by measuring.

ANSWERS Answers for the **Practice** part of the lesson appear in the separate **Practice and Reflect answer guide**.

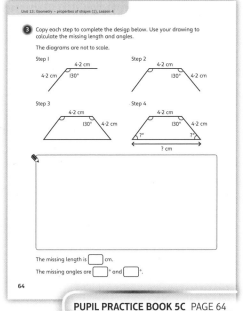

PUPIL PRACTICE BOOK 5C PAGE 63

PUPIL PRACTICE BOOK 5C PAGE 64

Reflect

WAYS OF WORKING Independent thinking

IN FOCUS Challenge children to draw 45-degree angles in different orientations. This emphasises the learning that there are multiple ways to position an angle, and that the orientation of the protractor helps them to draw angles at different orientations.

ASSESSMENT CHECKPOINT Ask children to check one another's drawings by measuring with a protractor. This will show whether children are drawing and measuring accurately.

ANSWERS Answers for the **Reflect** part of the lesson appear in the separate **Practice and Reflect answer guide**.

After the lesson

- Can children draw angles in different orientations?
- Can children explain what error has been made if the design 'goes wrong'?
- Are children confident following steps of a design independently?

PUPIL PRACTICE BOOK 5C PAGE 65

Calculating angles on a straight line

Learning focus

In this lesson, children will begin to understand that they can calculate missing angles on a straight line, based on their knowledge of 180° as a half turn.

Small steps

→ Previous step: Drawing lines and angles accurately
→ **This step: Calculating angles on a straight line**
→ Next step: Calculating angles around a point

NATIONAL CURRICULUM LINKS

Year 5 Geometry – Properties of Shapes
- Identify:
  - angles at a point and one whole turn (total 360°)
  - angles at a point on a straight line and $\frac{1}{2}$ a turn (total 180°)
  - other multiples of 90°.

ASSESSING MASTERY

Children can explain how to calculate the missing angles on a straight line, by reasoning about their knowledge of a half turn.

COMMON MISCONCEPTIONS

It is a common error to find the complementary angles to 200° rather than 180°, as children are used to finding number bonds to 100 in their calculations. Ask:
- *What should the angles total on a straight line?*

STRENGTHENING UNDERSTANDING

Children could practise the skill by creating a 'windscreen wiper'. As the line rotates to create angles of 10°, 20°, 30° and so on, children can find the number bonds to 180 to calculate the missing angle.

GOING DEEPER

Ask questions that challenge children to reason based on their knowledge of equal and unequal parts.

KEY LANGUAGE

In lesson: angles, half turn, degrees (°), right angle, quarter turn

Other language to be used by the teacher: total

STRUCTURES AND REPRESENTATIONS

angle diagrams

RESOURCES

Mandatory: protractor

Optional: paper semicircles, safety scissors

 In the eTextbook of this lesson, you will find interactive links to a selection of teaching tools.

Before you teach ⏸

- In this lesson, children will move from measuring angles to calculating them from known facts. Would children benefit from a lesson starter on refreshing calculation skills?
- Are there any resources that would be useful to underpin learning, for example a visual reminder of the degrees in a whole, half or quarter turn?

Discover

ASK

- Question ① a): *Does angle a look acute or obtuse? How can you be sure?*
- Question ① a): *What are the angles in a half turn?*
- Question ① a): *Can you check your estimate by measuring? What should you use to do this?*

IN FOCUS The main focus of question ① a) is for children to connect their understanding of angles in a half turn with the problem of finding the missing angle. Some children may revert to measurement, especially considering the effort they have put into learning that skill over the previous three lessons. Encourage children to compare the different approaches and to discuss how calculations may or may not be more efficient.

PRACTICAL TIPS This would be an excellent task for children to try out using paper. Provide children with semicircles of paper and then ask them to measure and cut different angles from a point marked on the straight line. They could then calculate the remaining angle and measure to check their predictions. This could be extended into a game where all children measure an angle and cut it away, and then as a class they try to match everyone's pairs.

ANSWERS

Question ① a): Angle a is 100°.

Question ① b): Max cuts two 90-degree angles.

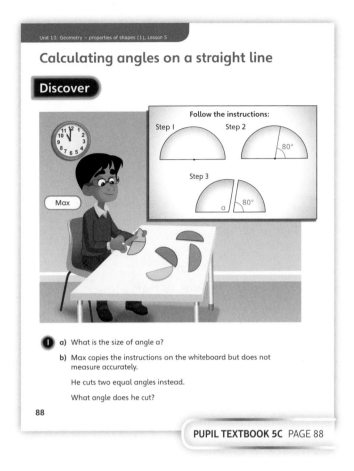

PUPIL TEXTBOOK 5C PAGE 88

Share

ASK

- Question ① a): *Which method is more efficient? Why?*
- Question ① a): *Can you explain why the subtraction method works?*
- Question ① a): *Would the subtraction method work for other angles?*

IN FOCUS The main focus of question ① a) is for children to recognise that it is often more efficient and accurate to use their calculation skills rather than measurement to find the missing angles, based on their understanding of the degrees in half a turn.

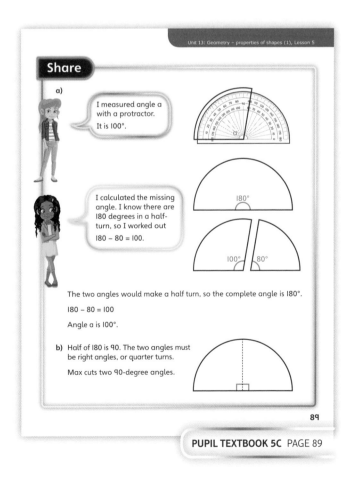

PUPIL TEXTBOOK 5C PAGE 89

Think together

WAYS OF WORKING Whole class teacher led (I do, We do, You do)

ASK

- Question **1**: *What is the total number of degrees in a half turn? What number do you need to subtract from?*
- Question **3**: *Which operation can you use if the 180° are split into five equal parts?*

IN FOCUS Question **2** requires children to measure the angles then find pairs that add to 180 to form a straight line, which reinforces that there are 180° along a straight line, as well as the concept of calculation that was introduced in the **Share** activity.

Question **3** looks at an angle split into equal parts and so requires a division, demonstrating that (depending on the calculation) different operations may be necessary.

STRENGTHEN Encourage children to explore the relationship between angles on a line by looking at the two scales on a protractor. What do they notice?

DEEPEN Challenge children to continue the exercise in question **3** with different straight-sided 2D shapes. They could draw these or use 2D shape manipulatives.

ASSESSMENT CHECKPOINT Question **2** helps to assess that children understand that angles on a straight line must add up to 180° and that this can be in many different combinations. Question **4** assesses children's understanding of both the angles within a square and the angles on a straight line.

ANSWERS

Question **1**: a = 140°, b = 105°, c = 10°

Question **2**: a = 120°, b = 155°, c = 35°, d = 60°, e = 90°, f = 25°
a and d fit together to make a straight line.
b and f fit together to make a straight line.

Question **3**: Each angle is 36°.

Question **4** a): The left-hand and right-hand angles would each have to be 45°.

Question **4** b): The left-hand angle would be 60° and the right-hand angle would be 30°.

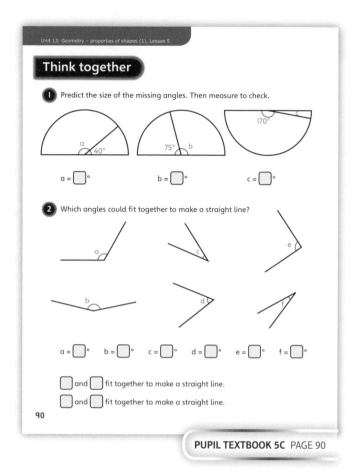

PUPIL TEXTBOOK 5C PAGE 90

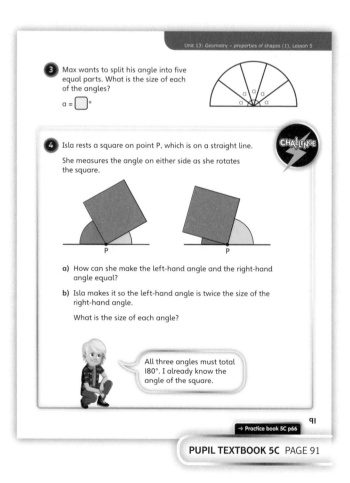

PUPIL TEXTBOOK 5C PAGE 91

Practice

WAYS OF WORKING Independent thinking

IN FOCUS Questions ❶ and ❷ reinforces the process of using the subtraction method to find missing angles. It is important to cement this understanding of the angles on a line making 180° so that they can complete the rest of the questions.

Question ❸ extends this learning by asking children to use both measurement and calculation. They must measure given angles then use calculation to find pairs and a triplet that sum to a straight line.

STRENGTHEN Encourage children to explore the bonds to 180° by totalling to 100, then adding on 80.

DEEPEN Extend learning in question ❹ by asking children to place a square along a straight line and measure one angle with a protractor. They can then swap with a friend to find the remaining angle.

ASSESSMENT CHECKPOINT Do children's answers to questions ❷ and ❹ show good understanding of the parts that sum to 180?

ANSWERS Answers for the **Practice** part of the lesson appear in the separate **Practice and Reflect answer guide**.

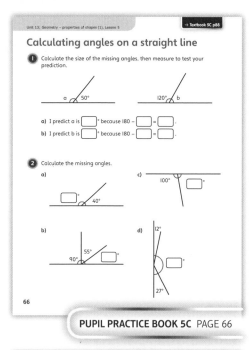

PUPIL PRACTICE BOOK 5C PAGE 66

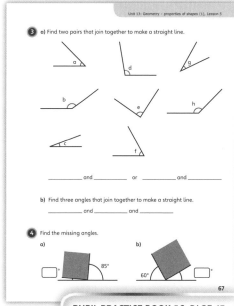

PUPIL PRACTICE BOOK 5C PAGE 67

Reflect

WAYS OF WORKING Independent thinking

IN FOCUS The **Reflect** question allows an opportunity for children to explain their understanding of angles along a straight line and also prove their calculation skills to 180.

ASSESSMENT CHECKPOINT Can children explain that he has summed to 190° instead of 180? Have they explained what the angle must actually be? Are children able to say which part Aki has said correctly (the measurement of a right angle) and where his error appeared?

ANSWERS Answers for the **Reflect** part of the lesson appear in the separate **Practice and Reflect answer guide**.

After the lesson

- Were children able to follow the chains of reasoning required when there are more than two angles on a straight line?
- Could children explain why the angles must sum to 180°, based on their knowledge of whole and half turns?

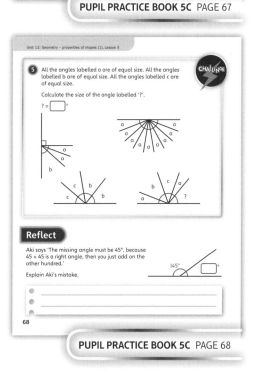

PUPIL PRACTICE BOOK 5C PAGE 68

Calculating angles around a point

Learning focus

In this lesson, children will learn to calculate missing angles around a point, by reasoning about the 360° in a whole turn.

Small steps

→ Previous step: Calculating angles on a straight line
→ **This step: Calculating angles around a point**
→ Next step: Calculating lengths and angles in shapes

NATIONAL CURRICULUM LINKS

Year 5 Geometry – Properties of Shapes
• Identify:
  – angles at a point and one whole turn (total 360°)
  – angles at a point on a straight line and $\frac{1}{2}$ a turn (total 180°)
  – other multiples of 90°.

ASSESSING MASTERY

Children can use reasoning to calculate missing angles around a point.

COMMON MISCONCEPTIONS

Some children may need support to structure the calculations where there are more than two angles around a point. Ask:
• *What is the whole and what are the parts? What calculations do you need to do to work out the missing part?*

STRENGTHENING UNDERSTANDING

Children can create and use the angle-makers to explore the way two parts of 360° vary as one increases and one decreases.

GOING DEEPER

Ask children to draw reflex angles. Can they identify the most efficient way to draw these when their protractor only goes as far as 180°?

KEY LANGUAGE

In lesson: angles around a point, **reflex angles**, degrees (°), quarter turn, whole turn, obtuse angle

Other language to be used by the teacher: half turn, acute angle, right angle

STRUCTURES AND REPRESENTATIONS

angle diagrams, 2D shapes

RESOURCES

Mandatory: paper or card circles

Optional: protractor, ruler

 In the eTextbook of this lesson, you will find interactive links to a selection of teaching tools.

Before you teach

• Are there any resources or visual aids that would help with this lesson? Making an angle-maker in advance would enable you to demonstrate this.
• How secure are children with their vocabulary (acute, right angle, obtuse)? Consider doing a quick refresher on this as a lesson starter.

Discover

Unit 13: Geometry – properties of shapes (1), Lesson 6

Calculating angles around a point

Discover

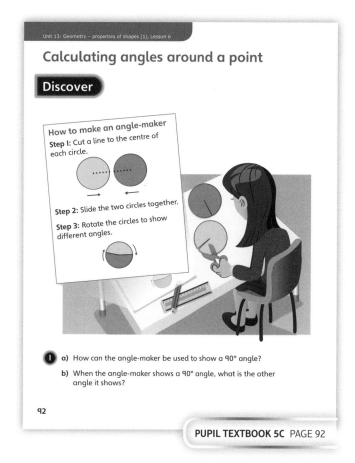

WAYS OF WORKING Pair work

ASK

- Question **1** a): *What do we call a 90-degree angle?*
- Question **1** b): *Why is one angle greater than 180°?*
- Question **1** b): *What calculation should you use to find the other angle?*

IN FOCUS The focus of questions **1** a) and b) is to explore the relationship between two angles that form a whole of 360°. By creating the angle-maker themselves children gradually find it easier to visualise how the angles fit together in a whole turn.

PRACTICAL TIPS Children could make angle-makers like those shown in the image. They should cut two paper circles of different colours and cut a line to the centre of each circle, then slide the two circles together. This then enables them to rotate the circles and show different angles.

ANSWERS

Question **1** a):

Question **1** b): The other angle the angle-maker shows is 270°.

Share

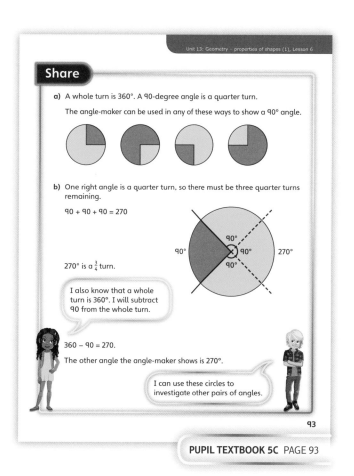

WAYS OF WORKING Whole class teacher led

ASK

- Question **1** a): *How could you show 90° in different orientations?*
- Question **1** b): *What is the same and what is different about the two different ways to calculate the 270-degree angle?*

IN FOCUS The main point of questions **1** a) and b) is for children to recognise that the whole turn is 360°, and how this can be used to calculate the missing angle around a point. It is important that they recognise how a subtraction can be a very useful calculation for questions like these and are able to explain why.

Think together

Whole class teacher led (I do, We do, You do)

ASK

- Question ❶: *What is the total of the parts you know? What is the whole?*
- Question ❶: *What calculation do you need to do to find the missing angle?*
- Question ❸: *How can you apply this to drawing an angle greater than 180°?*

IN FOCUS Question ❷ requires children to perform a multi-step calculation as there are three angles around a point. This reinforces that the angles around a point total 360°.

Question ❸ allows children to explore that one of the angles is a reflex angle. They may need to discuss how 'reflex' means greater than 180°.

STRENGTHEN Have children sketch the angles or make them with angle-makers. Allow them to explore the relationship between the parts and the whole using the angle-makers to create given angles, then calculate the other part to total 360°.

DEEPEN Question ❸ introduces new language in the form of reflex angles. Provide children with a selection of angles around a point which they must calculate, using the knowledge from this lesson, and also label as acute, right angle, obtuse, reflex.

ASSESSMENT CHECKPOINT Question ❷ requires good understanding of the concept of using calculation rather than measuring to find missing angles. Have children grasped that they need to use the knowledge that the angles around a point total 360°? Do they recognise the right angle and that it is 90°?

ANSWERS

Question ❶: The angles are 45° and 315°.

Question ❷: a) 230°, b) 120°, c) 182°

Question ❸ a): The reflex angle can be drawn by working out the complementary angles to 360° and drawing the remaining angle. So, to draw a 230-degree angle Jamilla can work out that 230 + 130 = 360, so the protractor can be used to measure 130°, then mark the angle that shows 230°.

Question ❸ b): Children draw their own reflex angles of 230° and 312°.

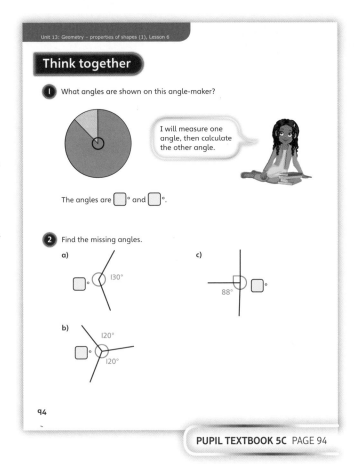

PUPIL TEXTBOOK 5C PAGE 94

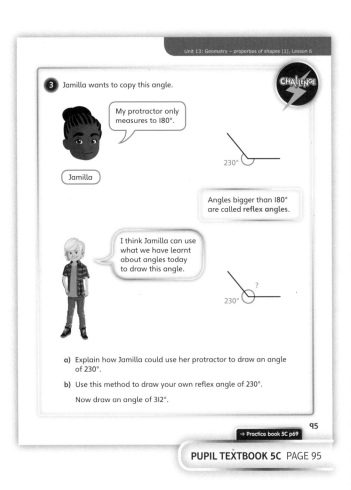

PUPIL TEXTBOOK 5C PAGE 95

Practice

WAYS OF WORKING Independent thinking

IN FOCUS Question ❶ is basic practice at finding the complementary angles to 360°, with the subtraction scaffolded to reinforce the efficient method of working out the missing angles.

Question ❷ requires children to calculate the missing angle where there are more than two parts. This shows that they need to add the given angles and then subtract the total from 360° to find the missing angle.

STRENGTHEN Some children may need to build their calculations step-by-step when working with more than two angles around a point.

DEEPEN Give children some examples of incorrect calculations and challenge them to find the mistakes. For example, the given angles could be added up incorrectly or the total could be more or less than 360°. Children could then set similar problems for a partner to solve.

THINK DIFFERENTLY Question ❺ requires children to remember the definition of an obtuse angle and use their reasoning skills to describe why Reena is unable to make four obtuse angles within the circle.

ASSESSMENT CHECKPOINT Question ❷ shows deep understanding of the key skill. Incorrect answers here might indicate that children have not grasped that there are 360° around a point or they may be relying on measuring rather than using calculation.

ANSWERS Answers for the **Practice** part of the lesson appear in the separate **Practice and Reflect answer guide**.

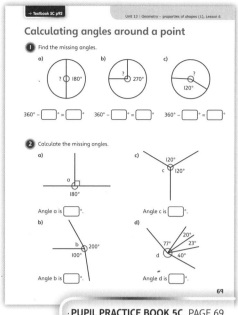

PUPIL PRACTICE BOOK 5C PAGE 69

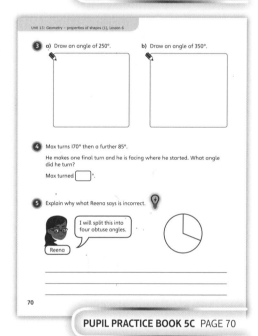

PUPIL PRACTICE BOOK 5C PAGE 70

Reflect

WAYS OF WORKING Independent thinking

IN FOCUS Children can find multiple solutions and explain the relationship between the two missing angles and the whole.

ASSESSMENT CHECKPOINT Can children explain the sum of the two missing angles and that there are various possibilities? Have they fully explained which number they are subtracting from to find these possibilities?

ANSWERS Answers for the **Reflect** part of the lesson appear in the separate **Practice and Reflect answer guide**.

After the lesson ⏸

- Can children explain the reasoning based on the total angle of a whole turn?
- Are children able to follow a chain of reasoning where there are more than two angles around a point?
- Are children confident with the vocabulary of acute, right, obtuse and reflex angles?

PUPIL PRACTICE BOOK 5C PAGE 71

Calculating lengths and angles in shapes

Learning focus

In this lesson, children will use reasoning about shapes to calculate missing angles and lengths. They use reasoning based on the properties of known lines, angles and shapes.

Small steps

→ Previous step: Calculating angles around a point
→ **This step: Calculating lengths and angles in shapes**
→ Next step: Recognising and drawing parallel lines

NATIONAL CURRICULUM LINKS

Year 5 Geometry – Properties of Shapes

Use the properties of rectangles to deduce related facts and find missing lengths and angles.

ASSESSING MASTERY

Children can explain their reasoning based on known properties, lengths and composites of shapes or parts of shapes.

COMMON MISCONCEPTIONS

Children may try to spot lengths or angles that look the same rather than using reasoning based on properties. Ask:
• *How do you know that these lengths must be the same?*

STRENGTHENING UNDERSTANDING

Children can use and transform paper versions of the shapes to be used in the problems, manipulating them by cutting and rearranging.

GOING DEEPER

Challenge children to make general statements about the angles in the diagonals of squares and rectangles.

KEY LANGUAGE

In lesson: angle, length, **interior angle**, parallelogram, degrees (°)

Other language to be used by the teacher: right angle, measure, calculate, obtuse angle, acute angle

STRUCTURES AND REPRESENTATIONS

angle diagrams, 2D shapes

RESOURCES

Mandatory: ruler

Optional: paper squares and rectangles

 In the eTextbook of this lesson, you will find interactive links to a selection of teaching tools.

Before you teach

• You might like to provide some 2D and 3D shapes for children to look at and find 90-degree angles.
• Are children confident in knowing that right angles are always 90°?

Discover

WAYS OF WORKING Pair work

ASK

- Question **1** a): *What size are the angles in the original square?*
- Question **1** a): *How would you calculate the angles in the triangles that are formed?*
- Question **1** a): *How are the lengths combined?*

IN FOCUS In question **1** a), the key is for children to recognise that the angles and side lengths of the triangles can be deduced based on the properties of the original squares. They need to recall known facts about squares.

Question **1** b) asks children to consider the length of a diagonal. They may want to explore how the diagonal of a square or rectangle is always longer than the side length. This could be an extra challenge to deepen learning.

PRACTICAL TIPS Children should create the parallelogram by cutting their own squares of paper in the way the instructions show. They can work in pairs with one square each and put them together to form two parallelograms. This will enable them to see exactly how the squares become the parallelograms.

ANSWERS

Question **1** a): The interior angles of the parallelogram are: 45°, 45°, 135° and 135°.

Question **1** b): Lee is correct about length A, but incorrect about length B.

Calculating lengths and angles in shapes

Discover

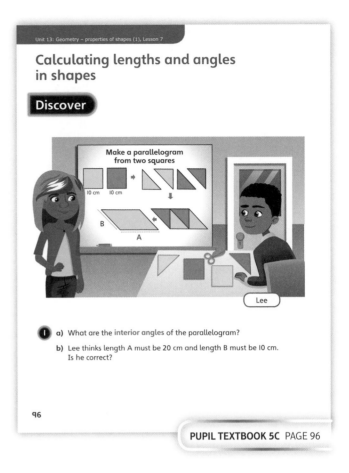

1 a) What are the **interior angles** of the parallelogram?

   b) Lee thinks length A must be 20 cm and length B must be 10 cm. Is he correct?

96

Share

WAYS OF WORKING Whole class teacher led

ASK

- Question **1** a): *How are the 90-degree angles halved in the triangles?*
- Question **1** a): *Why is there one 90-degree angle in each triangle?*
- Question **1** b): *Why is the diagonal length longer than 10 cm?*

IN FOCUS The key to this activity is to reason about the angles and lengths, based on the properties of the original squares. Children will notice that the diagonal of a square is always longer than its sides.

STRENGTHEN Although children should not need to re-measure or check with a protractor or ruler, some may find it increases their confidence in their calculations to do so.

Share

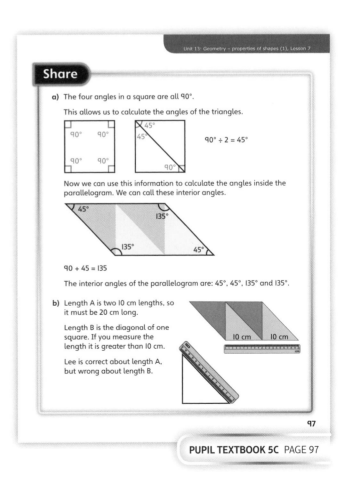

a) The four angles in a square are all 90°.

This allows us to calculate the angles of the triangles.

90° ÷ 2 = 45°

Now we can use this information to calculate the angles inside the parallelogram. We can call these interior angles.

90 + 45 = 135

The interior angles of the parallelogram are: 45°, 45°, 135° and 135°.

b) Length A is two 10 cm lengths, so it must be 20 cm long.

Length B is the diagonal of one square. If you measure the length it is greater than 10 cm.

Lee is correct about length A, but wrong about length B.

97

Think together

Think together

WAYS OF WORKING Whole class teacher led (I do, We do, You do)

ASK

- Question ❶ : *How can you use your knowledge that a right angle is 90° to help you?*
- Question ❷ : *Can you see how the shapes from Shape A have been rearranged to make Shape B?*
- Question ❷ : *Which of the measurements on the first shape should you use to help you?*

IN FOCUS Question ❶ focuses on finding the composite angles and applying prior knowledge of squares and triangles, as well as angles around a point, to work out angles without using a protractor.

Question ❷ challenges children to focus on deducing side lengths by calculating, based on the given dimensions.

Question ❸ explores the potential assumption that splitting any rectangle in half creates 45°, as the 90-degree angles may be seen to be halved by the process. Children should use or create different rectangles in different proportions to check this conjecture.

STRENGTHEN It may help children to use paper versions of all the shapes to support their reasoning, as these can be manipulated physically to support and prompt, but not replace, reasoning.

DEEPEN Children can be given paper squares and rectangles and experiment with ways of cutting them in half. What different angles do they make? Can they work out the answers without measuring?

ASSESSMENT CHECKPOINT Can children justify their reasoning for each stage, based on the properties of the shapes given?

ANSWERS

Question ❶ : p = 45°; q = 135°; r = 90°; s = 135°; t = 45°; u = 270°. All can be worked out without measuring.

Question ❷ : Length = 200 mm. Width = 45 mm

Question ❸ : Only in a square rectangle are the angles of 45° created when split in half diagonally.

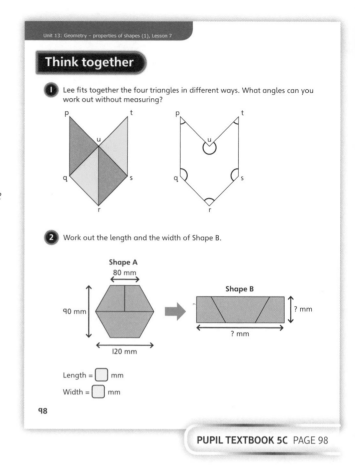

Think together

❶ Lee fits together the four triangles in different ways. What angles can you work out without measuring?

❷ Work out the length and the width of Shape B.

Shape A

80 mm
90 mm
120 mm

Shape B

? mm
? mm

Length = ☐ mm
Width = ☐ mm

98

PUPIL TEXTBOOK 5C PAGE 98

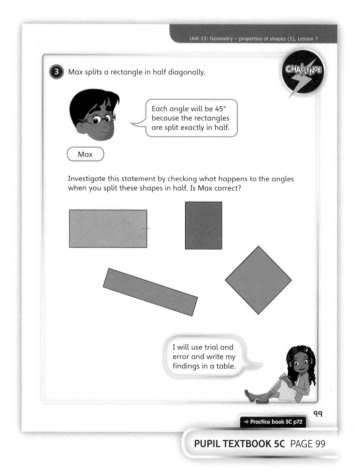

❸ Max splits a rectangle in half diagonally.

CHALLENGE

Each angle will be 45° because the rectangles are split exactly in half.

Max

Investigate this statement by checking what happens to the angles when you split these shapes in half. Is Max correct?

I will use trial and error and write my findings in a table.

99

→ Practice book 5C p72

PUPIL TEXTBOOK 5C PAGE 99

Practice

WAYS OF WORKING Independent thinking

IN FOCUS Question ① has been included as it allows children to practise the skill of deducing angles based on the properties of an original design.

Question ② requires children to recognise the composite angles and lengths shown.

Question ③ asks children to apply the reasoning from their understanding of angles on a straight line and at a right angle. This takes the knowledge from the previous lessons, on angles on a line and around a point, and begins to apply it to properties of shapes.

STRENGTHEN Support children by creating paper or card versions of the shapes to be manipulated in the ways shown in the problems. They could explore the effects of halving different squares.

DEEPEN Extend learning on question ① by asking children to cut up a square into smaller squares and rectangles and to then calculate the interior angles and side lengths of their new shapes.

ASSESSMENT CHECKPOINT Question ③ requires a deep understanding of how to make deductions about missing angles. Are children applying their knowledge of right angles and the sum of angles on straight lines and around points to calculate the answers?

ANSWERS Answers for the **Practice** part of the lesson appear in the separate **Practice and Reflect answer guide**.

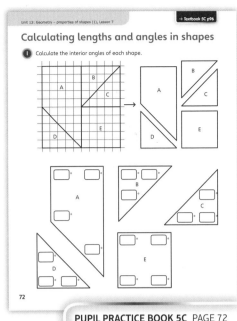

PUPIL PRACTICE BOOK 5C PAGE 72

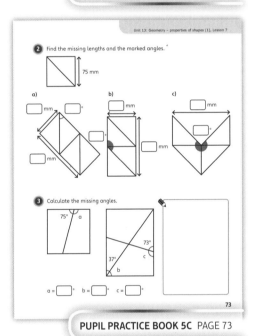

PUPIL PRACTICE BOOK 5C PAGE 73

Reflect

WAYS OF WORKING Independent thinking

IN FOCUS The **Reflect** section allows children to think back over the shapes they have worked on in this unit to decide if there are times when calculating is more efficient than measuring. It will provide them with an opportunity to fully digest the unit as a whole and reflect on how they will tackle geometry lessons in the future.

ASSESSMENT CHECKPOINT Can children justify when to measure and when to calculate, based on their knowledge of the properties of angles and shapes? Children should discuss how there are times when calculating is a more efficient or accurate method, but that sometimes it may be more practical to measure, where the calculations may not be clear, such as finding the length of a diagonal.

ANSWERS Answers for the **Reflect** part of the lesson appear in the separate **Practice and Reflect answer guide**.

After the lesson

- Were children able to explain their reasoning?
- Could children apply their knowledge of angles around a point or on a straight line?

PUPIL PRACTICE BOOK 5C PAGE 74

End of unit check

Don't forget the *Power Maths* unit assessment grid on p26.

WAYS OF WORKING Group work teacher led

IN FOCUS

- Question ② requires children to realise that they need to measure accurately using a protractor.
- Questions ④ and ⑤ ask children to calculate angles on a straight line and around a point and question ⑥ challenges children to find missing angles in a shape. To answer these questions they will need to apply what they have learnt about the sum of angles on straight lines and around points, and apply them in a variety of contexts.

ANSWERS AND COMMENTARY

Children who have mastered this unit will confidently be able to work out missing angles on a line and around a point without needing to use a protractor. Children can use their knowledge of the properties of squares, triangles and circles to calculate missing angles. Children can use a protractor accurately.

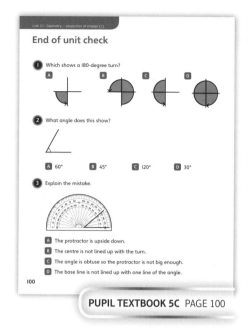

PUPIL TEXTBOOK 5C PAGE 100

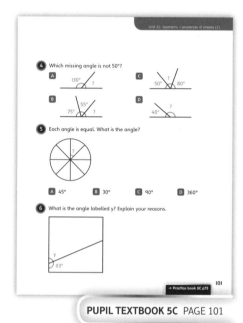

PUPIL TEXTBOOK 5C PAGE 101

Q	A	WRONG ANSWERS AND MISCONCEPTIONS	STRENGTHENING UNDERSTANDING
1	C	D shows they are unaware that a full turn is 360°.	Encourage children to sketch their ideas to support their reasoning.
2	A	C suggests that children have used the incorrect scale.	Model the different turns using manipulatives or by role playing with a group of children.
3	B	A shows children do not understand that a protractor may be oriented differently. C shows that children think angle is a measure of the size between two lines.	Revisit the three steps for measuring, using a protractor from Lesson 2.
4	D	B suggests children may not have added the 1s digits given.	Revisit 90-degree and 180-degree angles as quarter and half turns.
5	A	B suggests children may have estimated visually. C suggests children do not understand 90° as a quarter turn.	
6	67°	Incorrect answers suggest children are unaware that angles on a line add to 180°.	

My journal

WAYS OF WORKING Independent thinking

ANSWERS AND COMMENTARY In question ❶ a), children must not only put their new skills of using a protractor accurately to work but also call upon their understanding of how many degrees are in a whole turn. Look to see whether children use addition or subtraction.

For question ❷, children should notice that the angles formed where the internal square meets the external square are related. Encourage children to justify this reasoning based on the properties of the angles in a square, and linked with their understanding of finding angles around a point. This knowledge is also relevant for question ❶ b).

Children should feel that they can measure to check, or measure first and then explain any patterns they have noticed.

Question ❶ a): Groups of angles that fit together to form a whole turn are a, b, c, d or a, b, g.

Question ❶ b): The group of angles that fit together to form a straight line are a, b, c, f.

Question ❷: a = 70°, b = 20°.
They add up to 90°.

Power check

WAYS OF WORKING Independent working

ASK

- *What new skills have you learnt?*
- *Can you explain angles in a new way or using new vocabulary now?*
- *How confident do you feel about using a protractor?*

Power puzzle

WAYS OF WORKING Pair work

IN FOCUS Use this **Power puzzle** to give children the opportunity to explore the use of a protractor in more detail. Some children may enjoy creating their own patterns for people to follow as a deepening activity.

ANSWERS AND COMMENTARY Children may find that this task requires a few drafts and re-drafts. Encourage them by explaining that the protractor is one of the most challenging measuring tools that they will have to learn to use, but that once they have mastered it, they will be able to create accurate designs for their projects. They will also be able to use this skill in secondary school. Can children make a sensible decision on the length of each side so that it fits on the page?

After the unit ⏸

- Can children explain how to calculate missing angles on a line or around a point and justify their reasoning?
- Can children discuss the key challenges and common errors when measuring with a protractor?

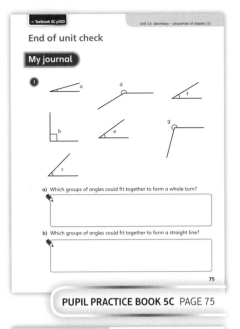

PUPIL PRACTICE BOOK 5C PAGE 75

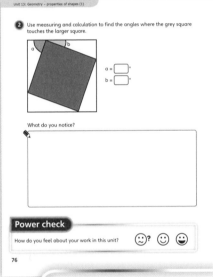

PUPIL PRACTICE BOOK 5C PAGE 76

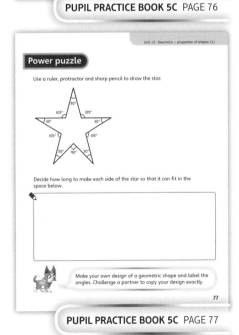

PUPIL PRACTICE BOOK 5C PAGE 77

Strengthen and **Deepen** activities for this unit can be found in the *Power Maths* online subscription.

Unit 14
Geometry – properties of shapes ❷

Mastery Expert tip! "When teaching this unit, I make sure children have access to construction and drawing materials so that they can explore and discuss their ideas by making physical or visual versions of the problems and their own conjectures. When using manipulatives, I make sure that these support and prompt reasoning, rather than replace it."

Don't forget to watch the Unit 14 video!

WHY THIS UNIT IS IMPORTANT

This unit is important because it builds on the previous unit of using rulers and protractors to identify angles and properties of shapes, helping children to practise and hone these new key skills. It develops learning from Years 3 and 4 to cement understanding of parallel and perpendicular lines as well as 2D and 3D shapes, encouraging children to predict results based on prior knowledge before proving them with the apparatus. This will prepare children for working with angles and drawing accurate shapes in Year 6.

WHERE THIS UNIT FITS

→ Unit 13: Geometry – properties of shapes (1)
→ **Unit 14: Geometry – properties of shapes (2)**
→ Unit 15: Geometry – position and direction

Before they start this unit, it is expected that children:
• have encountered the concepts of parallel and perpendicular lines in previous years
• can measure angles accurately
• recognise right angles in different orientations
• have knowledge of common 2D and 3D shapes.

ASSESSING MASTERY

Children who have mastered this unit will be able to identify and construct parallel and perpendicular lines, follow logical chains of reasoning about parallel and perpendicular lines in shapes, and apply their understanding of angles to regular and irregular shapes. They will also be able to visualise what a 3D shape will look like from different viewpoints.

COMMON MISCONCEPTIONS	STRENGTHENING UNDERSTANDING	GOING DEEPER
Children may not realise that to be regular, a polygon must meet **both** the following criteria: same size angles **and** same side lengths.	Encourage children to explore the variations of quadrilaterals that have sides the same length but different angles. This can be modelled with strips of paper or card joined with split pins, or on geoboards or with geostrips.	Investigate the properties of quadrilaterals and explore the relationship between a rhombus, parallelogram, rectangle and square.
Children sometimes may not recognise perpendicular lines when they are not oriented horizontally or vertically.	Encourage children to explore perpendicular lines in various orientations, using construction materials, rulers or string.	Children can investigate general statements about the diagonals of quadrilaterals and be able to explore these using geoboards.

WAYS OF WORKING

Use these pages to introduce the unit focus to children. Can children identify which groups of lines are not parallel and explain why? Discuss the key learning points and key language mentioned by the characters.

STRUCTURES AND REPRESENTATIONS

Arrow notation: these indicate and distinguish between different sets of parallel lines.

Right angles: The properties of right angles will recur and will be important for marking and recognising perpendicular lines.

2D representations of 3D shapes: children will need to visualise the solid shape from its 2D representation.

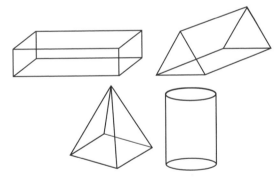

KEY LANGUAGE

There is some key language that children will need to know as part of the learning in this unit.

→ parallel
→ perpendicular
→ angle, right angle, interior angle
→ grid
→ regular, irregular
→ polygon, quadrilateral
→ 2D, 3D
→ viewpoint

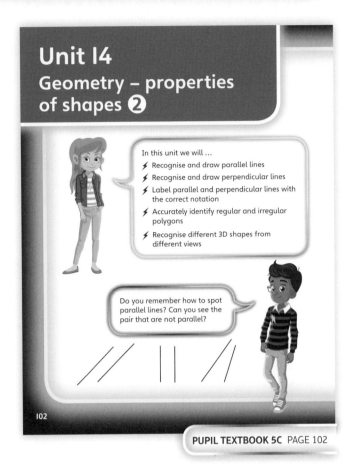

PUPIL TEXTBOOK 5C PAGE 102

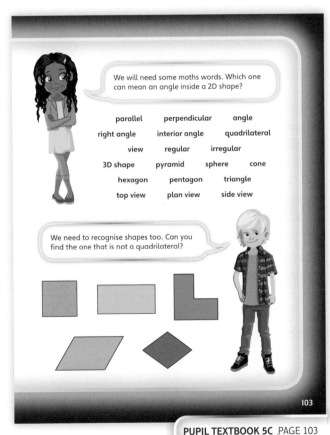

PUPIL TEXTBOOK 5C PAGE 103

Recognising and drawing parallel lines

Learning focus

In this lesson, children will develop their understanding of parallel lines, including the use of arrow notation to distinguish sets of parallel lines. Children will recognise and draw parallel lines in different orientations.

Small steps

→ Previous step: Calculating lengths and angles in shapes
→ **This step: Recognising and drawing parallel lines**
→ Next step: Recognising and drawing perpendicular lines

NATIONAL CURRICULUM LINKS

Year 5 Geometry – Properties of Shapes
- Use the properties of rectangles to deduce related facts and find missing lengths and angles.
- Identify:
  – angles at a point and one whole turn (total 360°)
  – angles at a point on a straight line and $\frac{1}{2}$ a turn (total 180°)
  – other multiples of 90°.

ASSESSING MASTERY

Children can use arrow notation to indicate sets of lines that are parallel and can use the properties of a grid to reason about parallel and non-parallel lines.

COMMON MISCONCEPTIONS

Children may think that parallel lines must be exactly the same length. Point to two parallel lines of different lengths. Ask:
- *Can these two lines be called parallel? Do you look at the length to find that out?*

Children may fail to recognise that there can be more than two lines parallel to one another. Ask:
- *Are all parallel lines in pairs?*

STRENGTHENING UNDERSTANDING

Encourage children to discuss different ways to describe parallel lines, recapping with them work from Year 3. Parallel lines are a constant width apart; they would never meet even if they continued forever, and they go in exactly the same direction.

GOING DEEPER

Challenge children to use the properties of a grid to create lines that are parallel. Encourage them to draw a line on a grid for a partner to draw a parallel line, based on the grid.

KEY LANGUAGE

In lesson: parallel, horizontal, vertical, arrow marking, diagonal

Other language to be used by the teacher: length, constant, width

RESOURCES

Mandatory: rulers

Optional: sticks

 In the eTextbook of this lesson, you will find interactive links to a selection of teaching tools.

Before you teach

- What do children remember about the word 'parallel'?
- Can children give examples of where they could see parallel lines?
- Do children know what 'horizontal' and 'vertical' mean?

Discover

Recognising and drawing parallel lines

Discover

WAYS OF WORKING Pair work

ASK

- Question **1** a): *How can you tell if two lines are parallel?*
- Question **1** b): *How far apart are these lines? Does it change?*
- Question **1** b): *Would these lines cross if they continued further?*

IN FOCUS Questions **1** a) and b) contain examples of parallel lines that are horizontal and vertical. They also contain clear non-examples, discussion of which should deepen understanding of the concept.

Children should have a good basic understanding of parallel lines from previous years' learning, but it will be important to recap the key ideas that parallel lines are a constant width apart and would never touch or cross, even if extended indefinitely.

PRACTICAL TIPS The gates in the image show parallel lines in the horizontal and vertical orientations very clearly. There will be many examples of parallel lines in the school environment. The class could go on a parallel line treasure hunt around the school, perhaps capturing many different examples on a digital camera, to be displayed or printed for inspection by the class.

ANSWERS

Question **1** a): All the horizontal and all the vertical lines on the gates are parallel.

Question **1** b): The diagonal lines on the gates are not parallel because if they continued they would cross over.

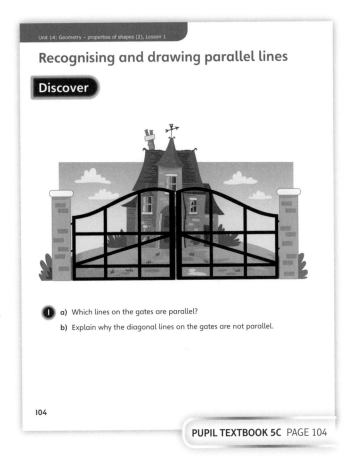

1 a) Which lines on the gates are parallel?

b) Explain why the diagonal lines on the gates are not parallel.

104

PUPIL TEXTBOOK 5C PAGE 104

Share

WAYS OF WORKING Whole class teacher led

ASK

- Question **1** a): *Why do some lines have one arrow mark, and others have two or three?*
- Question **1** b): *What is the proof that the diagonal lines are not parallel?*
- Question **1** b): *Can parallel lines ever be diagonal?*

IN FOCUS The focus in questions **1** a) and b) is on recapping the main definitions of parallel lines and learning how to use arrow notation to indicate different sets of parallel lines.

Children should discuss how all the vertical lines in this picture are parallel to each other – parallel lines do not have to come solely in pairs.

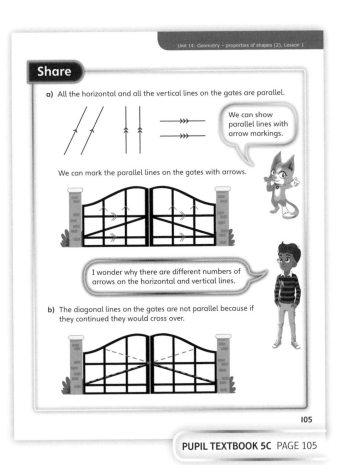

Share

a) All the horizontal and all the vertical lines on the gates are parallel.

We can show parallel lines with arrow markings.

We can mark the parallel lines on the gates with arrows.

I wonder why there are different numbers of arrows on the horizontal and vertical lines.

b) The diagonal lines on the gates are not parallel because if they continued they would cross over.

105

PUPIL TEXTBOOK 5C PAGE 105

Think together

WAYS OF WORKING Whole class teacher led (I do, We do, You do)

ASK

- Question ❶: *The gate has fallen, so the vertical lines are no longer vertical. Does this change whether the lines are parallel?*
- Question ❷: *How can you make sure you copy the shapes accurately?*
- Question ❸ a): *What letters do you use to describe a line?*
- Question ❸ c): *How will you make sure your lines are parallel?*

IN FOCUS Question ❶ has been included as it covers sets of parallel lines that are not oriented horizontally or vertically.

Question ❷ introduces the idea of sets of parallel lines within shapes. Children should be encouraged to notice the grids on which the shapes are drawn. Do they see how these can help them spot parallel lines?

Question ❸ introduces the notation for a line by naming the vertices, such as 'line BC'. Here children are required to use the properties of the grid to form and justify sets of parallel lines.

STRENGTHEN Encourage children to place long straight sticks or rulers over lines, to support their understanding of whether parallel lines cross if extended.

DEEPEN Challenge children to recognise that the properties of a grid can support their reasoning about parallel lines. Ask: *How can you use the grid to prove your lines are parallel?*

ASSESSMENT CHECKPOINT Question ❸ a) requires a deep understanding of parallel lines and the vocabulary introduced in this lesson. Are children using the grid lines to help make their identification of parallel lines more efficient?

ANSWERS

Question ❶: The vertical lines are parallel and the horizontal lines are also parallel. The rusted gate contains two sets of parallel lines that are now oriented 'diagonally' on the page.

Question ❷ a): The square contains two pairs of parallel lines.

Question ❷ b): The equilateral triangle contains no parallel lines.

Question ❷ c): The trapezium contains one pair of parallel lines.

Question ❷ d): The parallelogram contains two pairs of parallel lines.

Question ❸ a): Make sure children point to BC and EF.

Question ❸ b): AB is parallel to ED.

Question ❸ c): Children should use the grid lines to ensure their lines are parallel.

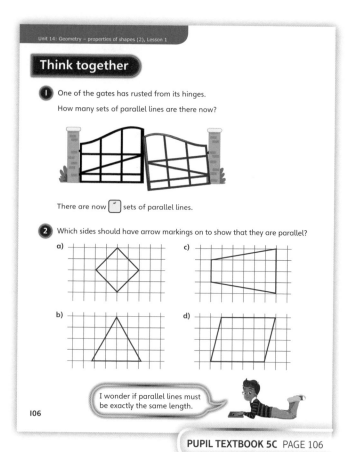

PUPIL TEXTBOOK 5C PAGE 106

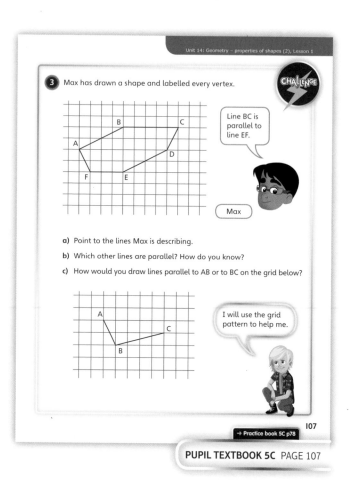

PUPIL TEXTBOOK 5C PAGE 107

Practice

WAYS OF WORKING Independent thinking

IN FOCUS Question ❶ is included here as it reinforces the skill of using arrow notation to indicate parallel lines.

Question ❷ requires children to recognise parallel lines in shapes and to remember to use the grid lines to aid them in this task.

Question ❸ focuses on the idea that parallel lines need not be the same length.

STRENGTHEN Encourage children to practise forming parallel lines by arranging pairs of pencils or rulers in different orientations.

DEEPEN Question ❺ challenges children to consider examples and non-examples of parallel lines, by using the properties of an isometric grid to deepen their understanding. Are children able to draw shapes of their own on isometric paper for their partner to find the parallel lines?

THINK DIFFERENTLY Question ❹ challenges children to consider hypothetical lines, which are not yet drawn, but which are indicated by vertex label notation.

ASSESSMENT CHECKPOINT Identifying and marking the parallel lines in different orientations in questions ❶ and ❷ requires a good understanding of the basic concept, allowing you to assess children's grasp of it through their answers.

ANSWERS Answers for the **Practice** part of the lesson appear in the separate **Practice and Reflect answer guide**.

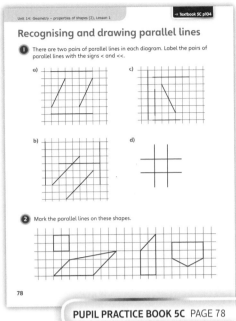

PUPIL PRACTICE BOOK 5C PAGE 78

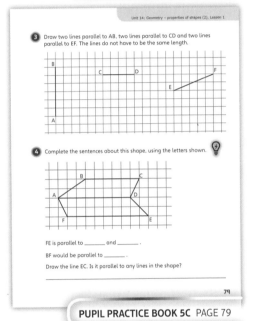

PUPIL PRACTICE BOOK 5C PAGE 79

Reflect

WAYS OF WORKING Independent thinking

IN FOCUS Children could sketch different drafts on a whiteboard or on scrap paper, then share their ideas with a partner, before deciding on the best way to meet the task.

ASSESSMENT CHECKPOINT Can children justify why there are two pairs of parallel lines based on the properties of the grid?

ANSWERS Answers for the **Reflect** part of the lesson appear in the separate **Practice and Reflect answer guide**.

After the lesson ⏸

- Do children recognise parallel lines in different orientations?
- Are all children confident in identifying parallel lines that are different lengths?
- Can children use the properties of a grid to draw and identify parallel lines, and justify when lines are not parallel?

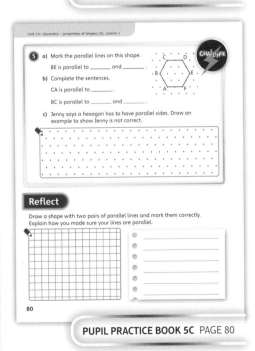

PUPIL PRACTICE BOOK 5C PAGE 80

Recognising and drawing perpendicular lines

Learning focus

In this lesson, children will build on their knowledge of angles to deepen their understanding of perpendicular lines, including recognising, labelling and drawing lines that are perpendicular to one another.

Small steps

→ Previous step: Recognising and drawing parallel lines

→ **This step: Recognising and drawing perpendicular lines**

→ Next step: Reasoning about parallel and perpendicular lines

NATIONAL CURRICULUM LINKS

Year 5 Geometry – Properties of Shapes
- Use the properties of rectangles to deduce related facts and find missing lengths and angles.
- Identify:
  - angles at a point and one whole turn (total 360°)
  - angles at a point on a straight line and $\frac{1}{2}$ a turn (total 180°)
  - other multiples of 90°.

ASSESSING MASTERY

Children can justify a statement that two lines are or are not perpendicular based on their understanding of right angles and the properties of a grid.

COMMON MISCONCEPTIONS

Children may not recognise that two lines can be perpendicular even if they do not touch or cross. Ask:
- *At what angle would these lines meet if they were both continued?*

Children may assume vertical lines or horizontal lines are always perpendicular to another line, even if the line is oriented differently/diagonally in relation to them. Ask:
- *Are all vertical lines perpendicular to other lines?*

STRENGTHENING UNDERSTANDING

Children should develop their understanding of right angles by exploring lines that cross at different angles, perhaps working as a group using lengths of string. They can vary the angle at which the lines cross, and call *Stop!* when they are perpendicular.

GOING DEEPER

Challenge children to complete rectangles in different orientations, by forming perpendicular lines at the vertices and by using the properties of a grid.

KEY LANGUAGE

In lesson: perpendicular, degrees (°), right angle, vertical, horizontal, box marking, protractor

Other language to be used by the teacher: right angle notation

RESOURCES

Optional: protractor, geostrips, geoboards

 In the eTextbook of this lesson, you will find interactive links to a selection of teaching tools.

Before you teach

- Can children recognise a 90° angle?
- Can children show how a horizontal and a vertical line would meet if they continued?
- Do children remember the word 'perpendicular' from learning in Year 3?

Discover

Unit 14: Geometry – properties of shapes (2), Lesson 2

WAYS OF WORKING Pair work

ASK

- Question **1** a): *What does the word 'perpendicular' mean?*
- Question **1** a): *What are you looking for to determine if the streetlamps are perpendicular?*
- Question **1** b): *How is the word 'perpendicular' different from the word 'vertical'?*

IN FOCUS Questions **1** a) and b) prompt children to discuss the meaning of the word perpendicular, which they originally met in Year 3. They may notice that one set of streetlamps look precarious. The important aspect to focus on is the difference in meaning between vertical and perpendicular, and how these meanings intersect.

Some children may discuss the relationship between vertical structures and engineering. Questions to encourage this are: *Why do you not build leaning structures? Why are some houses built in a way that is not perpendicular to the street?*

PRACTICAL TIPS This is presented as an engineering problem, and it could be recreated practically by pushing straws into modelling clay formed into the different gradients of the street. This could also be shown using gymnastics equipment raised to form different inclines.

ANSWERS

Question **1** a): The streetlamps on the top of the hill and on the right are perpendicular to the road because they make right angles.

Question **1** b): The streetlamps on the top of the hill are both vertical and perpendicular to the road, making right angles. This can be proved by using a protractor.

Share

WAYS OF WORKING Whole class teacher led

ASK

- Question **1** a): *Look at the little square. Have you seen this before? What does it tell us?*
- Question **1** a): *How can you check if an angle is a right angle?*
- Question **1** b): *Is something that is horizontal always perpendicular to something that is vertical?*

IN FOCUS In question **1** a), children recap that 90° angles are also called right angles, and then learn to use right-angle notation to indicate lines that are perpendicular. They should discuss how perpendicular lines need not be oriented horizontally and vertically. Children should become more confident recognising and using the box marking to indicate a right angle in different orientations.

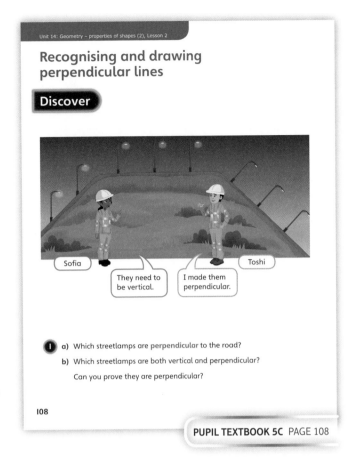

Recognising and drawing perpendicular lines

Discover

1 a) Which streetlamps are perpendicular to the road?

b) Which streetlamps are both vertical and perpendicular?

Can you prove they are perpendicular?

108

PUPIL TEXTBOOK 5C PAGE 108

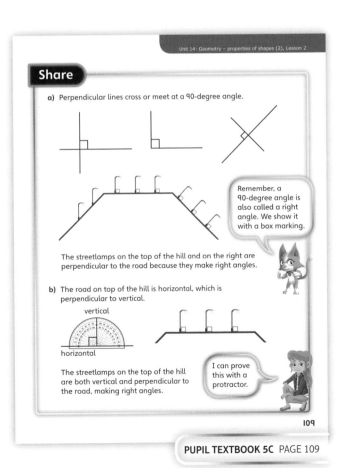

Share

a) Perpendicular lines cross or meet at a 90-degree angle.

Remember, a 90-degree angle is also called a right angle. We show it with a box marking.

The streetlamps on the top of the hill and on the right are perpendicular to the road because they make right angles.

b) The road on top of the hill is horizontal, which is perpendicular to vertical.

vertical

horizontal

The streetlamps on the top of the hill are both vertical and perpendicular to the road, making right angles.

I can prove this with a protractor.

109

PUPIL TEXTBOOK 5C PAGE 109

Think together

WAYS OF WORKING **WAYS OF WORKING** Whole class teacher led (I do, We do, You do)

ASK

- Question **1**: *How will you check which lines are perpendicular?*
- Question **2**: *Have you found all the perpendicular lines? Remember, they do not have to touch to be perpendicular to one another.*
- Question **2**: *Do you remember how labelling the vertices makes it easier to identify different lines?*
- Question **3**: *What do you know about the properties of rectangles to help you?*

IN FOCUS Question **1** prompts children to recognise perpendicular lines by using the properties of a grid (illustrated on a geoboard).

Question **2** discusses how two perpendicular lines do not necessarily meet or cross, but would cross at a right angle if they were extended.

STRENGTHEN Work with children to explore perpendicular lines through manipulating sticks, string or geoboards. For question **2**, children may find it helpful to draw out the shapes on squared paper and extend the lines and draw right angle markings to find which are perpendicular.

DEEPEN Question **3** challenges children to apply their understanding of perpendicular lines to the properties of rectangles, and to consider how to use the properties of a rectangle to construct perpendicular lines. Ask children to discuss different solutions for how to alter the shapes so that they are rectangles. Can children show how to draw rectangles in different orientations?

ASSESSMENT CHECKPOINT Can children explain clearly how they worked out which lines are perpendicular in question **2**?

ANSWERS

Question **1**: C and D show perpendicular lines.

Question **2** a): Lines CD and AF are perpendicular to AB.

Question **2** b): Lines JI, KL and GH are perpendicular to HI.

Question **3** a): Bella has not made rectangles as in a rectangle the adjacent sides need to be perpendicular.

Question **3** b): Accept any answer stating that rectangles must have 4 sides which must all be perpendicular.

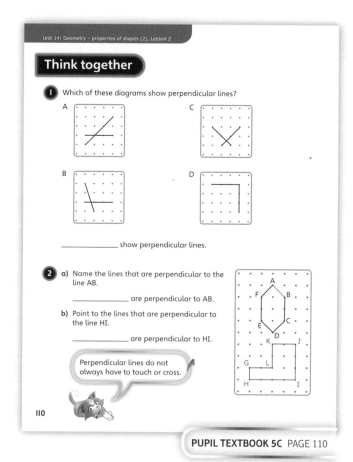

PUPIL TEXTBOOK 5C PAGE 110

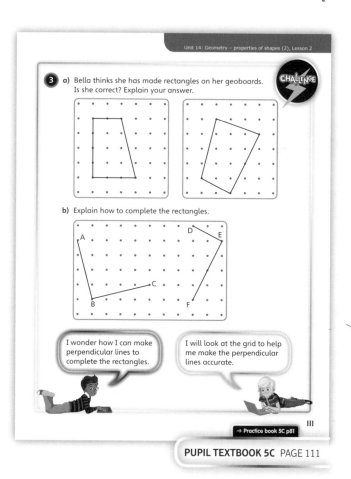

PUPIL TEXTBOOK 5C PAGE 111

Practice

WAYS OF WORKING Independent thinking

IN FOCUS Question ① focuses on marking perpendicular lines that cross in different orientations and recognising non-examples. It also helps to ensure children are confident marking right angles. Note that not all the lines meet at right angles.

Question ② practises the drawing of perpendicular lines, using the properties of the grid to support reasoning.

Question ③ has been included to support learning in identifying perpendicular lines in shapes.

Question ④ challenges children to use vertex notation to communicate about perpendicular lines.

STRENGTHEN Use construction materials to manipulate lines and shapes physically, and make versions of the shapes in the problems.

DEEPEN Question ⑥ challenges children to construct rectangles in different orientations by forming perpendicular lines as adjacent sides. Ask children to draw their own part-drawn rectangles to swap with a partner for them to complete.

THINK DIFFERENTLY Question ⑤ challenges children to construct a shape given information about the sides that are perpendicular, and ensures they understand the vertex notation.

ASSESSMENT CHECKPOINT Questions ③ and ④ require a good understanding of the key concepts of the lesson. Check that children have marked all of the perpendicular lines in question ③. Their true or false selections for question ④ will show their understanding of the key concepts and highlight any misconceptions they may have.

ANSWERS Answers for the **Practice** part of the lesson appear in the separate **Practice and Reflect answer guide**.

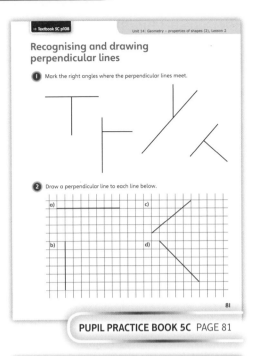

PUPIL PRACTICE BOOK 5C PAGE 81

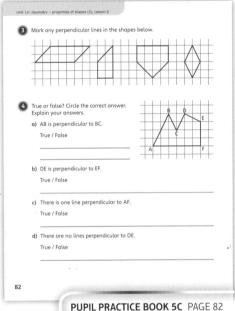

PUPIL PRACTICE BOOK 5C PAGE 82

Reflect

WAYS OF WORKING Independent thinking

IN FOCUS The **Reflect** question provides children with the opportunity to discuss the similarities and differences between the key vocabulary from Lessons 1 and 2 of this unit.

ASSESSMENT CHECKPOINT Can children confidently explain the difference in meaning between parallel and perpendicular?

ANSWERS Answers for the **Reflect** part of the lesson appear in the separate **Practice and Reflect answer guide**.

After the lesson

- Can children recognise perpendicular lines and justify them in terms of right angles?
- Are children able to use the properties of a grid to form perpendicular lines in diagonal orientations?

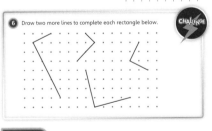

PUPIL PRACTICE BOOK 5C PAGE 83

Reasoning about parallel and perpendicular lines

Learning focus

In this lesson, children will develop their reasoning about parallel and perpendicular lines in relation to one another in shapes and patterns. Children will use angle and length properties to support their judgements.

Small steps

→ Previous step: Recognising and drawing perpendicular lines

→ **This step: Reasoning about parallel and perpendicular lines**

→ Next step: Regular and irregular polygons

NATIONAL CURRICULUM LINKS

Year 5 Geometry – Properties of Shapes
- Draw given angles, and measure them in degrees (°).
- Identify:
  - angles at a point and one whole turn (total 360°)
  - angles at a point on a straight line and $\frac{1}{2}$ a turn (total 180°)
  - other multiples of 90°.

ASSESSING MASTERY

Children can discuss, investigate and evaluate mathematical statements about parallel and perpendicular lines in shapes and in patterns.

COMMON MISCONCEPTIONS

Children may use single examples to prove a general statement, rather than considering all possible examples. Ask:
- *Is that always, sometimes or never true?*

STRENGTHENING UNDERSTANDING

Children should manipulate lines in shapes, using geoboards or by drawing on square dotted paper, to help visualise the question they are being asked.

GOING DEEPER

Children can investigate the angles created when different quadrilaterals are overlapped and can discuss which angles can and cannot be created.

KEY LANGUAGE

In lesson: parallel, perpendicular, diagonals (of a quadrilateral), quadrilateral, protractor

Other language to be used by the teacher: angle notation, right angle, parallel line notation, arrow marking

STRUCTURES AND REPRESENTATIONS

2D shapes

RESOURCES

Mandatory: protractor, ruler

Optional: paper strips, card strips, split pins, geoboards, square dotted paper

 In the eTextbook of this lesson, you will find interactive links to a selection of teaching tools.

Before you teach

- Can children identify different examples of parallel lines?
- Can children identify perpendicular lines?
- Can children describe different quadrilaterals? Do they know what is the same and what is different about them?

Discover

WAYS OF WORKING Pair work

ASK

• Question ❶ a): *What do you notice about the angle these lines cross at?*
• Question ❶ b): *How far apart is the red strip of paper from the other line?*
• Question ❶ b): *Which lines are parallel?*
• Question ❶ b): *Are there any perpendicular lines?*

IN FOCUS The main idea of questions ❶ a) and b) is to explore the relationship between lines that cross a set of parallel lines. Children consider how when a straight line crosses parallel lines it does so at the same angle each time, and that parallel lines are always the same distance apart.

PRACTICAL TIPS The task can easily be modelled practically, where children use strips of coloured paper and arrange them to match the image in the **Discover** context. This will also easily allow them to demonstrate their thinking when answering the questions.

ANSWERS

Question ❶ a): The plain red strip crosses each dotted strip of paper at the same angle of 150°.
Yes, the angle is the same each time.

Question ❶ b): Move the plain red strip so it is perpendicular to the dotted strips. The plain red strip will then be parallel to the stripy blue strip of paper. (children can show this practically if modelling with strips).

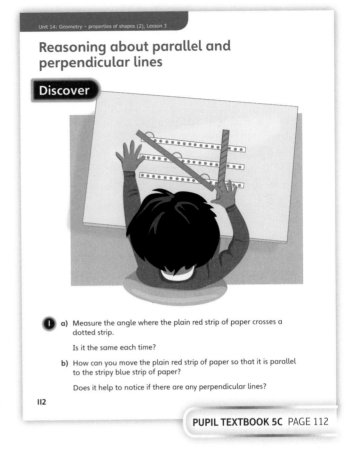

Reasoning about parallel and perpendicular lines

Discover

❶ a) Measure the angle where the plain red strip of paper crosses a dotted strip.

Is it the same each time?

b) How can you move the plain red strip of paper so that it is parallel to the stripy blue strip of paper?

Does it help to notice if there are any perpendicular lines?

112

PUPIL TEXTBOOK 5C PAGE 112

Share

WAYS OF WORKING Whole class teacher led

ASK

• Question ❶ a): *Can you measure the angles using your protractor? Can you show me how you use a protractor?*
• Question ❶ a): *Are all of the angles the same?*
• Question ❶ b): *Can you use a ruler to measure the distance of the plain red strip from the stripy blue strip as it crosses each dotted strip?*

IN FOCUS The focus in question ❶ is for children to notice that a line crosses parallel lines at the same angle.

Children may wish to explore this further, to test if it works in other cases, rather than simply accept it as true from one case.

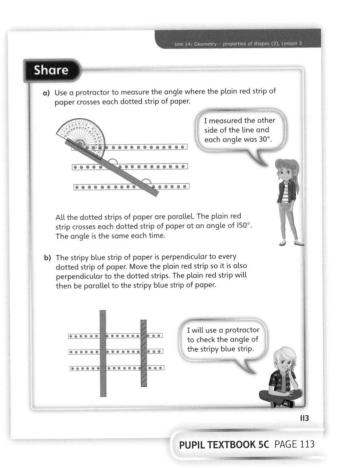

Share

a) Use a protractor to measure the angle where the plain red strip of paper crosses each dotted strip of paper.

I measured the other side of the line and each angle was 30°.

All the dotted strips of paper are parallel. The plain red strip crosses each dotted strip of paper at an angle of 150°. The angle is the same each time.

b) The stripy blue strip of paper is perpendicular to every dotted strip of paper. Move the plain red strip so it is also perpendicular to the dotted strips. The plain red strip will then be parallel to the stripy blue strip of paper.

I will use a protractor to check the angle of the stripy blue strip.

113

PUPIL TEXTBOOK 5C PAGE 113

Think together

Whole class teacher led (I do, We do, You do)

ASK

- Question **1**: *How will you check your lines are parallel? Can you find more than one answer?*
- Question **2**: *Can you explore the question further by folding your own rectangular piece of paper and predicting the number of parallel and perpendicular lines?*
- Question **3**: *Compare your statements with a partner's. Are they similar?*

IN FOCUS Question **1** focuses on testing other examples of lines that cross parallel lines at a constant angle.

Question **2** considers parallel and perpendicular lines in the context of folded paper. This will allow some children to make reasoned predictions.

STRENGTHEN Explore further examples of parallel and perpendicular lines by folding paper. Encourage children to make reasoned predictions and decisions based on the shape of the paper and the distances folded. Help children to look for known angles, such as right angles, and to use a ruler to measure equal lengths for the fold.

DEEPEN Question **3** begins to explore general statements about diagonals of quadrilaterals. Children should try to investigate and formulate statements about which quadrilaterals do or do not have perpendicular diagonals. Children could use square dotted paper or geoboards to create a range of quadrilaterals in different orientations.

ASSESSMENT CHECKPOINT Can children justify their answers with geometrical reasoning, rather than relying on a case-by-case test? Children with a solid grasp of the concepts will be able to explain their answers based on known angles, the properties of shapes and angles on lines.

ANSWERS

Question **1**: A line parallel to the plain red strip would cross the parallel green dotted lines at the same angle as the red strip.

Question **2**: The two long edges and central fold are all parallel, as are the short edge and the horizontal line created by the folded outside edges. The fold lines creating the top point are perpendicular to each other. The vertical sides and central fold line are all perpendicular to the short edge and to the horizontal line created by the folded outside edges.

Question **3** a): The kite, square and rhombus (A, B and D) have perpendicular diagonals.

Question **3** b): Astrid is correct; diagonals of a square intersect at a 90-degree angle and so are always perpendicular.

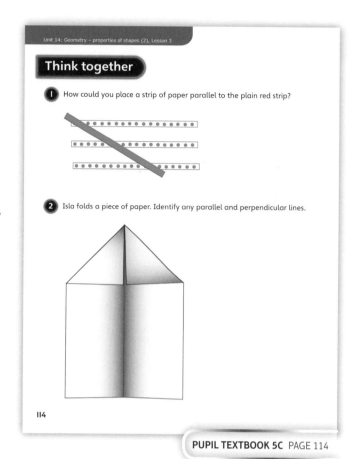

PUPIL TEXTBOOK 5C PAGE 114

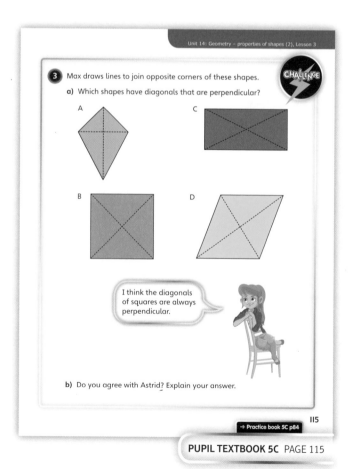

PUPIL TEXTBOOK 5C PAGE 115

Practice

WAYS OF WORKING Independent thinking

IN FOCUS Question ❶ continues to investigate the angles where straight lines intersect sets of parallel lines. This cements understanding that parallel lines cross at a constant angle. Question ❷ extends this further by asking children to investigate their own angles.

STRENGTHEN Encourage children to create and manipulate physical representations of the shapes, perhaps by using construction materials such as strips of card joined with split pins.

DEEPEN Question ❺ challenges children to use the properties of the given dots to form parallel and perpendicular lines. To challenge them further, you could ask children to explore forming parallel and perpendicular lines from different numbers of dots equally-spaced around a circle.

THINK DIFFERENTLY Question ❸ gives pairs of diagonals from which quadrilaterals need to be formed. Children are therefore working in reverse, constructing a shape from its diagonals. This allows them to develop their visualisation skills whilst thinking about the problem differently.

ASSESSMENT CHECKPOINT Questions ❸ and ❹ require a good understanding of the distinction between parallel and perpendicular lines. Look for children who are able to articulate the distinction between the two. Can children quickly spot that the diagonal lines in question ❸ d) are not perpendicular and can they therefore name which quadrilateral shape d) must be?

ANSWERS Answers for the **Practice** part of the lesson appear in the separate **Practice and Reflect answer guide**.

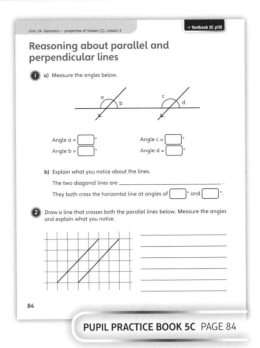

PUPIL PRACTICE BOOK 5C PAGE 84

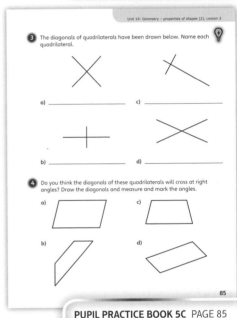

PUPIL PRACTICE BOOK 5C PAGE 85

Reflect

WAYS OF WORKING Independent thinking

IN FOCUS Children are given the opportunity to discuss their ideas, support them with reasons based on the properties of the paper, and then test them by folding. Children can then discuss the reasons behind whether their ideas produced perpendicular lines or not.

ASSESSMENT CHECKPOINT Can children explain the results based on the properties of shape and the structure of the folds they chose?

ANSWERS Answers for the **Reflect** part of the lesson appear in the separate **Practice and Reflect answer guide**.

After the lesson ⏸

- Do children justify their ideas using geometric reasoning?
- Are children confident and accurate when using the terms parallel and perpendicular in mathematical dialogue?

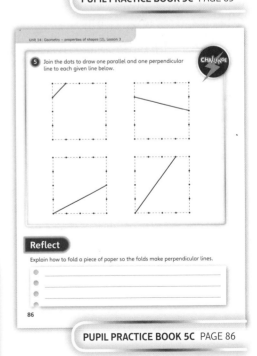

PUPIL PRACTICE BOOK 5C PAGE 86

Regular and irregular polygons

Learning focus

In this lesson, children will deepen their understanding of the concepts of regular and irregular polygons by considering them in terms of their knowledge of angles and lengths.

Small steps

→ Previous step: Reasoning about parallel and perpendicular lines
→ **This step: Regular and irregular polygons**
→ Next step: Reasoning about 3D shapes

NATIONAL CURRICULUM LINKS

Year 5 Geometry – Properties of Shapes

Distinguish between regular and irregular polygons based on reasoning about equal sides and angles.

ASSESSING MASTERY

Children can recognise common regular polygons and can justify why a given polygon does or does not meet the criteria necessary to be regular, based on angle size or lengths of sides.

COMMON MISCONCEPTIONS

Children may rely on visual intuition which will lead to misidentification in certain cases. Ask:
• *How can you tell for sure whether this shape is regular or irregular? What equipment can you use to check?*

STRENGTHENING UNDERSTANDING

Children should explore different shapes by manipulating them on geoboards or using construction materials to form models of 2D shapes. Encourage children to explore whether sides are the same length and to investigate the size of the angles in the shapes.

GOING DEEPER

Challenge children to consider how the properties of different grids restrict the formation of certain regular polygons. Do the properties of grids prevent children from making certain shapes with all the same length sides and the same sized angles?

Challenge children to make and justify general statements about regular polygons.

KEY LANGUAGE

In lesson: regular, irregular, polygon, rhombus, rectangle, octagon, pentagon, sides, angles

Other language to be used by the teacher: polygon, quadrilateral, vertices

STRUCTURES AND REPRESENTATIONS

2D shapes

RESOURCES

Mandatory: protractors, rulers

Optional: geoboards, squared paper, construction materials such as strips of card, split pins, geostrips

 In the eTextbook of this lesson, you will find interactive links to a selection of teaching tools.

Before you teach

• What do children remember about regular and irregular shapes?
• Can children define 'quadrilateral'?
• Do children know how to measure the angles in a given shape?

Discover

ASK

- Question **1** a): *What does 'polygon' mean?*
- Question **1** a): *How could you find the size of the interior angles?*
- Question **1** a): *Could the grid help identify the size of each angle?*
- Question **1** b): *What are the properties of a regular shape?*

IN FOCUS Question **1** a) encourages children to consider what is meant by the interior angles of a shape and discuss different ways to work out each angle. For question **1** b), children should discuss what is meant by the phrase 'regular polygon' in general and 'regular octagon' in particular.

PRACTICAL TIPS This could be made a practical task by giving children geoboards to model shapes on. Ask children to copy the octagon from the **Discover** task. Alternatively, children could draw the octagon onto squared paper, making sure they carefully match what they see in the picture.

ANSWERS

Question **1** a): Every interior angle is 135°. Isla is correct.

Question **1** b): The sides are not all the same length. Richard is not correct. This is an irregular octagon.

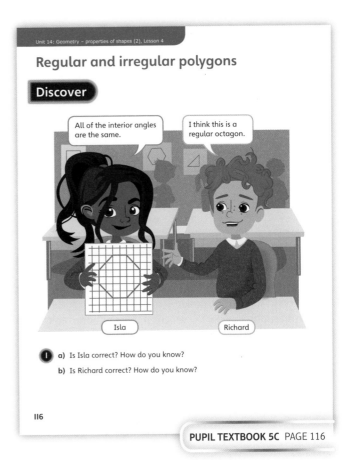

PUPIL TEXTBOOK 5C PAGE 116

Share

WAYS OF WORKING Whole class teacher led

ASK

- Question **1** a): *Which is the most accurate or efficient method for finding the size of these angles?*
- Question **1** a): *What do you notice when you compare each angle?*
- Question **1** a): *Can you always use the grid to find the size of an angle?*
- Question **1** b): *Can you prove that the diagonals are longer than the other lines? Are diagonal lines always longer?*

IN FOCUS The main point of question **1** is to recap the core concepts of regular and irregular polygons: that regular polygons have angles that are all the same and have sides that are all the same length.

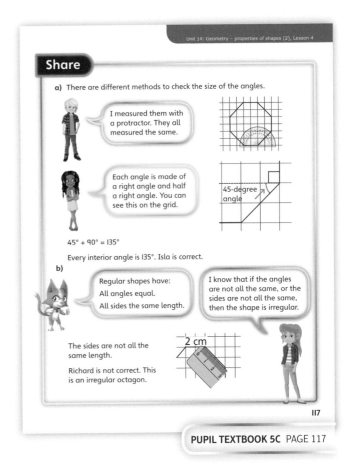

PUPIL TEXTBOOK 5C PAGE 117

Think together

WAYS OF WORKING Whole class teacher led (I do, We do, You do)

ASK

- Question **1**: *Is a shape definitely regular if its sides are all the same length?*
- Question **1**: *What two aspects do you need to check to decide if a shape is regular?*
- Question **2**: *Can you convince me that the angles are, or are not, all the same size?*
- Question **3**: *How many different regular quadrilaterals are there?*

IN FOCUS Question **1** focuses on the variations that cause irregularity: same lengths but different angles, same angles but different lengths, different lengths and different angle size. This reinforces how important it is for children to check everything before making a decision on whether a shape is regular or irregular.

Question **3** challenges children to consider how different geoboards and grids support different types of regular shapes.

STRENGTHEN It would be beneficial if children had access to geoboards to explore the construction of different regular and irregular shapes on different grids. Alternatively, children could make shapes with strips of card and split pins.

DEEPEN Challenge children to make and test general statements about regular and irregular shapes, such as 'A regular shape has right angles'.

ASSESSMENT CHECKPOINT Question **2** requires a sound understanding of the core concept about regular and irregular polygons. Look out for clear understanding of the two different aspects required for a regular polygon, both equal sides and equal angles. The question also allows assessment of accurate measuring skills with a ruler and protractor.

ANSWERS

Question **1**: The rhombus is irregular because the angles are not all the same size.
The rectangle is irregular because the sides are different lengths.
The hexagon is irregular because the sides are different lengths and the angles are not the same size.

Question **2**: Shape B is regular because all the sides are the same lengths and all the angles are the same size.

Question **3** a): Max should use the square-dotted geoboard for a regular quadrilateral (square, in different orientations) and Ambika should use the isometric geoboard for a regular hexagon.

Question **3** b): Max and Ambika could make squares on the square-dotted geoboard.
They could make equilateral triangles and regular hexagons on the isometric geoboard. It is also possible to make squares on the isometric geoboard.

Question **3** c): They cannot make regular pentagons or octagons on either geoboard.

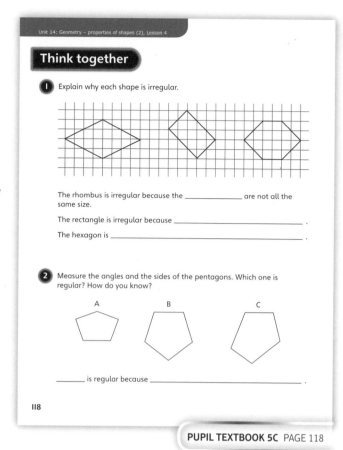

Think together

1 Explain why each shape is irregular.

The rhombus is irregular because the _____ are not all the same size.

The rectangle is irregular because _____ .

The hexagon is _____ .

2 Measure the angles and the sides of the pentagons. Which one is regular? How do you know?

A   B   C

_____ is regular because _____ .

118

PUPIL TEXTBOOK 5C PAGE 118

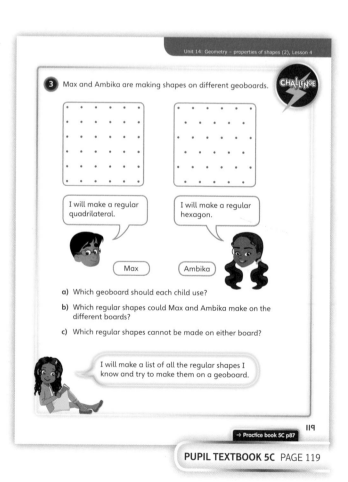

3 Max and Ambika are making shapes on different geoboards.

I will make a regular quadrilateral.

I will make a regular hexagon.

Max   Ambika

a) Which geoboard should each child use?

b) Which regular shapes could Max and Ambika make on the different boards?

c) Which regular shapes cannot be made on either board?

I will make a list of all the regular shapes I know and try to make them on a geoboard.

→ Practice book 5C p87

119

PUPIL TEXTBOOK 5C PAGE 119

Practice

WAYS OF WORKING Independent thinking

IN FOCUS Question ❶ requires children to reason about whether or not different polygons meet both the criteria for being regular. This cements the thinking that children need to look at both the angles and the lengths of the sides in order to determine whether a shape is regular.

Question ❷ prompts consideration of the case of regular triangles (equilateral triangles).

STRENGTHEN Encourage children to draw copies of the shapes in questions ❹ and ❺ onto squared or isometric paper, then cut them out and move them around to help visualise the shapes fitting together.

DEEPEN Deepen learning for question ❹ by providing children with new shapes and asking them to predict which shapes will join together to make a regular shape.

THINK DIFFERENTLY Question ❸ requires children to explain the mistaken assumption that having equal angles is sufficient to meet the requirements for a shape being regular.

ASSESSMENT CHECKPOINT Questions ❶ and ❷ cover the fundamental concepts. In question ❷, children may mistake a right-angled triangle for a regular shape, as it looks even. Use children's responses to check that they understand that both sides and angles have to be equal for a shape to be regular.

ANSWERS Answers for the **Practice** part of the lesson appear in the separate **Practice and Reflect answer guide**.

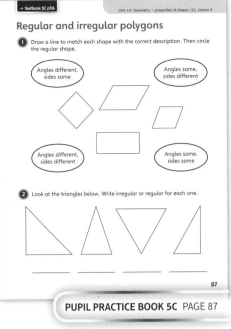

PUPIL PRACTICE BOOK 5C PAGE 87

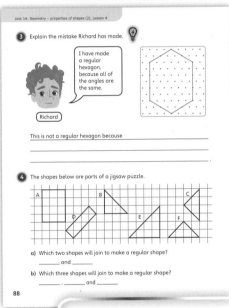

PUPIL PRACTICE BOOK 5C PAGE 88

Reflect

WAYS OF WORKING Pair work

IN FOCUS Children consider the points they have learnt throughout the lesson. Encourage them to explain to a partner the different ways of checking whether a shape is regular or irregular.

ASSESSMENT CHECKPOINT Do children include both angle size and side length as requirements for a regular shape?

ANSWERS Answers for the **Reflect** part of the lesson appear in the separate **Practice and Reflect answer guide**.

After the lesson ⏸

- Can children explain confidently that a shape must meet both criteria to be regular?
- Are children able to justify their reasoning based on the properties of the shapes or the grid on which the shapes are constructed?

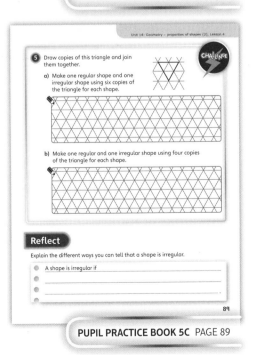

PUPIL PRACTICE BOOK 5C PAGE 89

Reasoning about 3D shapes

Learning focus

In this lesson, children will learn to recognise the different views of 3D shapes or collections when viewed from different positions.

Small steps

→ Previous step: Regular and irregular polygons
→ **This step: Reasoning about 3D shapes**
→ Next step: Reflection

NATIONAL CURRICULUM LINKS

Year 5 Geometry – Properties of Shapes

Identify 3D shapes, including cubes and other cuboids, from 2D representations.

ASSESSING MASTERY

Children can recognise and identify the different viewpoints of common 3D shapes and can reproduce the different views. Children are able to justify the views based on the properties of the 3D shapes themselves, and by visualising the properties of the solid shape from a 2D representation.

COMMON MISCONCEPTIONS

Some children may need support to identify the different viewpoints and to understand that a certain elevation creates a 2D shape. Ask:

• *What would this shape look like from the side or from above?*

STRENGTHENING UNDERSTANDING

Children could explore the concept further by shining a torch onto a shape and noticing the shapes of the shadows cast and how these shadows vary as the angle of the torch or the orientation of the shape varies.

GOING DEEPER

Challenge children to explore and categorise all the different viewpoints of the common 3D shapes that they have access to in class.

KEY LANGUAGE

In lesson: position, face, cylinder, prism, sphere, cuboid, cube, surface, triangle, square, viewpoint, **top view**, **plan view**, **side view**

Other language to be used by the teacher: square-based pyramid, cone

STRUCTURES AND REPRESENTATIONS

3D shapes

RESOURCES

Optional: models of 3D shapes, a torch

 In the eTextbook of this lesson, you will find interactive links to a selection of teaching tools.

Before you teach

• Which 3D shapes can children name and identify?
• Can children explain the definition of the face of a shape?

Discover

WAYS OF WORKING Pair work

ASK

- Question ❶ a): *What are the faces of the cylinder?*
- Question ❶ a): *Would the cylinder look the same from every angle?*
- Question ❶ b): *What is the same and what is different about the viewpoints marked A, B and C?*

IN FOCUS This is an introduction to the idea of viewing a shape from different positions and recording the view as a 2D shape. Children should visualise and discuss their ideas, then check these ideas for themselves.

PRACTICAL TIPS Children could explore this question using 3D shapes and shifting their own perspective to view a shape from the side or above. However, the learning will be more powerful if they spend time discussing what they expect to see before actually testing it for themselves.

ANSWERS

Question ❶ a): From position A, Emma can see only one face of the cylinder. The face is a circle.

Question ❶ b): Bella and Aki each have the same side view of the cylinder. They each see a rectangle.

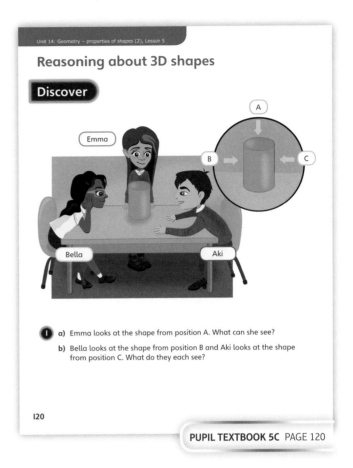

Reasoning about 3D shapes

Discover

❶ a) Emma looks at the shape from position A. What can she see?

b) Bella looks at the shape from position B and Aki looks at the shape from position C. What do they each see?

120

PUPIL TEXTBOOK 5C PAGE 120

Share

WAYS OF WORKING Whole class teacher led

ASK

- Question ❶ b): *How can Bella and Aki see a rectangle when the cylinder has a curved surface?*
- Question ❶ b): *Why do they not also see circles?*
- Question ❶ b): *What would change if the cylinder was positioned differently? What would stay the same?*

IN FOCUS The focus here is for children to explore the idea that different viewpoints will show different elevations, and that these are represented as 2D shapes. Children could explore this for themselves, using models of 3D shapes and physically moving around the shapes while they describe the different 2D elevations they see from different angles.

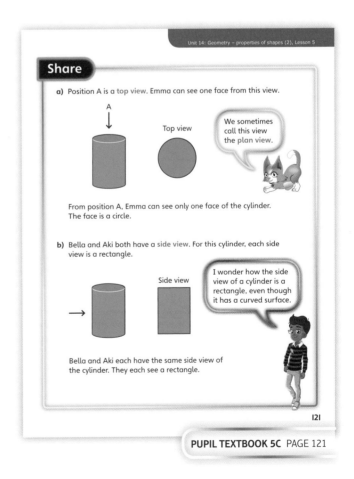

Share

a) Position A is a **top view**. Emma can see one face from this view.

Top view

We sometimes call this view the plan view.

From position A, Emma can see only one face of the cylinder. The face is a circle.

b) Bella and Aki both have a **side view**. For this cylinder, each side view is a rectangle.

Side view

I wonder how the side view of a cylinder is a rectangle, even though it has a curved surface.

Bella and Aki each have the same side view of the cylinder. They each see a rectangle.

121

PUPIL TEXTBOOK 5C PAGE 121

Think together

Whole class teacher led (I do, We do, You do)

ASK

- Question ❶: *What would this shape look like from above?*
- Question ❷: *What are the different faces of this shape?*
- Question ❷: *Which faces can you see from this angle?*
- Question ❷: *Will the side views be the same?*

IN FOCUS Question ❶ considers the views of a shape made from interlocking cubes.

Question ❷ challenges children to draw the different elevations of a prism by predicting and visualising what they expect the viewpoint to show.

Question ❸ challenges children to consider what an arrangement of different items would look like from above.

STRENGTHEN Children could explore variations on question ❶ by constructing different shapes from interlocking cubes and then viewing them from different viewpoints.

DEEPEN Challenge children to identify a shape given only its views: *From above it looks square, from each side it looks triangular. What shape can this be?*

ASSESSMENT CHECKPOINT Correctly answering question ❷ shows a good understanding of the properties of 3D shapes. Use children's responses to gauge their ability to recognise 3D shapes from different viewpoints.

ANSWERS

Question ❶: Option C could not be a view of this cube.

Question ❷: Andy can see a triangle.
Luis can see a rectangle.
Jamie can see a rectangle.

Question ❸: Max can see option B.

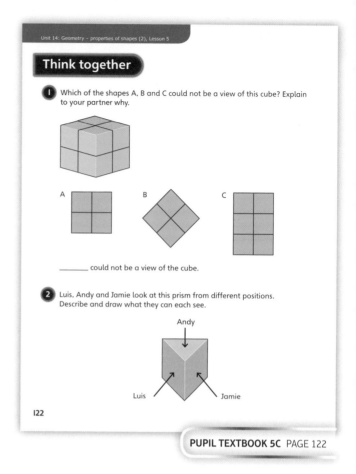

PUPIL TEXTBOOK 5C PAGE 122

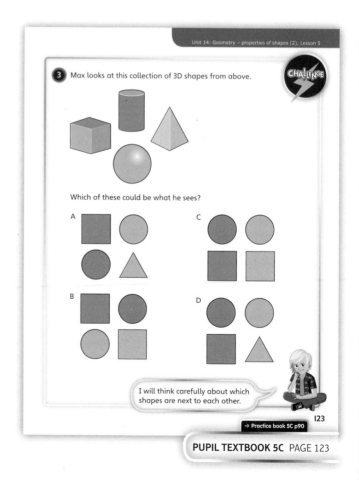

PUPIL TEXTBOOK 5C PAGE 123

Practice

WAYS OF WORKING Independent thinking

IN FOCUS Question ❷ looks at examples of possible views of cuboids and the views that are not possible. This is important as children need to understand which views are not possible in order to fully understand the required properties.

Questions ❸ and ❹ require children to reason about the properties and faces of common 3D shapes, and require children to consider the different possible aspects from different angles.

Question ❺ challenges children to reproduce a series of shapes based on what they would look like from a top view.

STRENGTHEN Children should explore different viewpoints by manipulating models of 3D shapes and shifting their perspective to notice how each view changes.

DEEPEN Question ❺ can be deepened by asking children to draw the 3D shapes if viewed from the side. Alternatively, give children a group of 2D shapes and ask children to predict which 3D shapes these could represent if viewed from above.

THINK DIFFERENTLY Question ❸ requires children to visualise the whole shape mentally by considering the different views from different positions.

ASSESSMENT CHECKPOINT Children can use their knowledge of the properties of 2D shapes to visualise the faces of 3D shapes. Look at children's answers to question ❷ to assess their visualisation and their answers to questions ❸ and ❹ to assess their knowledge of the properties of different shapes.

ANSWERS Answers for the **Practice** part of the lesson appear in the separate **Practice and Reflect answer guide**.

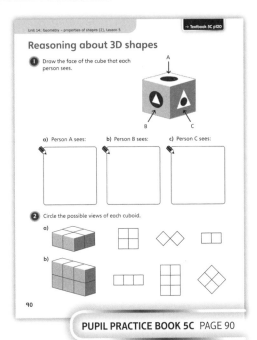

PUPIL PRACTICE BOOK 5C PAGE 90

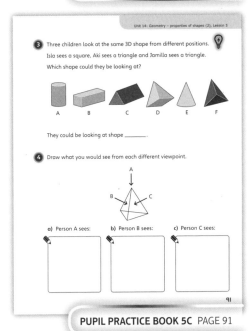

PUPIL PRACTICE BOOK 5C PAGE 91

Reflect

WAYS OF WORKING Independent thinking

IN FOCUS Children should perform this without using a model of the prism. The key skill is that they visualise the shape, rather than simply copy what they can see.

ASSESSMENT CHECKPOINT Have children drawn two rectangles and one triangle? Were they able to visualise the correct 3D shape without extra help?

ANSWERS Answers for the **Reflect** part of the lesson appear in the separate **Practice and Reflect answer guide**.

After the lesson ⏸

- Are children able to visualise what a shape will look like from different viewpoints?
- Can children justify their visualisations based on the properties of the 3D shapes?

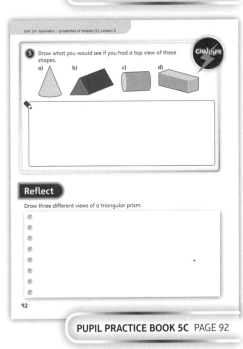

PUPIL PRACTICE BOOK 5C PAGE 92

End of unit check

> Don't forget the *Power Maths* unit assessment grid on p26.

WAYS OF WORKING Group work – adult led

IN FOCUS
- Question ❶ checks understanding of parallel lines in shapes.
- Question ❷ asks children to identify perpendicular lines and addresses the misconception that perpendicular lines must cross.
- Question ❸ challenges children to combine parallel and perpendicular concepts in shapes.
- Question ❹ tests understanding of regular and irregular shapes.
- Questions ❺ and ❻ check the skill of visualising a 3D shape from different viewpoints.

ANSWERS AND COMMENTARY Children who have mastered the concepts in this unit will be able to identify and construct parallel and perpendicular lines, follow logical chains of reasoning about parallel and perpendicular lines in shapes, and apply their understanding of angles to regular and irregular shapes. They will also be able to visualise what a 3D shape will look like from different viewpoints.

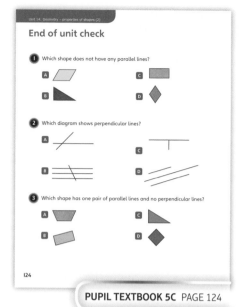

PUPIL TEXTBOOK 5C PAGE 124

PUPIL TEXTBOOK 5C PAGE 125

Q	A	WRONG ANSWERS AND MISCONCEPTIONS	STRENGTHENING UNDERSTANDING
1	B	A or D suggest children do not recognise that parallel lines can be oriented diagonally.	Allow children access to sketching and construction materials to support but not replace reasoning.
2	C	A or B suggest children think perpendicular lines must cross.	In question 6, encourage children to use squared paper to replicate the squares on each face of the cuboid.
3	A	B, C or D suggest children do not recognise perpendicular lines oriented diagonally.	
4	D	A, B or C suggest children do not fully understand how to recognise irregular shapes.	
5	A	D suggests children may be confused by the curved surface of the cylinder.	
6	Sketches of 2×1, 5×1 and 5×2 rectangles	Drawing squares suggests children have not visualised the cuboid correctly. Have children considered the width of each face?	

My journal

WAYS OF WORKING Independent thinking

ANSWERS AND COMMENTARY

Question **1** :

Children should use diagrams and annotations to explain how to draw parallel and perpendicular lines in different orientations on the different grids. They should explain how the different properties of the two grids mean that you have to adapt your strategy for drawing the two kinds of line. Explanations should show a good understanding of how to construct a variety of parallel and perpendicular lines. Ensure children have also included the arrow markings to identify their parallel lines.

Question **2** :

Children should draw three different hexagons and correctly label all the lines. When answering this question, look for children who experiment with different types of hexagon, both regular and irregular. Encourage them to predict whether a regular hexagon would have more parallel lines than an irregular one. Children should explain the thinking behind their prediction.

Check that children describe any lines with the correct terminology and are able to label the vertices and make reference to each line using vertices.

Power check

WAYS OF WORKING Independent thinking

ASK

- *What new skills have you learnt?*
- *Can you explain the difference between parallel and perpendicular lines?*
- *Are you confident in checking whether a shape is regular or irregular?*
- *Can you visualise what a 3D shape would look like from different positions?*

Power puzzle

WAYS OF WORKING Pair work or small groups

IN FOCUS Use this **Power puzzle** to give children the opportunity to explore the construction of a regular shape from an irregular shape.

ANSWERS AND COMMENTARY Although this may appear to be a simple folding task, many children will find this challenging.

Children who master the folds can continue to fold smaller and smaller squares as the strip left over decreases in size. Challenge children to explain why the shape becomes less square-like as the errors accumulate and an accurate fold becomes more challenging as the paper decreases in size.

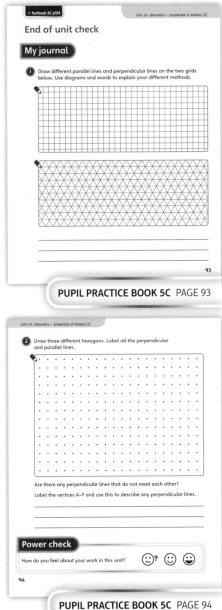

PUPIL PRACTICE BOOK 5C PAGE 93

PUPIL PRACTICE BOOK 5C PAGE 94

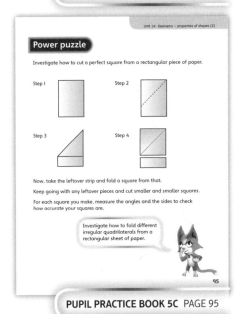

PUPIL PRACTICE BOOK 5C PAGE 95

After the unit ⏸

- Can children identify and construct parallel and perpendicular lines in different orientations?
- Are children able to reason whether a shape is regular or irregular, and check the angles carefully?
- Do children support their ideas with geometric reasoning?

Strengthen and **Deepen** activities for this unit can be found in the *Power Maths* online subscription.

Unit 15
Geometry – position and direction

Mastery Expert tip! *"I used the ideas of reflection and translation in Art. The children created reflective patterns and made pictures using one shape translated and reflected!"*

Don't forget to watch the Unit 15 video!

WHY THIS UNIT IS IMPORTANT

This unit teaches children about the position and orientation of shapes and how to reflect and translate points and shapes efficiently using coordinates. It builds on skills gained in Year 4 (plotting coordinates) and enables children to progress to problem solving involving position and direction in Year 6.

WHERE THIS UNIT FITS

→ Unit 14: Geometry – properties of shapes (2)

→ **Unit 15: Geometry – position and direction**

→ Unit 16: Measure – converting units

This unit builds on skills children will have gained in Year 4 – using coordinates in the first quadrant to plot points on a grid – and in previous Year 5 units on properties of shapes. It enables them to use these skills to plot reflections and translations. In Year 6, children will use coordinates in all four quadrants to complete reflections and translations, using them to solve problems.

Before they start this unit, it is expected that children:

- can plot and identify coordinates in the first quadrant
- can describe 2D shapes using appropriate vocabulary relating to their properties (vertex, parallel, vertical, horizontal)
- can describe positions of 2D shapes including left, right, up, down.

ASSESSING MASTERY

Children can plot and find coordinates of a reflected shape on a grid. They are able to use coordinates to find translations. Children confidently identify reflections and translations and describe them.

COMMON MISCONCEPTIONS	STRENGTHENING UNDERSTANDING	GOING DEEPER
Children may translate a shape vertically or horizontally instead of reflecting it.	Provide children with mirrors to explore reflections. Ask them to predict the reflection and then check by placing the mirror on the mirror line.	Children can explore drawing and plotting reflections in vertical and horizontal mirror lines on different types of paper such as square dotted paper, isometric paper and hexagonal grid paper.
Children may think that translation instructions (for example, left 5) refer to the distance between the original shape and the translated image, rather than the distance between each vertex on the original shape and the corresponding vertex on the image.	Ask children to cut out 2D shapes from squared paper so they can physically move them on a grid and place them in the new position. They should practise counting how far each vertex has moved: does this match the translation instruction?	Look at translations of more complex 2D shapes – for example, translations involving more than one step. Use coordinates without a grid for support: a translation of 4 left 3 up on (5,10) results in the coordinate $(5 - 4, 10 + 3) = (1,13)$.

WAYS OF WORKING

Use these pages to discuss with children the vocabulary and what they can remember about reading coordinates and reflections. Point out that Ash's diagram shows a reflection of a rectangle; the mirror line is shown by the dotted line. Revise reading and plotting coordinates, reminding children that a coordinate tells you how far away a point is from the origin, the coordinate (0,0). For example, (2,3) is 2 right 3 up from the origin. Briefly consider Dexter's diagram, which uses arrows to show the distance between two points. You may wish to use the terms right, left, up, down to compare the position of the two points in relation to each other.

STRUCTURES AND REPRESENTATIONS

Coordinate grids: A variety of coordinate grids in the first quadrant, on both squared paper and blank paper, are used in these lessons.

i)
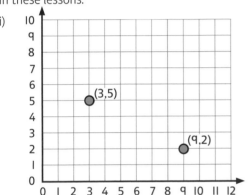

ii)
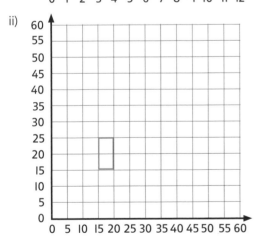

KEY LANGUAGE

There is some key language that children will need to know as part of the learning in this unit.

➜ reflection, translation

➜ mirror line

➜ coordinate, horizontal coordinate, vertical coordinate

➜ horizontal axis, vertical axis

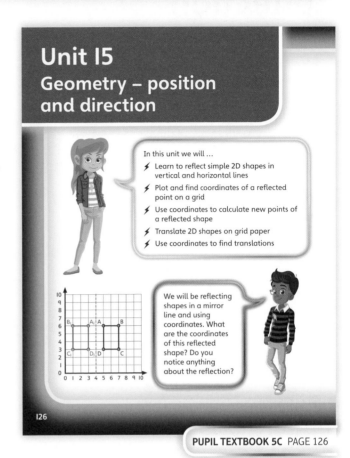

PUPIL TEXTBOOK 5C PAGE 126

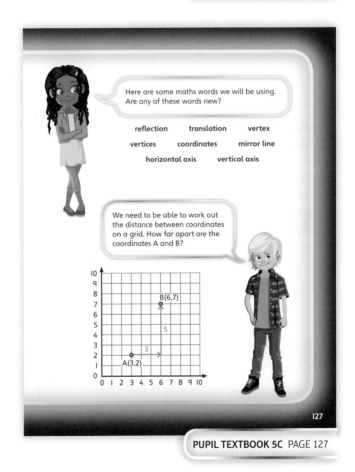

PUPIL TEXTBOOK 5C PAGE 127

Reflection

Learning focus

In this lesson, children will explore reflection. They will learn to reflect simple 2D shapes in vertical and horizontal lines. Children will explore drawing reflections on different types of paper (squared, square dotted, isometric).

Small steps

→ Previous step: Reasoning about 3D shapes
→ **This step: Reflection**
→ Next step: Reflection with coordinates

NATIONAL CURRICULUM LINKS

Year 5 Geometry – Position and Direction

Identify, describe and represent the position of a shape following a reflection or translation, using the appropriate language, and know that the shape has not changed.

ASSESSING MASTERY

Children can reflect simple 2D shapes in horizontal and vertical mirror lines. They confidently use the terms 'reflect', 'reflection' and 'mirror line' and understand that the shape does not change in size or shape but will face in a different direction (orientation). Children can accurately draw reflections in mirror lines on different types of paper and can identify whether a given reflection is correct. They are able to explain errors.

COMMON MISCONCEPTIONS

Children may simply transfer the shape to the other side of the mirror line, rather than reflecting it. Ask:
• *How many squares away from the mirror line is point A? Where should the reflected point be on the other side of the mirror line? Is each point the same distance away from the mirror line?*

STRENGTHENING UNDERSTANDING

Provide children with mirrors to explore reflections. Ask children to predict what the reflection will look like and then check by placing the mirror on the mirror line. Discuss, in detail, pictures and photographs of reflections. Cut 2D shapes out of thin card and model how the shape 'flips over' but does not change size or shape in a reflection. Mark a point with a dot to show where that point is when the shape has been reflected. Make sure reflected images are drawn accurately using the grid lines.

GOING DEEPER

Practise reflecting more complex shapes with several diagonal sides or by using different types of paper: squared, isometric or dotted. Ask children to draw and reflect the (capital) letters of the alphabet and place them in two groups: 1) reflection is different; 2) reflection is exactly the same (answers will vary depending on whether the mirror line is horizontal or vertical).

KEY LANGUAGE

In lesson: reflection, reflect, **mirror line**, vertex, symmetric, predict, isometric grid

Other language used by the teacher: mirror image, translation, orientation, flip over, position, direction

STRUCTURES AND REPRESENTATIONS

2D shapes

RESOURCES

Mandatory: mirrors, squared paper, square dotted paper, isometric paper, rulers

Optional: images of reflections

 In the eTextbook of this lesson, you will find interactive links to a selection of teaching tools.

Before you teach

• Are children able to use the correct language to describe 2D shapes: vertex, side, parallel, symmetric, right angle?

Discover

WAYS OF WORKING Pair work

ASK

- Question ❶ a): *What is a reflection?*
- Question ❶ a): *How many mirror lines are shown in this image?*
- Question ❶ a): *What happens to the shape when it is reflected? Does the shape change size?*
- Question ❶ b): *Does it matter if the reflection is not exactly on the grid lines?*

IN FOCUS The image shows a triangle with four mirror lines. Encourage children to place a mirror on each of the mirror lines, discussing what they can see. Explore what happens to the shape when it is reflected – ask: *Does the shape change?* It is important to spend a significant amount of time using the mirrors to develop children's understanding of what reflections look like. Children should also realise the importance of accurate drawing: make sure they use a ruler and ensure the shape is drawn on the grid lines.

PRACTICAL TIPS Provide children with mirrors, irregular 2D shapes and squared paper to explore reflections and mirror lines.

Demonstrate how to place the mirror on the mirror lines to see the reflections.

ANSWERS

Question ❶ a):

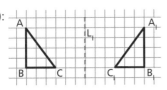

Question ❶ b):

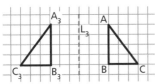

Share

WAYS OF WORKING Whole class teacher led

ASK

- Question ❶ a): *In which line are you reflecting the shape?*
- Question ❶ a): *What has happened to each vertex – where has it moved to?*
- Question ❶ b): *Where will each point/vertex of the shape be when you have reflected the shape?*
- Question ❶ b): *Can you check your answer using a mirror?*

IN FOCUS This part of the lesson shows, step-by-step, how to reflect a shape one vertex at a time. Show children how to count squares from the vertex to the mirror line. Ask children to draw the problem onto squared paper. Can they use a mirror to check their answers? Discuss if and how the shape has changed – ensure children understand that the shape has not changed in size or shape, only in position/orientation. Use a triangle cut out of thin card to model this, marking a dot at one of the vertices: show how the shape is 'flipped over' and where the vertex with the dot has moved to.

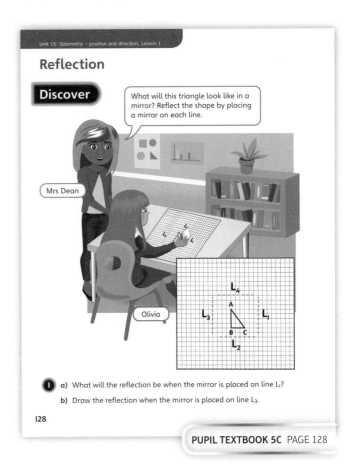

PUPIL TEXTBOOK 5C PAGE 128

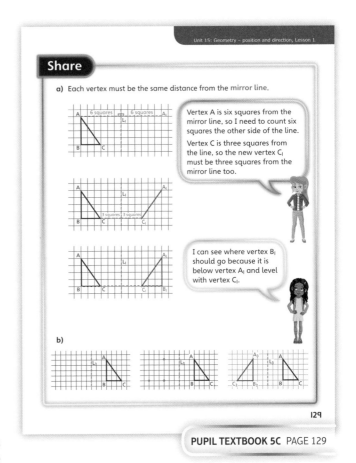

PUPIL TEXTBOOK 5C PAGE 129

Think together

Whole class teacher led (I do, We do, You do)

ASK

- Question **1**: *How far is each vertex from the mirror line?*
- Questions **1** and **2**: *Where will each reflected vertex be?*
- Question **3**: *Can you predict where to hold a mirror?*

IN FOCUS In questions **1** and **2**, children draw reflections of simple 2D shapes one vertex at a time and check their drawings using a mirror. Give children square dotted and isometric paper.

STRENGTHEN Ensure children have plenty of opportunities to check reflections with a mirror and to discuss what has happened to the shape and to each vertex of the shape.

DEEPEN Encourage children to practise drawing similar 2D shapes and reflecting them.

ASSESSMENT CHECKPOINT Can children draw the reflection in a mirror line one vertex at a time? Do they know to count squares to find the position of reflected vertices?

ANSWERS

Question **1**:

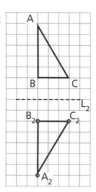

Question **2**: Bella has moved the shape up rather than reflecting it.

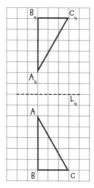

Question **3** a): To turn the 9 into a 6 you need to reflect the shape in mirror line 1 and then reflect in mirror line 2. Alternatively you could reflect in mirror line 2 and then in mirror line 1.

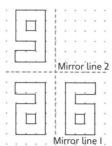

Question **3** b):

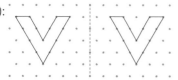

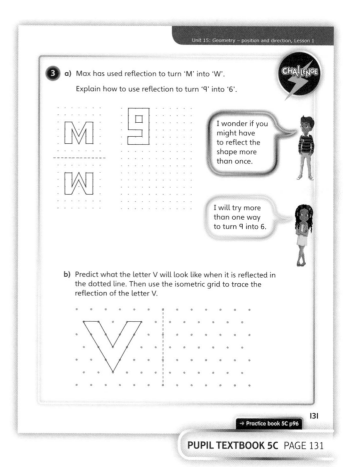

Think together

1 Complete the reflection of the triangle in L₂.

2 Bella drew the symmetric figure of ABC, reflected in the mirror line L₄.

Explain her mistake. Then draw the correct reflection on squared paper.

130

PUPIL TEXTBOOK 5C PAGE 130

3 a) Max has used reflection to turn 'M' into 'W'.

Explain how to use reflection to turn '9' into '6'.

I wonder if you might have to reflect the shape more than once.

I will try more than one way to turn 9 into 6.

b) Predict what the letter V will look like when it is reflected in the dotted line. Then use the isometric grid to trace the reflection of the letter V.

131

→ Practice book 5C p96

PUPIL TEXTBOOK 5C PAGE 131

162

Practice

WAYS OF WORKING Independent thinking

IN FOCUS Question **2** involves reflecting the numbers 5 and 3, drawn on square dotted paper so they look as they would on a digital clock face. Children may see the shapes as an S and a back-to-front E, so help them to recognise the numbers if necessary. Encourage children to check each drawing by placing a mirror on the mirror line.

STRENGTHEN Spend time exploring reflections by placing a mirror on the mirror line and discussing what happens to the shape. Encourage children to write capital letters or other numbers to see what they look like when reflected. Ask them to explain what has changed (orientation) and what has not changed (size and shape).

DEEPEN Ask children to draw and reflect the numbers 1 to 9 on squared, square dotted or isometric paper. Which paper is easier to draw numbers on? Which paper do children prefer and why?

THINK DIFFERENTLY In question **3**, children are given the original shape and the reflection and asked to draw the mirror line. Provide mirrors for children to check their answers.

ASSESSMENT CHECKPOINT Do children understand that reflected shapes do not change in size or shape but are positioned differently? Can children reflect shapes accurately by measuring the distance of each vertex from the mirror line?

ANSWERS Answers to the **Practice** part of the lesson appear in the separate **Practice and Reflect answer guide**.

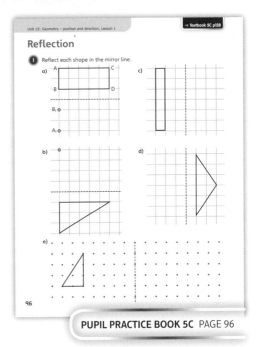

PUPIL PRACTICE BOOK 5C PAGE 96

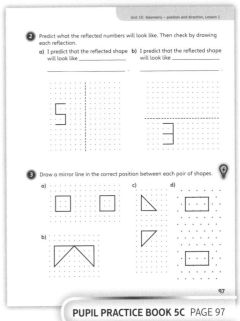

PUPIL PRACTICE BOOK 5C PAGE 97

Reflect

WAYS OF WORKING Independent thinking

IN FOCUS Prompt children by asking: *Which way is the arrow facing? Which way will the arrow be facing once reflected?* Children should identify that the arrow will point to the right (in the opposite direction) after it is reflected. Encourage children to draw the reflection on squared paper and check with a mirror.

ASSESSMENT CHECKPOINT Can children draw and describe reflections in a vertical mirror line accurately? Can they check their answer using a mirror?

ANSWERS Answers to the **Reflect** part of the lesson appear in the separate **Practice and Reflect answer guide**.

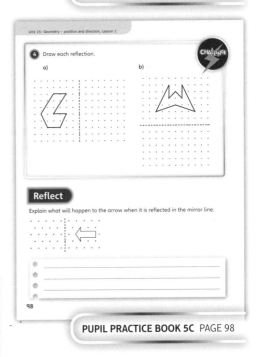

PUPIL PRACTICE BOOK 5C PAGE 98

After the lesson ⏸

- Can children draw reflections accurately?
- What misconceptions did children have relating to reflection?

Reflection with coordinates

Learning focus

In this lesson, children will find the coordinates of a reflected point on a grid. They will use coordinates to calculate new points rather than counting squares.

Small steps

→ Previous step: Reflection
→ **This step: Reflection with coordinates**
→ Next step: Translation

NATIONAL CURRICULUM LINKS

Year 5 Geometry – Position and Direction

Identify, describe and represent the position of a shape following a reflection or translation, using the appropriate language, and know the shape has not changed.

ASSESSING MASTERY

Children can use coordinates to find a reflected point on a grid. They are able to use coordinates to calculate the new point/vertex of a shape by adding or subtracting rather than counting squares. Children can find the coordinates of a reflected 2D shape by plotting each vertex.

COMMON MISCONCEPTIONS

Children may rely on counting squares rather than using coordinates to calculate points. Ask:
• *How could you work out the new coordinate without counting squares?*

When the mirror line is parallel to the axes, children may not see that part of the coordinate stays the same. Ask:
• *How can you tell that one number in this coordinate will stay the same?*

STRENGTHENING UNDERSTANDING

Provide children with coordinate grids to practise reflecting individual points before moving on to shapes. Ask children to work with a partner: partner A places red counters on a 10×10 grid and partner B places yellow counters to indicate the reflection of each point in a vertical mirror line ($x = 5$); then children swap roles. You may wish to encourage children to draw lines to the axes and use number line jumps to show an equal distance either side of the mirror line.

GOING DEEPER

Ask children to explore the coordinates of squares and rectangles set parallel to the axes on a 10×10 coordinate grid and their reflections. Which part of the coordinate stays the same when the mirror line is parallel to the horizontal or vertical axis? Encourage children to use addition or subtraction of the relevant coordinates to work out the reflected vertices, and to predict what will happen to these reflected vertices if the mirror line is moved.

KEY LANGUAGE

In lesson: reflection, reflect, mirror line, grid, coordinates, position

Other language to be used by the teacher: vertex, mirror image, translation, direction, orientation, horizontal axis, vertical axis

STRUCTURES AND REPRESENTATIONS

coordinate grids, 2D shapes

RESOURCES

Optional: mirrors, squared paper

 In the eTextbook of this lesson, you will find interactive links to a selection of teaching tools.

Before you teach

• Are children secure in reflecting simple shapes in a mirror line?
• Can children plot and find coordinates in the first quadrant?

Discover

WAYS OF WORKING Pair work

ASK

- Question **1** a): *How do you read coordinates? What are the coordinates of T?*
- Question **1** a): *Where is the mirror line?*
- Question **1** b): *How far away from the mirror line is coordinate (6,8)?*

IN FOCUS Encourage children to discuss the map. Can they identify the coordinates of point T and find the point (6,8) on the map? Ensure children are able to identify coordinates confidently.

What happens when children put a mirror on the mirror line? Note that it will show an image of where point T and the secret cave will be but will not show the new coordinates correctly.

PRACTICAL TIPS Provide children with mirrors to explore the reflection. Provide a copy of the coordinate grid with the mirror line in place so children can practise plotting and reflecting other points.

ANSWERS

Question **1** a): The true coordinates, T_1, of the treasure are (8,3).

Question **1** b): The coordinates of the secret cave are (4,8).

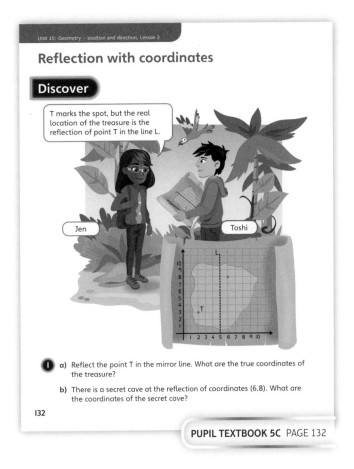

PUPIL TEXTBOOK 5C PAGE 132

Share

WAYS OF WORKING Whole class teacher led

ASK

- Question **1** a): *What do you need to do to answer the question?*
- Question **1** a): *What has happened to the vertical coordinate of the reflected point?*
- Question **1** b): *How have the coordinates of the reflected point been worked out? Which part of the coordinate has not changed?*

IN FOCUS Model how to use addition or subtraction to find new coordinates. For example, 5 + 3 = 8, so the horizontal coordinate is 8. Encourage children to use this method rather than counting squares. You could also discuss how adding (or subtracting) double the distance to the original horizontal coordinate will give the new horizontal coordinate – for example, in part a), 2 + 6 = 8; in part b), 6 – 2 = 4). Highlight that when the mirror line is vertical the vertical coordinate does not change. If the mirror line is horizontal, the horizontal coordinate will not change. Explore examples with the class.

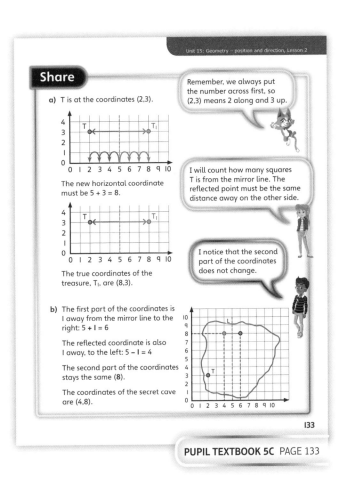

PUPIL TEXTBOOK 5C PAGE 133

Think together

Whole class teacher led (I do, We do, You do)

ASK

- Question **1**: *Where is the mirror line?*
- Question **2**: *How far are the coordinates from the mirror line? How can you use this to work out the coordinates of the reflection?*
- Question **3**: *What can you tell me about the coordinates of the rectangle? Which parts of the coordinates are the same/ different? How will this help you to find the coordinates of the reflected rectangle?*

IN FOCUS For questions **1** and **2**, concentrate on the method of adding or subtracting the distance from the mirror line to the original coordinate to work out the reflected coordinate. Explain that children can also add or subtract double this distance to or from the original coordinate. Ensure children understand which coordinate does not change when the mirror line is vertical (the vertical coordinate) or horizontal (the horizontal coordinate). In question **3** a), there are no grid lines; look out for children trying to draw them in, so they can count squares rather than adding or subtracting. Discuss how to work out how long and high the rectangle is using the coordinates (height = 14 − 11 = 3; length = 11 − 6 = 5).

STRENGTHEN For questions **2** and **3**, provide coordinate grid paper so children can explore drawing rectangles parallel to the axes. Ask them to write the coordinates of each vertex and identify which parts of the coordinates 'match' and which parts change. Encourage children to practise reflecting one rectangle in different mirror lines (vertical and horizontal) to consolidate which parts of the coordinates change and which do not. Relate the difference between original and reflected coordinates to the distance from the mirror line to the original rectangle.

DEEPEN Enable children to explore reflecting parallelograms in horizontal and vertical mirror lines.

ASSESSMENT CHECKPOINT Can children identify the new coordinates when a point is reflected? Can they identify the new coordinates when a rectangle is reflected? Can children calculate reflected coordinates without counting the squares?

ANSWERS

Question **1**: A_1 (2,5), B_1 (3,6), C_1 (7,1)

Question **2**: A_1 (8,11), B_1 (8,14), C_1 (3,14), D_1 (3,11)

Question **3** a): A_1 (6,5), B_1 (11,5), C_1 (6,2), D_1 (11,2)

Question **3** b): P (12,4), Q (12,10), R (9,7), P_1 (2,4), Q_1 (2,10), R_1 (5,7)

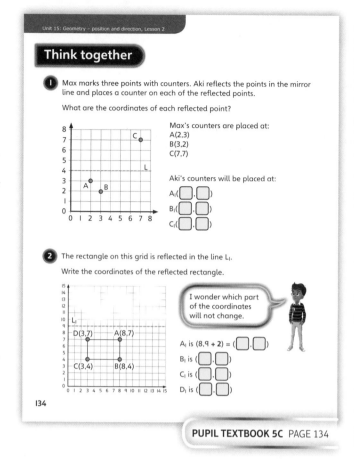

Think together

1 Max marks three points with counters. Aki reflects the points in the mirror line and places a counter on each of the reflected points.

What are the coordinates of each reflected point?

Max's counters are placed at:
A(2,3)
B(3,2)
C(7,7)

Aki's counters will be placed at:

A_1([ ],[ ])

B_1([ ],[ ])

C_1([ ],[ ])

2 The rectangle on this grid is reflected in the line L_1.

Write the coordinates of the reflected rectangle.

I wonder which part of the coordinates will not change.

A_1 is (8,9 + 2) = ([ ],[ ])

B_1 is ([ ],[ ])

C_1 is ([ ],[ ])

D_1 is ([ ],[ ])

134

PUPIL TEXTBOOK 5C PAGE 134

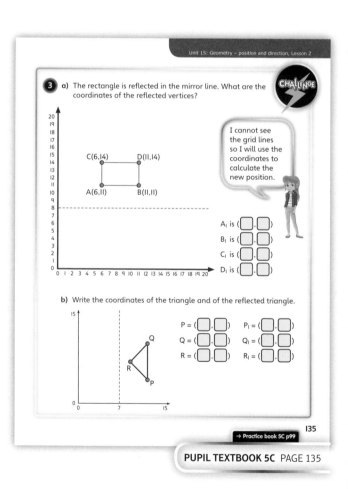

3 a) The rectangle is reflected in the mirror line. What are the coordinates of the reflected vertices?

CHALLENGE

I cannot see the grid lines so I will use the coordinates to calculate the new position.

A_1 is ([ ],[ ])

B_1 is ([ ],[ ])

C_1 is ([ ],[ ])

D_1 is ([ ],[ ])

b) Write the coordinates of the triangle and of the reflected triangle.

P = ([ ],[ ]) P_1 = ([ ],[ ])

Q = ([ ],[ ]) Q_1 = ([ ],[ ])

R = ([ ],[ ]) R_1 = ([ ],[ ])

135

→ Practice book 5C p99

PUPIL TEXTBOOK 5C PAGE 135

Practice

WAYS OF WORKING Independent thinking

IN FOCUS In question **6**, children will need to identify the coordinates of all the vertices. Two can be deduced from the markings on the axes: (22,14) and (22,20). Discuss how to find the length of the sides using the vertical coordinates given (20 – 14 = 6); this will allow children to identify the other two coordinates: (28,14) and (28,20). Some children may need to draw the reflected square and plot each point to see where it lies. Encourage more able children to just mark on the axes where the reflection will be.

STRENGTHEN In question **2**, discuss which parts of the coordinates stay the same and which are changed and by how much, depending on the distance from the mirror line. Can children see that you add or subtract double the distance from the mirror line to the horizontal or vertical coordinate? Do they understand that one part of the coordinate will not change when the mirror line is horizontal or vertical?

DEEPEN Give each child a 12×12 coordinate grid and ask them to mark the four vertices of a rectangle or square, plus a mirror line. Children then swap with a partner to work out the vertices of the reflected shape. Can they work out the new vertices even if the image does not lie within the grid they have?

THINK DIFFERENTLY In question **5**, fewer numbers are provided on the axes of the grid. Children should realise that they still have enough information to complete the task: they can use their knowledge of scales and number lines to find the correct coordinates for the reflected shape.

ASSESSMENT CHECKPOINT Can children calculate the reflected coordinates using addition or subtraction rather than by counting squares? Can children explain which part of the coordinate will/will not change with a given mirror line?

ANSWERS Answers for the **Practice** part of the lesson appear in the separate **Practice and Reflect answer guide**.

Reflect

WAYS OF WORKING Independent thinking

IN FOCUS Look out for mention of: identifying that one part of the coordinate will change and one will not; working out the distance from the mirror line; adjusting the horizontal coordinate by that distance for a vertical mirror line or adjusting the vertical coordinate for a horizontal mirror line (either by adding or subtracting double the distance or by adding/subtracting the distance from the mirror line).

If children use the image, they should refer to subtracting 6 (or 3 + 3) from the horizontal coordinate for the vertical mirror line, or subtracting 6 (or 3 + 3) from the vertical coordinate for the horizontal mirror line.

ASSESSMENT CHECKPOINT Can children explain how to calculate a reflected point using coordinates? Can they give an example when explaining?

ANSWERS Answers for the **Reflect** part of the lesson appear in the separate **Practice and Reflect answer guide**.

After the lesson

- Are all children confident in reading coordinates?
- Do children understand which coordinate does not change when reflecting in a line parallel to one of the axes (vertical or horizontal)?

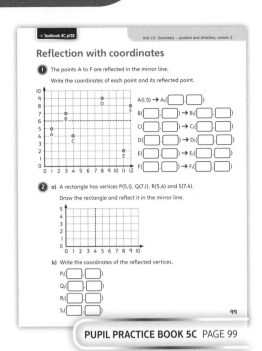

PUPIL PRACTICE BOOK 5C PAGE 99

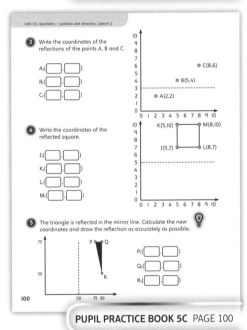

PUPIL PRACTICE BOOK 5C PAGE 100

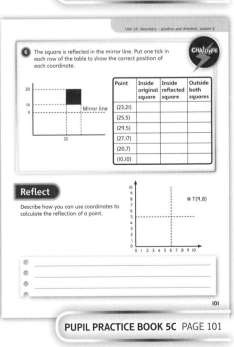

PUPIL PRACTICE BOOK 5C PAGE 101

Translation

Learning focus

In this lesson, children will explore translations. They will learn how to translate simple 2D shapes on grid paper by moving one vertex at a time. Children will understand that the shape has not changed.

Small steps

→ Previous step: Reflection with coordinates
→ **This step: Translation**
→ Next step: Translation with coordinates

NATIONAL CURRICULUM LINKS

Year 5 Geometry – Position and Direction

Identify, describe and represent the position of a shape following a reflection or translation, using the appropriate language, and know the shape has not changed.

ASSESSING MASTERY

Children can use appropriate language to describe translations: translation, direction, position, vertex, left, right, up, down. They can confidently complete translations of 2D shapes on a grid by moving one vertex at a time. Children understand and can explain that the shape has not changed in any way.

COMMON MISCONCEPTIONS

Children may slide the shape so the translation instruction is applied to the distance between the shape and its translation rather than the distance between corresponding vertices of the two shapes. Ask:
• *How many squares has this vertex moved? Does this match the instruction?*

STRENGTHENING UNDERSTANDING

Provide 2D shapes or cut out 2D shapes from squared paper, so children can physically move them on a grid and place them in a new position. Marking one of the vertices may also help. This will help children to understand that the shape does not change. They will be able to see clearly how far and in which direction the shape has moved.

If you have patio slabs in the school grounds, you could model translations on a large scale outdoors, using the patio squares as a grid and moving cardboard cut outs of shapes. Alternatively, draw a large grid in chalk.

GOING DEEPER

Look at moving more complex 2D shapes. Complete translations involving more than one step, first by plotting each vertex in turn, then by plotting one vertex and using the dimensions to complete the translation.

KEY LANGUAGE

In lesson: position, **translation**, triangle, vertex, coordinates, left, right, up, down, reflection, grid

Other language to be used by the teacher: vertices, 2D shape, distance, plot, translate, rectangle

STRUCTURES AND REPRESENTATIONS

2D shapes

RESOURCES

Optional: squared paper, square dotted paper, 2D shapes cut out of squared paper, chalk

 In the eTextbook of this lesson, you will find interactive links to a selection of teaching tools.

Before you teach

• Can children use the correct language to describe and identify 2D shapes: vertex, sides, parallel?
• Can children describe the change in position of a point on grid paper using right/left/up/down?

Discover

Unit 15: Geometry – position and direction, Lesson 3

WAYS OF WORKING Pair work

ASK

- Question **1** a): *What do the shapes represent?*
- Question **1** a): *In which directions could the bed move? If Bella wanted to move her bed into the top corner, would that be a movement left or right? Up or down?*
- Question **1** b): *Can you work out where the table will move to? Could Bella move her desk by the same amount?*

IN FOCUS Ensure children understand that this is a plan of a bedroom. Provide children with squared paper to draw the new position of the bed. Discuss moving other items, thinking about the maximum distance right/left/up/down each object can be moved.

PRACTICAL TIPS Children could create a plan of their own bedroom on squared paper and cut out each item of furniture from another sheet of paper, so they can physically move the items. Encourage them to explain the movements using the language of translation.

ANSWERS

Question **1** a): The new position of Bella's bed will be above the table.

Question **1** b): The table will now be in the bottom right corner of her room, near the desk.

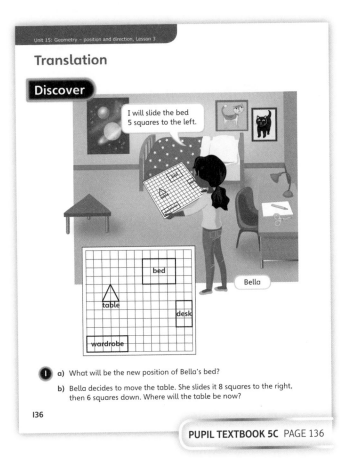

Translation

Discover

1 a) What will be the new position of Bella's bed?

b) Bella decides to move the table. She slides it 8 squares to the right, then 6 squares down. Where will the table be now?

136

PUPIL TEXTBOOK 5C PAGE 136

Share

WAYS OF WORKING Whole class teacher led

ASK

- Question **1** a): *What is a translation? Which movement comes first?*
- Question **1** a): *Where will each point/vertex of the shape be once you have translated the shape?*
- Question **1** b): *Has the size/orientation of the shape changed? What changes when you translate a shape?*
- Question **1**: *How is a translation different to a reflection?*

IN FOCUS Use question **1** a) to discuss what a translation is. Ensure children understand that a translation is a slide left or right, up or down on a grid and that the shape does not change in shape, size or orientation. Identify and discuss any misconceptions about what the translation instruction refers to: it is the distance each vertex moves, not the number of squares between the shape and its translation. Encourage children to use the vocabulary 'translate' and 'translation'. The convention for translations is to give the horizontal direction first, then the vertical (as with coordinates): it is important to establish this now.

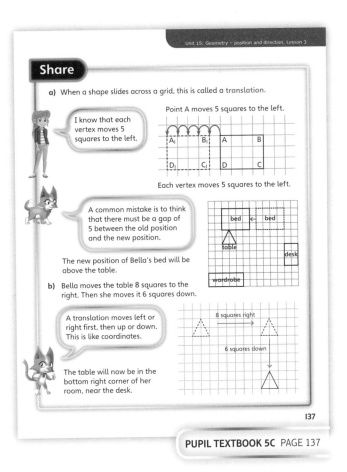

Share

a) When a shape slides across a grid, this is called a translation.

Point A moves 5 squares to the left.

I know that each vertex moves 5 squares to the left.

Each vertex moves 5 squares to the left.

A common mistake is to think that there must be a gap of 5 between the old position and the new position.

The new position of Bella's bed will be above the table.

b) Bella moves the table 8 squares to the right. Then she moves it 6 squares down.

A translation moves left or right first, then up or down. This is like coordinates.

8 squares right

6 squares down

The table will now be in the bottom right corner of her room, near the desk.

137

PUPIL TEXTBOOK 5C PAGE 137

Think together

Whole class teacher led (I do, We do, You do)

ASK

- Question ❶: *Where will each translated vertex be?*
- Question ❷: *What pattern do you see when you reverse a translation?*
- Question ❸: *What is the difference between a translation and a reflection?*

IN FOCUS In this section, children identify the translation between two shapes. In question ❷, the translations involve movement in two directions, so establish that the horizontal movement is stated first, followed by the vertical movement. The easiest way to identify a translation is to focus on a single vertex and work out how it has moved.

In question ❷, discuss how to reverse a translation. Ensure children recognise they need to do the opposite movements. For example left 1 down 2 becomes right 1 up 2.

Discuss the differences between a translation and a reflection using question ❸.

STRENGTHEN Give each child a sheet of squared paper with a shaded rectangle drawn in the middle, labelled A. Provide instructions for children to practise translating this rectangle, labelling the new positions B, C and so on. Begin with one direction only, then move on to translations in two directions.

DEEPEN Use the **Strengthen** activity, but give children a rectilinear shape to translate. Ask them to write the translations from one image to another and back again. Can they generalise about how the instructions change?

ASSESSMENT CHECKPOINT Can children translate a shape by plotting one vertex at a time? Can they identify the translation between two shapes using the correct vocabulary? Do children understand that a shape does not change its size or orientation when translated?

ANSWERS

Question ❶: The desk has moved 3 squares up.

Question ❷ a): A to B: 1 left 2 down; B to A: 1 right 2 up

Question ❷ b): C to D: 3 right 4 down; D to C: 3 left 4 up

Question ❷ c): The numbers stay the same, the directions are reversed.

Question ❸ a): C and E are reflections as the orientation/ direction has changed; B and D are translations as the orientation has not changed.

Question ❸ b): A to B: 2 left 2 up; A to D: 3 right 4 up

Question ❸ c) and d):

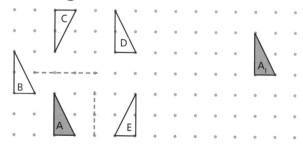

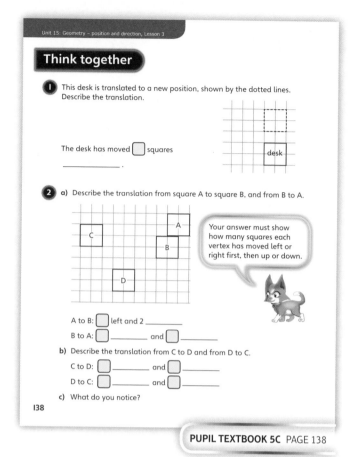

Think together

❶ This desk is translated to a new position, shown by the dotted lines. Describe the translation.

The desk has moved ☐ squares _____.

❷ a) Describe the translation from square A to square B, and from B to A.

Your answer must show how many squares each vertex has moved left or right first, then up or down.

A to B: ☐ left and 2 _____
B to A: ☐ _____ and ☐ _____

b) Describe the translation from C to D and from D to C.

C to D: ☐ _____ and ☐ _____
D to C: ☐ _____ and ☐ _____

c) What do you notice?

138

PUPIL TEXTBOOK 5C PAGE 138

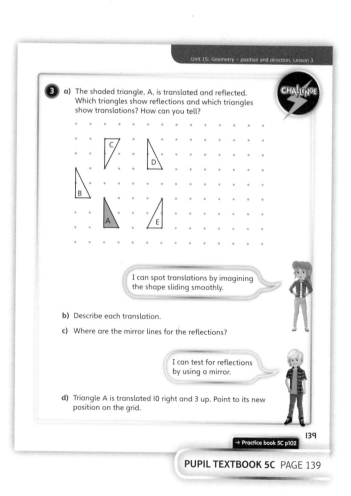

❸ a) The shaded triangle, A, is translated and reflected. Which triangles show reflections and which triangles show translations? How can you tell?

CHALLENGE

I can spot translations by imagining the shape sliding smoothly.

b) Describe each translation.

c) Where are the mirror lines for the reflections?

I can test for reflections by using a mirror.

d) Triangle A is translated 10 right and 3 up. Point to its new position on the grid.

139

→ Practice book 5C p102

PUPIL TEXTBOOK 5C PAGE 139

Practice

WAYS OF WORKING Independent thinking

IN FOCUS In questions ❶ and ❷, children practise translating shapes and identify a translation. In question ❸, children are required to reverse a given translation to identify the starting position of the original shape. They may need to follow a step-by-step approach to interpret what they are being asked to do. Establish that, when going back to the original shape, the instructions are reversed – so right becomes left and up becomes down – but the numbers stay the same.

STRENGTHEN With question ❹, provide a mirror so children can check if the shape has been reflected. Discuss whether the shape looks exactly the same (translation) or has changed in orientation (reflection), and why you can or cannot tell that with this shape.

DEEPEN To extend questions ❺ and ❻, provide children with squared or dotted grid paper and challenge them to create their own problems where one shape is split and parts are translated to form a different shape or picture.

THINK DIFFERENTLY In question ❹, children need to identify whether the movement is a translation or a reflection and explain how they know. The rectangle has not changed in shape, size or orientation but it has moved up, so it is a translation. Some children may need to check with a mirror to see where the reflection would be.

ASSESSMENT CHECKPOINT Can children describe a translation using the correct terminology and in the correct order? Can they translate a simple shape accurately? Do children understand that a translated shape does not change in size or shape but moves left/right, up/down? Can they describe the difference between a reflection and a translation?

ANSWERS Answers for the **Practice** part of the lesson appear in the separate **Practice and Reflect answer guide**.

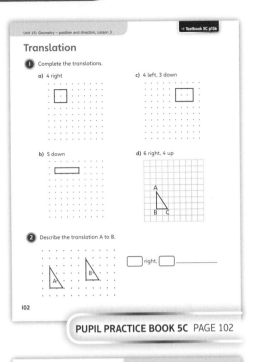

PUPIL PRACTICE BOOK 5C PAGE 102

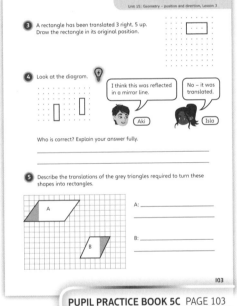

PUPIL PRACTICE BOOK 5C PAGE 103

Reflect

WAYS OF WORKING Independent thinking

IN FOCUS The challenge here is for children to think generally and use only the instructions to answer the question, demonstrating an understanding that to return a shape to its original position, the translation is reversed. For example, left becomes right and up becomes down. If necessary, children can draw a shape onto grid paper and work out the translation visually.

ASSESSMENT CHECKPOINT Can children explain how the translation instructions need to be reversed to return the shape to its original position?

ANSWERS Answers for the **Reflect** part of the lesson appear in the separate **Practice and Reflect answer guide**.

After the lesson

- Can children explain what is meant by the term translation?
- Can children draw translations accurately, using a ruler and keeping to the grid lines?
- Do children understand the difference between reflection and translation?

PUPIL PRACTICE BOOK 5C PAGE 104

171

Translation with coordinates

Learning focus

In this lesson, children will build on knowledge of translation from the previous lesson. They will use coordinates to find translations.

Small steps

→ Previous step: Translation
→ **This step: Translation with coordinates**
→ Next step: Metric units (1)

NATIONAL CURRICULUM LINKS

Year 5 Geometry – Position and Direction

Identify, describe and represent the position of a shape following a reflection or translation, using the appropriate language, and know the shape has not changed.

ASSESSING MASTERY

Children can use coordinates to calculate the new position after a translation. They understand that the shape has not changed in any way. Children can confidently plot the new coordinates of a point and/or shape on a coordinate grid.

COMMON MISCONCEPTIONS

Children may default to counting methods because they do not know which part of the translation to add to or subtract from each part of the coordinate. Ask:
• *Which direction does the horizontal coordinate show? Which direction does the vertical coordinate show? Which coordinate shows up or down?*

STRENGTHENING UNDERSTANDING

Provide children with a coordinate grid and counters. (Alternatively, you could mark out a large grid on the playground and children could move themselves as 'counters'.) Ask children to find the point (2,3) to begin. Then give a list of translations (for example: right 3, up 4; left 2, down 5; right 4, down 1) and ask children to practise using coordinates to find the new position of the counter. Always begin at the original point.

GOING DEEPER

Children can practise calculating a new position using coordinates by playing the game described in the **Discover** section of the **Pupil Textbook**, using a larger grid and 0–9 dice. Encourage them to add to (right/up) or subtract from (left/down) the starting coordinate using the translation numbers. Can they give a combination of two or more double translations (right/left **and** up/down) to get from one point to another?

KEY LANGUAGE

In lesson: translation, translate, coordinate, position, calculate, efficient, decrease, increase, horizontal coordinate, vertical coordinate, vertices, left, right, up, down

Other language to be used by the teacher: vertex, axis, horizontal axis, vertical axis

STRUCTURES AND REPRESENTATIONS

coordinate grids, 2D shapes

RESOURCES

Optional: squared paper, two different coloured dice

 In the eTextbook of this lesson, you will find interactive links to a selection of teaching tools.

Before you teach

• Can children describe the translation of a shape (left, right, up, down)? Can they identify left from right?
• Are children confident using and plotting coordinates?

Discover

Unit 15: Geometry – position and direction, Lesson 4

WAYS OF WORKING Pair work

ASK

- Question ❶ a): *What are the coordinates of the counters marked A and B?*
- Question ❶ a): *Look at the two dice. Could Andy have chosen a different translation? How many different possibilities are there with each pair of numbers?*
- Question ❶: *What translation would get from the yellow counter to the red one? What about red to yellow?*
- Question ❶: *Can you calculate the new coordinates by adding or subtracting instead of moving the counter?*

IN FOCUS Encourage children to explore the game practically using dice, counters and a grid. Discuss the current coordinates of the counters. Can children identify the new coordinates? What methods do they use? Do they move the counter physically and then determine the coordinates or can they use the coordinates to find the new position?

PRACTICAL TIPS Provide children with two different coloured dice, red and yellow counters and a coordinate grid so they can play the **Discover** game. Ask them to explore and apply the eight possible translations for each roll of the two dice. They can record their moves on the coordinate grid, but encourage them to use addition or subtraction to find the new coordinates.

ANSWERS

Question ❶ a): The coordinates of Andy's new position is (10,8).

Question ❶ b): A translation of 3 left, 4 down would win.

Share

WAYS OF WORKING Whole class teacher led

ASK

- Question ❶ a): *What is a translation?*
- Question ❶ a): *Who used Dexter's method? Who used Flo's method?*
- Question ❶ a): *Can you describe Flo's method to a partner?*
- Question ❶ b): *Is Bella's method the same as Dexter's or Flo's method?*
- Question ❶ b): *Use Bella's method to work out where the red counter could be with dice scores of 2 and 3.*

IN FOCUS Focus on Bella's/Flo's method by discussing how to use the coordinates to calculate the new position after a translation. To move right, add to the horizontal coordinate; to move left, subtract from the horizontal coordinate; to move up, add to the vertical coordinate; to move down, subtract from the vertical coordinate. Use the scores shown (6,3) to write and apply different translations to either the red or yellow counter using this method. There are eight possible translations.

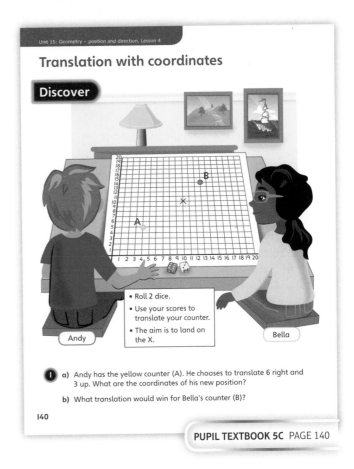

Translation with coordinates

Discover

- Roll 2 dice.
- Use your scores to translate your counter.
- The aim is to land on the X.

Andy   Bella

❶ a) Andy has the yellow counter (A). He chooses to translate 6 right and 3 up. What are the coordinates of his new position?

b) What translation would win for Bella's counter (B)?

140

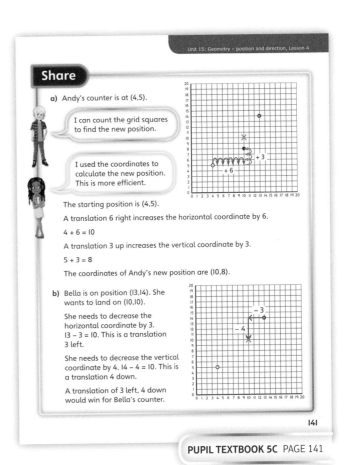

Share

a) Andy's counter is at (4,5).

I can count the grid squares to find the new position.

I used the coordinates to calculate the new position. This is more efficient.

The starting position is (4,5).

A translation 6 right increases the horizontal coordinate by 6.

$4 + 6 = 10$

A translation 3 up increases the vertical coordinate by 3.

$5 + 3 = 8$

The coordinates of Andy's new position are (10,8).

b) Bella is on position (13,14). She wants to land on (10,10).

She needs to decrease the horizontal coordinate by 3. $13 - 3 = 10$. This is a translation 3 left.

She needs to decrease the vertical coordinate by 4. $14 - 4 = 10$. This is a translation 4 down.

A translation of 3 left, 4 down would win for Bella's counter.

141

173

Think together

WAYS OF WORKING Whole class teacher led (I do, We do, You do)

ASK

- Questions **1** and **2**: *Does the translation affect the horizontal coordinates or the vertical coordinates?*
- Questions **1** and **2**: *Does the translation increase or decrease the coordinates?*
- Question **3**: *What needs to be done to the translation to reverse it?*

IN FOCUS The focus for all these questions is on children using the calculation method to find new points, rather than moving the shape on the grid. Talk through the fact that a translation right or up increases the relevant part of the coordinate, while a translation left or down decreases it. Make the link with coordinates: the horizontal coordinate is how far along (left or right) and the vertical coordinate is how far up or down.

STRENGTHEN Give children a coordinate grid marked with one point, A. Ask them to calculate the new coordinates after given translations, labelling each new point alphabetically; ensure children use the coordinate method rather than counting. Start with right/left **or** up/down before moving on to a combination. Then give examples that will allow children to practise reversing the translation and identifying translations between marked points by considering the changes in the coordinates.

DEEPEN Give children a list of six coordinates, A to F, and ask them to identify the two translations between each pair of coordinates without the support of a coordinate grid. For example A (6,11) and B (4,5) give A to B: 2 left, 6 down; B to A: 2 right, 6 up.

ASSESSMENT CHECKPOINT Can children calculate a new point using the coordinates? Do they know whether to increase or decrease the coordinate depending on the direction of the translation?

ANSWERS

Question **1**: A_1 (12,8), B_1 (13,5), A_2 (12,5), B_2 (13,2)

Question **2**: A_1 (14,10), B_1 (14,12), C_1 (16,12), D_1 (16,10)

Question **3** a): A (13,13), B (12,10), C (15,11)

Question **3** b): P (0,1), Q (2,3), R (3,0)

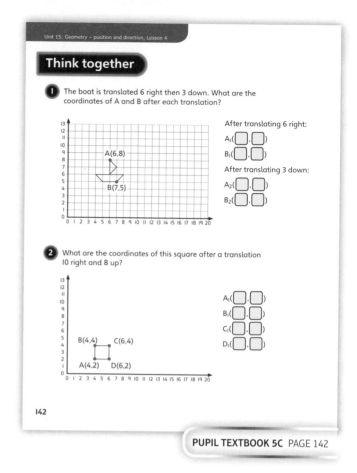

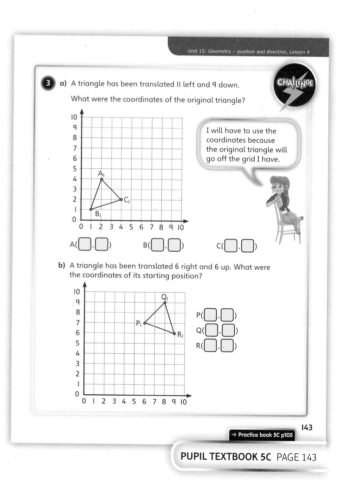

Practice

WAYS OF WORKING Independent thinking

IN FOCUS In question ❶, ensure children realise that each translation is applied to the coordinate immediately above it, not to the starting coordinate. Children will need to work out the final translation based on the ending position of point A. When the table is completed, the ending position in all columns should show a translation of 1 left, 7 up from the previous coordinate, or 3 right, 9 up from the starting coordinate – this is a useful check on accuracy. Encourage children to add or subtract rather than using the grid. The arrow diagram will help them to see which operation they need to use.

STRENGTHEN Give children a starting coordinate of (10,10) and a series of translations to perform on it, involving all four combinations: right and up (+ +); right and down (+ –); left and up (– +); and left and down(– –). You may wish to provide copies of the arrow diagram from question ❶ for reference.

DEEPEN Ask children to work in pairs. Each child draws a shape twice on a coordinate grid then asks their partner to work out the translation from one shape to the other. What translation would move the shape back to its original position?

ASSESSMENT CHECKPOINT Can children calculate a new point after a translation using the coordinates? Can they explain when to increase or decrease the coordinate, depending on the direction of the translation? Can children explain which coordinate to increase or decrease for each part of the translation?

ANSWERS Answers for the **Practice** part of the lesson appear in the separate **Practice and Reflect answer guide**.

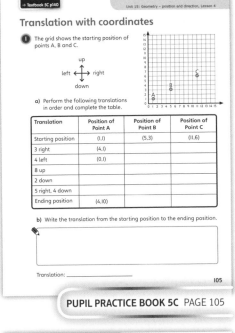

PUPIL PRACTICE BOOK 5C PAGE 105

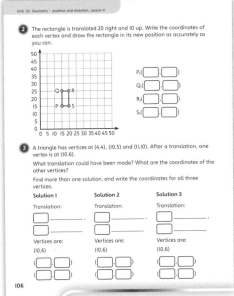

PUPIL PRACTICE BOOK 5C PAGE 106

Reflect

WAYS OF WORKING Independent thinking

IN FOCUS This question will help children to consider the methods they can use to work out the new position after a translation: coordinates or counting squares. Children should consider both methods.

ASSESSMENT CHECKPOINT Can children explain each method? Do they refer to the directions right, left, up and down? Do children mention increasing or decreasing the horizontal or vertical coordinate?

ANSWERS Answers for the **Reflect** part of the lesson appear in the separate **Practice and Reflect answer guide**.

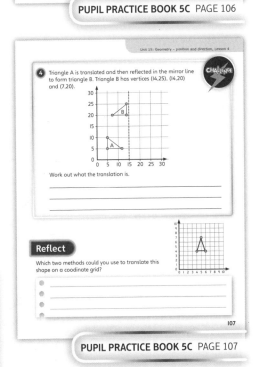

PUPIL PRACTICE BOOK 5C PAGE 107

After the lesson ⏸

- Do children still rely on counting squares to work out a translation?
- Do children understand the terms increase, decrease, horizontal coordinate and vertical coordinate in relation to translations?

End of unit check

Don't forget the *Power Maths* unit assessment grid on p26.

WAYS OF WORKING Group work adult led

IN FOCUS

- Question **1** will test children's ability to identify common errors in reflection and translation.
- Question **3** will ensure children are confident with left and right and know which instruction to follow first.
- Question **4** is a SATS-style question which will assess whether children remember that the vertical coordinate is unchanged when a mirror line is vertical.

ANSWERS AND COMMENTARY Children who have mastered the concepts in this unit will be able to plot and find coordinates of a reflected shape on a grid. They will be able to use coordinates to find translations. Children will also be able to confidently identify and describe reflections and translations.

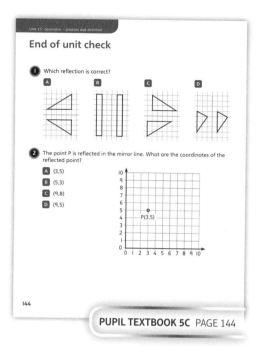

PUPIL TEXTBOOK 5C PAGE 144

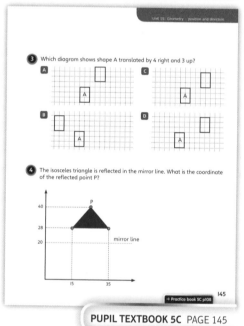

PUPIL TEXTBOOK 5C PAGE 145

Q	A	WRONG ANSWERS AND MISCONCEPTIONS	STRENGTHENING UNDERSTANDING
1	A	D suggests children do not understand the difference between reflection and translation.	Provide children with mirrors to explore reflections; ask them to predict the reflection and then check by placing the mirror on the mirror line.
2	D	A coordinates are just repeated; B suggests children have simply swapped the coordinates. C suggests they have added 3 to both parts of the coordinate.	Ask children to cut out 2D shapes from squared paper so they can physically move them on a grid and place them in the new position. This will help children to understand that the shape does not change. They will be able to see clearly how far and in which direction the shape has moved.
3	C	A shows 3 right, 4 up; B shows movement left instead of right; D shows 3 squares between the rectangles, not between the corresponding vertices.	
4	(25,0)	The mirror line is horizontal, so only the vertical coordinate is affected, but children also need to work out the horizontal coordinate (half-way between 35 and 15).	Practise using coordinates to find translations involving more than one move.

My journal

WAYS OF WORKING Independent thinking

ANSWERS AND COMMENTARY

Question **1** : A (53,25), B (67,25), C (77,25), D (82,13), E (72,13)

As the grid is blank, children will need to calculate the new coordinates using the distance from the mirror line. The mirror line is vertical, so the vertical coordinates of the reflection will be the same as those of the original shape. The mirror line is on the right-hand side of the shape, so the horizontal coordinates of the reflection will be greater than those of the original shape.

Question **2** : Note that both mirror lines will be between the grid lines, as shown here.

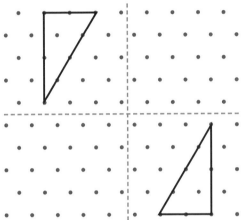

Power check

WAYS OF WORKING Independent thinking

ASK

- *What have you learnt about reflections?*
- *What have you learnt about translations?*
- *Are you confident with using coordinates?*

Power puzzle

WAYS OF WORKING Independent thinking

IN FOCUS Use this **Power puzzle** to see if children can independently create and reflect a design in four quadrants, using coordinates to plot accurately. Encourage children to sketch their design first. Begin with designs based on rectilinear shapes then suggest designs involving diagonal lines and more complex rectilinear shapes.

ANSWERS AND COMMENTARY If children complete the task successfully, this shows that they can plot the coordinates for a reflection in both horizontal and vertical mirror lines.

After the unit

- Are children confident with plotting coordinates?
- Do children use coordinates to plot a translation or reflection, or do they rely on counting squares?
- What misconceptions did children have and how can you address these before the next unit?

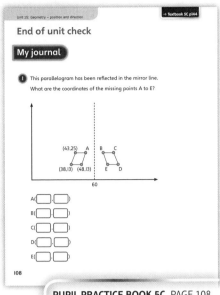

PUPIL PRACTICE BOOK 5C PAGE 108

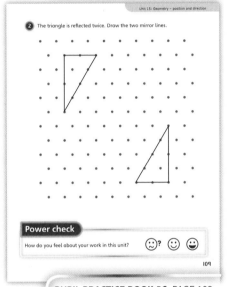

PUPIL PRACTICE BOOK 5C PAGE 109

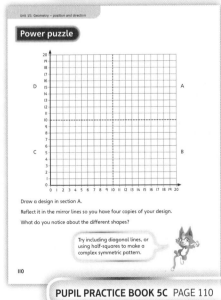

PUPIL PRACTICE BOOK 5C PAGE 110

Strengthen and **Deepen** activities for this unit can be found in the *Power Maths* online subscription.

Unit 16
Measure – converting units

Mastery Expert tip! "This unit lends itself to so many opportunities for meaningful, real-life application of maths concepts. Before starting the unit I identified as many instances as I could to make the concepts significant to my class, for example using local bus timetables and even a cookery lesson when I gave children a recipe entirely in imperial units!"

Don't forget to watch the Unit 16 video!

WHY THIS UNIT IS IMPORTANT

This unit consolidates children's existing knowledge of units of measurement and develops it further. It is a very practical unit in the sense that the skills children learn will be clearly applicable to real-life measurement situations and many of the problems will be ones they will face at some point in life: conversion between units (both metric and imperial), including conversion and scaling of amounts; and timetables, including converting between units of time when the conversion does not result in a whole number answer.

WHERE THIS UNIT FITS

→ Unit 13: Geometry – position and direction

→ **Unit 14: Measure – converting units**

→ Unit 15: Measure – volume and capacity

This unit builds on the concepts of measurement learnt in Year 4, particularly conversion between metric units. Children link their prior knowledge to bar models that will help them use these facts to convert units.

Before they start this unit, it is expected that children:
- can convert between different metric units of measure (whole number amounts) and between units of time
- can read and understand 24-hour clock times and convert between 24-hour and 12-hour clocks
- can calculate duration between two times.

ASSESSING MASTERY

Children can convert between units of mass, length and capacity (metric → metric, imperial → imperial and metric ↔ imperial) and between units of time, including where there is a remainder, and confidently apply this knowledge to solve problems. For each type of conversion, they can use reasoning to explain their methodology. Children can read information from timetables and use it to solve time-based problems.

COMMON MISCONCEPTIONS	STRENGTHENING UNDERSTANDING	GOING DEEPER
Children may confuse the operation needed to convert from one unit to another. Often this can be because they think that larger unit → smaller unit means larger amount → smaller amount (and so divide instead of multiplying).	Give children opportunities to measure simple lengths, masses and capacities using different units. Where possible, provide equipment that shows different units on the scale, for example different metric units and metric and imperial units. Emphasise the equivalence between units with bar models.	Encourage children to practise converting between unusual combinations of units, for example: *How tall is a 6-foot person in millimetres?* When working between several conversions in this way, ask children to draw a function machine or flow chart to show the steps they need to take. In the above example, convert feet into inches (× 12), inches into centimetres (× 2·5) and then centimetres into millimetres (× 10). Finally, challenge children to find one conversion that could replace the separate steps: in this case × 300 will convert directly from feet to millimetres.
Children may think that they can solve a problem without converting any units, just using the numbers even though they may be in different units.	Ask children to circle or point to all mentions of units of measurement in the question. Where possible, provide examples of the measurements so they can see that they need to convert to use the numbers together. Discuss which units it makes sense to convert in the context of the problem.	

Unit 16: Measure – converting units

WAYS OF WORKING

Use these pages to introduce the unit focus to children. Can children see how the number line helps us convert easily between two units of measurement? Find out how many words they recognise from the list of vocabulary, especially the imperial units.

STRUCTURES AND REPRESENTATIONS

Bar model: This model helps children to represent the equivalence between different units of measure. Children can then see the calculation that they need to do to convert one unit into another.

3 feet

I foot	I foot	I foot
12 inches	12 inches	12 inches

Number line: This model also helps children in considering the equivalence of units. It can help them to convert between two units quickly or to recognise where a measurement comes in terms of whole measures and parts (for example, 192 seconds is between 180 and 240 seconds, and so comes between 3 and 4 minutes). Number lines are also useful for working out durations between two times.

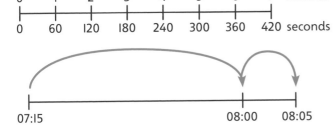

KEY LANGUAGE

There is some key language that children will need to know as part of the learning in this unit:

→ mass, capacity, length, time, quantity

→ metric units, gram, kilogram, millilitre, litre, millimetre, centimetre, metre, kilometre

→ imperial units, ounce (oz), pound (lb), stone (st), pint (pt), gallon, inch (in), foot (ft), yard (yd)

→ second, minute, hour, day, week, month, year

→ convert, equal to, equivalent, approximately, per, measure, remainder, multiple

→ timetable, 24-hour, digital, duration

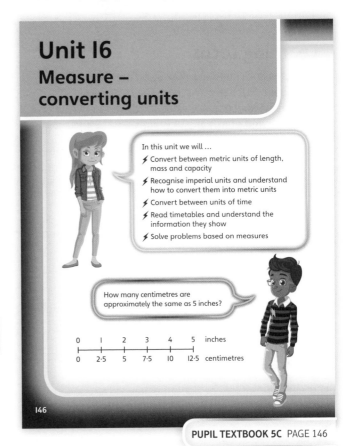

PUPIL TEXTBOOK 5C PAGE 146

PUPIL TEXTBOOK 5C PAGE 147

Metric units ❶

Learning focus

In this lesson, children will focus on metric units that begin with the prefix 'kilo'. They will apply their knowledge of place value to convert between kilograms and grams and vice versa.

Small steps

→ Previous step: Translation with coordinates
→ **This step: Metric units (1)**
→ Next step: Metric units (2)

NATIONAL CURRICULUM LINKS

Year 5 Measurement

Convert between different units of metric measure (for example, kilometre and metre; centimetre and metre; centimetre and millimetre; gram and kilogram; litre and millilitre).

ASSESSING MASTERY

Children recognise the relationship between kilometres and metres, and between kilograms and grams. They can then apply this information to convert from one unit of measure to another, choosing to multiply or divide according to the units involved.

COMMON MISCONCEPTIONS

Children may confuse the operation needed to convert from one unit to another. Often this can be because they think a larger unit must become smaller when converting to a smaller unit (and so they divide instead of multiplying) and vice versa. Ask:

• *Would you expect the number itself to increase or decrease when you convert from __ to __? Do you think you should multiply or divide?*

Children may think that they can multiply by 1,000 by writing three zeros on the end of a number, which does not work with decimals and can lead to confusion if encouraged as a strategy. Ask:
• *How does the value of a digit change when you multiply it by 1,000? ... divide by 1,000?*

STRENGTHENING UNDERSTANDING

To strengthen understanding, provide practical opportunities for children to measure and use kilometres and metres, and kilograms and grams in context. For example, provide metre measuring wheels and ask children to measure various distances around the school grounds in kilometres. Give them measuring scales set to kilograms and ask them to measure various objects in grams. Encourage children to work with measurements that involve decimals as well as whole numbers.

GOING DEEPER

Provide children with real-life data that shows distances of flights between cities in kilometres. Challenge them to design their own departure board of an airport where the distances are given in metres. Extend the task by providing data that has a mixture of units of measurement.

KEY LANGUAGE

In lesson: kilo, kilometre, metre, kilogram, gram, unit, convert, thousands, hundreds, tens, ones, tenths, mass, length

Other language to be used by the teacher: place value, hundredths

STRUCTURES AND REPRESENTATIONS

bar model, place value grid

RESOURCES

Optional: measuring wheels, sets of scales, digit cards

 In the eTextbook of this lesson, you will find interactive links to a selection of teaching tools.

Before you teach

• Are there ways you can adapt this lesson to link it to other lessons or curriculum work?
• How will you improve children's fluency when multiplying and dividing by 1,000?

Discover

Pair work

ASK

- Question ❶ a): *What are the different units of measurement you can see in the image? Why do you think long distances are usually measured in kilometres and not metres?*
- Question ❶ a): *Would you expect the number of metres from London to Berlin be a larger or smaller number than the one shown? Why?*
- Question ❶ b): *'6,000 is a lot more than 7, so Jen's bag is far too heavy.' What is wrong with this sentence?*
- Question ❶: *What do you need to do to convert from one unit into another? Why?*

IN FOCUS Use the picture to discuss whether any children have experience of travelling on an aeroplane and, in particular, of weighing luggage prior to boarding a plane. Discuss what the luggage limit means and why aeroplanes have luggage limits for passengers.

PRACTICAL TIPS Show children a bag and talk about the sorts of things they might like to take with them onto an aeroplane. Have about 20 different items at the front of the class (for example, a book, a packet of sweets, a bottle of water, a pillow). Encourage children to choose a selection of these items and then weigh the bag to see whether they are over the luggage limit or not. This activity will not only help children to understand the scenario, but will also provide them with estimation practice and, if the scales show grams, a chance to discuss the need to convert between units.

ANSWERS

Question ❶ a): It is 930,000 metres from London to Berlin.

Question ❶ b): 6 kg < 7 kg, so Jen can take her bag onto the plane.

Share

WAYS OF WORKING Whole class teacher led

ASK

- Question ❶: *What is similar about the two units of measurement being used at the airport? Do their names give you a clue about how to convert them?*
- Question ❶: *How does a place value grid help when multiplying or dividing by 1,000? Are there any other numbers you could use a place value grid to help to multiply or divide by?*
- Question ❶: *Think about the two conversions that you needed to do to work out the answers to both questions. What is the same? What is different? Why?*

IN FOCUS Both questions ❶ a) and b) use place value tables in order to model how to multiply and divide by 1,000. Check that children understand why this is such a useful way of representing the change in a number. They should be able to describe the effect on the digits when a number is multiplied or divided by 1,000.

PUPIL TEXTBOOK 5C PAGE 148

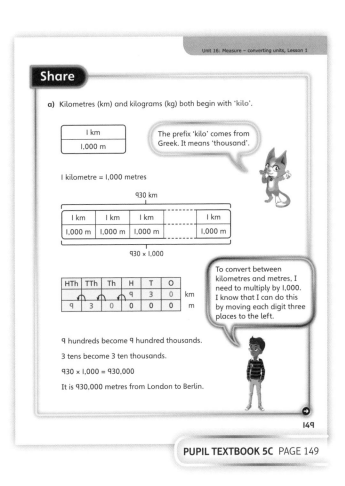

PUPIL TEXTBOOK 5C PAGE 149

181

Think together

Whole class teacher led (I do, We do, You do)

ASK

- Question **1**: *Do you expect that the number shown on the set of scales will be greater or less than 5·9? Why?*
- Question **1**: *Why do you multiply by 1,000 when converting from kilograms to grams?*
- Question **1**: *Can you give another example of a conversion where you need to multiply by 1,000?*
- Question **2**: *What is the same about this question and the previous one? What is different?*
- Question **2**: *What do you notice about the way that the value of each digit changes when the number is divided by 1,000?*

IN FOCUS Questions **1** and **2** provide children with real-life contexts to work with, providing a degree of scaffolding to help them work through their choices step by step. The structure helps them to consider whether they should convert by multiplying or dividing (and why), what they should multiply or divide by (and why) and the effect of this operation on the digits in the measurement.

STRENGTHEN To strengthen understanding of the effect of multiplying or dividing by 1,000, encourage children to draw place value grids and provide them with digit cards. Begin by modelling multiplying simple whole numbers by 1,000, emphasising the three-place shift to the left in each digit. Ask children what they notice about how the value of each digit changes. Challenge them to predict the new value of a digit when a number is multiplied or divided by 1,000.

DEEPEN Provide children with measurements given in different units, for example the mass of a rucksack is 5·9 kg and the mass of a suitcase is 5,200 g. Challenge them to compare the measurements and write them in order. Ask whether it matters which unit they decide to convert, and whether it affects the answer.

ASSESSMENT CHECKPOINT Use questions **1** and **2** to assess whether children can convert between metres and kilometres, and grams and kilograms. They should display a growing confidence when converting. Ensure they can explain clearly why and how place value grids are helpful.

ANSWERS

Question **1**: 1 kg = 1,000 g. To convert kg to g, multiply by 1,000. When we multiply by 1,000, the digits shift to the left by 3 places.
5·9 × 1,000 = 5,900
The scales will show 5,900 g when the rucksack is placed on them.

Question **2**: 1,000 m = 1 km. To convert m to km, divide by 1,000. The digits will shift to the right by 3 places.
260,500 ÷ 1,000 = 260·5
The plane travels 260·5 km.

Question **3**: Multiplying by 1,000 involves shifting digits 3 places to the left.
8·3 kg = 8,300 g

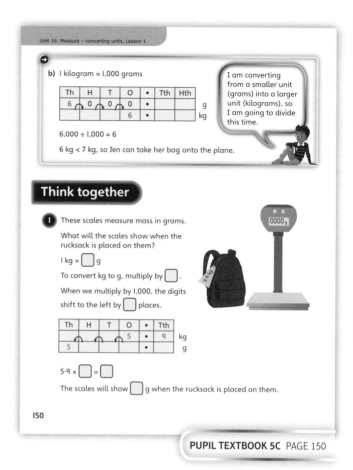

PUPIL TEXTBOOK 5C PAGE 150

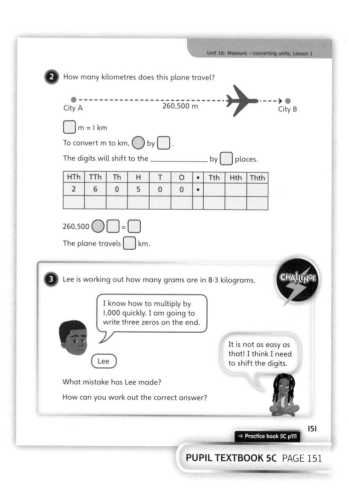

PUPIL TEXTBOOK 5C PAGE 151

Practice

WAYS OF WORKING Independent thinking

IN FOCUS Question **3** provides children with fluency practice, completing boxes to show what various measurements in kilograms and grams are equivalent to when converted. Parts e) and f) are designed to show that there can be two ways to represent the same measurements. Children should therefore convert into grams and into kilograms separately. Ask which part of the measurement they need to convert if they want to express the measurement in grams or kilograms, and how this affects the operation they use.

STRENGTHEN For question **2**, encourage children to express each conversion as larger units → smaller units, or vice versa. Ask them to explain whether they would expect the number to get larger or smaller. Check that children do not confuse the move from larger to smaller units with a change from larger to smaller numbers. Provide large sorting circles and the statements on pieces of card for children to discuss each one as a group.

DEEPEN Use question **6** to deepen children's reasoning skills. Observe whether any children can answer the question using mental methods and then challenge them to devise a rule that explains how they know the answer, for example, 'If an amount of grams is a multiple of 1,000 it will make a whole number of kilograms when it is converted.'

THINK DIFFERENTLY In question **5**, children need to express a distance in kilometres that is not a whole number of kilometres using only the digits 4, 5 and 0, but to give the possible distances in metres. They should recognise that the 0 does not belong in the tenths position. Suggest that they find all possible distances before converting. Challenge them to do the conversions mentally.

ASSESSMENT CHECKPOINT Use questions **1**, **3** and **6** to check that children are confident when applying their knowledge of converting between kilometres and metres, and kilograms and grams, in problem-solving contexts and as abstract conversions. They should display reasoning skills, explaining appropriate methods.

ANSWERS Answers for the **Practice** part of the lesson appear in the separate **Practice and Reflect answer guide**.

Reflect

WAYS OF WORKING Independent thinking

IN FOCUS This activity provides an opportunity to check children's methodology. They should recognise that they need to divide by 1,000 in order to convert from grams into kilograms and should be able to explain how this is done by shifting the digits 3 places to the right.

ASSESSMENT CHECKPOINT Look for children who can describe clearly and accurately how to convert 12,500 g into kilograms.

ANSWERS Answers for the **Reflect** part of the lesson appear in the separate **Practice and Reflect answer guide**.

After the lesson

- How well did the prompts and questions promote learning and how will you learn from this in the next lesson on metric units?
- How did children respond to the materials and approaches used? Were they adequately (or excessively) challenged by them?

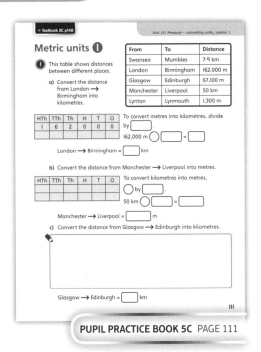

PUPIL PRACTICE BOOK 5C PAGE 111

PUPIL PRACTICE BOOK 5C PAGE 112

PUPIL PRACTICE BOOK 5C PAGE 113

Metric units ❷

Learning focus

In this lesson, children will focus on metric units that begin with the prefix 'milli'. They will apply their knowledge of place value to convert between millimetres and metres or centimetres, and between millilitres and litres.

Small steps

→ Previous step: Metric units (1)
→ **This step: Metric units (2)**
→ Next step: Metric units (3)

NATIONAL CURRICULUM LINKS

Year 5 Measurement

Convert between different units of metric measure (for example, kilometre and metre; centimetre and metre; centimetre and millimetre; gram and kilogram; litre and millilitre).

ASSESSING MASTERY

Children understand the relationship between millimetres and metres, millimetres and centimetres, and millilitres and litres. They are able to apply their knowledge when converting between these units of measure, choosing to multiply or divide according to the units involved.

COMMON MISCONCEPTIONS

Children may think that only 'kilo' units have a link with 1,000, because millimetres (and millilitres) are so small that it is hard to visualise how many fit into 1 metre (or litre) or possibly because they link 'milli' with one million. Ask:
• *What does 1 millimetre look like? How many millimetres do you think there are in 1 metre? Why?*

Children may confuse the operation needed to convert from one unit to another. They may link moving from a larger unit to a smaller unit to moving from a larger number to a smaller one (and so divide when they need to multiply). Ask:
• *Would you expect the number to increase or decrease when you convert from millilitres to litres? Do you think you should multiply or divide?*

STRENGTHENING UNDERSTANDING

To strengthen understanding, provide opportunities for children to measure and use millimetres and millilitres in context. For example, give children water bottles (for example, 500 ml), ask them to fill them with water and use a 1-litre measuring jug (marked in parts of a litre: 0·1, 0·2 and so on) to find out their equivalence in litres.

GOING DEEPER

Consider fractions of litres, centimetres and metres in terms of millilitres and millimetres. Ask children to express $\frac{1}{4}$ of a litre or $\frac{3}{4}$ of a metre in smaller units. Challenge children to identify more complex fractions ($\frac{3}{10}$ of a metre, $\frac{4}{1,000}$ of a litre).

KEY LANGUAGE

In lesson: milli, millimetre, centimetre, metre, millilitre, litre, unit, convert, place value, thousands, tens, tenths, ones, thousandths, length, capacity

Other language to be used by the teacher: hundreds, hundredths

STRUCTURES AND REPRESENTATIONS

bar model, place value grid

RESOURCES

Optional: bottles with different capacities in ml, rulers marked in cm and rulers marked in mm, metre rulers marked in mm, large sheets of paper, measuring jug

 In the eTextbook of this lesson, you will find interactive links to a selection of teaching tools.

Before you teach

• How might you scaffold questioning to help children to reflect on their assumptions?
• How will you bring practical opportunities to convert between metric units into the lesson?
• Are children confident multiplying and dividing by 1,000?

Discover

ASK

- Question **1** a): *Which part of the flower bed is 2 metres long?*
- Question **1** a): *The flower bed is measured in metres and the border fencing is measured in millimetres. Without unravelling the fencing, how can Ebo work out whether he has enough fence to go across the length of the flower bed?*
- Question **1**: *Can you think of any real-life objects that have about the same length or capacity of some of the measurements in the picture?*

IN FOCUS Discuss the situation that Ebo is in. Discuss when children might find themselves in a situation where they know the measurement of something, but the object they need to help them is measured in a different unit. Use the opportunity to brainstorm real-life scenarios where metric units need to be converted. Asking children to describe which part of the flower bed is 2 metres long is important as a tool to check that children understand the scenario and realise that 2 m refers to the length of the flower bed and not its perimeter.

PRACTICAL TIPS Provide pairs with pieces of string, labelled with their length in millimetres (for example, 900 mm). Set up two tables in the classroom a specific distance apart (for example, 1 m). Challenge children to predict whether their piece of string will reach across the gap. Ask what fact they need to know in order to know whether their piece of string will reach. Use the opportunity to reinforce the concept that 1 m = 1,000 mm.

ANSWERS

Question **1** a): 1,500 < 2,000, so Ebo does not have enough fencing to go across the flower bed.

Question **1** b): Alex has put 4·5 litres of water in the watering can.

Share

ASK

- Question **1** a): *Can you think of any other words that begin with the prefix 'milli'? Are any related to the number 1,000? (for example, milligram ($\frac{1}{1,000}$ of a gram), million (1,000 thousands), millisecond ($\frac{1}{1,000}$ of a second))*
- Question **1** a): *What does 'one thousandth' mean? Can you think of two ways to write this?*
- Question **1** a): *How does the bar model help you to convert from metres to millimetres?*
- Question **1** b): *If 1,000 ml is 1 litre, what is 500 ml in litres?*
- Question **1** b): *Do you think a watering can of this capacity would usually be marked in millilitres or litres? Why?*

IN FOCUS Both question **1** a) and b) use bar models to represent the problem visually. Ask children to explain how the bar models have been used to help solve the problem.

PUPIL TEXTBOOK 5C PAGE 152

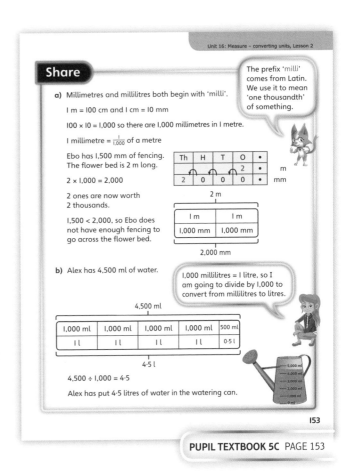

PUPIL TEXTBOOK 5C PAGE 153

Think together

WAYS OF WORKING Whole class teacher led (I do, We do, You do)

ASK

- Question ❶ a): *How do you expect each digit to change when millimetres are converted to centimetres?*
- Question ❶ b): *Can you think of a way to represent this problem using a bar model?*
- Question ❶ b): *How do the digits in the measurement change when litres are converted into millilitres?*

IN FOCUS As any conversion between metric units simply involves a shift of digits, challenge children to 'see' the answers without using a place value grid. Ask in which direction the digits will shift and why. Children should start to move away from visual representations and apply mental methods and reasoning.

STRENGTHEN For question ❶ provide children with rulers marked in millimetres and others marked in centimetres. Ask children to measure a blade of grass in centimetres and then in millimetres. What do they notice?

DEEPEN Question ❸ challenges children to consider the various relationships between units of length and capacity and the similarities between the two. Ensure children recognise that the relationship between a millimetre and a metre is the same as that between a metre and a kilometre. Challenge children to work out how many millimetres are in a kilometre.

ASSESSMENT CHECKPOINT Use questions ❶ and ❸ to assess whether children can convert between millimetres, centimetres and metres, and between millilitres and litres. They should recognise the relationship between 'milli' units and the concept of one thousandth and apply this correctly.

ANSWERS

Question ❶ a): There are 10 mm in 1 cm, so to convert mm into cm, divide by 10. $6 ÷ 10 = 0·6$. The flower is 0·6 cm tall.

Question ❶ b): There are 1,000 ml in 1 l. $0·7 × 1,000 = 700$. The bottle contains 700 ml.

Question ❷: To convert from a larger to a smaller unit, multiply. To convert from a smaller to a larger unit, divide.

Question ❸ a): 1 mm = $\frac{1}{1,000}$ of a metre, 1 ml = $\frac{1}{1,000}$ of a litre; 1 cm = $\frac{1}{100}$ of a metre; 1 m = 1,000 mm, 1 l = 1,000 ml; 1 m = 100 cm; 1 mm is 0·001 m or 1 m is 0·001 km, 1 ml is 0·001 l

Question ❸ b): Although they are concerned with different types of measurement, the digits are the same in each column of the table. Words which begin 'milli' are always one thousandth of the whole. The units of measurements are different, length is measured in millimetres, centimetres and kilometres. Capacity is measured in millilitres and litres.

PUPIL TEXTBOOK 5C PAGE 154

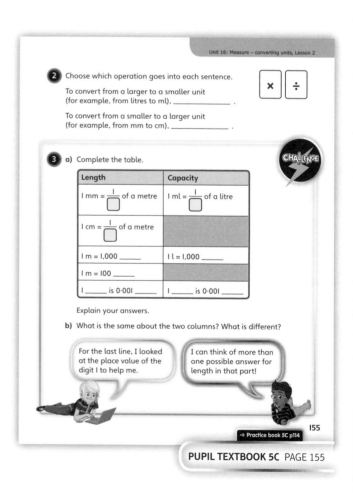

PUPIL TEXTBOOK 5C PAGE 155

Practice

WAYS OF WORKING Independent thinking

IN FOCUS Question ❸ has been designed to test children's understanding of the operations that are needed to convert between different metric units. The two key concepts that children need to apply are whether a conversion requires multiplication (larger → smaller unit) or division (smaller → larger unit) and also the amount that the value should be multiplied or divided by (dependent on the equivalence of one unit compared to another). Encourage children to explain their reasoning.

STRENGTHEN Provide children with metre rulers that clearly show millimetres and ask them to label their rulers to help convert between m and mm. For example, the top of the ruler could be labelled in metres (from 0 to 1, with each 0·1 m marked) and the bottom of the ruler in millimetres (from 0 to 1,000, with each 100 mm marked). Children might also find it helpful to mark the equivalence between 1 cm and 10 mm. Encourage them to use this representation when answering questions ❶ a), ❷ b) and so on.

DEEPEN In question ❻, children apply their knowledge of conversion between millilitres and litres in a problem-solving context. Three cups each have a capacity measured in millilitres and children need to make totals measured in litres using three cups. Observe those children who realise that it may be easier to convert the target numbers into millilitres and therefore explore numbers they can make by adding combinations of 100, 75 and 200 (rather than using litres and trying to make totals by adding combinations of decimals: 0·1, 0·75 and 0·2). Challenge children to find all the possible totals in litres that Amelia could make using one, two, three of four containers.

ASSESSMENT CHECKPOINT Use questions ❶, ❷ and ❹ to assess whether children are confident when applying their knowledge of metric conversions between metres and millimetres, centimetres and millimetres and litres and millilitres in problem-solving contexts and as abstract conversions. They should be able to demonstrate appropriate methodology and explain why it works.

ANSWERS Answers for the **Practice** part of the lesson appear in the separate **Practice and Reflect answer guide**.

Reflect

WAYS OF WORKING Independent thinking

IN FOCUS This reflection provides an opportunity to assess whether children can apply the concepts learnt during the lesson. While the latter part of the statement is correct (10 mm = 1 cm), the way to convert from cm to mm is not to divide by 10, but to multiply. Children will need to consider the statement carefully in order to identify the error. Encourage them to convert the measurement in order to check their answer.

ASSESSMENT CHECKPOINT Look for children who can describe how to convert from centimetres into millimetres.

ANSWERS Answers for the **Reflect** part of the lesson appear in the separate **Practice and Reflect answer guide**.

After the lesson

- Do you feel that the lesson objectives were achieved?
- Can children recognise when they need to convert units?
- Where did you provide feedback to push children to think more deeply or to learn more about process skills?

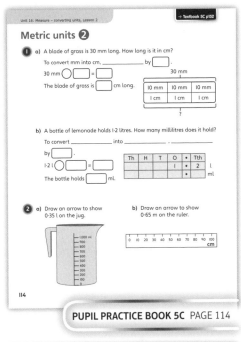

PUPIL PRACTICE BOOK 5C PAGE 114

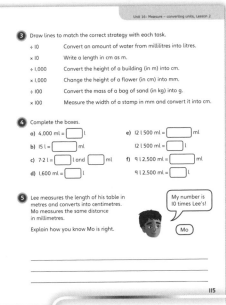

PUPIL PRACTICE BOOK 5C PAGE 115

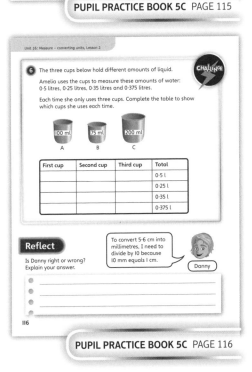

PUPIL PRACTICE BOOK 5C PAGE 116

187

Metric units ③

Learning focus

In this lesson, children will apply their knowledge of metric units of length, mass and capacity to problems that require calculating with different units. They will work with measurements that have different numbers of decimal places and fractions of units.

Small steps

→ Previous step: Metric units (2)
→ **This step: Metric units (3)**
→ Next step: Metric units (4)

NATIONAL CURRICULUM LINKS

Year 5 Measurement
- Use all four operations to solve problems involving measure [for example, length, mass, volume, money] using decimal notation, including scaling.
- Convert between different units of metric measure (for example, kilometre and metre; centimetre and metre; centimetre and millimetre; gram and kilogram; litre and millilitre).

ASSESSING MASTERY

Children are able to solve problems that require converting between metric units of measurement in order to calculate. They can apply their knowledge of fractions to work out fractions of larger units in terms of smaller units.

COMMON MISCONCEPTIONS

Children may think that they can solve a problem converting any units (i.e. just using the numbers from each measurement regardless of units). Ask them to point to all units in the question. Ask:
- *Do you need to convert to find the answer? Which measurement(s) will you need to change?*

When converting fractions of units of measurement (specifically mixed numbers), children may think that the fraction can be simply transferred across to the smaller unit (for example, $1\frac{1}{2}$ litres to 1,000·5 ml). Ask:
- *What is $\frac{1}{2}$ a litre the same as? So how would you write $2\frac{1}{2}$ litres as millilitres?*

STRENGTHENING UNDERSTANDING

Ensure that children use the structures and representations used in the previous lessons. Ask them to underline the parts of the problem that are most important. Provide blank bar models, number lines and place value grids with digit cards to help children model each problem and convert between metric units.

GOING DEEPER

Challenge children to create their own problems involving metric units of measurement. Begin by ensuring children recognise some of the common characteristics of conversion problems (i.e. information given in one or two units and the answer required in a different unit). Children can share their problems and explain how they think their problem ought to be solved.

KEY LANGUAGE

In lesson: convert, smaller, larger, unit, metre, centimetre, millimetre, litre, millilitre, kilogram, gram, heaviest, lightest

Other language to be used by the teacher: greater, more, less, fraction, decimal

STRUCTURES AND REPRESENTATIONS

number line, place value grid

RESOURCES

Optional: blank bar models, number lines and place value grids; digit cards, flashcards

 In the eTextbook of this lesson, you will find interactive links to a selection of teaching tools.

Before you teach

- How will you help to refine children's own representations for different problems?
- How can you improve the teaching of problem-solving and reasoning through this lesson?
- Are children confident naming which units of measurement are used for weighing, measuring distances and capacity?

Discover

Pair work

ASK

- Question ❶: *Where can you see different units of measurement in the picture?*
- Question ❶: *What facts do you know about these units of length and capacity? How many centimetres are in 1 metre? How many millilitres are in 1 litre?*
- Question ❶ a): *To be allowed on the roller coaster, does Isla's height need to be less than or greater than 1·45 m?*
- Question ❶ b): *Why is it tricky to add the fizzy drinks as they are? What could you do to help?*

IN FOCUS Discuss the sorts of height restriction signs that children have seen. These may include those at a theme park, bridge or barrier heights for traffic and so on. Discuss why height restrictions exist. Talk about the ruler and ask children to describe how they might work out the answer as the ruler shows a different unit of measurement.

PRACTICAL TIPS Provide tape measures marked in millimetres for children to measure each other. Give them different height restrictions in metres for them to work out whether they are shorter or taller than each height.

ANSWERS

Question ❶ a): 1·40 m < 1·45 m so Isla is not tall enough to go on the roller coaster.

Question ❶ b): Aki is buying 750 ml of fizzy pop altogether.

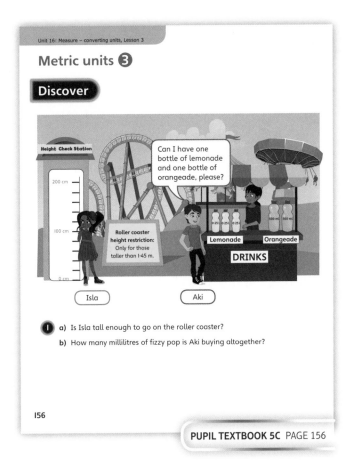

PUPIL TEXTBOOK 5C PAGE 156

Share

Whole class teacher led

ASK

- Question ❶ a): *How does the number line help you to convert between units?*
- Question ❶ a): *Can you think of another way to compare the two heights (instead of converting 140 cm into metres)?*
- Question ❶ b): *0·25 l is the same as $\frac{1}{4}$ of a litre. 500 ml is the same as $\frac{1}{2}$ of a litre. Can you explain why? How can you say the total (750 ml) as a fraction of a litre?*

IN FOCUS The number line used in question ❶ a) is a useful way of representing the equivalences between two different units of measurement. It is a model that is used in later lessons on imperial and metric units and so it is important that children recognise its importance at this stage. Give children time to practise using the line as a conversion tool by calling out different measurements and asking them to respond by using the number line to convert to the other unit of measurement.

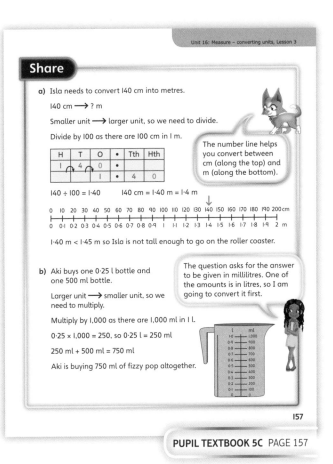

PUPIL TEXTBOOK 5C PAGE 157

Think together

WAYS OF WORKING Whole class teacher led (I do, We do, You do)

ASK

- Question ❶: *How do you think Ambika has estimated the masses of the cakes? What strategies might she have used?*
- Question ❶: *What does Ambika need to calculate?*
- Question ❶: *How could you find the same answer, but only convert once?*
- Question ❷: *Can you think of a mistake you could make when answering this question? What could you do to avoid it?*
- Question ❷: *How would you convert 300 cm into metres?*

IN FOCUS Questions ❶ and ❷ both incorporate an element of problem-solving that children will need to familiarise themselves with – the presentation of information in one unit and the requirement to give the answer in a different unit. It is important that children are able to identify this in a question. Encourage children to discuss potential errors (including giving the answer in the wrong unit) and to suggest ways of preventing them.

STRENGTHEN To strengthen children's understanding of the connections between metric units, use flashcards with equivalent measurements on each side (for example, 1 kg on the front and 1,000 g on the back). Once they are familiar with these equivalences, extend the activity to include the amounts in each problem, with children using the cards to form bar models. For example, in question ❶, children could model the first measurement (0·9 kg) by placing nine '0·1 kg' cards in a row. By turning over the cards, they show how the measurement is converted into nine lots of 100 g.

DEEPEN Question ❸ extends children's knowledge of metric units in context by introducing comparison and order into a problem that already involves reading scales. The character shout-outs highlight the easy mistake to make when answering this question and what needs to be done to avoid this mistake. Discuss each character's statement with the class. Challenge children to produce a similar problem on ordering lengths for a partner to answer.

ASSESSMENT CHECKPOINT At this point, children should be able to confidently apply their knowledge of metric units to solve problems that involve conversion. Check that children can describe the strategies they are using to find each answer and how and when they are converting between units.

ANSWERS

Question ❶: $0·9 \times 1,000 = 900$ $0·3 \times 1,000 = 300$
0·9 kg = 900 g   0·3 kg = 300 g
0·9 kg + 0·3 kg = 900 g + 300 g = 1,200 g
Ambika should guess a total of 1,200 g.

Question ❷: The roller coaster is now 597 m long.

Question ❸ a): A, D, B, C, E

Question ❸ b): Yes, you would get the same order.
Explanations should mention that the mass of each parcel is still the same, whether it is expressed in grams or kilograms. Converting to kilograms and then comparing or converting to grams and then comparing will both give the same order.

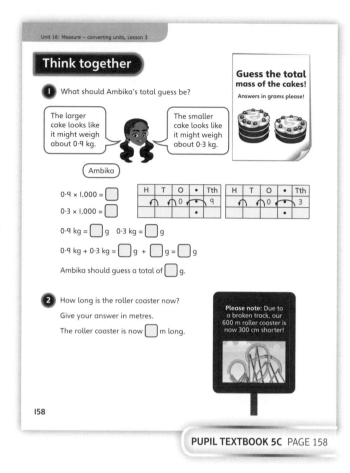

PUPIL TEXTBOOK 5C PAGE 158

PUPIL TEXTBOOK 5C PAGE 159

Practice

WAYS OF WORKING Independent thinking

IN FOCUS Question **3** explores the way that pairs of measurements can be converted in two different ways and the same answer expressed differently. Discuss the difference between the calculations on the left and those on the right. Check that children recognise that they are essentially the same calculation, but that the answer has been worked out in a different unit of measurement, and that the answers are equal.

STRENGTHEN Ask children to identify the different units used in each problem, highlighting them in some way. Ask questions about the problem, such as the unit asked for in the answer, the unit(s) given in the question, when they need to convert. Provide children with digit cards and encourage them to draw their own place value grids, shifting the digits physically. Children may also find it useful to cross out numbers in each problem once they have converted them and replace them with their equivalents.

DEEPEN Question **5** a) requires children to work through a series of steps to solve the problem: finding $\frac{1}{10}$ of a litre, adding it to 1 litre, then subtracting 300 ml. Challenge children to write the problem as a single number sentence (brackets will not be needed to express the order of operations: $1,000 \div 10 + 1,000 - 300$). Ask how the number sentence would be different if the question asked 'How many litres of squash does he have left?'

THINK DIFFERENTLY Question **4** first requires children to read scales showing masses in different ways. In some cases they need to work out the interval between each mark and hence the mass that is being shown. They then convert the masses so that they can order them.

ASSESSMENT CHECKPOINT Use questions **1** to **4** to assess whether children are confident when applying their knowledge of metric conversions in problem-solving contexts.

ANSWERS Answers for the **Practice** part of the lesson appear in the separate **Practice and Reflect answer guide**.

Reflect

WAYS OF WORKING Independent thinking

IN FOCUS This question has been designed to assess children's ability to add two different units of measurement. Look for children identifying which is the smallest unit and whether they identify that they could convert to either kilometres or metres.

ASSESSMENT CHECKPOINT Look for children who can apply their knowledge of metric units and can explain the strategies they used.

ANSWERS Answers for the **Reflect** part of the lesson appear in the separate **Practice and Reflect answer guide**.

After the lesson ⏸

- To what extent were children's various responses the ones that were anticipated: their ideas and questions, the obstacles they encountered, their misunderstandings and mistakes?
- How well do you feel they were able to express the strategies they chose to use? Do you feel that they have a broad knowledge of mental strategies to draw on?

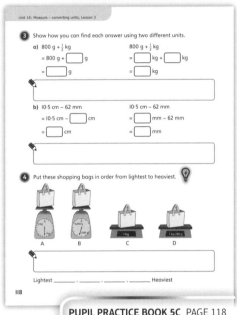

PUPIL PRACTICE BOOK 5C PAGE 117

PUPIL PRACTICE BOOK 5C PAGE 118

PUPIL PRACTICE BOOK 5C PAGE 119

Metric units 4

Learning focus

In this lesson, children will convert between all combinations of mm, cm, m and km, including splitting conversions into more than one step (for example, mm → m → km). Children will identify the values they need to use for any conversion and apply these in multi-step problem-solving contexts.

Small steps

→ Previous step: Metric units (3)
→ **This step: Metric units (4)**
→ Next step: Imperial units of length

NATIONAL CURRICULUM LINKS

Year 5 Measurement
• Use all four operations to solve problems involving measure [for example, length, mass, volume, money], using decimal notation, including scaling.
• Convert between different units of metric measure (for example, kilometre and metre; centimetre and metre; centimetre and millimetre; gram and kilogram; litre and millilitre).

ASSESSING MASTERY

Children can confidently apply their knowledge of metric units of length to solving problems that involve converting between and calculating with them. They are able to use reasoning to explain their methodology.

COMMON MISCONCEPTIONS

Children may think that they are limited to certain numbers when converting. For example, they may think that all conversions involving kilometres require multiplying and dividing by 1,000. Ask:
• *What facts do you know about the two units you need to convert between? How does this help you know how to convert from one unit to the other?*

Children may think that they are limited to certain units when converting, for example centimetres to the next smaller unit (millimetres) or the next larger (metres), but not directly to kilometres as they have less experience of this and the numbers involved are difficult to visualise (for example, 5 cm = 0·00005 km). Ask:
• *Which units of measurement could you convert a distance in millimetres into?*

STRENGTHENING UNDERSTANDING

Encourage children to make flashcard reminders of how to convert between mm and cm, cm and m, and m and km, including simple bar models or number lines as pictorial prompts. To convert between units more than one step removed (for example, cm → km), they can place their flashcards next to each other and talk about the way to find the answer in two jumps (cm → m → km: divide by 100, then divide by 1,000) or in one jump directly to km (divide by 100,000).

GOING DEEPER

Ask children to research distance-based world records, similar to those in question 5 of the **Practice Book**. They can use these facts to devise their own questions that require unit conversion for a partner to solve.

KEY LANGUAGE

In lesson: base metric unit, millimetre, centimetre, metre, kilometre, length, convert, decimal, unit

STRUCTURES AND REPRESENTATIONS

bar model, place value grid

RESOURCES

Optional: place value grids, digit cards, a selection of rulers showing different metric units

 In the eTextbook of this lesson, you will find interactive links to a selection of teaching tools.

Before you teach

• Although the focus of this lesson is on the relationship between metric units of length, how could you apply the rules more generally?
• Can children name the different units of measurement used for measuring length?

Discover

ASK

- Question **1** a): *If you made a similar 1 km chain of coins in a straight line from your school, where do you think would you get as far as? What have you used to help you estimate 1 km?*
- Question **1** a): *'1 km of coins means 1,000 pennies which equals £10·00.' What is wrong with this statement?*
- Question **1** b): *Can you explain why the children will raise more money if they place the coins on their sides? Use plastic counters to show what you mean.*

IN FOCUS Discuss the scenario and talk about whether children have ever seen coins used in this way. As well as chains of coins, children may have seen photos of floors covered with coins as a form of charity fundraising. Ask why they think 1p coins have been chosen for this question. Encourage children to estimate of the number of coins they think might stretch to 1 km and the value of this amount. Observe whether children's estimates are reasonable and whether any understand the link between the number of coins and their value (i.e. the number of coins divided by 100 gives the value in pounds).

PRACTICAL TIPS Provide children with some 1p coins. Ask them to measure the diameter and depth of each coin and discuss whether 1 cm and 1 mm (respectively) are accurate measurements. Challenge children to suggest the number of coins they would need to cover short distances (for example, 1 cm or 10 cm). Encourage them to translate this into a monetary value. By considering simpler distances, children are building the skills that can then be applied to the longer distances featured in **Discover**.

ANSWERS

Question **1** a): The children will need 100,000 1p coins to make a line 1 km long.
They will have raised £1,000 for charity.

Question **1** b): The children would raise £9,000 more if they placed the coins on their sides.

Share

ASK

- Question **1** a): *What do you think it means that the 'base metric unit of length is the metre'? What do you think is the base metric unit of capacity?*
- Question **1** a): *How do the names of each unit give you a clue as to what they are worth?*
- Question **1**: *What facts will help you to work out the answers quickly? How would the questions be more difficult if the children used a different coin to make a chain from?*

IN FOCUS Both questions have several parts to them and it is important that children can understand the purpose behind each step. Ask children to write a description of each step on a piece of card and arrange them to show the method (for example, find the number of coins in 1 m; calculate the value of 1 m of coins; work out the number of metres in 1 km; calculate the value of 1 km of coins).

PUPIL TEXTBOOK 5C PAGE 160

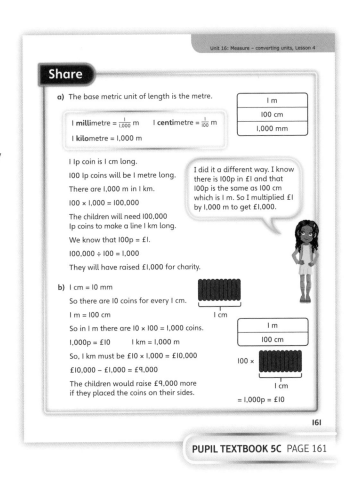

PUPIL TEXTBOOK 5C PAGE 161

Think together

Whole class teacher led (I do, We do, You do)

ASK

- Question ❶: *How many millimetres are in 1 cm? How many centimetres are in 1 m? How can you use these facts to convert from mm → m?*
- Question ❶: *What is the same about the methods? What is different? Explain which method you would choose.*
- Question ❷: *How would you convert $\frac{1}{2}$ to a decimal? How does converting $\frac{1}{2}$ to a decimal help? What other fractions can convert to decimals?*
- Question ❷: *How many centimetres are in 1 m? How many metres are in 1 km? How can you use these facts to convert cm to km in fewer steps?*

IN FOCUS Although questions ❶ and ❷ both show children a series of steps in converting between units, question ❶ also shows how to find the answer in one conversion. Discuss the advantages of both methods.

STRENGTHEN Provide place value grids and digit cards for children to use in questions ❶ and ❷ in order to strengthen children's understanding of how to convert in more than one step. Children should move the digit cards twice to model converting in two steps.

DEEPEN In question ❸ children should identify two pieces of information for each conversion: whether the units need to be multiplied or divided and by how much. They should be able to recognise that each number is a multiple of 10 and has a 1 followed by a number of zeros. Encourage children to spot patterns between their conversions (for example, m → mm involves × 1,000 or m → cm then cm → mm involves × 100 and then × 10, which is the same as × 1,000).

ASSESSMENT CHECKPOINT Use questions ❶ and ❷ to assess whether children can switch between different units of length, converting using one or two steps where necessary and applying their knowledge in problem-solving contexts. Their confidence when reasoning should be growing and they should be able to explain their methodology.

ANSWERS

Question ❶: 600 ÷ 10 = 60. 600 mm = 60 cm.
60 ÷ 100 = 0·6, 60 cm = 0·6 m
600 ÷ 1,000 = 0·6. 600 mm = 0·6 m
Olivia's chain of coins is 0·6 m long.

Question ❷: B, C, A; Max walks 50,000 cm.

Question ❸: All possible answers: mm → cm ÷ 10,
cm → mm × 10; mm → m ÷ 1,000,
m → mm × 1,000; mm → km ÷ 1,000,000,
km → mm × 1,000,000; cm → m ÷ 100,
m → cm × 100; cm → km ÷ 100,000,
km → cm × 100,000; m → km ÷ 1,000,
km → m × 1,000

Explanations should include that each number has a 1 and a number of zeros (accept any alternative answer that describes the fact they are all powers of 10).

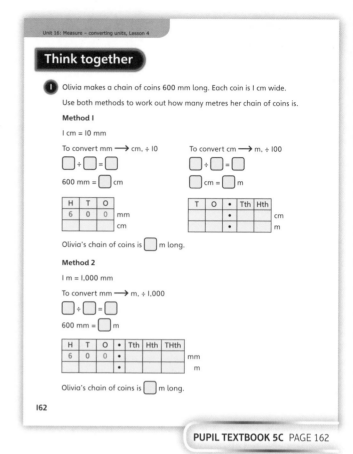

PUPIL TEXTBOOK 5C PAGE 162

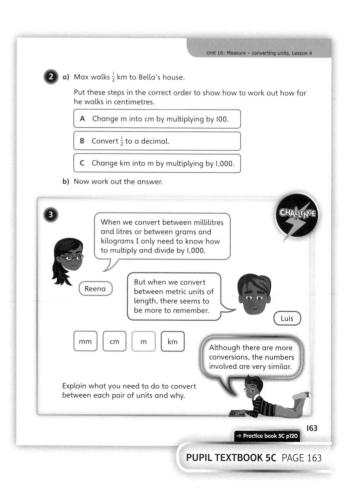

PUPIL TEXTBOOK 5C PAGE 163

Practice

WAYS OF WORKING Independent thinking

IN FOCUS Question ❶ consolidates children's understanding of the process of converting between units. They need to show when they need to multiply and when to divide. They then use the process outlined in question ❶ to answer question ❷.

STRENGTHEN Ask children to model question ❸ by providing them with digit cards and place value grids. Encourage them to convert each measurement into centimetres and model each shift in digits using the cards. Discuss why it is easier to order the measurements when they are converted to centimetres first. Ask whether they would get the same answer if they had converted the measurements into metres instead. Children could use rulers to measure each length (using the original units) and mark each height on the wall.

DEEPEN Ask children to make a poster showing how to convert between different units of length. They could illustrate it with examples of world records from question ❺ or their own research.

THINK DIFFERENTLY Question ❹ requires children to apply their knowledge of conversion to calculating perimeter. They need to understand that when finding perimeters and areas of shapes, it is very important that all the measurements are in the same unit.

ASSESSMENT CHECKPOINT Use questions ❷, ❸ and ❹ to assess whether children can apply their knowledge of metric units of length to solving multi-step problems that involve converting between units and calculating with the resulting numbers. Children should be reasoning confidently, explaining their methodology for each conversion.

ANSWERS Answers for the **Practice** part of the lesson appear in the separate **Practice and Reflect answer guide**.

Reflect

WAYS OF WORKING Independent thinking

IN FOCUS The aim of this activity is for children to display their knowledge of metric units in different ways. Although the obvious answer is that there are 10 mm in 1 cm, encourage children to give answers that equal part of a unit and remind them that 10 of one unit does not always have to equal 1 of another (for example, 10 cm in 0·1 m). Prompt them with questions such as: *What is 1 m in terms of kilometres? So, what is 10 m in terms of kilometres?* Encourage children to use their knowledge of conversion to help (for example, converting 10 cm into millimetres).

ASSESSMENT CHECKPOINT Look for children who are able to demonstrate their knowledge of metric units by suggesting appropriate ways in which each sentence can be completed.

ANSWERS Answers for the **Reflect** part of the lesson appear in the separate **Practice and Reflect answer guide**.

After the lesson ⏸

- Did children understand the issues and did they learn what was intended?
- The next few lessons deal with imperial and metric units of measurement. Do you feel that children's grasp of metric units is solid enough to apply their knowledge in this way without further consolidation?

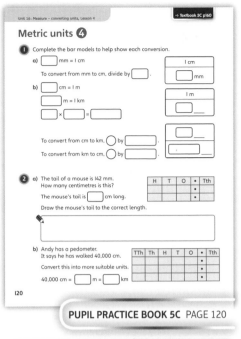

PUPIL PRACTICE BOOK 5C PAGE 120

PUPIL PRACTICE BOOK 5C PAGE 121

PUPIL PRACTICE BOOK 5C PAGE 122

Imperial units of length

Learning focus

In this lesson, children will be introduced to imperial units of length. They will understand the terms inches, feet and yards, convert between these and use approximations to convert from imperial to metric units.

Small steps

→ Previous step: Metric units (4)
→ **This step: Imperial units of length**
→ Next step: Imperial units of mass

NATIONAL CURRICULUM LINKS

Year 5 Measurement

Understand and use approximate equivalences between metric units and common imperial units such as inches, pounds and pints.

ASSESSING MASTERY

Children understand the term 'imperial units'. They can convert between common imperial units of length using given facts (12 inches = 1 foot, 3 feet = 1 yard). They can use given approximations to convert between imperial and metric units (for example, 1 inch is about 2·5 cm). Children are able to apply these skills when solving problems.

COMMON MISCONCEPTIONS

Children may think that it is not possible to convert between imperial and metric units. This may be because so far they have only worked with the metric system and any unit that does not fit this pattern of base units (the 'metre') cannot be converted. Ask children to show what they think 1 inch looks like and ask:
• *About how many centimetres do you think this is?*

Children may be unsure how to find the answer when more than one conversion is needed to solve a problem (for example, yards → metric: convert into inches and then centimetres). Ask:
• *What do you know? How can you use it to help?*

STRENGTHENING UNDERSTANDING

Give children extensive practical experience of an explorative nature in measuring, comparing and converting imperial units before embarking on problem solving. Give children rulers and tape measures that show inches and centimetres or inches and feet then ask them to measure different pieces of string that are whole inches long. Children are not expected to recognise each relationship just through measurement, but practical activities will build their understanding before starting on more abstract representations of these concepts.

GOING DEEPER

Encourage children to design their own 'Whodunnit?' problems in the style of the **Discover**, but extended to include comparison of different units of measurement (for example, four characters with heights given in inches, feet and inches, centimetres and metres, the tallest character being the culprit).

KEY LANGUAGE

In lesson: imperial units, metric units, **inch/inches** (in), **foot/feet** (ft), **yard** (yd), centimetre, metre, convert, approximately

STRUCTURES AND REPRESENTATIONS

bar model

RESOURCES

Optional: rulers and tape measures showing imperial and metric units, sticky labels

 In the eTextbook of this lesson, you will find interactive links to a selection of teaching tools.

Before you teach

• Based on previous lessons taught in this unit, are there any addition misconceptions you need to consider before this lesson?
• What real-life examples of imperial measurements can you use to reinforce the concepts of the lesson?

Discover

WAYS OF WORKING Pair work

ASK

- Question ❶: *What do you notice about the units of measure shown in the picture?*
- Question ❶: *When have you heard people use inches, feet or yards in real life?*
- Question ❶: *Can you show with your hands how long you think 1 inch / 1 foot / 1 yard is?*

IN FOCUS Imperial units of measure are introduced for the first time in this picture. It is important that time is spent talking about these new units before attempting to find the solution. Without discussing and exploring imperial units as a concept (particularly in real life), 'inches' and 'feet' do not hold any meaning and the conversion chart could be replaced with nonsense words and children could still calculate the answer (for example, if children knew that 1 zog ≈ 2·5 cm, they could still convert zogs into centimetres!).

PRACTICAL TIPS Provide lots of opportunities for children to explore the imperial measurements used in the picture. A fun idea might be to give children rulers or tape measures marked in inches and ask them to mark the various heights of the birds on a wall in chalk. The experience of measuring in a new unit will help children to both visualise its worth and (if they use tape measures) spot the equivalence between feet and inches by the markings.

ANSWERS

Question ❶ a): The penguin swallowed the ring.

Question ❶ b): The ostrich is 120 cm tall, which is the same as 1·2 m.

Share

WAYS OF WORKING Whole class teacher led

ASK

- Question ❶ a): *Why do you think the metric system might have made the heights easier to work with?*
- Question ❶: *Can you explain how the two bar models show the conversion between the units?*
- Question ❶ b): *Read Dexter's comment. Can you think of another '× 0·5' calculation that you can use to show what Dexter means?*

IN FOCUS There is an interesting difference between questions ❶ a) and b) and it is important that children spend time understanding this. In part a), children are given an exact equivalence (12 in = 1 ft) and in part b), they are given an approximation (1 in ≈ 2·5 cm). Provide rulers marked in inches and cm and ask children to draw a line 1 inch long and measure it very carefully in cm. They should see that 1 inch is just over $2\frac{1}{2}$ cm (or about 25·5 mm, actual measurement: 25·4 mm or 2·54 cm). Discuss why we approximate this to $2\frac{1}{2}$ cm and the usefulness of rounding in making calculations easier to work with. Ensure that children understand (and are reminded regularly) that all imperial → imperial conversions will be exact and all imperial ↔ metric conversions will be approximate.

PUPIL TEXTBOOK 5C PAGE 164

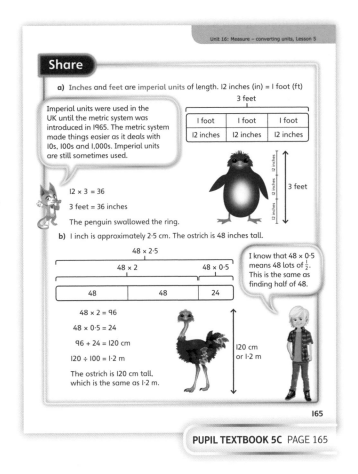

PUPIL TEXTBOOK 5C PAGE 165

Think together

Whole class teacher led (I do, We do, You do)

ASK

- Question ❶: *What strategy can you use to multiply a number by 12 and so convert feet into inches?*
- Question ❶: *The emu's height is an amount of whole feet with an amount of inches. Can you explain what to do with this amount of inches when you are converting into inches?*
- Question ❷: *Dexter uses two steps. How could you convert yards into inches using only one multiplication?*

IN FOCUS In question ❷, the partially completed bar model illustrates how to find the answer by converting from yards to feet (× 3) and then from feet to inches (× 12). Check that children understand these two steps. Ask if it is possible to convert yards to inches in one step. In effect, this is the same as removing the '3 ft' bar of the bar model, so each yard is clearly the same as 36 inches. The answer can therefore be found by multiplying 15 by 36.

STRENGTHEN Cut thick coloured strips of paper 1 yard long (two strips may need to be taped together!), 1 foot long and 1 inch long. For question ❷, challenge children to begin to make the bar model using the coloured strips, emphasising the equivalences between each unit. Ask how many 1 yard strips they will need to complete the bar model, how many 1 foot strips and how many 1 inch.

DEEPEN In question ❸, discuss Astrid and Ash's comments and why they might have to convert 1 foot and 1 yard into inches before converting into metric. Children can work in pairs to plan their strategies. Remind them to use various metric units (for example, 1 inch is approximately 25 mm and 1 yard is approximately 0·9 m). Give children different measurements for them to practise using their conversions.

ASSESSMENT CHECKPOINT Use questions ❶ and ❷ to assess whether children can use given facts to convert between imperial units of length and between imperial and metric units. They should be growing in confidence when applying these conversions in problem-solving contexts and be able to suggest appropriate strategies.

ANSWERS

Question ❶: 5 × 12 = 60; 60 + 3 = 63
5 feet 3 inches is equal to 63 inches. The emu is 63 inches tall.

Question ❷: 15 × 3 = 45, so 15 yards = 45 feet
45 × 12 = 540, so 15 yards = 540 inches
The pond is 540 inches wide.

Question ❸: Answers will vary. For example:
1 inch ≈ 2·5 cm, 25 mm, 0·025 m
1 foot ≈ 30 cm, 300 mm, 0·3 m (12 × 2·5 = 30)
1 yard ≈ 90 cm, 900 mm, 0·9 m (3 × 30 = 90)

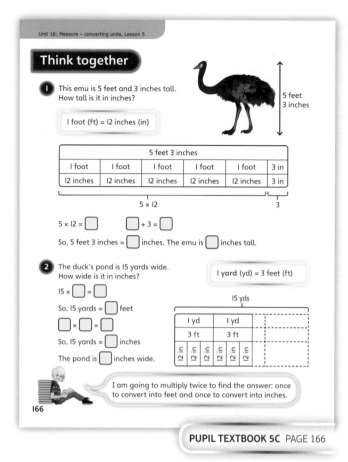

PUPIL TEXTBOOK 5C PAGE 166

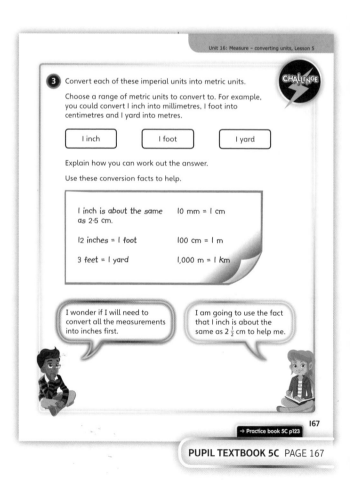

PUPIL TEXTBOOK 5C PAGE 167

Practice

WAYS OF WORKING Independent thinking

IN FOCUS In question **4** children compare pairs of imperial measurements given in different units. From their earlier work comparing metric units children should be aware that they can convert either one of the units. Ask whether there is more than one way to compare the measurements and which they find easier. Discuss whether conversions are easier with metric units and why. As well as the ease of multiplying and dividing by 10, 100, 1,000 and so on, the fact that the digits don't alter in metric conversions means that the answer can often be seen quickly without the need to do any real calculation.

STRENGTHEN For question **3**, children's understanding could be strengthened by providing them with rulers marked in inches and in centimetres, together with sticky labels to label the ruler in the same way as the one in the text.

DEEPEN Question **7** a) asks children to identify a mistake or misconception. As part of their explanation, encourage children to give more appropriate answers, correcting the mistake. Encourage children to discuss their thoughts first as there may be different possibilities (for example, in part a), Jamie may have confused feet for yards or for metres and may think (still incorrectly!) that a typical human is about 2 metres tall.

ASSESSMENT CHECKPOINT Use questions **2**, **4** and **5** to assess whether children can convert between imperial units and from imperial units to metric units using approximations. Children should be confident when applying their knowledge in problem-solving contexts.

ANSWERS Answers for the **Practice** part of the lesson appear in the separate **Practice and Reflect answer guide**.

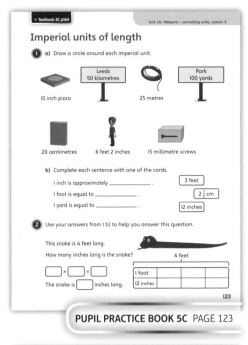

PUPIL PRACTICE BOOK 5C PAGE 123

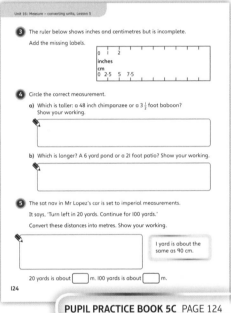

PUPIL PRACTICE BOOK 5C PAGE 124

Reflect

WAYS OF WORKING Independent thinking

IN FOCUS This activity provides an opportunity for children to summarise the information they have learnt about imperial units of length. Encourage them to think about imperial units as a whole and not just to write down the metric equivalents. Allow children time to work independently, writing down what they know, then discuss children's answers as a class.

ASSESSMENT CHECKPOINT Look for children who recognise that imperial units are part of a measurement system and that the units are related to each other. Children should know that imperial units can be converted into metric units but it will be an approximate value.

ANSWERS Answers for the **Reflect** part of the lesson appear in the separate **Practice and Reflect answer guide**.

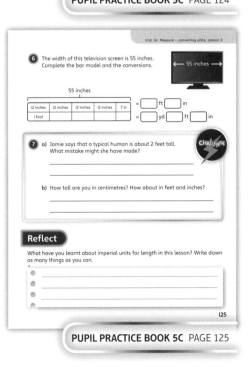

PUPIL PRACTICE BOOK 5C PAGE 125

After the lesson

- How well do you feel that children understand the general concept of imperial units of measurement as opposed to metric units?
- What misconceptions and mistakes did they make that you can take into account in the next lesson on imperial measures?

199

Imperial units of mass

Learning focus

In this lesson, children will be introduced to imperial units of mass. They will understand the terms ounces, pounds and stones, convert between them and use approximations to convert from imperial to metric units.

Small steps

→ Previous step: Imperial units of length
→ **This step: Imperial units of mass**
→ Next step: Imperial units of capacity

NATIONAL CURRICULUM LINKS

Year 5 Measurement

Understand and use approximate equivalences between metric units and common imperial units such as inches, pounds and pints.

ASSESSING MASTERY

Children can recognise common imperial units of mass and convert between them using given facts (16 ounces = 1 pound, 1 stone = 14 pounds). They can use given approximations to convert between imperial and metric units (for example, 1 oz is about 28 g). Children are able to apply these skills when solving problems.

COMMON MISCONCEPTIONS

Children may be unsure how to find the answer when more than one conversion is needed to solve a problem (for example, stones and pounds → metric: convert stones and pounds → pounds → grams). Ask:
• *What information does the question tell you? How can you use it to help?*

STRENGTHENING UNDERSTANDING

Provide children with practical experience of measuring, comparing and converting imperial units of mass before embarking on problem solving. Encourage children to investigate and explore as they measure using weighing scales that display both imperial and metric units. For example, ask them to weigh out 1 ounce of sand and to read how many grams this is. They are not expected to recognise each relationship just through measurement, but practical activities will build their understanding.

GOING DEEPER

Ask children to investigate the labelling on food products. They should find that many are labelled with both a metric mass and its imperial equivalent, where the metric value is a round number (for example, 500 g, 1 kg). However, some products (for example, jars of jam and packs of sausages) are labelled with only a mass of 454 g. Discuss why companies have not rounded up to 500 g or down to 450 g. Children may apply their knowledge from the lesson to see that 454 g is close to 448 g and is a way of approximating 1 lb. Even though these products are sold in a country using the metric system, they are still sold by the pound (or by the 454 g!). Children could also devise their own conversion problems based on one of the units on a label.

KEY LANGUAGE

In lesson: imperial units, metric units, **ounce** (oz), **pound** (lb), **stone** (st), gram, kilogram, convert, approximately, mass, long multiplication, estimate

STRUCTURES AND REPRESENTATIONS

bar model, number line, grid method, long multiplication

RESOURCES

Optional: weighing scales (imperial and metric), examples of masses (for example, 1 oz, 1 lb), two-sided flashcards for conversions, flashcards for imperial and metric units of mass, sticky labels

 In the eTextbook of this lesson, you will find interactive links to a selection of teaching tools.

Before you teach

• How do you plan to include practical experience of ounces, pounds and stones during the lesson?
• How might you develop and refine children's own representations of problems?

Discover

ASK

- Question ① a): *When have you heard people use ounces, pounds or stones in real life?*
- Question ①: *How heavy do you think 1 ounce or 1 pound is? Can you estimate the mass of objects in ounces/pounds?*

IN FOCUS Talk about the scenario. Explain that fruit and vegetables were sold by the pound and the ounce until fairly recently, when new laws said traders had to sell them using metric measurements (although they can still also display the imperial equivalent on the label). While units of length and capacity can be understood visually, it is more difficult for children to make links between units of mass and what they can see. When discussing the scenario, provide pre-weighed examples of 32 oz, 16 oz (1 lb), 4 oz and 1 oz to allow children to feel objects that weigh these amounts and make cognitive links between the words on the page and what they represent.

PRACTICAL TIPS Give children plenty of opportunities to explore imperial measures of mass. Provide sets of scales and materials (for example, sand, dried peas or modelling clay). Being able to actually measure amounts in a new unit should have the dual effect of ensuring children can gauge the value of ounces and pounds and (if the weighing scales show both units) spot the equivalence between these imperial units by noting the markings on the scale.

ANSWERS

Question ① a): Alex should ask for 2 lb of apples and $\frac{1}{4}$ lb (or 0·25 lb) of blueberries.

Question ① b): Alex's fruit will weigh about 1·008 kg.

Share

ASK

- Question ①: *In as few words as possible, describe what each question is asking you to do.*
- Question ① a): *How do the bar models help you to convert between units of measurement?*
- Question ① a): *Explain why 4 ounces is the same as $\frac{1}{4}$ of a pound. How could you write this as a decimal?*
- Question ① b): *36 × 28 is shown using the grid method. Can you think of a different method?*

IN FOCUS Challenge children to identify the moments in the calculations where they are converting from one unit to another. Draw arrows between units on the board and ask children to label these with the conversion calculation (for example, ounces → grams: × 28). Ensure that they understand why they need to multiply or divide (larger → smaller unit or smaller → larger, respectively) and how they know what value to multiply or divide by. For question ① b), discuss the different methods they might use to convert 36 oz into kilograms.

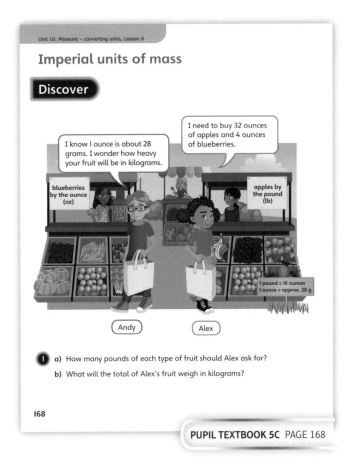

PUPIL TEXTBOOK 5C PAGE 168

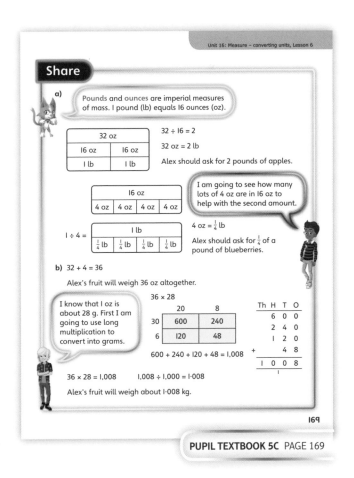

PUPIL TEXTBOOK 5C PAGE 169

Think together

Whole class teacher led (I do, We do, You do)

ASK

- Question **1**: *What do you know about ounces and grams that will help you find the answer?*
- Question **1**: *How would you complete the bar model?*
- Question **1**: *Can you explain how the written column method has been used to work out the answer to 28 × 15?*
- Question **1**: *Is there a different method you could use to multiply 28 by 15?*
- Question **2** a): *Which number features in all three calculations?*
- Question **2** a): *How would you alter the bar model to represent each individual calculation?*
- Question **2** b): *There is more than one way to find $\frac{3}{4}$ lb in ounces. Can you describe two ways?*

IN FOCUS Although the partially-completed bar model in question **1** has three layers, children should be able to see that the calculation is simply the number of ounces (15) multiplied by the number of grams per ounce (28). After discussing the method shown, ask children what other strategies they might use to find 28 × 15. Ask which method children think is the most efficient and why.

STRENGTHEN To strengthen children's understanding of the connections between units of mass, use flashcards with equivalent measurements on each side (for example, 1 lb and 16 oz). Children can use these flashcards to form their own bar models, for example in question **2** they could put four '1 lb' flashcards in a row that they then turn over to show how the mass is converted into four lots of 16 oz, which they can then discuss how to calculate.

DEEPEN Question **3** challenges children to begin thinking more independently about how to apply their knowledge of imperial units of mass. Ask them to discuss in pairs whether Astrid or Flo is correct and why. Choose different pairs to share their ideas with the rest of the group. Challenge children to work out how to convert from stones to grams and to make up problems using their conversion.

ASSESSMENT CHECKPOINT Use questions **1** and **2** to assess whether children can use given facts to convert between common imperial units of mass and between imperial and metric units. They should be growing in confidence when applying these conversions in problem-solving contexts and be able to suggest appropriate strategies.

ANSWERS

Question **1**: The raspberries weigh about 420 g.

Question **2** a): 4 lb = 16 oz × 4 = 64 oz;
10 lb = 16 oz × 10 = 160 oz;
$\frac{1}{2}$ lb = 16 oz ÷ 2 = 8 oz

Question **2** b): $\frac{1}{4}$ lb = 16 oz ÷ 4 = 4 oz, so $\frac{3}{4}$ lb = 4 oz × 3 = 12 oz

Question **3** a): The second set of scales will show 13·2 lb.

Question **3** b): The dog weighs 49 lbs, which is about 22·5 kg.

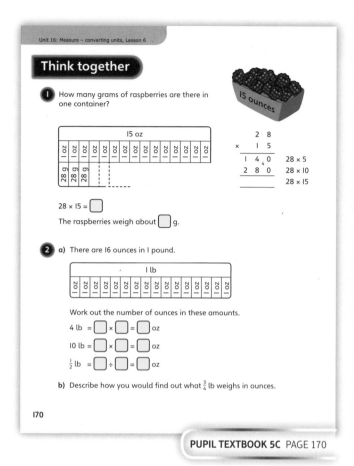

PUPIL TEXTBOOK 5C PAGE 170

PUPIL TEXTBOOK 5C PAGE 171

Practice

WAYS OF WORKING Independent thinking

IN FOCUS Question **4** presents children with a common misconception. When finding equivalences for mixed numbers, some children will convert the whole number, but then take the fraction and simply add it on the end. Discuss what the $\frac{1}{2}$ in $3\frac{1}{2}$ lb stands for – half of what? It is crucial that children see that this represents half of *something*.

STRENGTHEN Before children attempt question **1**, give them cards showing different units of mass (both imperial and metric). Ask children to sort these into two groups according to whether they are imperial or metric units. Then draw a large number line for question **1** for children to label using sticky labels. Encourage children to see a pattern in the multiples of 16. They can use their completed number line to help convert the measurements that follow.

DEEPEN In question **6**, encourage children to share their methods with a partner to help consolidate their understanding. Challenge children to estimate how heavy the giant octopus is in relation to an adult human. If an adult is said to weigh about 13–14 stone, then a giant octopus is about half the mass.

THINK DIFFERENTLY Question **5** provides children with a code to crack and a new imperial unit of mass to discover: the ton. To convert 10 lb into different units, children should convert from pounds to ounces by multiplying by 16 and use 1 lb ≈ 450 g to convert into grams and then kilograms.

ASSESSMENT CHECKPOINT Use questions **1**, **2** and **3** to assess whether children can convert between common imperial units and between imperial and metric units. They should be confident when applying their knowledge of imperial units of mass.

ANSWERS Answers for the **Practice** part of the lesson appear in the separate **Practice and Reflect answer guide**.

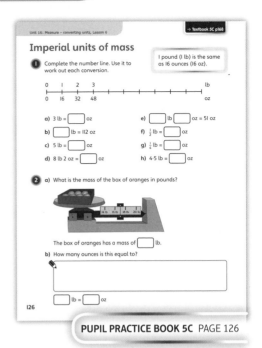

PUPIL PRACTICE BOOK 5C PAGE 126

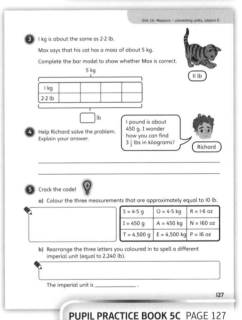

PUPIL PRACTICE BOOK 5C PAGE 127

Reflect

WAYS OF WORKING Independent thinking

IN FOCUS This activity provides an opportunity for children to apply the information they have learnt about pounds. Observe those children who use different strategies (for example, sketching a bar model or double number line). Encourage children to share their methods and discuss them as a group.

ASSESSMENT CHECKPOINT Look for children who can apply their knowledge of imperial and metric equivalences to express the given mass correctly in either grams or kilograms.

ANSWERS Answers for the **Reflect** part of the lesson appear in the separate **Practice and Reflect answer guide**.

After the lesson

- Are children confident in understanding that an ounce is smaller than a pound which is smaller than a stone?
- Do you feel that they are beginning to be more confident working with imperial measures? How might the final lesson (on capacity) deal with some of their more general misconceptions?

PUPIL PRACTICE BOOK 5C PAGE 128

Imperial units of capacity

Learning focus

In this lesson, children will be introduced to imperial units of capacity. They will understand the terms pints and gallons, convert between them and use approximations to convert from imperial to metric units.

Small steps

→ Previous step: Imperial units of mass
→ **This step: Imperial units of capacity**
→ Next step: Converting units of time

NATIONAL CURRICULUM LINKS

Year 5 Measurement

Understand and use approximate equivalences between metric units and common imperial units such as inches, pounds and pints.

ASSESSING MASTERY

Children can convert between common imperial units of capacity using given facts (8 pints = 1 gallon). They can use given approximations to convert between imperial and metric units (for example, 1 pint is about 570 ml). Children are able to apply these skills when solving problems.

COMMON MISCONCEPTIONS

Children may think that it is not possible to convert between units when more than one conversion is needed to solve a problem (for example, gallons → metric: convert gallons → pints → millilitres). Ask:
• *What do you know? How can you use it to help?*

STRENGTHENING UNDERSTANDING

Provide children with practical experience of measuring, comparing and converting imperial units of capacity before embarking on problem solving. Encourage children to measure exploratively using measuring jugs that display both imperial and metric units. For example, ask them to measure 1 pint of water and read how many millilitres this is. They can read other equivalences just by looking carefully at the jug.

GOING DEEPER

Give children facts about capacities measured in imperial units (for example, a bath holds 64 gallons, the Niagara Falls has 150,000 gallons of water rushing over it every second and the daily requirement of water for women is about 3 pints) or encourage them to find their own facts. Challenge them to devise their own conversion problems for a partner to solve (for example, the weekly water requirement for women in litres; the number of pints of water over the Niagara Falls every second; the number of litre jugs would it take to fill up a bath).

KEY LANGUAGE

In lesson: imperial units, metric units, **pint**, **gallon**, millilitre, litre, convert, approximately, capacity

STRUCTURES AND REPRESENTATIONS

bar model, number line

RESOURCES

Optional: measuring jugs (imperial and metric), liquid containers (for example, milk cartons, water bottles), paper rectangles

 In the eTextbook of this lesson, you will find interactive links to a selection of teaching tools.

Before you teach

• This lesson is the last in this series on imperial units. Are there any general misconceptions that you feel need to be addressed during the lesson?
• How might you help children to adapt their strategies when problem constraints are changed?

Discover

ASK

- Question **1**: *Where might you see imperial units of measurement in a supermarket?*
- Question **1**: *When have you heard people use pints or gallons in real life?*
- Question **1**: *What facts can you see in the image? How can you use these to help convert between units?*

IN FOCUS As with the previous lesson, talk about the fact that liquids were sold by imperial measures and, although shops now have to label products with metric units, people still use imperial measures (for example, milk in pint cartons, miles per gallon for fuel consumption). Discuss the facts shown in the picture and ask children to try estimating 1 pint. Encourage them to use reasoning and prior knowledge of capacity (for example, a 500 ml bottle of water fills about 2 mugs of water, so a pint must be just over 2 mugs of water).

PRACTICAL TIPS Give children opportunities to explore imperial measures of capacity. Provide the sorts of liquid containers found in supermarkets (milk cartons, water bottles and so on) and encourage children to find their capacity in pints using imperial measuring jugs. Physically measuring amounts in pints should have the dual effect of ensuring children can gauge the value of imperial units of capacity and (if the measuring jug shows both units) spot the equivalence between imperial and metric units by looking at the scale.

ANSWERS

Question **1** a): 2·28 litres are approximately the same as 4 pints.

Question **1** b): Mo has 3·42 litres of water.

Share

ASK

- Question **1** a): *Can you describe why the bar model, short multiplication and place value grid are all important in finding the solution?*
- Question **1** a): *Can you explain how to work out the answer without using a bar model?*
- Question **1** a): *A pint is just over $\frac{1}{2}$ a litre (500 ml). What would you expect 2 pints to be about the same as? What would you expect 4 pints to be?*
- Question **1** b): *What is $\frac{1}{4}$ of a gallon? How does this help? Can you think of a different way to solve this? Think of a way that uses subtraction to find $\frac{3}{4}$.*

IN FOCUS Both questions use bar models. Ask children to explain how they have been used to help find the solution. Spend time particularly considering the two bar models used to represent question **1** b), and how they show how to find $\frac{3}{4}$ by finding $\frac{1}{4}$ and multiplying by 3.

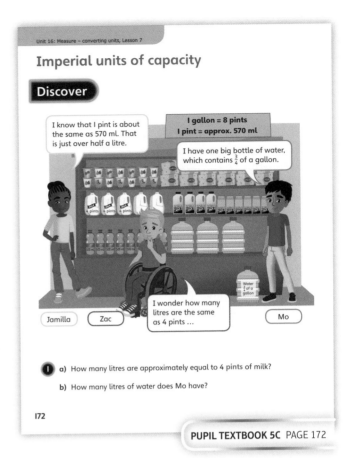

PUPIL TEXTBOOK 5C PAGE 172

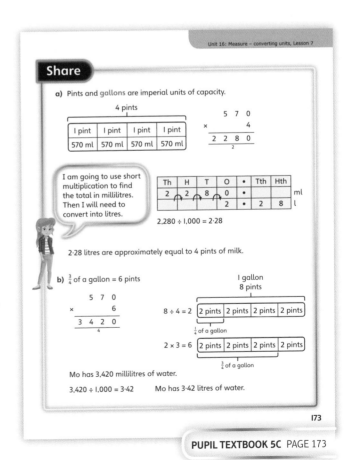

PUPIL TEXTBOOK 5C PAGE 173

Think together

Whole class teacher led (I do, We do, You do)

ASK

- Question **1** a): *Can you describe how to get from a capacity measured in pints to one measured in litres?*
- Question **1** a): *Can you think of a way to convert directly from pints to litres?*
- Question **1** a): *How would you alter the bar model and the method if the water carrier was $\frac{1}{3}$ the size?*
- Question **1** b): *How has the number line been used to show the difference between the water container's capacity and 1 gallon? How could you alter the number line to include millilitres?*
- Question **2**: *'Is a pint of milk more or less than two cans of lemonade?' Why is answering this is the same as answering the given question?*

IN FOCUS Question **1** scaffolds children's ability to visualise and calculate the conversions needed to find the answer using bar models and number lines. These are removed for questions **2** and **3**, although children may benefit from drawing their own pictorial representations as part of their working.

STRENGTHEN If children are finding question **1** a) challenging provide measuring jugs for children to find what 1 pint of water is in millilitres. Ask how many pints they need and what units they need to give the answer in. Then ask children to draw a sketch of what the question is asking. Children now attempt the problem.

DEEPEN Ensure children understand that question **3** is the sort of conversion problem that occurs in everyday life. Ask children to work in pairs and plan the steps needed to find the answer (for example, convert 1 gallon to pints, pints to ml, ml to litres, then subtract to find the difference). Challenge children to devise new, similar problems for a partner to solve.

ASSESSMENT CHECKPOINT Use questions **1** and **2** to assess whether children can use given facts to convert between common imperial units of capacity and between imperial and metric units. They should be growing in confidence when applying these conversions in problem-solving contexts and be able to suggest appropriate strategies.

ANSWERS

Question **1** a): $5 \times 570 = 2,850$.
$2,850 \div 1,000 = 2.85$. 5 pints are about the same as 2·85 litres.

Question **1** b): 3 pints is the difference.
1,710 millilitres is the difference.
$1,710 \div 1,000 = 1.71$. 1·71 litres is the difference.

Question **2**: 1 pint is approximately 570 ml.
Half a pint is approximately 285 ml.
So half a pint is less than a 330 ml can of lemonade.

Question **3**: Yes, the bucket can be filled and there will be 0·26 litres (or 260 ml) left over.

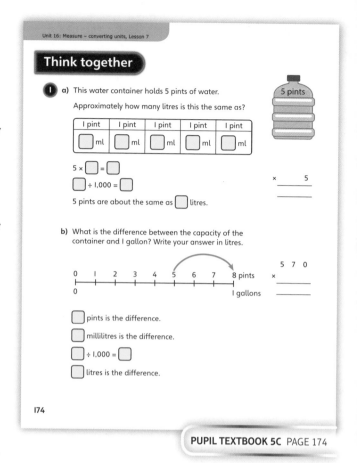

PUPIL TEXTBOOK 5C PAGE 174

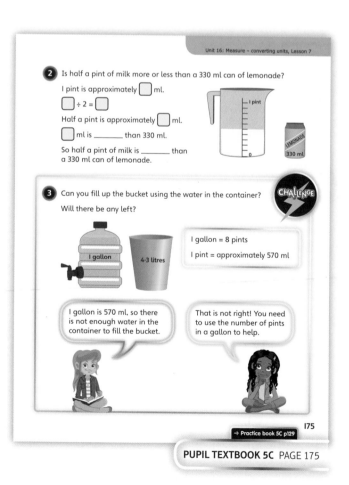

PUPIL TEXTBOOK 5C PAGE 175

Practice

WAYS OF WORKING Independent thinking

IN FOCUS In question **3**, children are expected to make the important link between gallons and litres. They can use the bar model from question **1** to find the equivalence of 8 pints in terms of litres. The answer, 4,560 ml, rounded to the nearest half litre is 4·5 litres (or $4\frac{1}{2}$ litres). As an extension, ask how many litres are nearest to $\frac{1}{2}$ a gallon.

STRENGTHEN For question **5**, encourage children to label the notches on the milk jug. Establish which two amounts the milk is between and thus that there are 3·5 pints. Provide rectangles of paper for children to create a bar model, writing that each whole pint is worth 570 ml. Ask them to cut one rectangle in half to represent half a pint and ask how many millilitres this is. Once children have calculated the answer in millilitres, provide place value grids where appropriate to support conversion from millilitres into litres.

DEEPEN Ask children to rephrase question **7** in their own words and then show how they might find the answer. The cost at petrol station A is straightforward to find, but B requires more reasoning, using $4\frac{1}{2}$ litres ≈ 1 gallon. Challenge children to suggest real-life situations when a calculation like this might be useful.

THINK DIFFERENTLY In question **6**, the only calculation that children need to do is 3 × 200 ml. They will then need to recognise that 600 ml is just over a pint.

ASSESSMENT CHECKPOINT Use questions **1** to **5** to assess whether children can convert between common imperial units and between imperial and metric units. They should be confident when applying their knowledge of imperial units of capacity.

ANSWERS Answers for the **Practice** part of the lesson appear in the separate **Practice and Reflect answer guide**.

Reflect

WAYS OF WORKING Independent thinking

IN FOCUS This activity provides an opportunity for children to apply what they have learnt in a real-life context, using prior knowledge of the equivalence between pints and millilitres. Children's explanations may go on to justify the number of litres they would decide to buy. An answer of 1·14 l shows that they are able to convert correctly. An answer of either $1\frac{1}{2}$ litres or 2 litres shows that children are considering the real-life scenario and have recognised that milk may possibly be sold only in half or whole litres, so have rounded their answer up.

ASSESSMENT CHECKPOINT Look for children who are able to convert 2 pints into litres by using known facts (1 pint ≈ 570 ml). Observe those children who round their answer up to the next half or whole litre.

ANSWERS Answers for the **Reflect** part of the lesson appear in the separate **Practice and Reflect answer guide**.

After the lesson

- Do you feel that children's misconceptions were addressed during the lesson? What reasons did children have for making these and what learning points did they show?
- How well do you think that children have understood and applied the new concept? Do you feel that they are ready to move on?

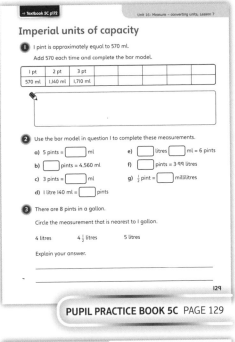

PUPIL PRACTICE BOOK 5C PAGE 129

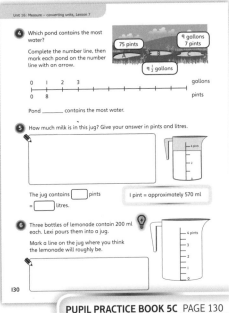

PUPIL PRACTICE BOOK 5C PAGE 130

PUPIL PRACTICE BOOK 5C PAGE 131

Converting units of time

Learning focus

In this lesson, children will solve problems where they have to convert between units of time, including those where there is a remainder.

Small steps

→ Previous step: Imperial units of capacity
→ **This step: Converting units of time**
→ Next step: Timetables

NATIONAL CURRICULUM LINKS

Year 5 Measurement

Solve problems involving converting between units of time.

ASSESSING MASTERY

Children can solve time-based problems confidently, where they are required to convert between units of time. They can make appropriate decisions about how to present their answers if there is a remainder (for example, 150 seconds = 2 minutes 30 seconds or 2·5 minutes).

COMMON MISCONCEPTIONS

Children may think that they can express remainders as decimals, as with metric measures (for example, 2 kg 500 g = 2·5 kg). However, 2 weeks 5 days cannot be expressed as 2·5 weeks and 3·25 hours is not 3 hours 25 minutes. Ask:
• *What proportion of a week is 5 days? Can you write this as a decimal?*
• *What does the decimal 0·25 in 3·25 hours represent? What fraction of an hour is the same as 0·25?*

STRENGTHENING UNDERSTANDING

To support children before the lesson, provide examples showing different units of time (for example, analogue and digital clocks, calendars), together with representations, to consolidate their knowledge of equivalences. Ask questions about equivalences, for example when looking at calendars ask how they show how many days in two weeks. Do the same for minutes, seconds and hours using analogue clock faces.

GOING DEEPER

Give children problems where they need to interpret decimals and fractions of different units of time. For example *A book order is going to be delivered in $3\frac{1}{2}$ weeks. How many days is this?; How many hours is the same as 4·5 days?* Ask children to explain what the fraction or decimal part represents and what mistake people might make. Extend the challenge to consider further examples (for example, 0·25, 0·75, $\frac{1}{4}$, $\frac{3}{4}$) where finding these parts of the unit is possible (for example, 0·25 hours in minutes or $2\frac{3}{4}$ days in hours).

KEY LANGUAGE

In lesson: remainder, multiple, second, minute, hour, day, week, month, year

STRUCTURES AND REPRESENTATIONS

calendar, bar model, number line

RESOURCES

Optional: analogue and digital clocks, calendars, year planners, interlinking cubes

 In the eTextbook of this lesson, you will find interactive links to a selection of teaching tools.

Before you teach

• This lesson applies the concepts of converting between units of time. How confident are children with these concepts?
• How can you improve the teaching of problem-solving and reasoning through this lesson?

Discover

WAYS OF WORKING Pair work

ASK

- Question ❶: *What different units of time can you see?*
- Question ❶ a): *How much longer than 1 month has Toshi had his phone? Why is it difficult to say for sure?*
- Question ❶ b): *How long does the whole battery on Amal's phone take to charge?*
- Question ❶ b): *How many minutes has Amal's phone been charging for?*

IN FOCUS Use the picture to discuss children's wider experience of this real-life scenario. For example, ask questions about how long they think they normally have to return an electrical item if it is not working, whether they think that 5 hours is a quick length of time to charge up a battery. Discuss when else they might think about units of time with a mobile phone (for example, length of a call, the number of free minutes, setting an alarm).

PRACTICAL TIPS Prior to the lesson, give children experience of everyday durations in the context of electronic devices. For example, children could time how long it takes for their class laptop to charge, explore advertisements for mobile phone deals that talk about free minutes or investigate the time it takes to download files on a computer. For each example, ask children to practise converting into alternative units of measurement.

ANSWERS

Question ❶ a): Toshi has had his phone for 5 weeks and 4 days.

Question ❶ b): 4 bars of Amal's battery should be charged fully. There are 15 minutes left until the next bar is charged.

Share

WAYS OF WORKING Whole class teacher led

ASK

- Question ❶ a): *What do you think Flo means by 'there will be a remainder'?*
- Question ❶ a): *How can you predict whether there will be a remainder when converting units of time?*
- Question ❶ a): *What does the 5 represent in the answer 5 remainder 4? What does the 4 represent?*
- Question ❶ b): *Can you give some amounts of minutes that are the same as a whole number of hours? Which two multiples of 60 does 285 minutes come between?*
- Question ❶ b): *Explain how the bar model represents the problem.*

IN FOCUS Both questions use bar models to represent the problem. Ask children to explain how the bar models have been used. In particular, challenge them to explain the relevance of the remainder at the end of the second bar. Check that children recognise that this leftover amount is less than a whole week or hour.

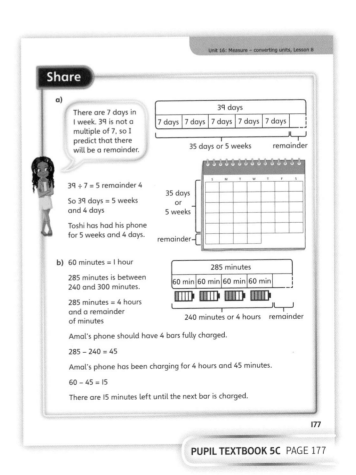

Think together

Whole class teacher led (I do, We do, You do)

ASK

- Question **1**: *What unit of time is given in the question? What unit is needed for the answer?*
- Question **1**: *What could you do to find out whether Amal's phone been downloading for a whole number of minutes or a whole number and part of a minute?*
- Question **1**: *How many minutes is 378 seconds in-between? How do you know?*
- Question **1**: *Can you explain how to work out the remainder of seconds?*
- Question **2**: *How is this question the same as question 1? How are they different?*

IN FOCUS The scaffolding for question **2** involves calculating 5 weeks in terms of days and then subtracting the number of days that have already gone. Ask children whether they can think of a different way to find the answer. They may be able to recognise that they could convert the number of days that have gone by into weeks and days and use this to find the difference.

STRENGTHEN If children need representations to help answer question **2**, refer back to the use of a number line in question **1**. Ask what else they could use that shows weeks and days clearly. Provide calendars (or × 7 grids) to help children count in multiples of 7 and quickly identify that 5 weeks are the same as 35 days. Discuss how they can use that fact to work out the number of days left.

DEEPEN Question **3** deepens children's understanding by giving them a series of durations in hours and asking them to translate these into clock times. As the durations are mostly greater than 24 hours, children will need to convert into days and hours (for example, 93 hours = 3 days 21 hours) and identify the effect that this will have on the day of the week as well as the time. Ask children to create a similar problem based on their school week.

ASSESSMENT CHECKPOINT Use questions **1** and **2** to assess whether children can give solutions involving conversion and comparison. Ensure children are able to explain clearly why and how they are using bar models to help solve each problem.

ANSWERS

Question **1**: 378 is between 360 and 420.
So there are 6 minutes and there will be a remainder of seconds.
378 – 360 = 18
Amal's phone has been downloading for 6 minutes and 18 seconds.

Question **2**: 5 weeks = 5 × 7 = 35 days
35 – 22 = 13
There are 13 days until the sale ends.

Question **3** a): On the ferry: 13:00 Tuesday;
arrived: 19:00 Tuesday;
visiting auntie: 13:00 Thursday;
theme park: 10:00 Friday

Question **3** b): Jen has 154 hours until she has to go home.

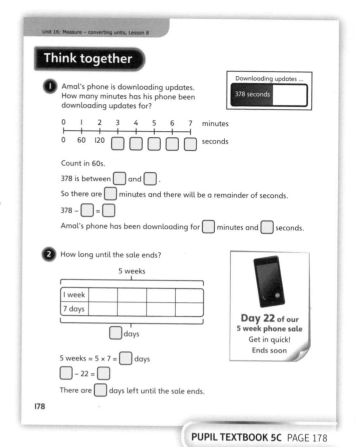

PUPIL TEXTBOOK 5C PAGE 178

PUPIL TEXTBOOK 5C PAGE 179

Practice

WAYS OF WORKING Independent thinking

IN FOCUS Question **3** addresses the common misconception that units of time behave in a similar way to metric units, with a remainder appearing to the right of the decimal point. It is essential that children make the link between the decimal and the fraction of an hour as their understanding depends on them recognising that 0·25 of an hour = $\frac{1}{4}$ of an hour (= 15 minutes), so 4·25 hours is the same as $4\frac{1}{4}$ hours or 4 hours 15 minutes.

STRENGTHEN Provide children who need further support with question **5** with scaffolding in the form of a list for them to fill in. They should write this out and fill in the gaps. '1 week = _ days; 1 day = _ hours; 1 hour = _ minutes; 1 minute = _ seconds.' Then ask them how they would convert each of these (for example, how they would work out the number of weeks there are if there are 21 days and how would they work out the number of days in 3 weeks).

DEEPEN Question **5** deepens children's understanding by challenging them to consider the combinations of operations needed to convert across several units. Encourage children to apply their knowledge of larger and smaller units (i.e. larger → smaller unit requires multiplication) to work out the final units. Ask them to draw sets of function machines for two conversions, one larger → smaller unit and one smaller → larger unit.

THINK DIFFERENTLY In question **4**, children are presented with four durations of summer holidays expressed using different units. Ask why the different durations are tricky to compare and what they need to do to make it easier.

ASSESSMENT CHECKPOINT Use questions **1** to **3** to assess whether children are confident when solving problems where they need to convert between units of time that are not whole amounts. They should display reasoning skills, explaining appropriate methods and thinking with confidence.

ANSWERS Answers for the **Practice** part of the lesson appear in the separate **Practice and Reflect answer guide**.

Reflect

WAYS OF WORKING Pair work

IN FOCUS This activity provides an opportunity to check children's methodology. Initially, children should think individually and decide on a method, which they then explain to their partner. They should mention that 1 year = 12 months and that 30 is not a multiple of 12, so the answer is not a whole number of years. They should describe how they would use this information, for example 'I would count in 12s until I got near to 30. This would show the years and then the remainder is the number of extra months.' Encourage children to compare their methods.

ASSESSMENT CHECKPOINT Look for children who describe clearly and accurately how to convert 30 months into years and months.

ANSWERS Answers for the **Reflect** part of the lesson appear in the separate **Practice and Reflect answer guide**.

After the lesson ⏸

- How did children respond mathematically to the problems and how did the mathematical processes develop during the lesson?
- Did you provide feedback to push them to think more deeply or to learn more about process skills?

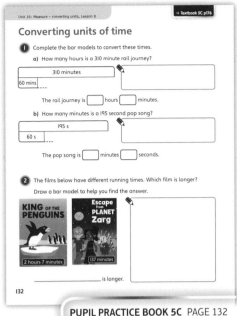

PUPIL PRACTICE BOOK 5C PAGE 132

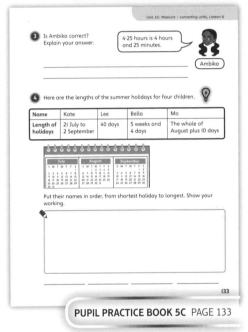

PUPIL PRACTICE BOOK 5C PAGE 133

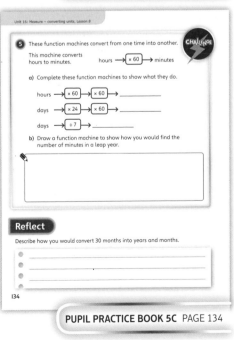

PUPIL PRACTICE BOOK 5C PAGE 134

Timetables

Learning focus

In this lesson, children will learn to use timetables, applying their knowledge of 24-hour times to read arrival and departure times and calculate durations.

Small steps

→ Previous step: Converting units of time
→ **This step: Timetables**
→ Next step: Problem solving – measure

NATIONAL CURRICULUM LINKS

Year 5 Measurement

Solve problems involving converting between units of time.

ASSESSING MASTERY

Children can read information from timetables accurately. They can apply their knowledge of timetables to solve time-based problems confidently, including where they need to convert between units of time.

COMMON MISCONCEPTIONS

Children may think that a journey is read from left to right, across the row of the timetable, instead of down a column. Ask:
• *Use your finger to trace the journey that one single bus/train makes. How many times does it stop? What time does it finally arrive? What do you think a row of the timetable shows?*

Children may think that timetables should show every time mentioned in a problem. For example, with 'Olivia arrives at Boston at 10 o'clock and catches the next train …', children become confused because they cannot locate 10:00 on the timetable. Ask:
• *What is the first train after Olivia arrives? What time does it leave?*

STRENGTHENING UNDERSTANDING

It is essential that children's use of timetables is made as relevant as possible to their own lives. Where possible, take photos of local bus stops and ask children to match them up with a timetable. Children can document their journeys on buses and compare the times the bus stopped with the scheduled times. For children who do not use public transport regularly, start by using timetables that apply to them (a school timetable or cinema showing times). These will not be as complex as bus or train timetables and so will provide a useful introduction.

GOING DEEPER

Challenge children to devise their own bus timetables with several columns, showing at least five buses, at least five stops, at least one bus not stopping so regularly (and therefore quicker) and with consistent times between stops. They can then create their own problems for a partner to solve, based on their timetables.

KEY LANGUAGE

In lesson: timetable, 24-hour, digital, duration, hour, minute, departs/departure, arrives/arrival

STRUCTURES AND REPRESENTATIONS

timetable, analogue clock face, number line

RESOURCES

Optional: different kinds of timetables, analogue clock faces with movable hands, mini whiteboards, paper strips

 In the eTextbook of this lesson, you will find interactive links to a selection of teaching tools.

Before you teach

• This lesson requires a prior knowledge of 24-hour times. How well do you feel children understand this way of representing times? Does this skill need consolidating first?
• How can you link this lesson to other lessons or the use of timetables in everyday life?

Discover

Unit 16: Measure – converting units, Lesson 9

WAYS OF WORKING Pair work

ASK

• Question ❶: *Where have you seen a timetable like this before? Have you ever needed to use one?*
• Question ❶: *Put your finger at the top of a column and move it downwards. What does this column show?*
• Question ❶: *Put your finger at the start of a row and move it from left to right. What does this row show?*
• Question ❶: *How many buses are shown on this timetable? How often do they leave?*

IN FOCUS Use the picture as a way to introduce children to the concept of timetables. Talk about how each column has been labelled with a bus name. Tell children to put their finger at the top of a bus route and follow its journey. Ask questions about the bus's journey.

PRACTICAL TIPS Provide pairs with timetables showing local bus routes or film times at a local cinema. Many children will never have used a timetable and the more relevant it is to your school's locality, the better. Ask them to look at the way the times are written (layout, 24-hour) and what each column and row represents. Encourage pairs to share their findings.

ANSWERS

Question ❶ a): Emma arrives at school at 08:05 (five minutes past 8).

Question ❶ b): Bus C arrives at school at 08:35.

PUPIL TEXTBOOK 5C PAGE 180

Share

WAYS OF WORKING Whole class teacher led

ASK

• Question ❶ a): *Why do you think timetables are usually written in 24-hour digital time?*
• Question ❶ a): *Emma leaves at twenty-five to 8: what time will this look like on the timetable? Which bus does Emma catch?*
• Question ❶ a): *How do you know what time Emma will arrive at school?*
• Question ❶ b): *How does the number line show how long each bus takes?*
• Question ❶ b): *Why do you think the clock faces show 15 minutes being added up to 08:00 and then the remaining 35 minutes separately?*

IN FOCUS Question ❶ b) employs a method children will be familiar with from previous work when bridging an o'clock time. Both the number line and the clock faces show time being added up to an o'clock time and then from the o'clock time to the final time. When used in timetables, the 24-hour clock reduces confusion between am and pm times and makes it easier to calculate duration over several hours, although children have not had to use this strategy here. For example, 8:30 am to 1:30 pm is 5 hours – this is easier to see when written as 08:30 to 13:30 because 8 + 5 = 13.

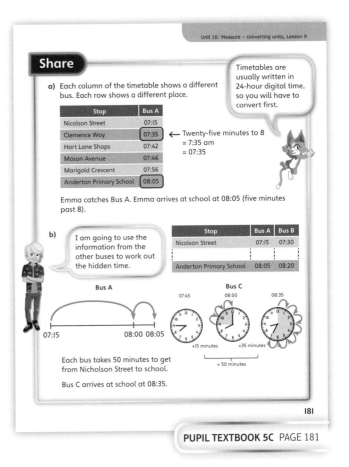

PUPIL TEXTBOOK 5C PAGE 181

Think together

WAYS OF WORKING Whole class teacher led (I do, We do, You do)

ASK

- Question **1**: *Compare this timetable to the timetable in* **Discover**. *What is the same? What is different?*
- Question **1**: *What does each column show? Each row?*
- Question **1** a): *How can you find which train Lexi gets on?*
- Question **1** a): *Describe Lexi's arrival time in two ways.*
- Question **1** b): *How can you find which train Andy gets on?*
- Question **1** b): *How will you find the duration of the journey? How does the representation of the clocks help?*
- Question **2**: *Can you find this part of the timetable? What time does the train leave? What time does it arrive?*
- Question **2**: *Why does the number line show two separate jumps? How does this help?*
- Question **2**: *All the trains take the same time to get from Birchfield to Ashtown Parkway. Can you prove this by using a number line and working out the time using different trains?*

IN FOCUS Encourage children to use the large timetable as much as possible and to locate the relevant times and trains within the whole timetable, rather than using the small timetable representations. For question **2**, you may find it useful to initially ask the question separately, without getting children to consider the supporting image of part of the timetable. Ask whether it matters which train they choose. Then go on through the methodology shown.

STRENGTHEN To strengthen children's understanding of the relationship between a train's journey and the timetable, provide analogue clock faces. Encourage children to draw a line on a mini whiteboard and then talk through the journey of one of the trains. At every station, children should make the new time on their analogue clock and label the time and station on their time line. This should help translate the columns of the timetable into something that resembles a journey from A to B. Children could apply this modelling technique to find answers.

DEEPEN Use question **3** to discuss when a train might not stop at particular stations. Ask why they would expect the express train to be quicker than the next train, without looking at the times. If children find a duration in hours and minutes, encourage them to convert before comparing and calculating. Ask children to discuss Flo's comment in pairs and to find the answer using her method. They can compare the 14:13 and 15:13 trains: the 15:13 leaves one hour later but arrives only 40 minutes later, so is 20 minutes quicker.

ASSESSMENT CHECKPOINT Use questions **1**, **2** and **3** to assess whether children are growing in confidence when reading timetables. They should be able to identify departure and arrival times and calculate durations, using representations to help. They should understand how to apply these skills in problem-solving contexts.

ANSWERS

Question **1** a): Lexi arrives in Ashtown Central at 15:50.

Question **1** b): It takes 24 minutes to get to Birchfield.

Question **2**: It takes 32 minutes to get from Birchfield to Ashtown Parkway.

Question **3**: The express train is 20 minutes quicker.

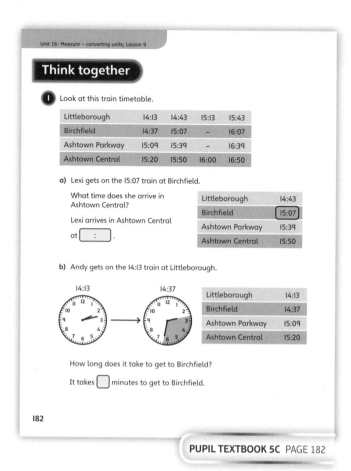

PUPIL TEXTBOOK 5C PAGE 182

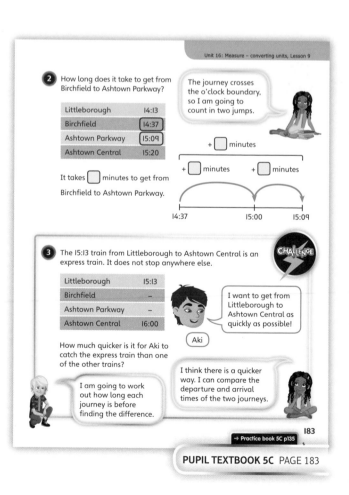

PUPIL TEXTBOOK 5C PAGE 183

Practice

WAYS OF WORKING Independent thinking

IN FOCUS Question ❷ shows a timetable that seems to have times missing. Discuss what children think these gaps mean. Ask which station would be the next stop if they caught the 06:31 train from Grantham. Children may spot similarities in the different train journeys. For example, the first and the fourth trains have a similar journey (no stop at Rauceby), also the second and third trains (no stops at Thorpe Culvert or Havenhouse) and the fifth and sixth trains (no stops at any of these three stations).

STRENGTHEN Encourage children to focus on the relevant part of the timetable by providing them with two pieces of paper to cover up the timetable either side of the particular column or row that they need to look at. They may also benefit from drawing timeline representations of journeys on mini whiteboards as described in **Think together**.

DEEPEN Question ❸ challenges children to devise their own school bus timetable given certain parameters. Establish that they can write in two times immediately from the information they are given and ensure they understand how to find the other times. Ask children to create a similar set of instructions for producing a timetable for a bus to their school.

ASSESSMENT CHECKPOINT Use questions ❶ and ❷ to assess whether children can read timetables with confidence, identifying departure and arrival (or start and end) times and calculating durations accurately. They should be able to apply these skills confidently in problem-solving contexts.

ANSWERS Answers for the **Practice** part of the lesson appear in the separate **Practice and Reflect answer guide**.

Reflect

WAYS OF WORKING Independent thinking

IN FOCUS This activity encourages children to consider why the 24-hour clock is used in timetables. Possible answers may include the following: it is not possible to get confused between whether a time is am or pm; it is easier to calculate the duration of something with 24-hour clock times, particularly when it goes across 12:00; the lack of 'am' and 'pm' means that the times take less space on the timetable!

ASSESSMENT CHECKPOINT Look for children who are able to explain why timetables use 24-hour clock times by referring to some of the benefits of using 24-hour over 12-hour times.

ANSWERS Answers for the **Reflect** part of the lesson appear in the separate **Practice and Reflect answer guide**.

After the lesson ⏸

- To what extent were children's various responses the ones that were anticipated: their ideas and questions, the obstacles they encountered, their misunderstandings and mistakes?
- What percentage of children do you feel mastered the lesson? How confident do you think they will be when using timetables in everyday situations?

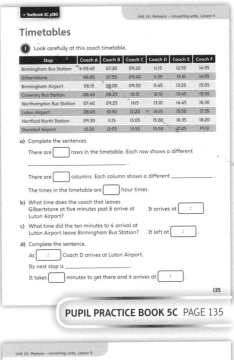

PUPIL PRACTICE BOOK 5C PAGE 135

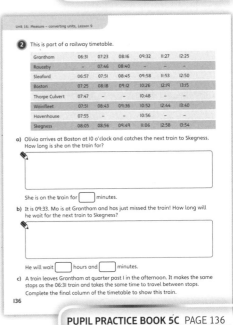

PUPIL PRACTICE BOOK 5C PAGE 136

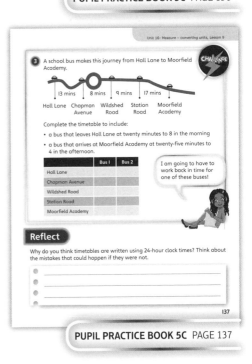

PUPIL PRACTICE BOOK 5C PAGE 137

Problem solving – measure

Learning focus

In this lesson, children will apply their knowledge of converting units to solving problems. These will include a range of problem types, including those that involve applying multiplication and/or division facts to solve scaling problems.

Small steps

→ Previous step: Timetables
→ **This step: Problem solving – measure**
→ Next step: What is volume?

NATIONAL CURRICULUM LINKS

Year 5 Measurement

Use all four operations to solve problems involving measure [for example, length, mass, volume, money] using decimal notation, including scaling.

ASSESSING MASTERY

Children can apply their knowledge of converting between units of measurement (metric → metric and metric ↔ imperial, using approximate equivalences) in the process of solving a range of problems. Children apply their knowledge of multiplication and division in particular when converting and solving scaling problems.

COMMON MISCONCEPTIONS

Children may think that they can compare or calculate using amounts without converting when it is necessary, failing to check that two amounts are in the same unit first. Ask:
• *What unit of measurement will your answer be in? What will you need to do to find the answer?*

STRENGTHENING UNDERSTANDING

Prepare children for this lesson by encouraging them to look back through the previous nine lessons and the different conversions they have learnt, including the equivalences between imperial and metric units. Show children flashcards with different conversions written on (for example, mm → cm). Encourage them to match these up with a list of operations written on the board (mm → cm: ÷ 10). Ask children to justify their decisions and use the opportunity to refresh their knowledge of what each unit is equivalent to.

GOING DEEPER

Find examples of simple recipes that serve 2, 5 or 10 people (numbers that are fairly easy to divide a measurement by). Challenge children to develop their knowledge of scaling by exploring the ways they can alter these recipes to make different amounts. For example, this makes 10 pancakes: 100 g plain flour, 1 pinch of salt, 2 large eggs, 300 ml milk. Ask children to alter the ingredients to make 12 pancakes. Children will need to think carefully about how to alter a pinch of salt and 2 eggs.

KEY LANGUAGE

In lesson: unit, measure, quantity, convert, centimetre, metre, millilitre, litre, gram, kilogram, ounce, pound, pint, inch, yard, per

Other language to be used by the teacher: approximately, kilometre, millimetre, gallon, foot, for every, scaling, value

STRUCTURES AND REPRESENTATIONS

number line, bar model

RESOURCES

Optional: measuring tape (cm), set of scales (g), string, dried rice and pasta, analogue clock faces with movable hands, strips of paper, rulers, flashcards

 In the eTextbook of this lesson, you will find interactive links to a selection of teaching tools.

Before you teach

• This lesson draws together everything children have learnt in unit 16. What misconceptions and mistakes will you look out for?
• Where might you give children more opportunities to develop their reasoning skills?

Discover

ASK

• Question ❶: *List these categories of measurement (capacity, mass, length and time) in order of most to least important in the kitchen. Why did you choose that order?*
• Question ❶: *Why is it important for Reena and Lee to solve their problems? What might be the result if they do not?*

IN FOCUS Talk about the different types of units of measurement involved in cookery. Length may be the least obvious one; examples include the diameter of a pizza (a recipe for a 10-inch pizza), the size of a cake tin or baking tray or the depth of an ingredient ('Roll out the icing until it is about half a centimetre thick'). Discuss when children might need to convert between measurements when baking.

PRACTICAL TIPS Set up very simple activities where these sorts of problems are explored practically. For example: provide a measuring tape that only shows centimetres and ask children to cut a piece of string that measures about 5 inches; give children 90 g of pasta without telling them how heavy it is and explain that this is enough for 3 people – ask them to find out how much pasta is needed for 1 person or 4 people.

ANSWERS

Question ❶ a): Reena needs to convert ounces → grams:
56 g oats, 112 g brown sugar, 112 g butter, 140 g flour

Question ❶ b): 5 cooking apples, 70 g oats, 140 g brown sugar, 140 g butter, 175 g plain flour

Share

ASK

• Question ❶ a): *How do you convert from ounces into grams? How do you know this?*
• Question ❶ a): *How can Dexter use doubling to help convert the different amounts of ounces?*
• Question ❶ a): *Can you think of two methods to convert 5 oz – one using addition and one using subtraction?*
• Question ❶ b): *If a recipe is for 1 person, how can you work out the quantities for 5 people? Can you explain what Flo is suggesting?*
• Question ❶ b): *How does the bar model show the method? Can you describe what to do?*

IN FOCUS Explain that converting units and altering recipes to make different amounts are common real-life problems that anyone who cooks or bakes has to solve regularly. For question ❶ b), encourage children to think about how the recipe might be written differently to be more helpful to Lee. Introduce the term 'scaling' as a way of describing how to make something larger or smaller, whilst keeping everything in proportion.

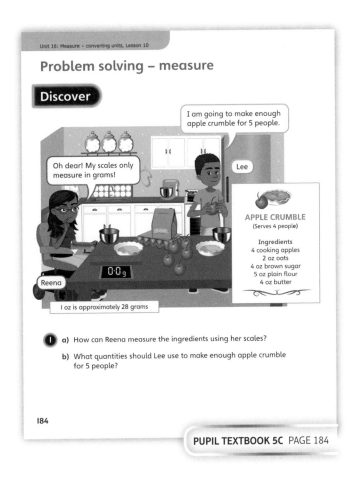

PUPIL TEXTBOOK 5C PAGE 184

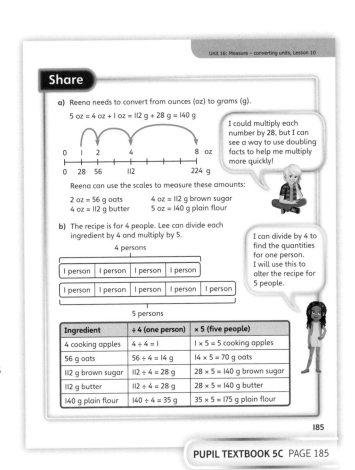

PUPIL TEXTBOOK 5C PAGE 185

Think together

Whole class teacher led (I do, We do, You do)

ASK

- Question **1** a): *Can you predict the number of cartons Jamie needs without calculating anything?*
- Question **1** a): *How is the bar model useful in helping to solve the problem? How would you complete it?*
- Question **2**: *Is 17:10 the start or the end time of Danny's baking? Do you need to work backwards or forwards to find the answer?*
- Question **2**: *What could you do to represent this problem visually? How might it help you to find the answer?*
- Question **3**: *What does 'best value' mean?*

IN FOCUS When answering question **1** a), encourage children to consider how they might predict the answer using mental methods. For example, if they know that 2 litres = 2,000 ml and that a pint of milk is just over 500 ml, they can predict that they will need to open four pints of milk to get the 2,000 ml that they need. They should then use the bar model and calculate whether their prediction is correct.

STRENGTHEN Support children when working backwards in question **2** by proving them with analogue clocks with movable hands. Encourage them to make the end time (17:10) on their clocks and then count 55 minutes backwards to represent the time in the oven and a further 25 minutes backwards to represent the preparation time. Discuss how they can check whether the start time is correct by counting forwards from 15:50.

DEEPEN When considering question **3**, establish why the bags of sugar are difficult to compare (they are all the same price, they all look the same but the units of measurement are all different). Ask whether the best value bag is going to be the one that weighs the least or the most. Discuss why Dexter suggests that the gram is the best unit of measurement to convert them into and whether there any other units they could convert into. Give children similar problems to solve using length or capacity.

ASSESSMENT CHECKPOINT Use questions **1** and **2** to assess whether children are displaying more confidence when applying their knowledge of unit conversion in problem-solving contexts. They should know how to use given representations and models to help support their working.

ANSWERS

Question **1** a): Jamie needs to open 4 cartons of milk.

Question **1** b): Jamie will have 280 ml left over.

Question **2**: The latest time Danny should start preparing is 15:50 (ten minutes to 4).

Question **3**: A: 1·4 kg = 1,400 g, B: 10 oz = 280 g, C: 1,250 g, D: 2 lb = 900 g
Bag A is the best value.

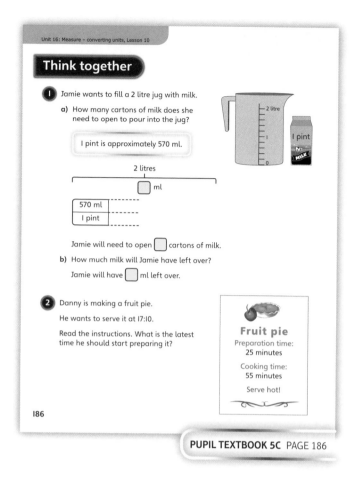

PUPIL TEXTBOOK 5C PAGE 186

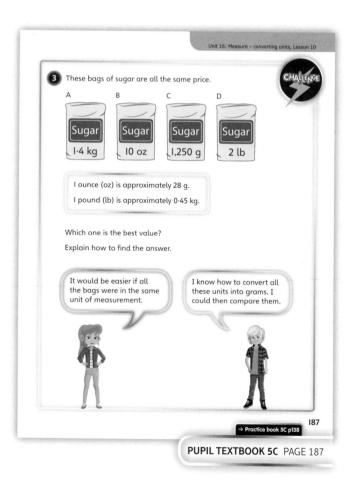

PUPIL TEXTBOOK 5C PAGE 187

Practice

WAYS OF WORKING Independent thinking

IN FOCUS Encourage children to consider at which point in each question they need to convert between units. In some instances, children can work out the answer just as easily by converting at the beginning or at the end, for example in question **4** : calculate 1·6 ÷ 10 = 0·16 kg and then convert into 160 g, or convert 1·6 kg into 1,600 g and then calculate 1,600 ÷ 10 = 160 g. Discuss whether it makes a difference which method they use.

STRENGTHEN For question **5**, encourage children to make actual-size bar models, measuring and cutting strips of paper 1 m and 90 cm (≈ 1 yd) long. Give children time to consider the problem in pairs, using these concrete representations to help. They may choose different ways to find the cheaper option, ranging from visual reasoning to calculating the answer.

DEEPEN Question **7** can be used to deepen children's problem-solving skills as it contains several calculation steps (find the total of four frames, subtract from total length, divide by 3 for the size of one gap) and also incorporates the need to convert between metric units. Discuss which unit it is easier to work in: centimetres because 1·25 – 0·8 is more difficult to subtract than 125 – 80. Say that there are now 5 frames and ask how this changes the calculations.

ASSESSMENT CHECKPOINT Use questions **1** to **6** to assess whether children can apply their knowledge of unit conversion confidently. They should be using representations and models to help support their working where necessary. They should identify times when they need to convert between units and recognise how to do this. They should display reasoning skills, explaining appropriate methods and thinking with confidence.

ANSWERS Answers for the **Practice** part of the lesson appear in the separate **Practice and Reflect answer guide**.

Reflect

WAYS OF WORKING Pair work

IN FOCUS In this reflection, children explain how they would apply what they have learnt about converting between units and about the values of metres and inches in terms of centimetres. Initially, children should think individually and decide on a method, which they can then explain to their partner. Children should include the equivalence of 1 m with 100 cm and that 1 inch is approximately the same as 2·5 cm. Encourage children to compare their methods, identifying what is the same and what is different.

ASSESSMENT CHECKPOINT Look for children who describe how to convert 1 m into centimetres and then use their knowledge of the approximate length of an inch in cm.

ANSWERS Answers for the **Reflect** part of the lesson appear in the separate **Practice and Reflect answer guide**.

After the lesson

- How did the discussions between children go and how did they reason?
- How much do you feel that the success of this lesson reflects the success of the unit as a whole?

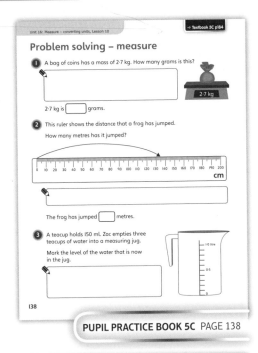

PUPIL PRACTICE BOOK 5C PAGE 138

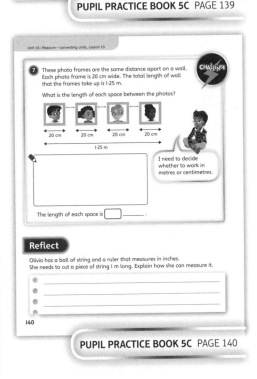

PUPIL PRACTICE BOOK 5C PAGE 139

PUPIL PRACTICE BOOK 5C PAGE 140

End of unit check

Don't forget the *Power Maths* unit assessment grid on p26.

IN FOCUS

- Questions **1**, **2**, **4** and **6** are all designed to assess children's confidence with converting units. Questions **1** and **4** require them to convert between metric units and question **6** between imperial and metric units, while question **2** assesses their understanding of the method of conversion.
- Questions **3** and **5** are both concerned with time. Question **3** assesses children's ability to convert from a time in hours and minutes into minutes, and question **5** requires them to identify information from a timetable.
- Question **7** is a SATs-style question where children need to convert between units of time to order durations.

ANSWERS AND COMMENTARY

Children who have mastered this unit will be able to convert between units of mass, length and capacity (metric → metric, imperial → imperial and metric ↔ imperial), between units of time, including where there is a remainder, and confidently apply this knowledge to solve problems. They can use reasoning to explain their methodology. Children can read information from timetables and use it to solve time-based problems.

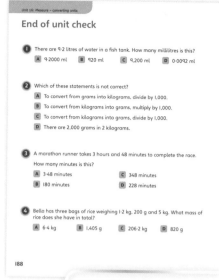

PUPIL TEXTBOOK 5C PAGE 188

PUPIL TEXTBOOK 5C PAGE 189

Q	A	WRONG ANSWERS AND MISCONCEPTIONS	STRENGTHENING UNDERSTANDING
1	C	D shows that the child has divided instead of multiplying.	Play matching pairs games using flashcards where children are given measures expressed in different units (for example, 4·5 litres) and must find their matching partner (for example, 4,500 ml).
2	C	Not choosing C suggests that the child is unsure of the correct operation required to convert g ↔ kg.	
3	D	A and C suggest that the child has an incorrect understanding of how to convert a time into minutes.	
4	A	B and C suggest that the child has not converted all the measurements into the same unit.	Provide opportunities to measure simple lengths, masses and capacities using different units. Where possible, provide equipment that shows different units on the scale.
5	B	C suggests an incorrect identification of 09:55.	
6	D	A suggests an incorrect understanding of the equivalence between inches and cm (using 1 cm = 2·5 inches).	
7	$4\frac{1}{2}$ min, 300 s, 5 min 10 s, $\frac{1}{4}$ hr	Some children may assume that 300 seconds is the longest duration because it involves the highest number and that $\frac{1}{4}$ hour is the smallest because it is the only one less than 1.	

My journal

WAYS OF WORKING Independent thinking

ANSWERS AND COMMENTARY Explanations may vary, but should refer to the equivalence between the units.

a) 1·2 litres = 1,200 millilitres. There are 1,000 ml in 1 litre and
$1.2 \times 1,000 = 1,200$.

b) 490 minutes = 8 hours 10 minutes. There are 60 minutes in 1 hour, so 8 hours = 480 minutes because $8 \times 60 = 480$. There are 10 minutes remaining, so the answer is 8 hours and 10 minutes.

c) 60 inches = 1·5 metres. 1 inch is about 2·5 cm, so 60 inches equals $60 \times 2\frac{1}{2}$ or $60 + 60 + 30 = 150$ cm. There are 100 cm in 1 m, so $150 \div 100 = 1.5$ m.

If children are finding working out how to answer the questions challenging, discuss what they know about the units in the question. Change the number in the question to an easier number and ask them to describe how they would work out the answer and then encourage them to use this method to answer the actual question.

Power check

WAYS OF WORKING Independent thinking

ASK

- *Do you think you would be able to convert between two metric units on your own?*
- *If you were reminded of the approximate value, do you think you would be able to convert between a metric measurement and an imperial measurement?*
- *What would you say the difference is between metric and imperial units?*

Power play

WAYS OF WORKING Pair work

IN FOCUS The purpose of this **Power play** is to continue to consolidate children's familiarity with reading data from timetables in a game context. The activity challenges children to consider the various ways that the timetable can be read – vertically (considering one train's journey), horizontally (considering the trains that visit one station) and calculating durations.

ANSWERS AND COMMENTARY Answers will vary. Facts might include information such as:
- a correct reading of the time in 12-hour vocabulary
- a reference to another time in the same column
- a reference to another time in the same row
- a reference to the duration.

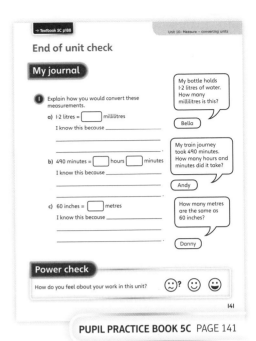

PUPIL PRACTICE BOOK 5C PAGE 141

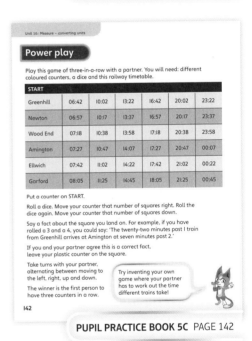

PUPIL PRACTICE BOOK 5C PAGE 142

After the unit ⏸

- Are children familiar with the different metric and imperial units of measurement?
- Can children confidently read timetables?
- How do you feel that the unit assessment went?

Strengthen and **Deepen** activities for this unit can be found in the *Power Maths* online subscription.

Unit 17
Measure – volume and capacity

Mastery Expert tip! "When I taught this unit, I encouraged children to work together in small groups to make storage boxes by recycling card boxes, shoe boxes or old containers. I asked children to estimate the volume of the storage boxes they made. We then used the boxes to store some of our maths resources and gave the rest to the local nursery."

Don't forget to watch the Unit 17 video!

WHY THIS UNIT IS IMPORTANT

This unit introduces the concept of volume and capacity, giving children a tangible way to measure and compare a shape's size. Until now, children will have been able to say whether a shape is longer or shorter, wider or narrower, and will have been able to measure a shape's length, width and area. However, this unit now provides them with the tools to measure the amount of space taken up by an object.

Volume is introduced through children using non-standard units and seeing how many of these units will fit within a shape. Children will learn to measure volume by counting the number of cubes that fit within a shape. Although the relationship between length, width and height is not expounded in this unit, children may still recognise informal links between the three concepts from their activities when counting cubes. These links will provide a foundation for further development of the concept of volume in Year 6.

WHERE THIS UNIT FITS

→ Unit 16: Measure – converting units

→ **Unit 17: Measure – volume and capacity**

This unit builds on children's understanding of the properties of cubes, cuboids and different solids. It extends children's basic comprehension of how to measure and calculate the area of a shape to estimating the amount of space taken up by an object and the amount a container can hold.

Before they start this unit, it is expected that children:
- understand what is meant by a 3D shape and are able to identify the space inside it
- understand simple properties of cubes and cuboids.

ASSESSING MASTERY

Children who have mastered this unit will understand that the volume of a 3D shape is the amount of space taken up by an object, while capacity is defined by the amount a container can hold. Children will be able to confidently estimate the volume of 3D shapes. They can do this by counting the number of cubes in each layer, then adding the results. Children are able to recognise that this is an estimation of volume and can explain why this is the case. Children can confidently estimate capacity in different situations. Children are able to recognise and explain the differences between capacity and volume.

COMMON MISCONCEPTIONS	STRENGTHENING UNDERSTANDING	GOING DEEPER
Children may confuse volume and capacity and may not be able to differentiate between the two.	Give children simple tasks that involve them exploring volume and capacity more generally. For volume, provide unit cubes or multilink cubes to support discussion. For capacity, provide different-sized containers. Explain that only containers have capacity.	Ask children to explore the differences between volume and capacity by setting investigative challenges. For example, make a sorting circle for children to sort items according to volume and capacity.
Some children may view the estimation process as a form of calculation, providing the actual volume, because it involves counting.	It is important children understand that when estimating, the answer can vary. Discuss with children why the answers may vary and what an acceptable answer is.	Challenge children to predict volumes of different shapes.

Unit 17: Measure – volume and capacity

WAYS OF WORKING

Use these pages to introduce the concept of the volume of 3D shapes and the capacity of containers to the whole class, checking their understanding of how volume and capacity differ. Also introduce the importance of estimating volume and capacity.

STRUCTURES AND REPRESENTATIONS

3D shapes made of unit cubes: Models like this allow children to count the number of cubes in each solid in order to measure volume.

Models like this allow children to count the number of cubes that will fit inside a container to measure capacity.

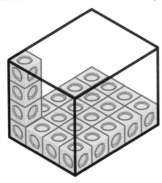

KEY LANGUAGE

There is some key language that children will need to know as part of the learning in this unit:

- volume, capacity, solid, liquid, container
- cube, cuboid, triangular, prism
- 3D shapes, objects
- calculate, estimate, compare, count, accurately, order, amount, irregular, prediction, exact
- unit (cm) cubes, units of measurement, measure
- less, more, less than (<), more than (>), largest, smallest, least, greatest, equal
- space inside
- height, length, width, size, tall
- layer, slice
- multiple, total, take away, whole, part, almost half, identical
- litre (l), millilitre (ml)

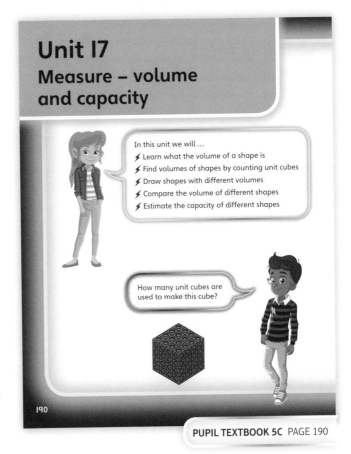

What is volume?

Learning focus

In this lesson, children will be introduced to the concept of the volume of a 3D shape. They will measure this by counting the unit cubes used to make each shape.

Small steps

→ Previous step: Problem solving – measure
→ **This step: What is volume?**
→ Next step: Comparing volumes

NATIONAL CURRICULUM LINKS

Year 5 Measurement

Estimate volume [for example, using 1 cm³ blocks to build cuboids (including cubes)] and capacity [for example, using water].

ASSESSING MASTERY

Children can confidently explain what volume is. Children can use unit cubes to make solids of different volumes and draw the shapes they make on an isometric grid.

COMMON MISCONCEPTIONS

Children last studied capacity in Year 3 and should recognise volume, but may not fully understand it. Children may confuse volume and capacity and have trouble differentiating between the two. Some children link volume to loudness and are unable to understand what volume represents. Ask:
• *What do you understand by volume? What do you understand by capacity?*

It is important to clarify that volume refers to the amount of space taken up by an object and capacity refers to the amount a container can hold.

STRENGTHENING UNDERSTANDING

To strengthen understanding, give children simple tasks that involve exploring volume and capacity more generally. Provide containers or bottles of differing sizes, glasses with coloured liquids in them and unit cubes or multilink cubes to support discussion. Explain that only containers have capacity. Ask: *What is the maximum volume this bottle or container can hold? What is the volume of the liquid in it? How many cubes are used to make this solid? What is the volume of this solid?*

GOING DEEPER

Ask children to explore the differences between volume and capacity by setting investigative challenges for them to explore. For example, use two hoops to make sorting circles at the front of the classroom and label them 'Volume' and 'Capacity'. Place containers and solids inside the hoops, making mistakes on purpose (for example, place a bottle full of liquid outside the hoops rather than in the middle) and encourage children to spot the mistakes. Ask: *Can volume and capacity be equal? Can the volume of a container have a greater value than the capacity of a container?*

KEY LANGUAGE

In lesson: volume, 3D shapes, **unit cubes**, amount, space, object, measure, cuboid, identical

Other language used by the teacher: capacity, height, length, width, space inside, units of measurement, layer

RESOURCES

Mandatory: cubes, isometric paper

Optional: a variety of measuring items, different size bottles and containers

 In the eTextbook of this lesson, you will find interactive links to a selection of teaching tools.

Before you teach

• Can you think of any misconceptions that children may have when measuring volume?
• How can you use your school environment to introduce and reinforce the concept of volume?

Discover

Pair work

ASK
- Question ① a): *Is there a way you could measure the volume of each shape?*
- Question ① a): *Should you add all the cubes in the shape or just the ones that are visible?*
- Question ① b): *If the shapes have the same volume, why do you think they look different?*

IN FOCUS Question ① a) encourages children to begin talking about what volume is. Challenge children by asking: *How can two shapes have equal volumes? If you turn the shape around, would the volume change? What happens if you move one of the cubes from the second layer and place it on the first layer?* Draw out the concept of the space that a shape takes up and that the volume is the amount of 3D space the shape occupies.

PRACTICAL TIPS Give children cubes to build the solids shown in the **Discover** picture. Examining how the solids are constructed by building them for themselves will help children develop their understanding of volume. Ask them to build other shapes using the same cubes and describe what they see.

ANSWERS

Question ① a): Yes, Zac is correct. Volume means the amount of space that an object fills. Volume can be measured by using unit cubes.

Question ① b):

Share

Whole class teacher led

ASK
- Question ① a): *What does the word 'volume' mean? When have you heard it used before? (Loudness)*
- Question ① b): *What do you notice about the way the cubes have been arranged? Are there other ways that the cubes can be arranged?*
- Question ① b): *Would the volume increase if you put the cubes one above the other to make a tall tower?*

IN FOCUS Questions ① a) and b) help children understand how to use cubes as non-standard measures to compare the volume of two shapes. It is necessary that children make connections between the cubes used to make each solid and its volume. It is important for children to make the solids used in this task themselves so that they can see what the volume of 6 unit cubes looks like.

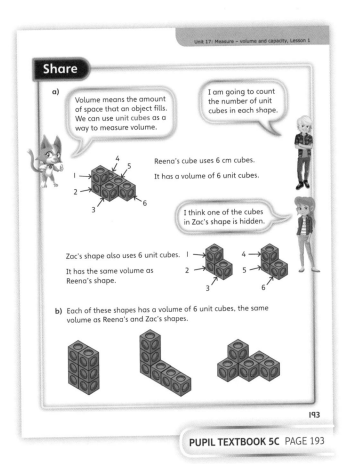

Think together

Whole class teacher led (I do, We do, You do)

ASK

- Question **1** : *Can you describe the shapes that you see? How many layers are there? How many cubes are there in each layer? How do you need to arrange the cubes into the shapes? Is there a right way and a way to do it?*
- Question **2** : *How many different shapes can you make? Can you make a cuboid? Can you make a different cuboid? Will the volume change? Is it possible to make a cube?*
- Question **3** : *How easy is it to draw shapes using isometric paper? What do you have to remember?*

IN FOCUS Question **1** leads children through calculating the volume of solids when not all the cubes are visible. Encourage children to discuss their methods of counting the cubes with each other. Allow children to share their most efficient ways of calculating the volume with the whole class.

STRENGTHEN For question **1**, encourage children to make the shapes shown in the pictures. This way, they will realise that some drawings of shapes have hidden cubes. For question **2**, give children opportunities to discuss their method of making shapes using a certain number of unit cubes. Encourage children to make a cuboid as well as other shapes. Ask: *What is the maximum number of layers the shape could have? How do you know?*

DEEPEN In question **3** b), ask children to make the different solids using the 10 cubes used in the question. Can they make two cubes and a cuboid? Encourage them to discuss the difference between the shapes they make. Ask: *Can you draw the shapes on isometric paper?*

ASSESSMENT CHECKPOINT Children should recognise what volume refers to and understand that this is a measure of the amount of space that an object fills. Children should be able to confidently suggest ways to measure volume using non-standard units of measurement.

ANSWERS

Question **1** a): 8 unit cubes

Question **1** b): 8 unit cubes

Question **1** c): 20 unit cubes

Question **1** d): 20 unit cubes

Question **2** : Independent answers – children should create three different 3D shapes using 12 cubes in total.

Question **3** a):

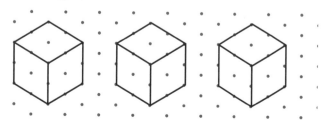

Question **3** b): 3 unit cubes, 3 unit cubes, 4 unit cubes

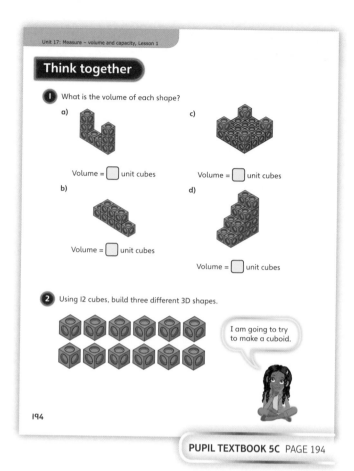

PUPIL TEXTBOOK 5C PAGE 194

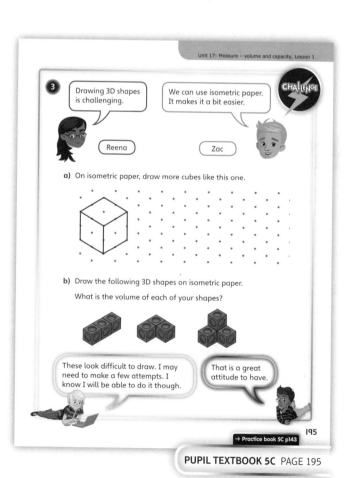

PUPIL TEXTBOOK 5C PAGE 195

Practice

WAYS OF WORKING Independent thinking

IN FOCUS Questions ❶ and ❷ allow children to consolidate their understanding of measuring volume of shapes using unit cubes. Questions ❸ and ❹ are designed to assess children's understanding of the definition of volume as the space inside a 3D shape. The questions draw children away from finding the volume by counting the cubes that they see. Ask: *How can you find the volume when you cannot see all the cubes? How can you ensure you have not forgotten any?* The more practice children have with making different solids with a given number of cubes, the easier it will be for them to visualise the shapes.

STRENGTHEN Extend questions ❶ and ❷ by asking children to physically make the different shapes using multilink cubes. Ask children to place the shapes in different positions. Ask: *Describe the shape you see now. Has the volume changed?*

DEEPEN For questions ❺ and ❻, ask children to calculate the volume of each shape. Encourage children to consider the relationship between a shape's dimensions and its volume. To extend understanding even further, children could play the game 'What am I?' One child describes a shape, while another makes it. Emphasise the importance of using the correct mathematical language.

ASSESSMENT CHECKPOINT At this point in the lesson, children should be confident in finding the volume of different solids. Children should be able to make different shapes with a given volume. They can draw cubes and cuboids on isometric paper.

ANSWERS Answers to the **Practice** part of the lesson appear in the separate **Practice and Reflect answer guide**.

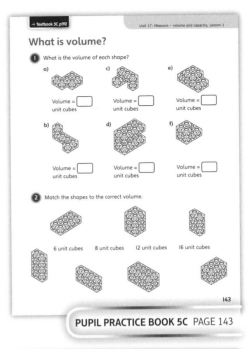

PUPIL PRACTICE BOOK 5C PAGE 143

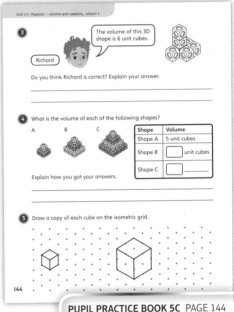

PUPIL PRACTICE BOOK 5C PAGE 144

Reflect

WAYS OF WORKING Independent thinking

IN FOCUS This question provides an opportunity to check children's understanding of volume and the methodology they will use in calculating volume. The aim of the question is that children are not necessarily asked to calculate the volume of a specific shape but to explain clearly what the volume represents and how they would find it. To extend understanding, ask: *Can different shapes have the same volume?*

ASSESSMENT CHECKPOINT Are children able to define and measure the volume of a shape correctly?

ANSWERS Answers for the **Reflect** part of the lesson appear in the separate **Practice and Reflect answer guide**.

After the lesson

- Have children mastered what volume is?
- Could more opportunities be given for children to explain the concept of volume?
- What opportunities can be provided for children to calculate volume outside of this lesson?

PUPIL PRACTICE BOOK 5C PAGE 145

Comparing volumes

Learning focus

In this lesson, children will learn how to compare shapes according to their volumes.

Small steps

→ Previous step: What is volume?
→ **This step: Comparing volumes**
→ Next step: Estimating volume

NATIONAL CURRICULUM LINKS

Year 5 Measurement

Estimate volume [for example, using 1 cm³ blocks to build cuboids (including cubes)] and capacity [for example, using water].

ASSESSING MASTERY

Children can confidently compare the volume of 3D shapes, measuring their volume accurately by counting cubes, then comparing both values to see which is larger. Children can apply this skill to order several shapes according to their volumes.

COMMON MISCONCEPTIONS

Children may compare a shape's volume visually by the way it looks, rather than by counting cubes and comparing volume. They may ignore all three dimensions of 3D shapes and compare volumes by comparing the height of the shape, rather than considering all aspects. Ask:

• *What do you need to do to work out which shape has the largest volume? What is the length, width and height of the shape?*

STRENGTHENING UNDERSTANDING

Give children the same number of cubes and ask them to build different cuboids and 3D shapes. Place the shapes in different positions and orientations and ask children to compare their volumes. Ask: *If you were to order the shapes, how would you do this?* Allow children to touch the shapes and see for themselves that they have the same number of cubes. If children assumed that the tallest shapes had the largest volume, ask them to look at the shapes again and discuss this misconception with the whole class. Allow time for children to explore the shapes and repeat the activity with a different number of cubes.

GOING DEEPER

Challenge children by asking: *Is it always, sometimes or never true that 3D shapes with the same height have equal volumes?* Encourage children to reason and support their answer with examples, rather than simply saying yes or no.

KEY LANGUAGE

In lesson: compare, volume, 3D shapes, cube, cuboid, irregular, unit cube, layer, greatest, more, smallest, order, least, greater than (>), prediction

Other language to be used by the teacher: less than (<), count, solid, measure, accurately, multiply, total, take away, size

STRUCTURES AND REPRESENTATIONS

3D shapes

RESOURCES

Mandatory: cubes

Optional: ruler, square dotted paper, isometric paper

 In the eTextbook of this lesson, you will find interactive links to a selection of teaching tools.

Before you teach

• Are children confident in making 3D shapes?
• Do they understand what volume is?

Discover

WAYS OF WORKING Pair work

ASK

- Question **1** a): *Can you predict who has built the 3D shape with the greatest volume just by looking? Why do you think this shape has the greatest volume?*
- Question **1** a): *How are the shapes the same? How are they different?*
- Question **1** b): *How many cubes does Isla's shape have? How many cubes does Emma's shape have?*

IN FOCUS Talk about the **Discover** picture and encourage children to describe what they see. They will already have plenty of experience of looking at two shapes and choosing the one that looks larger. Now they are required to find the volume of each shape by counting cubes and then comparing both values to find the shape with the greatest volume.

PRACTICAL TIPS Provide children with activities similar to the one shown in the **Discover** picture. Give children two or three shapes. Ask them to compare the volumes. Ask: *What do you have to do to make the volumes of the shapes equal? How many more cubes do you need to add? Why? Show me. Is there another way to do it?* Listen for children who realise that they can add or remove cubes to make the volumes equal.

ANSWERS

Question **1** a): Emma has built the shape with the greatest volume.

Question **1** b): Isla needs to add four more cubes to her shape.

Share

WAYS OF WORKING Whole class teacher led

ASK

- Question **1** a): *What information do you need to know to be able to compare the volumes? Can you tell which shape has the greatest volume just by looking? How could you check which shape has the greater volume?*
- Question **1** b): *How many more cubes does Isla need to add? What would the shape look like now? Is there only one way to do it?*
- Question **1** b): *How would you describe the shapes you made? How many layers does the shape have? How many cubes are required to make each layer? Can you see all the cubes used to make each shape?*

IN FOCUS Question **1** a) consolidates children's understanding of measuring volume by counting cubes. Question **1** b) develops children's understanding of how adding or removing unit cubes changes the volume of a shape. The question is important as it allows children to see how shapes with the same volume can look different. Encourage children to explore the different shapes that can be made in question **1** b).

PUPIL TEXTBOOK 5C PAGE 196

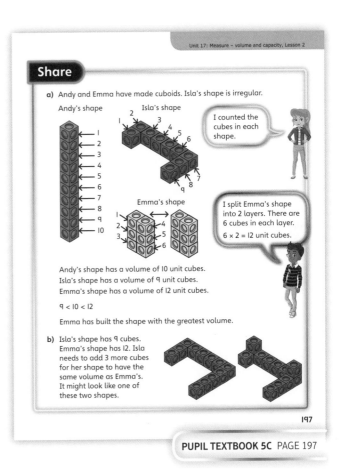

PUPIL TEXTBOOK 5C PAGE 197

Think together

WAYS OF WORKING Whole class teacher led (I do, We do, You do)

ASK

- Question **1**: *What method can you use to compare the volumes accurately?*
- Question **2**: *Can you see all the cubes in each shape?*
- Question **2**: *What steps do you need to take to put these shapes into size order?*
- Question **3** b): *What is different about Isla's shape?*

IN FOCUS Questions **1** and **2** take children through the steps needed to compare the volume of 3D shapes. First, children should find the volumes by counting cubes. They should then compare the values to see which is smaller or larger. For question **2**, children are expected to use their comparison to write each volume in order. Question **3** a) requires children to factor in hidden cubes when measuring and comparing volume.

STRENGTHEN For questions **1** and **2**, give children cubes so that they can make the shapes themselves. When working on question **2**, discuss with children how they can find the volume of shapes with 'hidden cubes'. The more practice children have in making different shapes, the better their visualisation of the 3D shapes will be. Discuss how multiplication can be used instead of addition to find the number of cubes in each layer.

DEEPEN In question **3**, discuss the importance of using the same size cubes when comparing shapes. To deepen children's understanding further, discuss the volume of a shape made from plastic building blocks and a shape made from real-life bricks. Show children pictures or provide them with examples of shapes made from different size cubes or blocks. Ask: *What do you need to consider when comparing volumes? Does a shape made from bigger cubes have a larger volume?* Allow children time to explore and generalise.

ASSESSMENT CHECKPOINT Children should understand that to compare volumes, they need to first find their values, then compare them. They need to consider not only the number of cubes used to make the shape, but also ensure the size of the cubes used are equal.

ANSWERS

Question **1**: Emma's shape is made of 12 unit cubes.
Isla's shape is made of 13 unit cubes.
12 < 13
Emma's shape has the smaller volume.

Question **2**: Shape A = 16 cubes
Shape B = 20 cubes
Shape C = 18 cubes
The order from least to greatest volume is: shape A, shape C, shape B

Question **3** a): Both shapes have equal volumes as they use an equal number of cubes. Emma is correct. Andy is forgetting about the hidden cube in Emma's shape.

Question **3** b): Isla's shape has a larger volume because she uses bigger cubes.

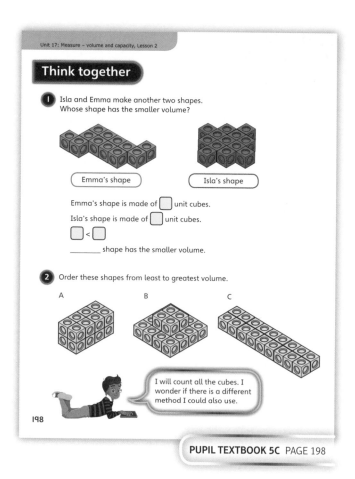

PUPIL TEXTBOOK 5C PAGE 198

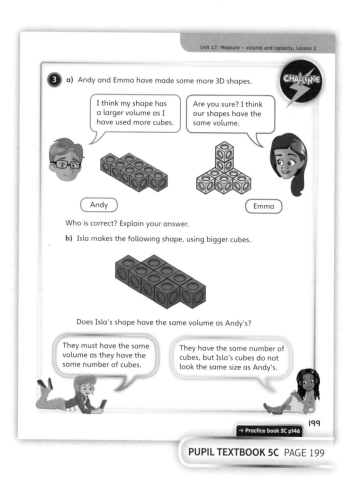

PUPIL TEXTBOOK 5C PAGE 199

Practice

WAYS OF WORKING Independent thinking

IN FOCUS Question **3** encourages children to think carefully about what volume represents. They need to read the clues given and identify the shapes that belong to each child. It may be beneficial to revisit what 'a third of', 'half' and 'more than' mean. Ask: *What is the question asking? What do you know? How can you find the volume of each shape? Which clues are you using? Is there another way to find the volume?* Encourage children to give clear reasons for their answers and ensure that they do not just give numbers when calculating the volumes, but use the correct unit for the volume too; for example, they say 'the volume is 10 cubes', rather than 'the volume is 10'.

STRENGTHEN If children need support to count hidden cubes in shapes accurately, provide them with cubes and ask them to model each of the shapes in questions **1** to **3** concretely. Encourage children to be systematic in their approach. Ask: *How can you record the information to ensure you have not missed any cubes?* Children could count and write the totals of each layer of cubes as they go, then add the results up to find the overall volume of each shape.

DEEPEN Question **5** involves reasoning about the relationship between the length, width and height of a shape and its volume. This is another opportunity to clarify the misconception that the taller the shape is, the larger the volume will be. Provide children with cubes so that they can make the shapes themselves and allow plenty of opportunities to discuss their estimates and results.

ASSESSMENT CHECKPOINT Children should be working confidently to find volumes by counting cubes and then comparing and ordering those volumes. Children should be able to use reasoning to explain their answers and make generalisations.

ANSWERS Answers to the **Practice** part of the lesson appear in the separate **Practice and Reflect answer guide**.

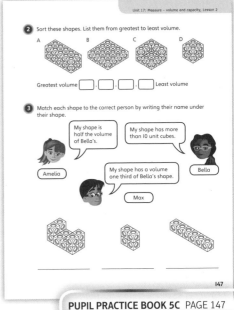

PUPIL PRACTICE BOOK 5C PAGE 146

PUPIL PRACTICE BOOK 5C PAGE 147

Reflect

WAYS OF WORKING Independent thinking

IN FOCUS This question asks children to explain how shapes that are made up of the same number of cubes, and therefore have the same volume, can still be different shapes. Their answers should include an explanation along the lines of volume being the amount of 3D space a shape occupies. Children can demonstrate that if two shapes are made from the same number of cubes, than they share the same volume, no matter the shape.

ASSESSMENT CHECKPOINT Look for children who can explain the importance of using the same unit of measurement when comparing shapes.

ANSWERS Answers for the **Reflect** part of the lesson appear in the separate **Practice and Reflect answer book**.

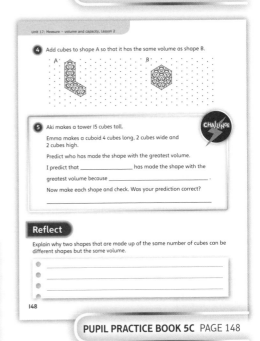

After the lesson

- How confident are children when comparing the volume of shapes?
- Are children now less reliant on comparison by sight? Do they understand why it is important to measure before comparing the volume of shapes?

PUPIL PRACTICE BOOK 5C PAGE 148

Estimating volume

Learning focus

In this lesson, children will apply their knowledge of volume to estimate the volume of 3D shapes and consider how accurate their estimates are.

Small steps

→ Previous step: Comparing volumes
→ **This step: Estimating volume**
→ Next step: Estimating capacity

NATIONAL CURRICULUM LINKS

Year 5 Measurement

Estimate volume [for example, using 1 cm³ blocks to build cuboids (including cubes)] and capacity [for example, using water].

ASSESSING MASTERY

Children can confidently estimate the volume of 3D shapes. They can do this by counting the number of cubes in each layer then adding the results. Children are able to recognise that this is an estimate of volume and can explain why their answer is an estimate and how accurate it is.

COMMON MISCONCEPTIONS

Children may view the estimation process as a form of calculation, providing the actual volume, because it involves counting. Other children may assume that the answer or the method of calculation doesn't matter as it is only an estimate. Ask:
• *What is the difference between estimating and calculating an exact value? Why is estimating important?*

It is important to use the correct vocabulary in the lesson ('estimate', 'approximately', 'about') and for children to understand that estimating is an important skill, first and foremost in determining how reasonable an answer is.

STRENGTHENING UNDERSTANDING

It is important children understand that, when estimating, the answer can vary. Discuss with children why the answers may vary and what an acceptable answer is. For example, if a solid is made of 12 cubes, but children estimate the volume to be 4 cubes by counting only the cubes on one of the faces, then you may suggest children check the answer again. Ask: *How many layers does your shape have? How many cubes are there in each layer? How do you know that you have included all the parts in your estimation?*

GOING DEEPER

Challenge children to predict the volume of different shapes. Ask: *What would be a fair answer? What would not be a realistic answer? How do you know?* Provide children with the same solid shown in different orientations. Ask: *Does your method of estimation change? Will your method affect your answer?*

KEY LANGUAGE

In lesson: estimate, volume, 3D shapes, triangular, prism, unit, cubes, layer, slice, exact, compare, accurate, sphere

Other language to be used by the teacher: whole, part, almost half, less than (<), more than (>)

STRUCTURES AND REPRESENTATIONS

3D shapes

RESOURCES

Mandatory: cubes

Optional: 3D shapes drawn on square dotted paper, modelling clay

 In the eTextbook of this lesson, you will find interactive links to a selection of teaching tools.

Before you teach

• How confident are children with the concept of estimation generally?
• How will you link their prior knowledge to the concept of estimation of volume?

Discover

ASK

- Question **1** a): *Can you describe the shape Jamilla has estimated the volume of? How can you estimate its volume?*
- Question **1** a): *How can you split the shape to make your calculations easier?*
- Question **1** b): *Why do you think you are being asked to estimate, rather than calculate, the volume of the shape? When might it be beneficial to estimate and not calculate?*

IN FOCUS Ask children to suggest how the shapes shown in the **Discover** picture differ from those they have been using so far. Pay attention to the language children use when describing the shapes. Children should note that the shape is made from three different layers or three different parts or cuboids. Ask: *When might someone need to estimate the volume of a shape?* For example, it is needed when deciding whether a toy will fit in a suitcase or box. Encourage children to look at the **Discover** picture again and ask: *Which of the shapes will it be easiest or most difficult to estimate the volume of?*

PRACTICAL TIPS Play estimation games where children are split into two teams. Display one 3D shape made from cubes and, without counting cubes, ask each team to predict the volume of the shape. Begin with simple shapes like cubes and cuboids, then gradually make them more complex. As the shapes grow in complexity, talk about the method children use and discuss different methods with the whole class.

ANSWERS

Question **1** a): Jamilla estimated the volume of a triangular prism. An estimate of the volume of the triangular prism is 90 cubes.

Question **1** b): The volume is an estimate. It is not exact because there would still be space left in the triangular prism if it were filled with cubes.

Share

WAYS OF WORKING Whole class teacher led

ASK

- Question **1** a): *Why do you think it is important to find the cubes in each layer first, then add them together?*
- Question **1** a): *How does Ash's method work? What does a 'slice' mean?*
- Question **1** b): *How is this method an 'estimation'? Isn't it just a way to 'calculate' volume?*

IN FOCUS Question **1** a) requires children to consider various methods of estimating the volume of a shape. Prior to discussing each of the illustrated steps in question **1** a) with children, remind them of what the aim of the task is. Ask: *Why is 90 cubes the volume of the 3D shape, but only an estimation of the volume of the prism?* For question **1** b), ensure that children understand the estimate is less than the actual shape as the cubes could fit inside the prism with space to spare.

PUPIL TEXTBOOK 5C PAGE 200

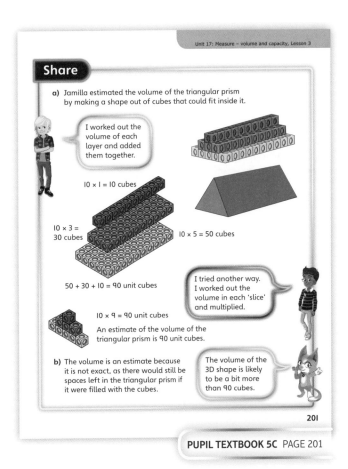

PUPIL TEXTBOOK 5C PAGE 201

Think together

Whole class teacher led (I do, We do, You do)

ASK

- Question **1**: *Before you start counting the cubes, estimate the volumes. What are you basing your estimates on? What makes some of these shapes difficult to estimate? Will you split the shapes into smaller parts? How can you make sure that you have counted all the cubes in each shape?*
- Question **2**: *Is it possible to use cubes to estimate any object in the classroom? What method can you use? Is there only one method? How can you ensure your estimation is accurate?*

IN FOCUS Although questions **1** and **2** both require children to estimate volumes by changing the shapes into cubes and cuboids, then adding the results, it may be worthwhile starting each activity by asking them to make a more informal quick estimation. Ask: *Without counting anything, what do you estimate the volume of this shape to be?* Challenging children to do this first will help them build visual connections between shapes and their estimated volumes.

STRENGTHEN Provide children with cubes that they can use to model the objects. Alternatively, provide boxes in which the objects can fit. Ask: *How many cubes did you use to make the model? Is your model bigger or smaller than the actual object? Can the shape fit in the box? What is the volume of the box? If the object fits in the box, will its volume be less or more than the volume of the box?*

DEEPEN Question **3** is designed to challenge children into thinking more deeply about what it means to use estimation to compare the volume of different shapes and objects. It is important that children are able to apply their prior knowledge of estimation. To extend their understanding, ask: *What would happen if you used bigger cubes to make each model? Will that affect the estimation or the comparison of the volumes?*

ASSESSMENT CHECKPOINT At this point, children should be working with greater confidence, using the different methods they have been taught to estimate the volume of the shapes and objects. Children should be able to provide accurate estimates and compare their estimates by volume.

ANSWERS

Question **1** a): 30 cubes

Question **1** b): 30 cubes

Question **1** c): 27 cubes

Question **2**: Independent answer

Question **3** a): Children could compare the volume of each ball by making a model of each shape with cubes, then counting the cubes to find the estimated volumes.

Question **3** b): Children should be able to say that while the height of the object is important, they also need to consider the width and length of an object.

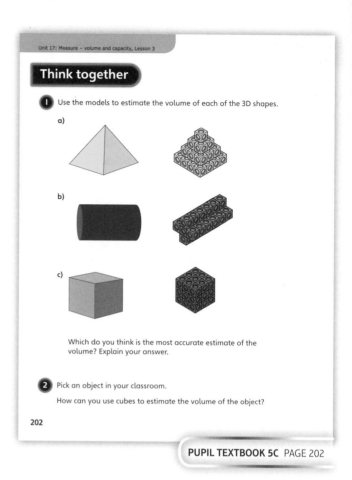

PUPIL TEXTBOOK 5C PAGE 202

PUPIL TEXTBOOK 5C PAGE 203

Practice

WAYS OF WORKING Independent thinking

IN FOCUS Children are asked to consider what the volumes of a hemisphere, sphere, cylinder and cuboid are in question **3** – a concept they have not had to deal with before this lesson. Ask: *How many different ways can you use to estimate the volume of these shapes? Does it matter that they have curved faces?*

STRENGTHEN Provide children with measuring cubes and modelling clay. Ask them to make a sphere and a cylinder. Ask: *Can you predict how many cubes the volume is?* Ask children to change the shape into a cube or cuboid, then compare it to the volume of the cubes. Ask: *How many cubes make each shape? What is your estimation of the volume?* Although this is not the method children will be encouraged to use all the time, it is a useful way to strengthen their understanding of how to estimate by 'changing' the shapes into cubes and cuboids first.

DEEPEN Question **6** is a challenge requiring several steps. Lead children through the process. Ask: *How do you find objects with a volume of less than 10 cubes? What do 10 cubes look like?* The question is designed to get children to consider appropriate methods. Thereafter, they are required to use their chosen method to complete the table. Ask: *Will you need up to 1,000 cubes to estimate the volume of large objects? What method can you use? Do you need to split the shape into layers?*

ASSESSMENT CHECKPOINT At this point in the lesson, children should be confident when estimating the volume of 3D shapes and objects. They should display a secure knowledge of a strategy to help them estimate, and will be able to use their estimation to compare the volume of the objects. They should be able to recognise that their calculations are an estimate of the volume and explain why this is.

ANSWERS Answers to the **Practice** part of the lesson appear in the separate **Practice and Reflect answer guide**.

Reflect

WAYS OF WORKING Independent thinking

IN FOCUS This question is used to help children look back on the strategies they have used in the lesson while estimating the volume of their hand. Some children may suggest drawing around the hand and then using cubes to change the drawing to a 3D shape. Other children may place cubes on their hand and count how many cubes the hand can hold. Whichever method they use, children should demonstrate their understanding of how estimation is used to calculate the volume of different objects.

ASSESSMENT CHECKPOINT Identify those children who have a correct methodology, demonstrating a confident understanding of how to use cubes to estimate the volume of the hand.

ANSWERS Answers for the **Reflect** part of the lesson appear in the separate **Practice and Reflect answer book**.

After the lesson

- How did you challenge children to think more deeply about estimating the volume of a shape?
- Do children now understand the concept of estimating the volume of any shape?

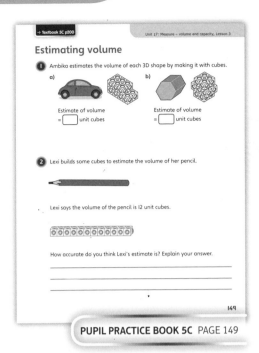

PUPIL PRACTICE BOOK 5C PAGE 149

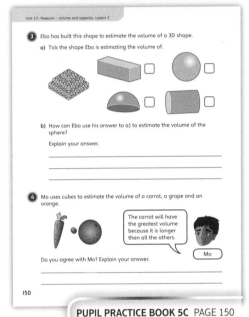

PUPIL PRACTICE BOOK 5C PAGE 150

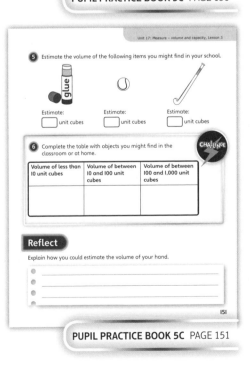

PUPIL PRACTICE BOOK 5C PAGE 151

Estimating capacity

Learning focus

In this lesson, children will estimate and order capacity. They will explain the differences between volume and capacity.

Small steps

→ Previous step: Estimating volume
→ **This step: Estimating capacity**

NATIONAL CURRICULUM LINKS

Year 5 Measurement

Estimate volume [for example, using 1 cm³ blocks to build cuboids (including cubes)] and capacity [for example, using water].

ASSESSING MASTERY

Children can confidently estimate capacity in different situations. Children are able to recognise and explain the differences between capacity and volume.

COMMON MISCONCEPTIONS

Children may think that a tall, thin container has a greater capacity than a short, wide one. Ask:
• *What does capacity mean? How can you measure it? What is the difference between capacity and volume? How can you estimate the capacity of each container?*

This is an extremely common misconception and one that it is important to combat by using the vocabulary of estimation ('estimate', 'approximately', 'about') at all times during the lesson.

STRENGTHENING UNDERSTANDING

Show children bottles and jugs of different shapes and sizes and ask them to predict their capacity. Set up an activity area and encourage children to use sand, rice or water to measure and compare the capacity of different items. Explain to children that capacity is defined by the amount a container can hold. It is always measured in litres or millilitres. For example, a bucket that can hold up to 10 litres of liquid has a capacity of 10 litres. However, if the bucket is half full, the volume of liquid in the bucket is 5 litres. Capacity is the maximum volume that each container can take. Provide children with different containers. Ask: *Can you compare the capacity of your shape with that of a partner's? Have you estimated in the same way?*

GOING DEEPER

Show children a container half full with 6 cubes and explain that the volume of cubes in this container is 6 cubes. Ask them to predict the capacity of the container. Challenge children to use litres and millilitres instead of cubes, and set their own estimation problems for partners to solve. Encourage them to ask for both the volume and capacity to be calculated, ensuring that all children can differentiate between the two.

KEY LANGUAGE

In lesson: estimate, capacity, container, smallest, greatest, millilitre (ml), litre (l), wide, tall, more, cubes, accurate, least, less than (<), volume

Other language to be used by the teacher: measure, liquid, less, more than (>)

RESOURCES

Mandatory: cubes

Optional: 1 litre bottles, cylinders, jugs, containers of different sizes, rice, sand

 In the eTextbook of this lesson, you will find interactive links to a selection of teaching tools.

Before you teach

• How confident are children with the concept of estimation?
• What practical activities could children do to practise estimation?

Discover

WAYS OF WORKING Pair work

ASK

- Question **1** a): *What facts do you know from this picture that will help you estimate how much the glass holds?*
- Question **1** a): *When estimating, why is it important to think about what you know and use it to help? Can you think of a way to check your estimate and find out the actual capacity of the glass?*
- Question **1** b): *How much does a small bottle of water hold? What do you measure liquid with? How can you use these measurements to order the containers?*

IN FOCUS When discussing question **1** a), encourage children to begin by suggesting a variety of ways that they can measure the capacity of the glass. Children may compare the glass to a bottle of water and discuss whether the glass contains more or less water than the bottle. Encourage children to use the correct mathematical language in their discussions. This is a good opportunity to clarify any misconceptions children may have.

PRACTICAL TIPS Discuss situations where children may have estimated the capacity of similar items, for example when cooking at home or at school. Display bottles and containers that children have come across before, such as bottles of the following sizes: 330 ml, 500 ml or 1 litre. Ask: *Do you know what the capacity of this bottle is? How do you know?* Then refer back to the **Discover** picture. Ask: *Can you use the bottles in front of you to estimate the capacity of the containers in the picture?*

ANSWERS

Question **1** a): You can estimate that the glass holds between 180 ml and 250 ml of water.

Question **1** b): Smallest capacity to greatest capacity: Sauce bottle, milk bottle, pan, watering can, fish tank.

Share

WAYS OF WORKING Whole class teacher led

ASK

- Question **1** a): *What are you measuring here, volume or capacity?*
- Question **1** a): *How is this method 'estimation'? Isn't it just a way to 'calculate' capacity?*
- Question **1** b): *What is your method of estimating the order? What did you compare each of the containers with?*
- Question **1** b): *Where have you seen the measurement of litres and millilitres before?*

IN FOCUS Spend some time discussing the concept of capacity and volume and the values that children actually estimate. Ensure children understand that the capacity of a glass will not change if there is no liquid in it. Discuss the strategies used to estimate the capacity and how known facts can help make a thoughtful guess about the capacity of a container.

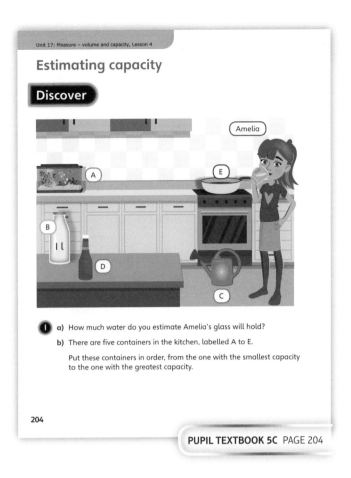

PUPIL TEXTBOOK 5C PAGE 204

PUPIL TEXTBOOK 5C PAGE 205

Think together

WAYS OF WORKING Whole class teacher led (I do, We do, You do)

ASK

- Question **1**: *What facts do you know that will help you estimate? Why can there only be one answer for each item?*
- Question **2**: *Will the capacity of each glass change if you poured in a different amount of juice? What does capacity measure? How does the fact that 100 ml of juice was poured into each glass help you estimate the capacity of the glasses?*

IN FOCUS Question **1** provides opportunity for children to estimate informed by known facts. Ensure children have access to containers and pictures of containers and items with different capacities. Some children may suggest that the teapot could have a capacity of 2 litres or 20 litres. Discuss that there are containers of all different sizes and that could be a possible answer; however, they have to choose the best estimate or the one that they have come across the most.

STRENGTHEN To support understanding of question **2**, children could use a bar model to calculate the capacity of each glass. Ensure that children understand that this is still an estimation as they are relying on the visual representation of each glass to determine what fraction of the glass is full of juice.

DEEPEN Question **3** is designed to challenge children into thinking more deeply about what it means to estimate the capacity of the colander and the different strategies that can be used to measure capacity. Deepen children's understanding by encouraging them to discuss the advantages and disadvantages of using each method.

ASSESSMENT CHECKPOINT At this point, children should be working with greater confidence, using the method they have been taught to estimate capacity in different scenarios. Children should understand the need to estimate based on what they know and have come across in their everyday life.

ANSWERS

Question **1** a): 500 litres

Question **1** b): Accept 500 ml (for 1 or 2 people) or 2 litres (large teapot for several people).

Question **2**: A: 300 ml, B: 300 ml, C: 175 ml, D: 200 ml

Question **3**: Children could discuss methods including using water, sand, flour or cubes to estimate capacity, depending on the item in question. They may also discuss putting a certain volume of materials into each container to see how much space remains.

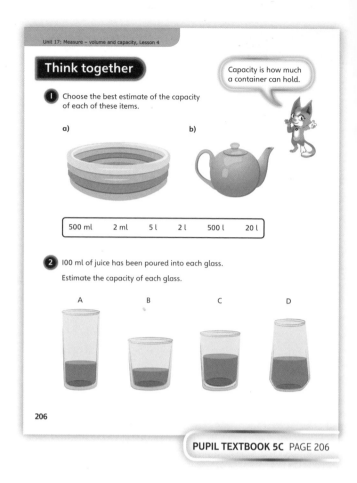

PUPIL TEXTBOOK 5C PAGE 206

PUPIL TEXTBOOK 5C PAGE 207

Practice

WAYS OF WORKING Independent thinking

IN FOCUS In question ❶, the options children have to choose from do not allow for a variety of possible answers. Instead, only one answer is appropriate each time. The question applies children's knowledge of estimating based on what they already know.

STRENGTHEN Strengthen children's estimation skills in question ❷ by providing them with concrete examples of bottles and jugs that contain 2 litres of liquid. Ask: *Given what you have been shown, which of the items can hold 2 litres of water or more?* In question ❺, provide children with opportunities to pour water from a bottle into 200 ml glasses. These real representations will help children visualise what the questions are asking more easily.

DEEPEN Deepen children's understanding in questions ❹ and ❺ by asking them to use a bar model to represent each problem. In question ❹, ask: *How much water was poured into each vase? What fraction of the vase is full? How much more water do you need to add so that the vase is completely full?* Encourage children to use reasoning to justify their answer. Children need to read question ❺ carefully. Ask: *How many glasses did Richard pour? How many ml of water is that?* Extend the challenge in question ❺ by asking children to estimate the capacity of the full bottle if the bottle is $\frac{3}{5}$ full instead. Ask: *Can you predict whether the capacity would be more or less than previously?*

THINK DIFFERENTLY The **Think differently** question in this lesson requires children to estimate the capacity of a bottle based on the volume poured from it. Ensure that children break the questions down into steps, first working out how much liquid has been subtracted from the full bottle, then finding out how much this volume represents ($\frac{1}{5}$), and finally working out the capacity based on $\frac{1}{5}$ being 400 ml.

ASSESSMENT CHECKPOINT At this point in the lesson, children should be confident when estimating the capacity of different jugs, bottles and containers. They should display a secure knowledge of using volume and capacity to estimate, compare and problem solve.

ANSWERS Answers to the **Practice** part of the lesson appear in the separate **Practice and Reflect answer guide**.

Reflect

WAYS OF WORKING Independent thinking

IN FOCUS Use this question to check children's reasoning. Pay attention to whether children can differentiate between capacity and volume. This is another opportunity to clarify any misconceptions they may have. Encourage children to give real-life examples of measuring volume and capacity to support their answers.

ASSESSMENT CHECKPOINT Look for children who are able to explain clearly what capacity and volume measure and then highlight the differences between them.

ANSWERS Answers for the **Reflect** part of the lesson appear in the separate **Practice and Reflect answer book**.

After the lesson

- To what extent do you feel that children understand how to estimate capacity?
- What opportunities can you provide inside and outside the classroom for children to estimate capacity and volume?

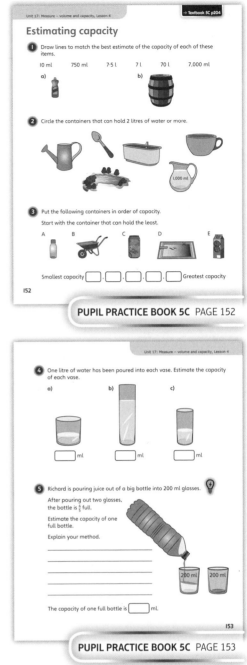

PUPIL PRACTICE BOOK 5C PAGE 152

PUPIL PRACTICE BOOK 5C PAGE 153

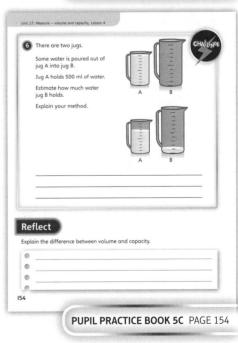

PUPIL PRACTICE BOOK 5C PAGE 154

End of unit check

Don't forget the *Power Maths* unit assessment grid on p26.

Group work adult led

IN FOCUS

- Question **1** assesses children's ability to find the volume of a solid.
- Question **2** assesses children's ability to find the volume of a shape by counting the cubes within it.
- Question **3** assesses children's ability to find and compare the volume of different solids.
- Questions **4** and **5** assess children's ability to estimate the capacity of containers.
- Questions **6** and **7** are SATs-style questions, which assess children's ability to estimate the capacity of different containers using different methods.

ANSWERS AND COMMENTARY

Children who have mastered the concepts in this unit will be able to define the terms 'volume' and 'capacity' and describe the differences between them. They will be able to measure and estimate the volume of different 3D shapes, ordering objects by their volume. They will know how to measure capacity and be able to use volumes to estimate the capacity of different containers, as well as ordering them by capacity.

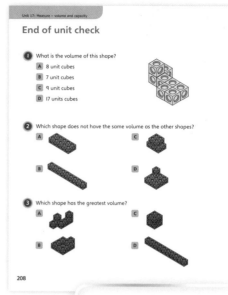

PUPIL TEXTBOOK 5C PAGE 208

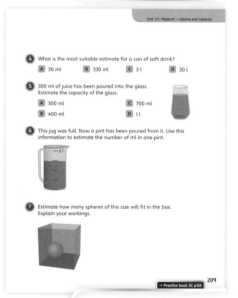

PUPIL TEXTBOOK 5C PAGE 209

Q	A	WRONG ANSWERS AND MISCONCEPTIONS	STRENGTHENING UNDERSTANDING
1	A	B or C suggest that children are unable to calculate volumes of shapes with 'hidden cubes'. D suggests that they have confused volume with area.	Strengthen understanding of the general concept of volume by providing children with opportunities to use concrete resources (such as plastic 3D shapes and cubes) to measure shapes or estimate the number of cubes that fit inside a shape.
2	B	A, C and D suggest that children have either miscounted or compared volumes incorrectly.	
3	D	A, B and C suggest that children have miscounted cubes.	
4	B	A, C and D suggest that children are unsure about what the capacity represents.	Allow children to make the shapes themselves so that they can understand what volume actually means and how they are using what they know to find it.
5	B	A suggests that children have confused volume and capacity.	
6	500–600 ml	1,500 ml suggests that children are finding the volume of the liquid left rather than the liquid poured from the jug.	
7	8	Children may not consider that they can fit in as many spheres as possible to fill the box.	

My journal

WAYS OF WORKING Independent thinking

ANSWERS AND COMMENTARY Possible answers are:

- Split the shapes horizontally into three different layers, then add the layers. Children have access to cubes and can make each of the layers in the shape. They add the number of cubes in each layer to find the volume of the whole shape.

- Split the shape into three equal slices. The volume of the shape = the number of cubes in one of the slices multiplied by 3.

If children need support to explain how to calculate the volume, encourage them to make the shape and ask: *How many cubes can you see? How many cubes are there on each of the layers?*

Power check

WAYS OF WORKING Independent thinking

ASK

- *What did you know about volume and capacity before you began this unit? What do you know now?*
- *Do you think you would be able to find the volume of any solid made of cubes on your own?*

Power puzzle

WAYS OF WORKING Pair work or small groups

IN FOCUS Use this **Power puzzle** to see if children can explore different ways of estimating the volume of a football and the volume of a classroom. Children should be able to use their knowledge of estimation and the properties of a cube to predict the number of footballs that could fit into their classroom.

ANSWERS AND COMMENTARY Answers depend on the size of each classroom. Possible answers to finding the most accurate estimate are:

- Children find the number of cubes needed to make one football. They estimate the number of cubes that could fit in the classroom.
- Children fit the football in a box. They estimate the number of boxes that can fit into the classroom.

Completing the Power puzzle shows that children understand what volume means and can estimate the volume of shapes of different dimensions.

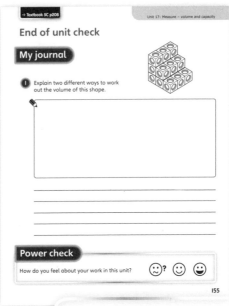

PUPIL PRACTICE BOOK 5C PAGE 155

PUPIL PRACTICE BOOK 5C PAGE 156

After the unit ⏸

- How did children respond to the materials and approaches used to estimate volume and capacity? Were they adequately (or excessively) challenged by them?

Strengthen and **Deepen** activities for this unit can be found in the *Power Maths* online subscription.

Published by Pearson Education Limited, 80 Strand, London, WC2R 0RL.

www.pearsonschools.co.uk

Text © Pearson Education Limited 2018
Edited by Pearson, Little Grey Cells Publishing Services and Haremi Ltd
Designed and typeset by Kamae Design
Original illustrations © Pearson Education Limited 2018
Illustrated by Laura Arias, John Batten, Fran and David Brylewski, Diego Diaz, Nigel Dobbyn and
Nadene Naude at Beehive Illustration; Emily Skinner at Graham-Cameron Illustration; and Kamae.
Cover design by Pearson Education Ltd
Back cover illustration © Diego Diaz and Nadene Naude at Beehive Illustration.

Series Editor: Tony Staneff
Consultants: Professor Liu Jian and Professor Zhang Dan

The rights of Liu Jian, Josh Lury, Catherine Casey, Belle Cottingham, Zhou Da, Zhang Dan, Zhu Dejiang, Wei Huinv, Hou
Huiying, Zhang Jing, Huang Lihua, Yin Lili, Liu Qimeng, Paul Wrangles and Zhu Yuhong to be identified as authors of this work
have been asserted by them in accordance with the Copyright, Designs and Patents Act 1988.

First published 2018

22 21 20 19 18
10 9 8 7 6 5 4 3 2 1

British Library Cataloguing in Publication Data
A catalogue record for this book is available from the British Library

ISBN 978 0 435 19044 6

Printed in Slovakia by Neografia

www.activelearnprimary.co.uk

Note from the publisher
Pearson has robust editorial processes, including answer and fact checks, to ensure the accuracy of the content in this
publication, and every effort is made to ensure this publication is free of errors. We are, however, only human, and
occasionally errors do occur. Pearson is not liable for any misunderstandings that arise as a result of errors in this
publication, but it is our priority to ensure that the content is accurate. If you spot an error, please do contact us at
resourcescorrections@pearson.com so we can make sure it is corrected.